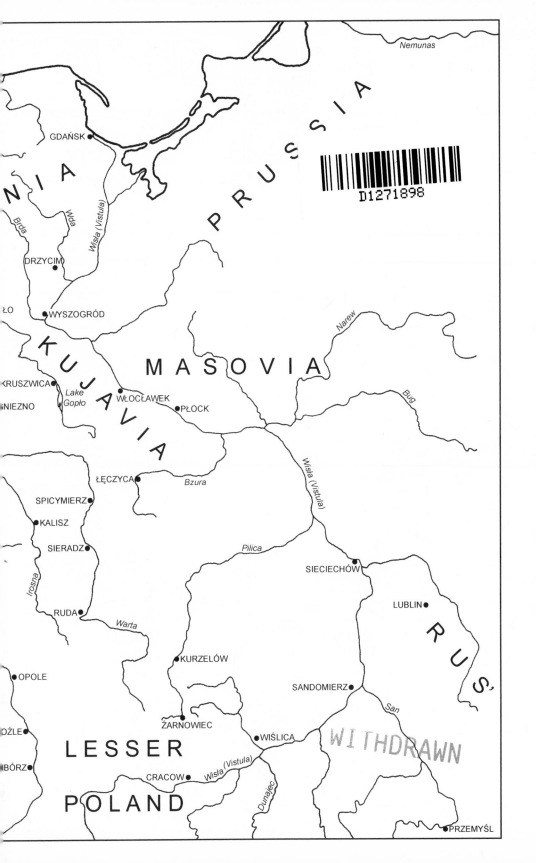

GDAŃSK

PRUSSIA

Nemunas

NIA

Brda

Wda

Wisła (Vistula)

DRZYCIM

ŁO

WYSZOGRÓD

KUJAVIA

MASOVIA

Narew

KRUSZWICA

Lake Gopło

WŁOCŁAWEK

PŁOCK

Bug

GNIEZNO

ŁĘCZYCA

Bzura

Wisła (Vistula)

SPICYMIERZ

KALISZ

SIERADZ

Pilica

Irosna

SIECIECHÓW

LUBLIN

RUŚ

RUDA

Warta

KURZELÓW

OPOLE

SANDOMIERZ

OŹLE

San

ŻARNOWIEC

WIŚLICA

BÓRZ

LESSER

CRACOW

Wisła (Vistula)

Dunajec

POLAND

PRZEMYŚL

GESTA PRINCIPUM
POLONORUM

———◦◦◦———

THE DEEDS OF THE PRINCES
OF THE POLES

CENTRAL EUROPEAN
MEDIEVAL TEXTS

VOLUME 3

General Editors

JÁNOS M. BAK
URSZULA BORKOWSKA
GILES CONSTABLE
GÁBOR KLANICZAY

Series Editor

FRANK SCHAER

GESTA PRINCIPUM POLONORUM

THE DEEDS OF THE PRINCES OF THE POLES

Translated and annotated by
PAUL W. KNOLL and FRANK SCHAER

With a preface by
THOMAS N. BISSON

CEU PRESS

Central European University Press
Budapest New York

English edition published in 2003 by
Central European University Press

Original title: *Galli Anonymi cronicae et gesta ducum sive principum
Polonorum / Anonima tzw. Galla kronika czyli dzieje książąt i
władców polskich*, ed.
Carolus/Karol Maleczyński, Monumenta Poloniae Historica, nova series,
tomus II (Cracow: Polska Akademia Umiejętności, 1952)

Translated by Paul W. Knoll and Frank Schaer

An imprint of the Central European University Share Company
Nádor utca 11, H-1051 Budapest, Hungary
Tel.: +36-1-327-3138 or 327-3000, Fax: +36-1-327-3183
E-mail: ceupress@ceu.hu
Website: www.ceupress.com

400 West 59th Street, New York, NY 10019, USA
Tel: +1-212-547-6932, Fax: +1-212-548-4607
E-mail: mgreenwald@sorosny.org

ISBN 963 9241 40 7 Cloth

Library of Congress Cataloging-in-Publication Data

Gallus, Anonymus, 1066–1145.
[Chronicon. English]
Gesta principum Polonorum = The deeds of the princes of the Poles /
translated and annotated by Paul W. Knoll and Frank Schaer ; with a
preface by Thomas N. Bisson.
p. cm. – (Central European medieval texts, ISSN 1419-7782 ; v.
3)
Includes bibliographical references and index.
ISBN
1. Poland–History–To 1572. I. Title: Deeds of the princes of the
Poles. II. Knoll, Paul W. III. Schaer, Frank. IV. Title. V. Series.
DK4190.M37213 2003
943.8'022–dc21
2003007636

Printed in Hungary by Akadémiai Nyomda Kft., Martonvásár

CONTENTS

GENERAL EDITORS' PREFACE

While interest in the medieval and early modern history of the Central European region is definitely growing, knowledge of the medieval languages in which the story is usually told (mainly Latin) has been declining for some time. Just as historians in the rest of Europe appreciated the value of modern language translations in presenting a picture of their country's history, so central Europeans too have done their best to translate their past chroniclers into the local vernaculars. However, very little has been done to make these highly important narrative sources available to readers not familiar with the relevant Central European languages.

The General Editors' plan is, therefore, to follow the example of such highly acclaimed enterprises as the *Oxford* (previously *Nelson) Medieval Texts* by launching a series of narrative sources on medieval Bohemia, Croatia, Hungary, Poland, and their neighboring countries. Each volume will contain the Latin (or medieval vernacular) text, an English translation, an introductory essay, annotations, indexes, and the usual scholarly apparatus, edited by the best experts in the region and beyond. Since these sources are mostly available in good, relatively recent critical editions, *Central European Medieval Texts* will print the original language texts with only select textual variants. However, extensive notes will be added on features, persons, and institutions of the region perhaps less known to persons outside it.

It is envisaged that a volume will be published yearly, so we hope that the series will have made the most important narrative and

[vii]

hagiographical sources of the region available within a decade or two.

The General Editors would like to take the opportunity to invite colleagues working on such texts to join the team of scholars editing *Central European Medieval Texts*, so that the series can proceed with good speed to deliver editions and translations of first-class quality. Readers, in turn, are encouraged to communicate to the General Editors their comments on the volumes and their suggestions for further texts to be included in the series.

J. M. B. – U. B. – G. C. – G. K.

PREFACE

The present edition will be recognized as a landmark in the study of medieval history. This assertion may seem puzzling on its face. For the text in question is the earliest extant Polish national chronicle, and it has long been known, having been printed and reprinted since the sixteenth century; moreover, it is accessible in a competent critical edition published just fifty years ago. Yet the work has hardly been known outside Poland (and Germany). It has never made it into the constellation of grand narratives recognised by medievalists everywhere—Bede, Thietmar, William of Malmesbury, Orderic Vitalis, for example—as transcending local circumstances. Like its subject—the Poles—this text has been marginalized in the conspectus of a historiography native to northwestern Europe. That situation is happily changing as the myopic "Europe" of the Cold War recedes in time, inviting a new focus on the larger Europe of an abiding, more truthful past.

This improving perspective ensures that a new edition accompanied by an English translation will bring a major text of the Middle Ages to the notice of many who have never heard of it. But this will be a new text, in a considerable sense, even for its devotees, for it is here for the first time liberated from the confusing attribution to "a Frenchman" (*Gallus*) with which it has been burdened since the eighteenth century. The text is resolutely anonymous in its earliest surviving manuscript, which provides in a rubric the quasi-title, here restored, that surely comes close to its author' s conception: "chronicles and deeds of the dukes or princes of the Poles." That the author was a French monk remains a likely possibility, but that presumption should no longer distract readers from the love of Poland and the values of Latin Christendom that suffuse the anonymous chronicle. Nor will this writer, who wished "not to eat Polish bread in vain," be any less agreeable and inscrutable in his pages for being nameless.

Composed in the early twelfth century—we know very nearly when, as the editors show—*The Deeds of the Princes of the Poles* is a precious historical record in three broad respects: it preserves and embroiders upon early Slavic traditions of dynastic origins, it gives a sober and plausible account of eleventh-century dynastic history in Poland, and it provides a muffled, yet uniquely informative impression of the strains and tensions within early Polish society that help to explain disruptions in dynastic power towards 1025–30 and again after 1090. That it may have been composed substantially to glorify Duke Bolesław III (1102–38) and commemorate his deeds in no way diminishes the wider and deeper interest of the history that precedes. In ·this respect the work may be likened to the narrative or versified commemorations of deeds in western lands during the century after the Norman Conquest, yet few if any of the western texts can match the Polish *Deeds* for human interest and authorial insights into the complexities of medieval societal formation. Page after captivating page sparkles with vitality and imagination, somewhat as if Henry of Huntingdon and Geoffrey of Monmouth had been run together. Few authors of the Middle Ages can have left his readers with so many urgent questions to ask him, yet it is largely thanks to this one that we know what to ask about early Poland at all. Scholars and general readers alike will experience the allure of a text that moves us with the power and touches of a fine storyteller.

This is one of the great chronicles of medieval European history. The present editors deserve the thanks of readers everywhere for rendering it accessible as never before.

Thomas N. Bisson

ABBREVIATIONS

GENERAL ABBREVIATIONS

ad a.	*ad annum* ('for the year')
b.	born
bk.	book/liber
ch.	chapter/caput
d.	died
fl.	*floruit*
GpP	*Gesta principum Polonorum* (the present edition)
MS(S)	manuscript(s)
n.s.	nova series/new series/neue Serie
PAU	Polska Akademia Umiejętności (Polish Academy of Arts and Sciences)
PAN	Polska Akademia Nauk (Polish Academy of Sciences)
PWN	Państwowe Wydawnictwo Naukowe (State Scholarly Publishing House)
trans.	translated by
UP	University Press
vol.	volume
†	(marks corrupt text)

TITLES CITED IN ABBREVIATED FORM

APH

Acta Poloniae Historica. Warsaw: Inst. Hist. PAN, 1946—.

CHP

Cambridge History of Poland: From the Origins to Sobieski (to 1696). Vol.1, ed. William F. Reddaway. Cambridge: Cambridge UP, 1950.

Cosmas, Chron. Boh.

Kronik von Böhmen/Cosmae Pragensis Chronica Boemorum. Ed. Bertold Bretholz. MGH. SSrG, n.s. 2. Berlin: Wiedmann, 1923.

Europas Mitte

Wieczorek, Alfried, and Hans-Martin Hinz, ed. Europas Mitte um 1000: Beiträge zur Geschichte, Kunst und Archäologie. Stuttgart: Konrad Theiss Verlag, 2000.

Europe's Center

Wieczorek, Alfried, and Hans-Martin Hinz, ed. Europe's Center Around 1000: Contributions to History, Art and Archaeology. Stuttgart: Konrad Theiss Verlag, 2000 [English version of articles from Europas Mitte, without illustrations].

Franklin-Shepard, *Rus*

Franklin, Simon, and Jonathan Shepard, *The Emergence of Rus 750–1200*. London: Longman, 1996.

FvS

Freiherr vom Stein-Gedächtnisausgabe. Ausgewählte Quellen zur Deutschen Geschichte des Mittelalters. Darmstadt: Wissenschaftliche Buchgesellschaft, 1956—.

Gumplowicz, Zbigniew

Gumplowicz, Maximilian Ernst. "Zbigniew, Grossherzog von Polen." In Zur Geschichte Polens im Mittelalter: zwei kritische Untersuchungen über die Chronik Balduin Gallus, pp. 1–126. Innsbruck: Wagner'sche Universitätsbuchhandlung, 1898. Reprint, Aalen: Scientia, 1969.

Grodecki-Plezia, *Kronika*
Roman Grodecki, trans. *Anonim tzw. Gall: Kronika polska* (The Anonymus known as Gallus: the Polish Chronicle). Ed. Marian Plezia. Biblioteka Narodowa 1/59. Wrocław: Zakład Narodowy im. Ossolińskich, 1975.

KMTL
Korai magyar történeti lexikon, 9–14. század (Dictionary of early Hungarian history, ninth–fourteenth centuries.) Ed. Gyula Kristó, Pál Engel, and Ferenc Makk. Budapest: Akadémiai, 1994.

Kossmann
Polen im Mittelalter. Vol. 1, *Beiträge zur Sozial- und Wirtschaftsgeschichte*. Marburg: Herder Institut, 1971. Vol. 2, *Staat, Gesellschaft und Wirtschaft im Bannkreis des Westens*. Ibid., 1985.

LexMA
Lexikon des Mittelalters. 9 vols. Munich: Artemis, 1980–1999.

Mal.
Maleczyński, Carolus/Karol. *Galli Anonymi cronica et gesta ducum sive principum Polonorum/Anonima tzw. Galla kronika czyli dzieje książąt i władców polskich.* MPH n.s. 2. Cracow: PAU, 1952.

MGH
Monumenta Germaniae Historica/Die deutschen Geschichtsquellen des Mittelalters, 500–1500.
DD: Diplomata
Dt. Chr.: Deutsche Chroniken
SS: Scriptores
SS AA: Scriptores Antiquissimi
SSrG: Scriptores Rerum Germanicarum in usum scholarum separatim editi

MPH — Monumenta Poloniae Historica/Pomniki Dziejowe Polski. Ed. August Bielowski. PAU Lviv: Nakladem Własnym, 1864–1970.

MPH n.s. — Monumenta Poloniae Historica. Pomniki Dziejowe Polski, various editors, 1956—.

MPL — Patrologiae cursus completus: Patrologia latina. Ed. J.-P. Migne. Paris: Garnier, 1844–55; 1862–65. Facsimile reprint, Turnholt: Brepols, 1999.

QMAeN — *Questiones Medii Aevi Novae.* Warsaw, 1996—.

PSB — *Polski słownik biograficzny* (Polish biographical dictionary). Wrocław: Zakład Narodowy im. Ossolińskich, 1959—.

PVL — *Povest' vremennych let* (Tale of by-gone years). Vol. 1. Ed. and trans. S. Lihachev. Leningrad: Nauka,1950.

Regino, *Chron.* — *Jahrbücher von Fulda; Regino, Chronik; Notker, Taten Karls. Quellen zur karolingischen Reichsgeschichte.* Ed. Reinhold Rau. 3d ed. Berlin: Rütten und Loening, 1960.

Simon, Topik I and II — Gertrud Simon, "Untersuchungen zur Topik der Widmungsbriefe mittelalterlicher Geschichtsschreiber bis zum Ende des 12. Jahrhunderts," Teil I, *Archiv für Diplomatik* 4 (1958): 52–112; Teil II, Ibid. 5/6 (1959/60): 73–153.

SRH — *Scriptores rerum Hungaricarum tempore ducum regumque stirpis Arpadianae gestarum.* Ed. Emericus Szentpétery. Budapest: Egyetemi Nyomda, 1937–38. Reprint (with afterword and appendix by Kornél Szovák and László Veszprémy), Budapest: Nap Kiadó, 1999.

SSS   *Słownik starożytności Słowiańskich* (Dictionary of Slavic antiquities). Ed. Gerard Labuda et al. 7 vols. Wrocław: Ossolineum, 1961–82.

Thietmar,   Thietmar von Merseburg, *Chronik*. Ed. R.
Chron.   Holzmann, rev. ed. Werner Trittmilch. FvS 15. Darmstadt: Wissenschaftliche Buchgesellschaft, 1957.

For the sigla of manuscripts, see below, p. xx.

Classical authors and biblical passages are cited in the usual abbreviated forms.

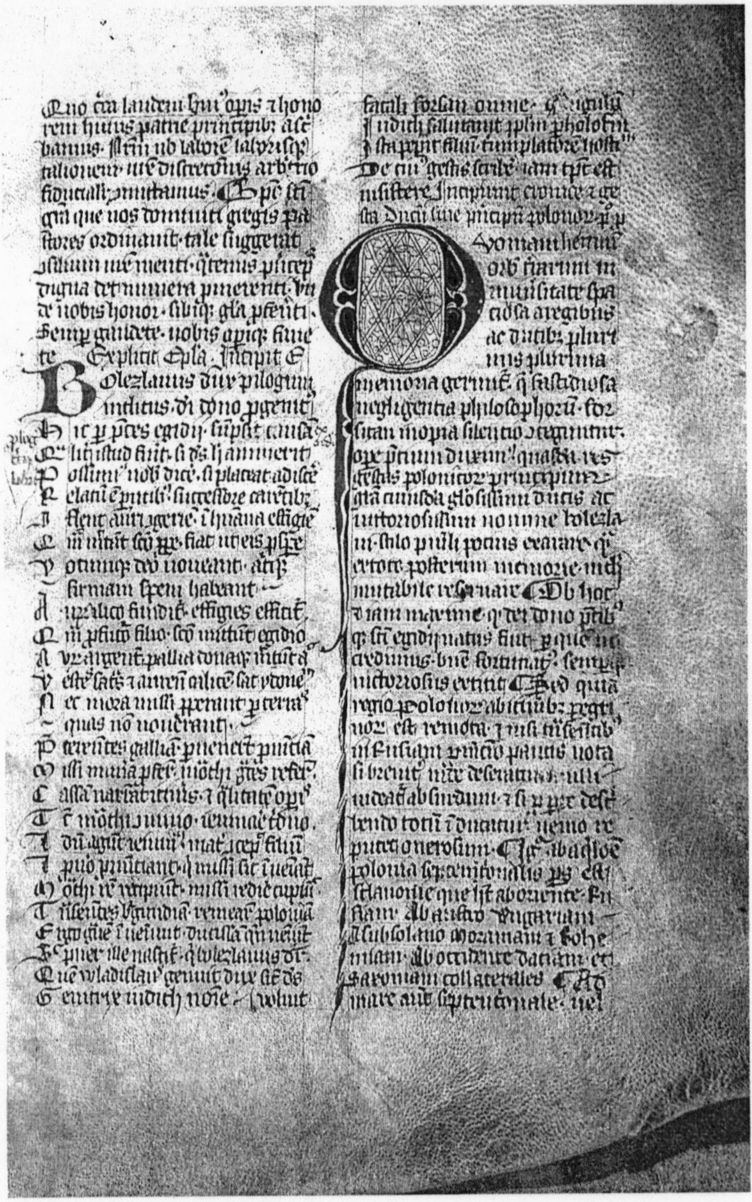

Fig. 1. Warsaw, National Library, MS BOZ cim. 28, fol. 20v
(with permission of the National Library, Warsaw)

LIST OF FIGURES, MAP,
AND GENEALOGICAL TABLE

FIGURES

MAP

GENEALOGICAL TABLE

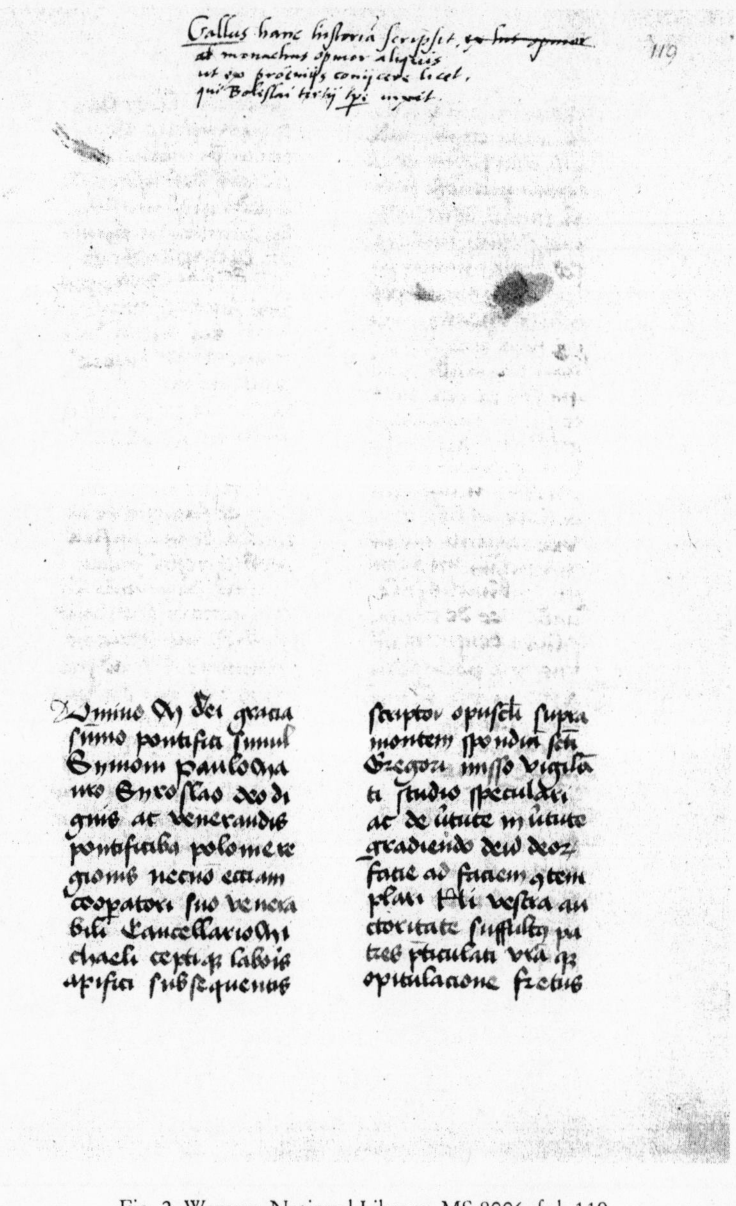

Fig. 2. Warsaw, National Library, MS 8006, fol. 119
(with permission of the National Library, Warsaw)

EDITORS' INTRODUCTION

IN COOPERATION WITH WOJCIECH POLAK

The anonymous work we have chosen to title *Gesta principum Polonorum/The Deeds of the Princes of the Poles* (henceforth: *GpP*) has been studied by scholars for some two centuries, yet many issues regarding it are still subject to debate. These include the person of the author and his context, the precise date of the work's composition, the author's motives in writing, his sources of information (written or oral), his reception of heroic and mythical traditions, and his choice of style and discourse. In what follows we seek to summarize the prevailing hypotheses and present the scholarly consensus, if such exists, without going into the details of learned controversies. References to these are given in our notes sparingly, especially as far as the inclusion of Polish titles is concerned; for those who read the East European vernaculars, the relevant handbooks and bibliographies will give sufficient orientation.[1]

---

[1] A good summary of this scholarship with extensive bibliography, including titles in languages other than Polish, is in Norbert Kersken, *Geschichtsschreibung im Europa der "nationes": Nationalgeschichtliche Gesamtdarstellungen im Mittelalter*, Münstersche Historische Forschungen, 8 (Cologne: Böhlau, 1995), esp. pp. 491–9. Of the older handbooks, see, e.g., Heinrich Zeissberg, *Die polnische Geschichtsschreibung des Mittelalters* (Leipzig: Hirzel, 1873; reprint: Cologne: Böhlau, 1968), pp. 26–9; Pierre David, *Les sources de l'histoire de Pologne à l'epoque des Piasts (963–1386)* (Paris: Les belles lettres, 1934), pp. 35–55; Max Manitius, *Geschichte der lateinischen Literatur des Mittelalters* (Munich: Beck, 1931), 3:407–11; *LexMA* 4:1099; *Repertorium fontium historiae Medii Aevi primum ab Augusto Potthast digestum, nunc cura collegii historicorum e pluribus nationibus emendatum et auctum* 3:416–7 (Rome: Istituto storico italiano per il Medio Evo, 1964) s.v. "Chronicon et gesta etc."

MANUSCRIPTS AND EDITIONS

No original or near-contemporary copy of the *GpP* survives. Our knowledge of the text depends primarily on three late-medieval copies. The earliest is in the so-called Codex Zamoyscianus, formerly in the library of the counts of Zamość, presently in the National Library in Warsaw (Ms. BOZ cim. 28, fols. 20v–54v). It is a parchment codex containing historical and hagiographical writings, written around 1380–92, most probably in Cracow (Fig. 1). Until the beginning of the fifteenth century this manuscript was in the library of the Łaski family,[2] whence it came into the hands of the Gniezno canon, Sędziwoj (Sandivogius) of Czechło (died in 1476), a friend of the historian Jan Długosz, who himself made use of the *GpP* (perhaps from this very copy) in compiling his *Annales*. This text (Z) is considered to be the best and most complete version.

A second copy, made for Sędziwoj in 1434–39, is in the so-called Sędziwoj Codex (*S*), a paper manuscript now in the Library of the Czartoryski Museum in Cracow (Ms. 1310, fols. 242 to 307)—hence also referred to as Codex Czartoryscianus—and containing in addition to the *GpP* other historical, hagiographical and legal texts. As this text was copied directly from the Zamoyski manuscript, its variant readings have no textual significance.

There is as well a third and independent witness, in the so-called Heilsberg codex (*H*), named for the place where it was kept between the mid-sixteenth and the eighteenth centuries—Lidzbark Warmiński, in German: Heilsberg—but today preserved in the National Library in Warsaw (Ms. 8006, fols. 119–247; see Fig. 2). This paper manuscript was written around 1469–71, based on a text from Cracow (of ca.1330), which reached Łekno

[2] The Łaski were aristocrats who supplied Poland with high officials and prelates, the best known being Jan Łaski, chancellor and primate of Poland in the early sixteenth century; see *PSB* 18:225–55.

in 1378 and then to the canons regular in Trzemeszno;[3] later it belonged to the historian Bishop Martin Kromer (1512–89).[4] Here too the *GpP* is one item in a collection of historical writings. The text in the Heilsberg manuscript is incomplete, ending with chapter 15 of Book III and omitting chapters entirely or partially. Especially notable is the omission of chapters 27–8 of Book I, which refer to the decline of King Bolesław II and his conflict with Bishop (St.) Stanislas of Cracow, in place of which were inserted appropriate passages from the Life of the saint (the so-called *Tradunt*, written before 1340).[5] With its many errors and omissions the text of the *GpP* in the Heilsberg manuscript is in a much more corrupt state than *Z* and *S*, yet it preserves a number of convincing variant readings and some additional words and phrases.

The *GpP* was apparently used by Peter of Byczyna in compiling his *Chronica Principum Poloniae*,[6] which thus may count as a further witness (*Chr*). The early thirteenth-century chronicler, Master Vincent (called Kadłubek), also had access to a now lost copy of the text.

Thus the extant copies of the chronicle can be divided into two traditions, the first represented by *Z* and its derivative *S*, the

---

[3] The most recent discussion is Wojciech Drelicharz, "Rękopis Piotra z Szamotul, zwany kodeksem heilbergskim i jego geneza" [The manuscript of Peter of Szamotuly, called the Heilsberg Codex, and its origin], in K. Ożóg and St. Szczur, ed., *Polska i jej sąsiedzi w późnym średniowieczu* (Cracow: Towarzystwo Naukowe "Societas Vistulana," 2000), pp. 255–72.

[4] On Kromer, see *New Catholic Encyclopedia* (New York: MacGraw-Hill, 1967–79), 8:264.

[5] Edited by Bandtkie on pp. 324–80 of his *Martini Galli Chronicon* (as at n. 10 below).

[6] *Chronica principum Poloniae/Kronika książąt polskich*, ed. Zygmunt Weclewski, MPH 3, pp. 423–578 (Lviv: Schmidt, 1878; reprint: Warsaw: PWN, 1961); see Kersken, *Geschichtsschreibung*, pp. 516–22, with bibliography; see also *Repertorium fontium historiae Medii Aevi* 3:417–8.

second by *H*. For the textual significance of this, see further below and under Editorial Principles.[7]

The first printed edition of the *GpP* was published in 1749 in Gdańsk on the basis of *H* by Gottfried Lengnich, who baptised the author Martinus Gallus.[8] Twenty years later this text was republished by Lawrence (Wawrzyniec) Mizler de Kolof in his collection of historical writings on Poland and Lithuania.[9] In preparing the 1824 Warsaw edition Jan Wincenty Bandtkie also took *S* into consideration.[10] Since *H* was lost between 1831 and the 1890s, the editions in the *Monumenta Germaniae Historica*[11]

---

[7] For a detailed discussion (including a *stemma codicum*) of the relations of the various witnesses of the *GpP*, both extant and reconstructed, see Karol Maleczyński, "Wstęp" [Preface], in *Galli anonymi cronica et gesta ducum sive principum Polonorum/Anonima tzw. Galla kronika czyli dzieje książąt i władców polskich*, MPH n.s. 2 (Cracow: PAU, 1952), pp. XXII–XXXI, Latin version pp. CV–CXI [henceforth: Mal.]; a simplified manuscript filiation, omitting a number of intermediary copies postulated by Maleczyński, is given by Zofia Budkowa in a review of Maleczyński's edition in *Przegląd Historyczny* 44 (1953): 423–6, and accepted by Jacek Wiesiołowski, *Kolekcje historyczne w Polsce średniowiecznej XIV-XV wieku* [Historical collections in medieval Poland, fourteenth-fifteenth centuries] (Wrocław: Zakład Narodowy im.Ossolińskich, 1967), pp. 19–20, 31–4.

[8] Gottfried Lengnich, ed., *Vincentius Kadlubko et Martinus Gallus scriptores historiae Polonae vetustissimi cum duobus anonymis ex ms. bibliothecae episcopalis Heilsbergensis editi* (Gdańsk: n.p., 1749).

[9] [Laurentius Mizler de Kolof, ed.] *Historiarum Poloniae Et Magni Ducatus Lithuaniae Scriptorum Quotquot Ab Initio Reipublicae Polonae Ad Nostra Usque Tempora Extant Omnium Collectio Magna . . . Edidit . . . Laur. Mizlerus De Kolof Regni Poloniae Historiographus, In Sereniss. Regis Polon. Aula Consiliarius Et Medicus Cum Indice Locupletissimo* (Warsaw: Mizler, 1776).

[10] [Joannes V. Bandtkie, ed.] *Martini Galli Chronicon ad fidem codicum : qui servantur in Pulaviensi tabulario celsissimi Adami principis Czartoryscii, palatini regni Poloniarum / denuo recensuit . . . Joannes Vincentius Bandtkie* (Warsaw: Regia Societas Philomathicae Varsoviensis,1824).

[11] Edited by J. Szlachtowski and P. Koepke in *Chronica et annales aevi Salici*, ed. Georg Heinrich Pertz, MGH SS IX, pp. 418–78 (Hanover: Hahn, 1851; reprint, 1983). This text was also reprinted in Migne PL 155: 833–936.

and the old *Monumenta Poloniae Historica*[12] were based solely on Z and S. The edition of 1898 prepared by Ludwik Finkel and Stanisław Kętrzyński was based on Z alone.[13] A facsimile editon of the latter manuscript was later published by Julian Krzyżanowski.[14] The most recent and complete critical edition—the text of which is reproduced in the present volume with minor corrections and variations—was prepared by Karol Maleczyński in 1952 within the new series of *Monumenta Poloniae Historica*.[15] He not only collated Z, S, and H, but also consulted Chr and occasionally Kadłubek for the reconstruction of the text.

A full translation of the GpP into Polish was prepared by Roman Grodecki in 1923, the text of which, reedited and annotated by Marian Plezia, appeared first in 1965.[16] A Russian translation by Ljudmila Mikhailovna Popova was published in 1961.[17] A com-

---

[12] MPH 1, ed. A Bielowski, pp. 379–484 (Lviv: Gubrynowicz i Schmidt,1864).

[13] Ludovicus Finkel and Stanislaus Kętrzyński, ed., *Galli anonymi chronicon*, Fontes rerum Polonicarum in usum scholarum 1 (Lviv: Societas Historica Leopolitana, 1899).

[14] Julian Krzyżanowski, ed., *Galla Anonima Kronika. Podobizna fotograficzna rękopisu Zamoyskich z wieku XIV/Galli Anonymi Chronica codicis saec. XIV. Zamoscianus appellati reproductio palaeographica* (Warsaw: Towarzystwo Naukowe Warszawskie, 1946).

[15] As above, n. 7. This edition profited much from the philological study of Marian Plezia, *Kronika Galla na tle historiografii XII w.* [The chronicle of Gallus in the context of the historiography of the twelfth century], Rozprawy Wydziału Historyczno-Filozoficznego PAU, ser. 2, vol. 46, no. 3 (Cracow: PAU, 1947) [henceforth: *Kronika Galla*], an extensive review of which by J. Hammer was published in *Speculum* 24 (1949): 291–5.

[16] Roman Grodecki, trans., *Anonim tzw. Gall Kronika polska* [The Anonymus known as Gallus: the Polish Chronicle], ed. Marian Plezia, Biblioteka narodowa 1/59 (Wrocław: Zakład Narodowy im. Ossolińskich, 1975) [henceforth: Grodecki-Plezia, *Kronika*].

[17] Ljudmila Mikhailovna Popova, ed. and trans., *Gall Anonim, Khronika u deianiia kniazei ili pravitelei polskikh*, Pamiatniki srednevekovoi istorii narodov Tsentralnoi i Vostochnoi Evropy (Moscow: Akad. Nauk SSSR, 1961).

plete translation into German was prepared in 1978 by Joseph Bujnoch, who utilized both the Latin text of the critical edition and the Polish translations, as well as recent German literature for the annotations.[18] Parts of Book I have appeared in Italian and Japanese translation.[19]

TITLE, AUTHOR, AND DATE OF COMPOSITION

Concerning the original title of the work, the only clue we have is what appears in the headings to the introductory parts of the Zamoyski manuscript. In the rubric of the letter prefacing the entire work it is called *cronica Polonorum*. The proem opening Book I has the heading *Incipiunt Cronice et gesta ducum sive principum Polonorum*. Unfortunately, there is no proof that this rubric—or the chapter headings in general—formed part of the original work, especially as several chapters have none. However, the term *gesta* is a quite appropriate one for a work concentrating on the deeds of princes (see further below).[20]

[18] Josef Bujnoch, *Polens Anfänge: Gallus Anonymus, Chronik und Taten der Herzöge und Fürsten von Polen*, Slawische Geschichtsschreiber 10 (Graz: Styria, 1978). Extensive selections in German had appeared in: Richard Roeppel, *Geschichte Polens* (Hamburg: Friedrich Perthes, 1840); Maximilian Ernst Gumplowicz, *Zur Geschichte Polens im Mittelalter: zwei kritische Untersuchungen über die Chronik Balduin Gallus* (Innsbruck: Wagner'sche Universitätsbuchhandlung, 1898; reprint, Aalen: Scientia, 1969); Oskar Kossmann, *Polen im Mittelalter*, 2 vols. (Marburg: Herder-Institut, 1971–85); and elsewhere.

[19] J. W. Woś, "La cronaca di Gallo Anonymo," *Annali della Scuola Normale Superiore di Pisa, Classe di lettere e filosofia*, ser. 3, vol. 11 (1981), pp. 165–79; M. Araki, "Tokumei no Garu Nendaiki, Dai Ikkan: Hon'yaku to chushaku [The Chronicle of Gallus Anonymus, volume 1, translation and notes], *Okayama Daigaku Hogaku-kai Zasshi* 42 (1993): 178–212; 44 (1994): 287–334.

[20] Our choice of title has the practical advantage of avoiding confusion with the late medieval *Chronica Principum Poloniae*. On the genre of *gesta* and its contemporary parallels, see the Preface, above, and Thomas N. Bisson, "On not eating Polish bread in vain: Resonance and Conjuncture in the Deeds of the Princes of Poland (1109–1113)," *Viator* 29 (1998): 279–88.

The *GpP* remains the only source of information regarding its author. It has been hypothesized ever since the sixteenth century that his place of origin was France, and to this his customary name, Gallus, has been linked. The latter derives from a note by Kromer to be found at the top of fol. 119 of *H* (see Fig. 3): *Gallus*

Fig. 3. Bishop Kromer's note on Warsaw, National Library, MS 8006, fol. 119

hanc historiam scripsit, monachus, opinor, aliquis, ut ex proemiis coniicere licet qui Boleslai tertii tempore vixit. Unfortunately we have no information to judge on what basis Kromer made this ascription of authorship, or whether he intended "Gallus" as a proper name or to indicate the author was (or at least that he believed him to have been) a Frenchman. Nevertheless, this name became standard from the time of the first printed edition. A further variant, Martin Gallus—the result of Lengnich's misunderstanding of a passage in Długosz—had long vogue in German scholarship.[21] In the late nineteenth century, Maximilan Gumplowicz argued that the author was a certain Balduin Gallus, assumed to have been a bishop of Kruszwica; this view, briefly accepted by some, does not stand scrutiny.[22]

[21] See Jan Długosz, *Annales seu Cronicae incliti Regni Poloniae*, lib. 1–2, ed. Jan Dąbrowski (Warsaw: PWN, 1964), pp. 106, 141. What Lengnich took to be a reference to our author is rather to another chronicle of universal history unknown to us but similar in kind to the work of Martin of Opawa; see David, *Les sources*, p. 51, and on that chronicle, *LexMA* 2:1962 and 6:349–50.

[22] Maximilian Gumplowicz, *Bischof Balduin Gallus von Kruszwica, Polens erster lateinischer Chronist*, Sitzungsberichte der Kaiserlichen Akademie der Wissenschaften in Wien, Philosophisch-Historische Classe, vol. 132, H. 9 (Vienna: Tempsky, 1895).

There is little doubt that the author was a monk. In the letter preceding Book III he writes about "the place of [his] profession" (*locus professionis*), to which he intended to return with his completed work.[23] He may possibly have held some minor benefice in Poland, if his self-description as "a dispenser of a modest fare" (*dispensator obsonii*) is not merely a conventional expression of humility, or if the expression "not eating the bread of the Poles in vain" is taken in a broader sense of enjoying hospitality in the country.[24] An additional puzzle regarding his identity and his position in Poland is represented by the repeated references to undefined persons "ill-willed" or "envious" of the author, against whom he defends himself or whose censure he affects to disregard.[25] This may again be a mere *topos*,[26] perhaps with a hint that the products of his French literary training were not entirely to the taste of his Polish colleagues. However, they could allude to political adversaries of his patrons, or at persons indeed envious of his trusted position as a foreigner.

Certainly the writer was not a Pole, for in addressing the clergy of Poland he calls himself "an exile and a sojourner among you" (*exul apud vos et peregrinus*).[27] He could hardly have been a Czech or a German, as he is notably ill-disposed towards these nations. Significant is his fairly precise knowledge of the history of Hungary. The fact that he mentions six Hungarian rulers (five kings and a prince) and includes a reference, unnecessary for the narration, to an unidentified Hungarian church *de Bazoario*

[23] See p. 211. Henceforth passages in the *GpP* will be quoted in Roman numerals for Book/*Liber*, followed by either Epist. (etc.) or Arabic numerals for chapter/*capitulum*, together with the page number in the present edition.

[24] II:Epist, p. 111; III:Epist., p. 211.

[25] See, e.g., I:Epist., p. 5; II:3, p. 123; II:12, p. 139; III:Epist., p. 215.

[26] The literary tradition of defending one's work against malicious critics went back to Antiquity and was widespread in medieval writings; see Simon, Topik, I:91–3.

[27] III:Epist., p. 211. Though the notion of life on earth as a mere *peregrinatio* was a *topos*, it is more reasonable to take this phrase literally here.

suggests that he had some connections with that country.[28] At the same time, it is most unlikely that he would actually have been a Hungarian (or a Slav from Hungary, as has also been proposed), since the *literati* of that country were themselves exclusively foreign in the early twelfth century.

In fact, present scholarly consensus would seek the author's origins rather in Western Europe. Among the regions with which he has been connected are Provence, the Loire valley, and Flanders. Provence is suggested by the several references to the monastery of Saint-Gilles in Provence, including the description of the journey there by the Polish emissaries and the miraculous birth of the *gesta*'s hero through the prayers of the saint.[29] Given his knowledge of matters Hungarian, a development of this hypothesis links him to Somogyvár in south-western Hungary, site of the Hungarian daughter-house of Saint-Gilles and regularly populated by French monks.[30]

Maleczyński, however, proposed Flanders as a possible place of origin. His arguments are mainly based on literary analysis and on parallels between the *GpP* and certain chronicles from Normandy and southern England.[31] However, rhythmic prose similar to that found in our text was known over a much wider region than Flanders, and the genre of *gesta* was familiar in many regions outside the area proposed by Maleczyński, as far south as the

---

[28] See M. Plezia, "Ungarische Beziehungen des ältesten polnischen Chronisten," *Acta Antiqua Academiae Scientiarum Hungaricae* 7 (1959): 285–95. On the church, see below, n. 3, p. 77.

[29] I:Epil., pp. 7–11; I:Proem., p. 11.

[30] Founded 1091; the author includes it into the itinerary of Bolesław's pilgrimage (III:25, p. 277, n.2).

[31] E.g. between the threnody to Bolesław I the Brave in the *GpP* and the *planctus* mourning the death of Lanfranc, archbishop of Canterbury, by an anonymous monk from Crowland Abbey—a parallel recently questioned in Andrew Breeze, "The Crowland *Planctus de morte Lanfranci* and the Polish *Galli Anonymi Cronica*," *Revue bénédictine* 101 (1994): 421.

county of Barcelona and Sicily.[32] Indeed, stylistic features—to be discussed below—would rather point to central France, and especially the neighborhood of Tours. On the basis of his argument that the oldest Vita of St. Adalbert was written in Liège, Johannes Fried in a recent study suggests not only that the author was schooled there but also that it was through that Vita that he obtained his knowledge of early eleventh-century Poland.[33] Sev-

---

[32] Among the various *gesta* of the age the one perhaps closest to ours is *The Gesta Normanorum ducum of William of Jumiège, Orderic Vitalis and Robert of Toringny*, ed. and trans. Elisabeth M. C. Van Houts, 2 vols. (Oxford: Oxford UP, 1992–5). Among other more or less comparable works, mention might be made—without assuming any direct connection—of Suger, *Vie de Louis VI le Gros*, ed. Henri Waquet, Les Classiques de l'histoire de France au Moyen Age 11 (Paris: Champion, 1929), and the *Gesta comitum Barcinonensium*, ed. Louis Barrau Dihigo and Jaume Massó Torrents, Cròniques catalanes, no. 2, 2 vols. (Barcelona: Institut d'Éstudis Catalans, 1925). More are listed in Plezia, *Kronika Galla*, pp. 54–7, and Bisson, "On not eating," pp. 279–81. Plezia, "Ungarische Beziehungen," pp. 287–90, points out several parallels to those parts of the Hungarian chronicles believed to have been written in the late eleventh century, especially the passages about King (St.) Ladislas. Even if the existence of such an "*Ur-Gesta*" is now seriously doubted—see, e.g., György Györffy, *Krónikáink és a magyar őstörténet: Régi kérdések új válaszok* [Hungarian Chronicles and Ancient History: Old questions, new answers] (Budapest: Balassi, 1993)—possible connections cannot be excluded.

[33] Johannes Fried, "Gnesen-Aachen-Rom, Otto III. und der Kult des hl. Adalbert: Beobachtungen zum Älteren Adalbertsleben," in *Polen und Deutschland vor 1000 Jahren: Die Berliner Tagung über den "Akt von Gnesen,"* ed. Michael Borgolte (Berlin: Akademie Verlag, 2002), pp. 267–9. This hypothesis would need to be refined by additional study of the Liège school; such an inquiry might include the possibility of a personal relationship between our author and Cosmas of Prague, who spent several years in Liège, perhaps at the same time as the author of *GpP*—a question on which neither J. Bujnoch, "Gallus Anonymus und Cosmas von Prag: Zwei Geschichtsschreiber und Zeitgenossen," in *Osteuropa in Geschichte und Gegenwart*, ed. H. Lemberg, P. Nitsche, and E. Oberländer (Cologne and Vienna: Böhlau, 1977), pp. 301–15, nor Kersken, *Geschichtschreibung*, p. 493, n. 3.9, ventures a definite opinion.

eral other suggestions, including links to Venice, are too weak
to be considered seriously.[34]

In the light of all this it seems fair to assume that the anonymous
was a monk in some way connected to the monastery of Saint-
Gilles, that he had been educated somewhere in France (perhaps
in the region of Tours) and/or Flanders, and that he may even
have spent some time in the monastery of Somogyvár in Hungary. In all likelihood he came to Poland in the early twelfth
century (see below)—perhaps for the specific purpose of writing
such a work—and started working on the *GpP* soon after.[35]

The kingdom of Poland grew as a result of the predominance of
the Polanian rulers of the region around Gniezno (an area later
termed Wielkopolska or Greater Poland),[36] and had become a
Christian state more than hundred years before the *GpP* was
composed. While the so-called Piast dynasty was able to extend
its power both north and south of the core area, in the 1030s a
decline set in due to internal uprisings and extended wars with
the neighbors, above all with Bohemia, which frequently controlled Silesia and what came to be called Małopolska or Lesser
Poland (that is, the area around Cracow). The monarchy gradu-

[34] See Dorota Borawska, "Gallus Anonim czy Italus Anonim" [Gallus Anonymus or Italus Anonymus] *Przegląd Historyczny* 56 (1965): 111–9. The article
identifies the Venetian archdeacon Johannes Maurus with the Cracow bishop
Maur, who is also regarded as the author of the *GpP*.

[35] An alternative hypothesis—which cannot be dismissed out of hand—based
on the basis of the extensive eulogy of young Mieszko, who returned from
Hungarian exile and died soon thereafter in 1098, and the description of his
funeral, which reads in part like an eye-witness report, proposes that the author
belonged to the young prince's entourage and arrived in Poland with him.

[36] Aleksander Gieysztor, "Die Herrschaft der Piasten in Gnesen," *Bohemia* 40
(1999): 79–86; Jerzy Strzelczyk, "Polen im 10. Jahrhundert," in *Europas Mitte*,
1:446–58; idem, "Die Piasten und Polen," ibid., 1:531–6; cf. *The Centre of
Europe*, pp. 287–98. Still useful for the early period is Tadeusz Manteuffel, *The
Formation of the Polish State: The Period of Ducal Rule, 963–1194* (Detroit:
Wayne State UP, 1982).

ally recovered from the later eleventh century onwards with ups
and downs in both international standing and internal development.[37] However, the time when it is assumed the author arrived
and set to work was one of internal conflicts whose exact course
is not discernible in the sources but coincided with the final
chapter in a struggle between Bolesław III Wrymouth (1102–38)
and his older half-brother Zbigniew. The latter, having been
expelled from the country by Bolesław after years of civil war
and temporary truces, returned to Poland and made peace with
his brother once again; however, around the year 1111 he was
blinded on Bolesław's order.[38] This act of cruelty, made worse
by Bolesław having broken his oath of reconciliation, seems to
have provoked an opposition against him. The situation must
have posed considerable danger for the prince, as he decided to
perform a ritual of public penance. Against the background of
this political constellation, the writing of a *gesta* aimed at legiti-
mating Bolesław III as the true, divinely protected *dominus
naturalis* of Poland, scion of a dynasty that had ruled the country
"since times immemorial," may well have been deemed timely.
The second last chapter of Book III, describing the penitential
pilgrimage (perhaps an eye-witness report), is conceived most

[37] For the history of Poland in the eleventh and twelfth centuries in general,
see *Cambridge History of Poland: From the Origins to Sobieski (to 1696)*, vol.
1, ed. William F. Reddaway (Cambridge: CUP, 1950) [=*CHP*], pp. 16–84;
Norman Davis, *God's Playground: A History of Poland*, 2 vols. (Oxford:
Clarendon, 1982), 1:3–82; Aleksander Gieysztor, ed., *History of Poland* (Warsaw: PAN, 1968), pp. 56–80; now also Christian Lübke, "Frühzeit und Mittelalter (bis 1569)," in *Eine kleine Geschichte Polens*, ed. R. Janowski, Ch.
Lübke, and M. G. Müller (Frankfurt: Suhrkamp, 2000), pp. 20–150; and for an
archaeologically based overview, P. M. Barford, *The Early Slavs: Culture and
Society in Early Medieval Eastern Europe* (London: The British Museum Press,
2000), esp. pp. 261–7.

[38] While this event is not directly referred to in the *GpP*, it is alluded to in
Cosmas, *Chron. Boh.*, III:34, p. 205; see below, III:25, p. 274. For the date
1111, see Janusz Bieniak, "Polska elita polityczna XII wieku" [The Polish
political elite in the twelfth century], in *Społeczeństwo Polski średniowiecznej:
Zbiór studiów* [The society of medieval Poland: A collection of studies], ed.
Stefan K. Kuczyński (Warsaw: PWN, 1985), 2:49, n. 156.

conspicuously as a kind of justificatory pamphlet—which indeed could be said as well of the entire *GpP*—with little narrative content but with elaborate rhetorical embellishment.

While the *GpP* itself contains no direct information about the time of its composition, internal evidence suggests the second decade of the twelfth century. The Polish bishops included in the initial dedicatory letter, Simon, Paul, Maur, and Żyrosław, held their respective sees simultaneously between 1112 and 1118. Moreover, as the *GpP* presents Palatine Skarbimir of the Awdańcy kindred in a very positive light, it must have been written before his unsuccessful revolt, which seems to have taken place in 1117 or a year later.[39] The most likely date *ante quem* is thus the year 1117/18.[40] As for the *terminus post quem*, the narrative ends with the pilgrimage of Bolesław III, which probably dates to 1112–3, the last chapter of the work referring mainly to earlier events.[41]

[39] The Annals of the Cracow Chapter (*Rocznik kapituły krakowskiej*), written around 1266–7 but going back to now lost "*Annales deperditi*," date the revolt to 1117, the Old Annals (*Rocznik dawny*), written ca. 1120 (also based on earlier lost ones) and thus closer to the event, to 1118; see *Annales Cracovienses priores cum calendario*, ed. Zofia Kozłowska-Budkowa, MPH, n.s., 5 (Warsaw: PWN, 1978), pp. 51 and 15.

[40] Gumplowicz, *Bischof Balduin*, p. 24, argues for an earlier date, maintaining that King Coloman of Hungary, who died in early 1116, is treated as being alive; this, however, is not borne out by the text.

[41] Certain passages in the *GpP* have been read as hints of its having been written after the reign of Bolesław III—for example, II:29, p. 171, where the "progeny" of the Pomeranian Duke Świętobór are said to have been faithless to Poland, or II:19, p. 155, where it is said that the Cumans never again attacked Poland "during Bolesław's reign"—but these may also be read in a rhetorical or "prophetic" sense, or could even be later interpolations. By contrast, the author's words about Bolesław's regretting what he had done to his brother (III:25, p. 273) sound very much as if they were written while the duke was still alive.

The environment in which the author moved while working on the *GpP* can only be surmised. But the opening reference to the chancellor Michael as his *cooperator* who inspired his work and helped him in it, and the address to the ducal chaplains in the letter introducing Book III, would direct attention to the *capella*, the ducal chapel (at this time already in Cracow), which may have also been the nucleus of the later royal chancellery.[42] In such a milieu, among educated people familiar with affairs of the state, the author could well have found the sources for the information he transmits.[43]

Several passages in the *GpP* suggest that the author was connected in some way with the Awdańcy kindred. Chancellor Michael was a member of that family, as was the palatine Skarbimir, one of the very few magnates singled out by name for praise. Also of this family was another Michael ("the Old"), who advises the prince at the siege of Kołobrzeg.[44] The Awdańcy, a family of Norse origin, came to Poland most probably via Rus' as professional warriors of Bolesław I the Brave during his campaign against Kiev in 1018; they formed part of the group of political supporters of Bolesław II, whom they followed into

---

[42] I:Epist., p. 3, n. 5; III:Epist., p. 211. On the royal chapel and its probable role in the spread of literacy in medieval Poland, see Gerard Labuda, "Miejsce powstania kroniki Anonima Galla" [The places of origin of the chronicle of Gallus Anonymus], in *Prace z dziejów Polski feudalnej ofiarowane Romanowi Grodeckiemu w 70 rocznicę urodzin*, ed. Z. Budkowa et al. (Warsaw: PWN, 1960), pp. 107–21 and Anna Adamska, "'From Memory to Written Record' in the Periphery of Medieval Latinitas: The Case of Poland in the Eleventh and Twelfth Centuries," in *Charters and the Use of the Written Word in Medieval Society*, ed. K. Heidecker (Turnhout: Brepols, 2000), pp. 83–100.

[43] Other hypotheses have sought to connect the author with, e.g., the episcopal court of Poznań, or with the Benedictine monastery of Lubin or its dependency Jeżow in Masovia, but do not stand up to scrutiny, not least for chronological reasons regarding the dates of the monastic foundations.

[44] II:28, p. 171. This Michael is identified by genealogists as the senior of the kindred at that time.

Hungarian exile, but under Bolesław III Wrymouth they returned and again became part of the ruling elite.[45]

The anonymous probably left Poland soon after the assumed date of writing the work. If he was indeed connected with the Awdańcy, the decline in their political importance after the aforementioned rebellion of Skarbimir may have entailed the loss of one basis of his support in Poland. Whatever the case, if according to his declared intentions he returned to his home monastery it is likely that he had done so by 1118. Nothing further is known of him.

GENRE, STRUCTURE, FORM, AND STYLE

The choice of genre was suggested by the political aim of the work, namely the historical legitimization of the ruling dynasty and its contemporary representative, Bolesław III. *Gesta* were very much in vogue in Latin Europe in the author's time. They have the common characteristic of adapting dynastic myth to the legitimization of territorial domination in an age of growing stability of such rule. As the name suggests, *gesta* concentrate on the (usually martial) deeds of the rulers, and present the history of a region (of which they often include in the initial chapters a description in the form of a *laus terrae,* or praise of the land) through the history of its ruling dynasty.[46] In contrast to "chronicles" and "histories," authors of *gesta* do not usually

[45] Teresa Kiersnowska, "O pochodzeniu rodu Awdańców" [Concerning the provenance of the Awdańcy family], in *Społeczeństwo Polski średniowiecznej* [The society of medieval Poland], ed. Stefan K. Kuczyński (Warsaw: PWN, 1992), 5:57–72; Bieniak, "Polska elita," 2:25–32.

[46] According to Bisson's count ("On not eating," p. 279) the author refers to "deeds" (*gesta*) no less than seventeen times in the *GpP*. For the genre in general, see E.M.C. Van Houts, *Local and Regional Chronicles,* Typologie des sources du Moyen Age occidental, fasc. 74 (Turnholt: Brepols, 1995); on their ecclesiatical counterparts, see M. Sot, *Gesta episcoporum, gesta abbatum,* ibid., fasc. 37 (ibid., 1981).

attempt to give a general picture of the age, and avoid exploring wider connections and causal or other explanations.[47] They may not even observe strict chronological order. As a rule, *gesta* put a special emphasis on the achievements of contemporary rulers, and are often inspired by current political needs. In this sense they attempt to fulfil what may be termed propaganda functions.

In common with virtually all medieval history-writing, *gesta* aim at setting an example of the good and the bad for the edification of the reader (in this case perhaps better described as the listener, as the author mentions more than once that he intends his work to be recited).[48] In the *GpP* stories are told and virtues listed as examples to successors, and the ways of earlier rulers or their courts are set implicitly or explicitly in contrast to the author's own times.[49] In this sense the work also functions as a kind of "mirror of princes." But within that tradition the emphasis, especially in the case of the work's protagonist, Bolesław III, is on martial virtues, both in hunting and war alike, the *exempla*

---

[47] For the on-going discussion of the genres of medieval history-writing, see, e.g., Herbert Grundmann, *Geschichstschreibung im Mittelalter: Gattungen—Epochen—Eigenart* (Göttingen: Vandenhoeck & Rupprecht, 1965); Bernard Guenée, *Histoire et culture historique dans l'Occident médiéval* (Paris: Aubier Montaigne, 1980); Adriaan H. B. Breukelaar, *Historiography and Episcopal Authority in Sixth-Century Gaul*, Forschungen zur Kirchen- und Dogmengeschichte, 57 (Göttingen: Vandenhoek & Ruprecht, 1994).

[48] Explicitly stated at II:Epil., p. 115; at III:Epist., p. 213, the reference is more general, to the recital of heroic deeds "in schools and in palaces." This question is discussed in detail by Karolina Targosz, "*Gesta principum recitata*: 'Teatr czynów polskich władców' Galla Anonima" [*Gesta principum recitata*: 'A theatre of the deeds of the Polish rulers' of Gallus Anonymus], *Pamiętnik Teatralny* 29 (1980): 152–67.

[49] The moral program is spelled out most explicitly in I:10, p. 51, and III:Epist., p. 213–5, but see also the I:Proem., p. 11; I:16, p. 67; I:23, p. 89; I: 26, p. 93; II:11, p. 137; etc. In I:2, p. 23, he points to the less "haughty" court of princes of the past; in I:11, p. 55, to the spiritual rather than secular concerns in the missions of Bolesław; in I:12, p. 59, to the peasants' happiness rather than fear at the coming of the travelling court; in II:35, p. 185, to the danger of the division of rule between equals; and so on.

regarding the administration of merciful justice and good government being drawn from the earlier periods, mainly the reign of Bolesław I. Nor, in contrast to many contemporary *specula principum*, is much space given to expressly Christian virtues, apart from general references to rulers' piety, their foundation of churches, and the propagation of Christianity among the pagans. Only in the chapter on Bolesław III's pilgrimage do we encounter a fairly detailed description of personal piety.

The declared subject of the *GpP* is the life and times of Bolesław III Wrymouth: at the outset the author says that it is because of him that he describes the acts of his predecessors.[50] This premise defines the structure of the work as a whole. Most of Book II and all of Book III are devoted to the deeds of Bolesław III, only Book I telling the story of his ancestors, and this one, too, culminating in the miraculous birth of the hero. The first five chapters of the work pass from legendary beginnings to the conversion of Mieszko I (960–92) to Christianity.[51] Twelve chapters describe the times of his successor, Bolesław I the Brave (992–1025), emphasizing the latter's good government, riches, and campaigns against pagans and Kievan Rus'. The best-known episode in this narrative is the famous meeting with Emperor Otto III in the year 1000 in Gniezno, which is preceded by a few sentences on St. Adalbert. Through the deeds of Mieszko II Lambert (1025–34) and Casimir I the Restorer (1038–58) the author presents first the decline and then the reconstruction of

---

[50] I:Proem., pp. 11, 15.

[51] The anonymous monk places much less emphasis on the "discontinuity" between pagan and Christian past than most medieval historians do. Rather, some kind of divine approval is granted already to the pagan ancestors of the dynasty. Moreover, the Christianisation of Poland in general is not described, only the baptism of the duke at the insistence of his Czech wife (I:5, pp. 29–31). Nor, if one disregards the author's interpretation of the sudden healing of the blind child Mieszko (I:4, pp. 27–9)—taken metaphorically as the transition from pagan blindness to Christian enlightment—is any "miraculous" event introduced, as is usually the case in such conversion narratives (though the earlier story of Piast and his guests does include one).

the kingdom. The chapters dedicated to Bolesław II the Bold describe his struggles with Poland's neighbors, and with intentional obscurity allude to the circumstances of his fall; his conflict with Bishop (St.) Stanislas is only hinted at before passing on to his exile to Hungary.[52] The book ends with the accession of Bolesław III's father, Duke Władysław Herman (1081–1102) and the birth of the *gesta*'s hero.

Book II begins with reign of Władysław Herman and soon introduces the two protagonists of the rest of the *GpP*, Bolesław III and his stepbrother Zbigniew. First, the conflict of the young princes with their father—and more particularly, with his palatine Sieciech—is described in detail, ending with the division of the realm and the death-bed testament of Władysław Herman.[53] Thereafter the author focuses on the manifestations of the ever more visible qualities and virtues of Bolesław and the growing conflicts with his brother. Besides tales of his youthful exploits the book contains detailed descriptions of military campaigns in Bohemia and Pomerania. Book III continues in the same vein, giving extensive coverage to the imperial campaign of 1109 against Poland and ever more successful fights against the

[52] In this case the author may have had to tread on slippery ground, for it is unclear whether or not Władysław Herman, the father of his hero, was implicated in the opposition to Boleslaw II which culminated in the execution of Bishop Stanislas—hence the carefully balanced sentence "neither do we forgive a traitor bishop, nor do we commend a king . . . " (I:27, p. 97). On this, see the detailed analysis in Tadeusz Grudziński, *Boleslaus the Bold, Called also the Bountiful, and Bishop Stanislaus: The Story of a Conflict*, trans. Lech Petrowicz (Warsaw: Interpress, 1985), pp. 89–106.

[53] The original position of Zbigniew—whether senior or not—has been a major point of dispute among historians. Gumplowicz ("Zbigniew, Grossfürst von Polen," in *Studien*, pp. 1–123) devoted a long study to proving that he was a legitimate duke of Poland, or co-ruler with his brother, according to their father's wish. On the other hand, the otherwise well-informed Cosmas of Prague nowhere mentions that Bolesław III, whom he clearly disliked, sought to deny his brother's senior position. His final fate is another matter the author has difficulty reporting; his presentation of excuses and explanations in III:25 is a masterpiece in "shaping history."

Czechs and Pomeranians, often tied to the "treacherous" actions of Zbigniew. It ends rather abruptly (on which more below) with the downfall of Zbigniew and Bolesław's expiatory pilgrimage to Hungary.[54]

Each book starts with a dedicatory letter. In Book I the addressees are all the bishops of Poland, listed by name; in Book II, Bishop Paul and Chancellor Michael; and in Book III, the ducal chaplains and other ecclesiastics in Poland. These letters are rich in the traditional *topoi* of dedications, and include the author's justification of his undertaking the task and a commendation of the fruit of his efforts for the approbation of the addressees; they end (especially for Books I and III) with hints at the author's deserved recompense, and are rounded off with an "Epilogue" in verse.

Within this framework the narrative displays a number of different registers. It begins in established story-telling style: "There was a duke in the city of Gniezno. . . ." Thereafter elements from classical biography and hagiographical miracle stories mingle with anecdotal detail and "battle memoirs" (evidently derived from eyewitnesses, in view of their vividness and precision).[55] Again following ancient example, fitting embellishment is provided in the form of fictive speeches (deathbed addresses, exhortations to battle, or exchanges between enemies) as well as by

[54] Kersken (p. 523) points out that "contemporary history" in the *GpP* takes up almost half of the text, notably more than in comparable *gesta* and national histories.

[55] Some incidents, such as the mysterious night shadows frightening the warriors at Nakło, the battle of the offal between the camp-followers of Bolesław I and the Ruthenians, and the women strawberry-gatherers disarming an enemy soldier must have been remembered because of these quaint or comic motifs, or because of some otherwise memorable element, as when Polish troops almost mistook their comrades for the enemy (II:3, p. 121; I:10, pp. 53–5; II:49, p. 209; III:23, p. 265; II:49, p. 209). Once the author even spells out that he is narrating a battle because of its novelty: *quoddam . . . prelium novitate facti satis memorabile referamus* (I:10, p. 51).

"letters" presumed to be written by rulers. The more or less chronological narrative of major events is frequently interrupted with eulogies of the main hero (be it Bolesław III himself or his model the first Bolesław),[56] as well as the edificatory and crypto-critical comments referred to above. What is entirely missing—though this is not uncommon in the genre of *gesta*—is an annalistic approach to the course of history (contrast here the near-contemporary chronicle of Cosmas of Prague).

The author shows a broad familiarity with ancient mythology and literature, even if his knowledge is hardly profound and at times inaccurate.[57] The influence of his reading is manifested throughout the text, although the only works he alludes to explicitly are the *Bellum Iugurthinum* of Sallust and an unidentified work he calls *historia principalis*.[58] Sallust seems to have been his favorite author—the borrowings and echoes being too numerous to be noted every time in our commentary.[59] Allusions and even verbatim quotations from other classical writers (Vergil, Ovid, and Horace) have also been detected, and he seems to have known such Christian authors as Boethius and Sulpicius Severus, as well as perhaps the historians Regino of Prüm and Thietmar of Merseburg. To be sure, the source of his knowledge may well have been limited to passages in the *excerpta* and *florilegia* used in the schools. The same holds true for the

[56] See Brigitta Kürbis, "Zum Herrscherlob in der Chronik des Gallus Anonymus (Anfang 11. Jahrhundert): '*Laudes regiae*' am polnischen Hof?," in *Patronage und Klientel: Ergebnisse einer polnisch-deutschen Konferenz*, ed. H-H. Nolte, Beihefte zum Archiv für Kulturgeschichte, 29 (Cologne: Böhlau, 1989), pp. 51–67.

[57] For example, he confuses Amphitrion and Amphitrite (I:Proem., p. 13) and perhaps Cleopatra and Dido (III:Epist., p. 215); nor are his biblical citations free from confusion (e.g. II:49, p. 209, n. 1).

[58] It has been suggested that this refers to the *Antiquitates Iudaicae* of Josephus Flavius, but this is highly debatable.

[59] See R. J. Kras, "Dzieła Sallustiusza w warsztacie Anonima zw. Gallem" [The works of Sallust in the workshop of the Anonymous callled Gallus], *Roczniki Humanistyczne* 50 (2002), fasc. 2, 3–51

occasional echo of philosophical terms, above all the notions of *natura* and *naturalis*, important in ancient as well as Christian philosophy.[60]

However, not surprisingly, the most extensively used authority is the Bible. Among Old Testament books he refers often to Genesis, Job, and the historical books Kings and Maccabees. As a monk he would also have been familiar with the daily routine of monastic life, thus the words of the psalms very often find their way into his text. He also cites the Gospels and several of the Epistles.

These Biblical echoes are found at different levels. There are direct borrowings, such as the phrase *per speculum in enigmate* in the vision preceding the death of Bolesław I.[61] On occasion these function independently of their biblical context, or even with contrary meanings: for example, where Bolesław III fighting against his enemies is compared to a lion in words which in the original text apply to Satan.[62] Elsewhere, quotations and echoes emphasize the message of a given passage. For example, *Quis puer iste erit*, originally referring to John the Baptist, is applied to Bolesław III Wrymouth, or the *visitavit nos oriens ex alto* of Luke's gospel foretelling the birth of Christ is used here in reference to the birth of Bolesław I the Brave.[63] Finally, there are narrative elements harkening back to Biblical precedents, such as the visit of two mysterious travelers in the cottage of Piast,

---

[60] See II:Epist., p. 111; on the important notion of *dominus naturalis*, see below, p. liii.

[61] I:16, p. 69 (=1 Cor. 12:13).

[62] II:36, p. 185 (=1 Pet. 5:18). Similarly, the author compares his hero to a fire-breathing dragon (II:39, p. 191; III:3, p. 231), a creature which in biblical texts and in medieval imagination in general is usually seen as an evil creature, indeed a metaphor for Satan.

[63] I:6, p. 31 (cf. Luke 1:78). However, the reference may also allude to the baptism of Bolesław's father Mieszko.

generally taken to be modeled on the angelic visitation of Abraham at Mamreh.[64]

In literary terms the *GpP* is an important and very elegant example of rhythmic (and often rhymed) prose. The author presents himself as a person well versed in this field; among the reasons he gives for undertaking his work is the wish "to keep up my practice in composing."[65] It has been noted that in many respects he was ahead of his time, a point investigated and underscored by Karl Polheim and Tore Janson in their detailed studies of rhythmic prose.[66] In this regard the prose of the *GpP* is similar to the style of writing taught and practiced in the region of Tours and known to us most particularly from the works of Hildebert of Lavardin.[67]

[64] I:1, p. 17. However, such numinous visitors are not unknown in classical texts, e.g., the story of Philemon and Baucis (see Ovid, *Met.* 8.616ff.).

[65] III:Epist., p. 211: *ut . . . dictandi consuetudinem conservarem.*

[66] K. Polheim, *Die lateinische Reimprosa* (Berlin: Weidmann, 1925), pp. 56–87; T. Janson, *Prose Rhythm in Medieval Latin from the 9th to the 13th Century*, Studia Latina Stockholmiensia, vol. 20 (Stockholm: Almquist & Wiksell, 1975), pp. 73–4. The combination in the *GpP* of the so-called *cursus velox* with the *cursus spondaicus* is notable, for the latter was not commonly used in the rhythmic prose of that period.

[67] Janson, *Prose Rhythm*, pp. 73–6; M. Plezia, "Les relations littéraires entre la France et la Pologne au XIIe siècle," *Bulletin de l'Association Guillaume Budé* 42 (1983): 67–78. For the relevant parallels, see M. Plezia, "Nowe studia nad Gallem Anonimem" [New studies on Gallus Anonymus], in *Mente et litteris: O kulturze i społeczeństwie wieków średnich* [*Mente et litteris*: On the culture and society of the Middle Ages], ed. H. Chłopocka (Poznań: Wydawnictwo Naukowe Uniwersytetu im. Adama Mickiewicza w Poznaniu, 1984), pp. 114–5. On the other hand, comparable stylistic features are found in the Venetian "Translation of Saint Nicolas"—a fact which has given rise to speculations about our author's possible Italian origin (cf. note 34, p. xxix, above).

The author of the *GpP* uses virtually all the *flores rhetorici* prescribed in the *artes dictandi* of the time.[68] Besides the formal *cursus*, many other rhythmic elements and internal as well as external rhymes appear. These rhythmic and rhymed elements may have been intended to enhance the understanding and memorizing of the text by its performers and perhaps also its audiences. Not atypically for medieval Latin, the text incorporates even the occasional hexameter, a form classically unrhymed but here embellished by internal rhyme.[69] Rhythmic and rhymed clauses are frequent, and can at times be arranged to read as couplets or triplets of verse.[70] However, besides these the *GpP* contains passages specifically intended as verse, and included in the text according to the principles of *prosimetrum*. Besides the Epilogues there are several complete poems, such as the lament over Bolesław the Brave and a shorter one in which Duke Casimir encourages his warriors. There are as well two "songs," one attributed to Polish warriors reaching the shores of the Baltic Sea and one allegedly sung by the soldiers of Emperor Henry V;[71] these may go back to an actual oral tradition, although it is hard to see how the second, praising the enemy, could have really been much more than an exercise in poetic imagination.[72]

In addition, the author's Latin is replete with metaphors, similes and *topoi*, some familiar, others less so. It is perhaps surprising

---

[68] The most widely used medieval handbooks of style, for example that of Alberic of Monte Cassino, may not yet have been known to the author, but there were several other guides in circulation; see Martin Camargo, *Ars dictaminis, ars dictandi*, Typologie des sources du Moyen Age occidental, fasc. 60 (Turnhout: Brepols, 1991).

[69] E.g. at the head of II:Epil., p. 114, or at the end of Book I, p. 108.

[70] We have been more selective than the critical edition in printing these as "verse"; see below, p. lxiii.

[71] II:28, p. 171; III:11, pp. 241–3.

[72] Praise of Bolesław III by his enemies appears elsewhere as well; for example, at II:17, p. 153, he is styled by the Pomeranians "the wolf's son," and at II:33, p. 179, he is acknowledged as invincible.

to find several metaphors borrowed from the hunt, hardly the most likely activity to be familiar to a monastic author.[73] While the battle scenes occasionally hearken back to classical (or Biblical) models or suggest orally transmitted epic narratives, they are frequently constructed in very original ways, with a most skilful choice of words and arrangement of clauses, linked by alliteration and internal rhymes. Contrasts and parallelisms, onomatopoeia, and sudden changes into the historical present conjure up lively images of the heat of battle—again strikingly precise and "professional" descriptions of military activity and technology from the pen of a monk. Several of these scenes (for instance, the "parade" of Bolesław the Brave's troops at Gniezno, or the anecdote of Bolesław II and the poor cleric)[74] are presented in such vivid and "theatrical" detail that it would be not be hard to imagine them reproduced on stage. Reading these, Marian Plezia was reminded of the *Galerie des Batailles* in the Château of Versailles, where exact historical details are presented according to high artistic standards and ways of construction.[75]

Irony and humor are not typical features of twelfth-century narratives, but the author seems to have a subtle sense for both. Irony is usually aimed at "foreigners," as in the story of Prince Isiaslav and his "dearly purchased kiss,"[76] but sometimes it is goodhearted "folk" humor, as in the story of the poor cleric. The ironical vein is most conspicuous in the treatment of Emperor Henry's campaign of 1109, the dead bodies preserved and sent back to Germany in salt being described as the "tribute" he

[73] E.g. II:27, II:37. Most have ancient literary precedents, but the addition of the dragon (II:39, p. 191 and III:3, p. 231) to the menagerie of classical beasts— lions, bears, Molossan hounds, etc.—is an interesting innovation; compare the author's original treatment of classical motifs at III:23, p. 266, n. 2.

[74] I:6, p. 35; I:26, pp. 93–7.

[75] Plezia, *Kronika Galla*, p. 79.

[76] I:23, pp. 89–91.

gained from Poland.[77] Indeed, one wonders where the author intended to draw the line at times—how far elements of the grotesque represent mere "entertainment" for his listeners or where these shade into ridicule. Certainly there seems a degree of overstatement in the account of the gifts sent by Bolesław I to Emperor Otto—everything from tablecloths to cutlery!—or the caricature of the ladies of that time unable to walk under the burden of all their gold and jewelry.[78]

Special mention should be made of the stylistic handling of the narrator's relationship to his reader/listener. The author addresses not only his patrons, recommending his work for their favor, but quite often, as when he draws a moral, his imaginary audience as well. He clearly intends them to share his view of the past when he excuses an omission with some formula like "it would be tedious for you to listen...."[79] In some cases this seems to be a subterfuge for hiding something that does not fit his political purpose: "intentional forgetting" might be the proper term.

A notable quality of the narrative is the way it plays with the time of narrated events and the "time" of his writing (and of his audience's hearing/reading). So, for example, at the point of Casimir's exile in Germany, the author interjects, "let us now leave Casimir to relax with his mother," and then returns to events in Poland.[80] Again he—surely ironically—leaves the Emperor Henry "to enjoy his stroll through the forests of Poland,"

---

[77] III:9, p. 239, III:15, p. 247.

[78] I:6, p. 39; I:12, p. 57. See Gert Althoff, "Symbolische Kommunikation zwischen Piasten und Ottonen," in *Polen und Deutschland vor 1000 Jahren: Die Berliner Tagung über den "Akt von Gnesen,"* ed. Michael Borgolte (Berlin: Akademie, 2002), pp. 303–6.

[79] I:8, p. 49; I:15, p. 65; I:27, p. 97; II:7, p. 133; II:16, p. 149, etc.

[80] I:18, p. 77.

and turns to narrating further military actions of Bolesław.[81]
Another mark of the author's handling of time is seen in those
cases in which he displays knowledge of future events; thus the
account of the fate of Zbigniew, in particular, is told from the
beginning with an awareness of its tragic finale.[82]

It has long been debated whether the *GpP* is complete in the
form as we have it. The narrative ends with the surrender of
an unnamed "another castle" (*castrum aliud*) on the Polish-
Pomeranian frontier. The rubric speaks of the submission of
Nakło—an event which, it seems, did subsequently come to pass,
but according to this chapter the siege was broken off, and no
further mention is made of the castle or its fate. This lack of a
clear-cut, convincing ending, together with the author's repeated
allusions to his enemies (and perhaps the fall of his assumed
patrons, the Awdańcy), have led some to conclude that he was
forced to stop work abruptly in the face of opposition of some
kind. Perhaps, too, his comments on the Zbigniew affair (III:25)
were unwelcome and caused offence. In purely literary terms one
feels that the work could fittingly have concluded with the long
twenty-fifth chapter on Bolesław's pilgrimage.[83]

---

[81] III:3, p. 231.

[82] E.g. II:5, p. 129, where it is written that Zbigniew "earned . . . what was later
to happen," or in II:35, p. 185, where the author (or perhaps one of the wise
men of Poland) foretells that Zbigniew "has fallen grievously . . . from where
he will not afterwards be able to be raised."

[83] At any rate, in the early thirteenth century the manuscript used by Kadłubek
already ended where the text known to us does. Plezia (*Kronika Galla*, pp.
72–73) notes several other chronicles, e.g. Albert of Aachen's *Historia Hi-
erosolymitana*, Eadmer's *Historia novorum in Anglia*, and Helmold's *Chronica
Slavorum*, and even one of the author's favorite models, Sallust's *Catilina*, all
of which lack a well-defined close. It has been suggested that the point of
including a description of two successful sieges (and perhaps the planned
continuation over one or more chapters, including, e.g., the final conquest of
Nakło) may have been to make plain that in spite of everything Bolesław still
enjoyed the full support of divine grace as proven by his victories against the
pagans.

SOURCES

As far as we can judge, the historical information in the *GpP* comes largely from oral traditions of one sort or another (though how he might have accessed these, not being a native of the country he lived in and wrote about, is another question).[84] However, it has been argued that the author also had access to written sources. Explicit mention is made only of a "book of the martyrdom" of Saint Adalbert, cited in the context of the meeting in Gniezno. Since none of the known legends of Saint Adalbert written before the author's time deals with the events in Gniezno, the author's source must have been a text now lost.[85] Another piece of information that may go back to a written source is the list of the number of troops of Bolesław the Brave.[86] The words *fidelis recordatio* 'faithful record' (or 'recollection')[87] regarding the deeds of the early Christian rulers of Poland have been seen as a reference to annalistic sources; however, none of

---

[84] That he was not wholly ignorant of the vernacular is shown by the occasional inclusion of Slavic words and etymologies.

[85] On the problem of the earliest Life of St. Adalbert, see Fried, "Gnesen-Aachen-Rome." It has also been suggested that the author had access to another, now lost Passion of St. Adalbert, written perhaps by Bruno of Querfurt; see Reinhard Wenskus, *Studien zur historisch-politischen Gedankenwelt Brunos von Querfurt*, Mitteldeutsche Forschungen, 5 (Munich and Cologne: Böhlau, 1956), pp. 202–46.

[86] I:8, p. 47. See now R. Barnat, "Siły zbrojne Bolesława Chrobrego w świetle relacji Galla Anonima" [The forces of Bolesław the Brave in the light of the account of Gallus Anonymous], *Przegląd Historyczny* 88 (1997): 223–35, with bibliography. The presence in the list of the stronghold of Giecz, a castle of no significance after its destruction by the Czechs in 1038, suggests the knowledge derives from some no longer identifiable early eleventh-century written source; see Teresa Krystofiak, "Giecz," in *Europas Mitte*, 1:464–7, cf. *Europe's Centre*, pp. 299–300.

[87] I:3, p. 24.

the old annals known from later sources contain material relevant to the period in question.[88]

Besides these, it is not impossible that the author used notes from calendars. Several dates from the liturgical year appear in the narrative.[89] However, most are connected with the deeds of Bolesław III, for which more direct information would have been available from contemporaries. Besides, their symbolic or religious significance in the narrative could have long preserved them in memory and oral tradition.[90] For example, the battle with the pagan Pomeranians took place around the feast of St. Michael, a saint closely connected with the Christianization of pagans and the defeat of heathen cults. Another victory is dated to the feast of the Assumption of the Virgin, which was also the day of Bolesław's knighting.[91]

Apart from the oral sources touched on previously—the accounts of participants and eyewitnesses (which seem to reach as far back as the times of Bolesław II the Bountiful)—another type of oral source seems to have been old dynastic legends. These would derive from the genealogical tradition of the ruling dynasty with its concomitant mythical elements.[92] Such informa-

---

[88] On lost annals and their questionable use by our author, see now Wojciech Polak, "Uwagi w sprawie rocznikarskiego źródła *Kroniki* Galla Anonima [Remarks about annalistic sources of the *Chronicle* of Gallus Anonymus], *Roczniki Humanistyczne*, 47 (2000) fasc. 2: 447–60.

[89] See II:1, 2, 18, 25; III:1, 5, 25, 26 (pp. 116, 119, 153, 163, 221, 233, 279, 283). Plezia, *Kronika Galla*, 191–2, lists 14 instances, beginning in 1089.

[90] See Wojciech Polak, "Czas w najstarszej polskiej kronice" [Time in the oldest Polish chronicle], Zeszyty Naukowe Katolickiego Uniwersytetu Lubelskiego 39, no. 3–4 (1996): 48–9.

[91] II:3, p. 121; III:26, p. 283; II:18, p. 153.

[92] An example is perhaps the mysterious downfall of Pumpil and his progeny, apparently opponents of the Piasts, which is introduced by the words: *narrant etiam seniores antiqui* ... (I:3, p. 22). For the reliability of the *GpP* on the early Piasts, see Kazimierz Jasiński, *Rodowód pierwszych Piastów* [The genealogy of the first Piasts] (Warsaw and Wrocław: Uniw. Wrocławski, 1993), 45–6; see also n. 108, p. lii, below.

tion was usually preserved in the memory of the political elites
in view of its importance for the legal, political, and ideological
aspects of succession. Anecdotes about the behavior of rulers,
both those which demonstrate their superiority vis-a-vis others
(such as Bolesław's humiliation of the Russian prince Izjaslav),
their mercy and magnanimity (the duke's pardoning certain
rebels at his wife's plea), or their generosity (Bolesław the
Bountiful's bounty to a poor cleric) may have been preserved in
the tradition of court circles.[93] Naturally, the author selected and
edited these traditions in accordance with the main purpose of
his work, not without borrowings from literary tradition. Thus,
his presentation of the reign of Bolesław I the Brave is fashioned
not only according to the image of a golden age in days gone by,
but with the idea that the third Bolesław would be able to return
the realm to that desired state of affairs, its "pristine state."[94]
Moreover, since these various traditions may have reached the
author in an incomplete or fragmentary way, it is not surprising
that the *GpP* often includes contradictory information, which
the author seems at no pains to reconcile.[95]

THE *GpP* AS A HISTORICAL SOURCE

As a source of historical information the *GpP* clearly has its
limitations—not the least being that not a single date is preserved
in the entire text—yet for all that it is the only surviving account

---

[93] I:23, pp. 89–91; I:13, pp. 59–63; I:26, pp. 93–7.

[94] II:20, p. 157.

[95] Most notably personalities and motives seem to be handled inconsistently
(at least by modern standards). For example, having been repeatedly portrayed
as duplicitous and perjured in the Sieciech affair, Duke Władysław is nevertheless described in his "obituary" as "that good and gentle man." Again, though
he casts Zbigniew as his brother Bolesław's evil, or at best misguided counter-
part, the author dismisses his alleged plans to murder his brother as not
compatible with the personality of "a quite humble and quite simple man"
(II:21, p. 157; III:25, p. 273).

of the history of Poland before the early twelfth century. Despite
the tendentious nature of the narrative it contains much about
the history of the country that we know from no other
source—though this very fact casts doubts on the reliability of
the information, which we usually have no means to verify.

As the *GpP* concentrates on the wars and victories of the
dynasty, the expansion of Polish lordship, and conflicts with
neighbors, what may be termed external relations provide the
central focus of the narrative. These include two major incidents
involving Poland's relations with the medieval Empire: the visit
of Otto III in 1000, and the invasion by Henry V in 1109.
Otherwise, the conflicts described are mostly with Poland's
southern neighbors, the Czechs, and the northern pagans, the
Pomeranians: resisting and avenging the incursions of both, and
the gradual conquest of Pomerania are ongoing subplots of the
narrative.[96] But even these are subsumed into the main "message": the praise of the valor of exemplary rulers, and in particular
that of Bolesław III. Earlier campaigns are reported selectively
and with little precision,[97] but generally presented as victorious
and as resulting in permanent conquests, while relations with the
neighbors are often connected to internal conflicts, especially in
Book III, in terms of Zbigniew's "treacherous" contacts with
foreigners.

The treatment of domestic affairs is largely subordinated to the
dominant theme of dynastic progress or conflict. In this respect,
the author is especially careful to control the narration. Thus he
does not allow his picture of the golden age of Bolesław I to be
overshadowed by the interdict imposed upon Poland by archbishop Gaudentius (or his successor), which must have taken

[96] On the history of Pomerania in the eleventh and early twelfth centuries, see
the literature in I:Proem., p. 30, below.

[97] Notable is the almost complete silence on the protracted and complicated
conflicts with the Empire and with Poland's western neighbors (Saxony,
Misnia).

place during his reign.[98] The great pagan (or servile, or "feudal") revolt around 1030 receives detailed coverage, rare among contemporary writings, whereas a notable omission is the 1031-2 rebellion of Bezprym against Mieszko II Lambert. Otherwise even major internal developments—the reconstruction that must have taken place in the reigns of Casimir "the Restorer" and his son Bolesław II—are omitted in favor of activities conferring military glory. Domestic affairs come again to the forefront with the appearance on the scene of the sons of Władysław Herman, Zbigniew and Bolesław, whose conflicts first with their father and then those between themselves receive detailed albeit very subjective coverage. However, there is no information on the nature or identity of the supporters of Zbigniew, who is portrayed as surrounded by "evil counselors" and "foolish men" whose advice pushes him towards disaster. About the government of Bolesław III we learn nothing at all.

In spite of the fact that the spread of Christianity and the organization of the church was a central issue in early medieval Poland, such information as the *GpP* conveys on church history is far from reliable or extensive—notwithstanding the author's promises to sing the praises of Poland's prelates.[99] The author gives summary treatment even to the highly significant foundation of the archbishopric of Gniezno. An enigmatic reference hints at the existence in Poland of two church metropolies.[100] Besides a few references to foundations and consecrations of churches,[101] the *GpP* is rather vague about the rulers' actual ecclesiastical and monastic sponsorship, although this was regarded as one of the main tasks and virtues of medieval rulers.

---

[98] I:19, p. 81. It is mentioned only in passing and in connection with the description of the calamities of a later reign, accompanied by one of the author's typical asides that the events occurred for "reasons unknown to me."

[99] I:Epist., p. 5; III:Epist., p. 112.

[100] I:11, p. 55.

[101] I:11, p. 55; I:21, p. 87; II:33, p. 177; etc.

While other *gesta* frequently list heroic deeds of ancestors of famous kindreds, the *GpP* contains few references to individual magnates or great men as supporters of the dynasty. Besides the Awdańcy, only the tutor of Bolesław III, Wojsław, the *comes* Żelisław, and the cupbearer Dzierżek are mentioned by name.[102] One commoner is singled out in the *GpP*, a soldier who rescued Casimir in a battle and was ennobled in consequence, but he remains nameless.[103]

It would be tedious—to borrow a formula from the anonymous—to list the many aspects of the study of early Poland which have been based on information derived from the *GpP* on matters military, toponymical, administrative, and even social.[104] It is true, however, and typical for the genre, that the anonymous takes little care to be specific about the different levels of leaders and nobles or of the various kinds of office-holders. It is also difficult to discern when the author is recording surviving memory from the previous century and when he is projecting the conditions of his own time into the past. However, recent archaeological research has in some points supported data from the *GpP*.[105]

Historians, mainly of the previous generations, who tended to study medieval narratives essentially as sources that transmit historical "facts," have scrutinized the *GpP* for "reliable data," with limited success. Only in rare cases can the data in the *GpP* be tested from other sources. For example, the list of names of

[102] II:14, p. 141; II:25, p. 165; III:23, p. 265.

[103] I:20, p. 85.

[104] See, for example, Karol Modzelewski, "Comites, Principes, Nobiles: The structure of the ruling class as reflected in the terminology used by Gallus Anonymus," in *The Polish Nobility in the Middle Ages: Anthologies*, ed. A. Gąsiorowski, Polish Historical Library 5 (Wrocław: Zakład Narodowy im. Ossolińskich, 1984), pp. 177–206; also Kossmann, *passim*.

[105] See, e.g., Michał Kara, "Anfänge der Bildung des Piastenstaates in Lichte neuer archäologischer Ermittlungen," *QMAeN* 5 (2000): 58–85.

the children of Mieszko I and Bolesław the Brave can be completed from the chronicle of Thietmar, the *Annales Hildesheimenses*, and the document titled *Dagome iudex*. The dates of
some of the rulers are also found in the old Polish annals. Much
regarding Polish-Czech contacts and related details can be
checked in Cosmas of Prague, and a few references to Polish
matters also appear in the Hungarian chronicles, the original
parts of which may go back to the eleventh century. Bolesław
the Brave's campaign against Kiev and his marriage contacts with
Rus' are also mentioned in the *Povest' vremennykh let* and by
Thietmar. German sources contain important, though problematic, information on the fate of Mieszko II's queen, Richeza, and
their son Casimir the Restorer. For the times of Bolesław III
Wrymouth, where the account in the *GpP* is more complete, the
foreign sources bring opposing points of view and sometimes
also a different set of facts. The invasion of Poland by Emperor
Henry V is mentioned by several German sources, for example
the chronicle of Ekkehard of Aura, the *Annalista Saxo*, and
various annals.[106]

Whether supported by external evidence or not, the *GpP* remains a source of fundamental importance for the early medieval
history of Poland.[107] But, first and foremost, it is unique in
allowing us to reconstruct the self-perception of the political

---

[106] For specific references to these parallel sources, see the notes to the text
and translation, below.

[107] The *GpP* is the only text presenting genealogical information on the ducal
dynasty before the reign of Mieszko I. The author of the *GpP* included specific
details concerning the times of Bolesław I the Brave such as the occupation of
part of Saxony and Northern Hungary, data on the number of his forces, and
the ban placed on Poland. For the reign of Mieszko II and Casimir the Restorer
our text is the only source of information on such matters as the castration of
Mieszko by the Czechs, the circumstances of the rebellion of Miecław, and the
revolt of the 1030s. Only in the *GpP* do we find information on the loss of
Pomerania by Bolesław the Bountiful, or about Polish internal affairs under
Władysław Herman and the relations between Bolesław and Zbigniew (however one-sided his presentation may be).

elite of Poland in the early twelfth century, especially of those circles that were the author's sponsors and assumed audience. It reflects—and may even have influenced—their view of their country's past and present.[108]

LORDSHIP,
LAND, AND THE COURSE OF HISTORY

The *GpP* emphasizes the close relationship between the dynasty and the land it ruled.[109] Notable is the use of family metaphors: Poland is described as a widow after the death of Bolesław the Brave, and is likened to a grieving mother at the premature demise of the young Mieszko. The death of Bolesław the Brave brings about a decline from the golden age, just as his virtues "gilded the whole of Poland." A similarly personal note is contained in his death-bed speech, in which the future savior of Poland is foretold as coming from the loins of the dying monarch and is compared to a shining jewel attached to the hilt of his sword.[110]

[108] See the various studies of Jacek Banaszkiewicz listed in the Bibliography (pp. 293–4, below) and further Roman Michałowski, "*Restauratio Poloniae* dans l'idéologie dynastique de Gallus Anonymus," *APH* 52 (1985): 5–43; Czesław Deptuła, *Galla Anonima mit genezy Polski: Studium z historiozofii i hermeneutyki symboli dziejopisarstwa średniowiecznego* [The myth of the origin of Poland in *Gallus Anonymus*: a study in historiosophy and the hermeneutics of the symbols of medieval historiography], 2nd ed. (Lublin: Instytut Europy Środkowo-Wschodniej, 2000); idem, "Ideologia Polski jako państwa morskiego w średniowiecznym dziejopisarstwie polskim" [The ideology of Poland as a marine country in the medieval Polish historiography], *Zeszyty Naukowe Katolickiego Uniwersytetu Lubelskiego* 18, no. 4 (1975): 3–17.

[109] In comparison to similar contemporary writings, the *GpP* seems to place much emphasis on the country, as against the dynasty (cf. Bisson, "On not eating," p. 288, who terms it "more national than dynastic"). The author himself emphasizes that his intention is to write "to the honor of the country" (III:Epist., p. 215), yet it seems that he saw country and dynasty as intimately connected.

[110] I:6, p. 31, I:16, p. 69.

The members of this dynasty are the *domini naturales* of Poland. This expression is used first by the author in the context of the major rebellion of the 1030s, and then by the young princes Bolesław and Zbigniew when asking for the support of the citizens of Wrocław.[111] It may be regarded as one of the key notions of the whole work. Loyalty is expected from subjects to their "natural lords," whereas rebellion or challenge to the rule of the dynasty is seen as a turning upside-down of the natural order. "Natural" in medieval discourse refers to what God has created, what is unquestionably right and what reflects the proper *ordo* in this world. Thus *domini naturales* may be understood as the God-given lords of the land whose right to rule is, so to say, beyond any doubt.[112]

Even though the origin of the dynasty is not expressly numinous (as in many other such myths), the figure of the plowman has far-reaching mythical implications.[113] However, the "low ori-

---

[111] The expression is not otherwise widely used, either in the author's time or before. Galbert of Bruges, writing a few decades later, applies it to Count Charles in the sense of his being the 'legitimate, hereditary ruler,' and Orderic Vitalis, also writing in the 1130s, applies it to the Duke of Normandy in connection with a knight who after decades of flight because of a crime returns to the fealty of the duke, his (native) *dominus naturalis*. See respectively *The Murder of Charles the Good, Count of Flanders by Galbert of Bruges*, trans. James Bruce Ross, rev. ed. (New York: Harper & Row, 1967), Introduction p. 79, and *The Ecclesiastical History of Orderic Vitalis* IX: 15, ed. and trans. Marjorie Chibnall, 6 vols. (Oxford, Oxford UP, 1975), 5:157.

[112] I:19, p. 81; II:16, p. 147.

[113] Some would see the figure of the plower of the earth as mythically connected with the notions of agriculture, fertility, and primitive nurture, comparing it with the myth of the Czech Přemysl, ancestor of the dukes of Bohemia; see in general Jacek Banaszkiewicz, "Königliche Karrieren von Hirten, Gärtnern und Pflügern: Zu einem mittelalterlichen Erzählthema vom Erwerb der Königsherrschaft," *Saeculum* 33 (1982): 265–86. However, it is notable that our work does not explicitly make such a connection; rather, the emphasis is on the hospitality of the poor *arator* (or *agricola*, *rusticus*), in contrast to the *inhumanitas* of the townspeople.

gin" of the ancestor that does not disqualify his progeny's claim to leadership, which rests on their "probity" (*probitas*), a quality seen both as the basis of divine selection and one which at the same time repeatedly earns approval from on high. The prophesy regarding the beginning of the dynasty—expressed in the words of the "angelic" visitors—is confirmed by miracles involving its members, from the food-multiplication at the outset to the birth of Bolesław III at the intervention of St. Giles. Approval from on high is further manifest in the divine assistance forthcoming to the rulers in their struggles against enemies (mainly heathen) and in their victories in battle. The author frequently spells out what was a common tenet in the Middle Ages, that God decides the fate of battles and that victory is a sign of divine approval.[114] Moreover, in several passages it is implied that the dukes' actions are performed at divine command and that Poland's cause is God's cause.[115] Yet in all this there is never mention of the ecclesiastical confirmation of any of the Polish kings,[116] and only in one sentence, referring to the conflict between Bolesław II and Bishop Stanislas, is it implied that the ruler, like the prelate, was anointed.[117] Clearly, not the formal royal title, but actual successful lordship, expressed in the ability to command the

---

[114] See, e.g., II:5, p. 129.

[115] E.g., III:Epist., p. 215.

[116] As far as we know, among the dukes and kings described in the GpP, besides Bolesław the Brave (in 1025), Mieszko II and Bolesław II were crowned and in all likelihood anointed in 1025 and 1077 respectively; for the latter, see Lampert of Hersfeld, *Annales*, ed. Oswald Holder-Egger, MGH SSrG [38], (Hanover: Hahn, 1894), p. 284.

[117] I:27, p. 7: *non debuit christus in christum peccatum quodlibet corporaliter vindicare*. On this see Brigitta Kürbis, "'Sacrum' and 'profanum' in Polish Mediaeval Historiography: Views on Social Order," *Questiones Medii Aevi* 2 (1981): 27; idem, "Zum Herrscherlob," p. 56.

loyalty of a retinue, to secure victory in war, and to defend the country are seen as the essential qualifications of the prince.[118] This theme is especially clearly elaborated in the description of the deeds of Bolesław III, who as a youth continuously grows in virtue and exhibits ever more evidence of such abilities. Yet even a non-ruling member of the dynasty, the young Mieszko, is described in superlatives. While the anonymous does not argue for the nobility by descent for his princes (as is done in several comparable *gesta*), his dukes acquire the qualities needed in "natural lords" by their "probity," demonstrated by exemplary deeds.[119] That in the description of the virtues of Bolesław III the two typically "noble" activities—war and hunt—are the exclusive subjects is certainly no coincidence.[120]

Another important theme in the *GpP* is the "ancient liberty" of Poland. Even though these exact words are used only once, when the author characterizes the campaign of Henry V as an arrogant attempt to destroy the *libertatem antiquam Poloniae*, there are

[118] On this view reflected in the *GpP* and other comparable narratives, see Thomas N. Bisson, "Princely Nobility in an Age of Ambition (c. 1050–1150)," in *Nobles and Nobility in Mediaeval Europe*, ed. A. J. Duggan (Woodbridge: Boydell, 2000), pp. 101–13. It is worth noting that the author expresses these views most succinctly in the (surely imaginary) song of German warriors (III:11, pp. 241–3) praising Bolesław III as defender of Poland, lord of the land, ruler over not merely a duchy, but rather a kingdom, even an empire!

[119] See Deptuła, *Galla Anonima mit*, pp. 293–300. A contemporary of the author, Petrus Alfonsi (1062–1110), lists seven *probitates* in his guidebook on manners: *equitare, natare, sagittare, cestibus certare, aucupare, scaccis ludere, versificari* 'riding, swimming, archery, boxing, fowling, playing chess, and making verses' (Alfons Hilka & Werner Söderhjelm, ed., "Petri Alfonsi *Disciplina Clericalis*: I, Lateinischer Text," *Acta Societatis Scientiarum Fennicæ* 38/4 (1911): 10). Thus probity could also refer to quite definite noble or knightly skills.

[120] On idea of the "heredibility" of virtue in this context, see Bronisław Geremek, "Temporal Imagination in Polish Medieval Historiography," *Questiones Medii Aevi* 2 (1981): 50.

several references to the "liberty" of the country, notably in the two imperial encounters (the meeting in Gniezno, and the exchange between Bolesław III and Henry V); moreover, the author claims that Poland, although often attacked by enemies, was never "completely subdued."[121] Reading between the lines, it emerges that the main element of this *libertas* is that Poland was not obligated to pay tribute to anyone (above all, to the Empire), whereas others (e.g. the Ruthenians) are compelled to pay tribute to the dukes of Poland. At the same time, this liberty does not exclude the possibility of the latter giving "aid and counsel" for the benefit of Christianity —in keeping with their role as "brother and helper," according to the words put in the mouth of Otto III to characterise the Polish monarch.[122]

All contemporary *gesta* have their particular perceptions of the relationship of people, land, and dynasty to each other. The *GpP*

---

[121] II:6, p. 37; III:1, p. 227; III:5, p. 233; III:14, p. 247; I:Proem., p. 15. That some early rulers did temporarily accept the obligation to pay tribute mainly for territories belonging to the empire is, understandably, not mentioned in the *GpP*. The author's concept of *libertas* is quite close to that of Saxon historians of the late eleventh century (e.g., Widukind of Corvey, Bruno, or Lampert of Hersfeld), who also emphasize freedom from tribute as the essential element of the collective liberty of a people. The Saxon interpretation is discussed with extensive references to the texts—including borrowings from Sallust common with the *GpP*—by Karl Leyser, "Von sächsischen Freiheiten zur Freiheit Sachsens: Die Krise des 11. Jahrhunderts," in *Die abendländische Freiheit vom 10. zum 14. Jahrhundert: Der Wirkungszusammenhang von Idee und Wirklichkeit im europäischen Vergleich*, ed. Johannes Fried, Vorträge und Forschungen 39 (Sigmaringen: Thorbecke 1991), pp. 67–84. Our author may also have been influenced by the notion of the *libertas ecclesiae*, a central issue of the Gregorian reform, on which see now Rudolf Schiefer, "Freiheit der Kirche: Vom 9. zum 11. Jahrhundert," ibid., pp. 49–66, with references to the older literature.

[122] III:2, p. 229; I:6, p. 37.

does not include an *origo gentis*, as most similar works do,[123] but has a definite view of the land. The prefatory *laus terrae* confers on Poland an elevated status within the broader context of the Slavic lands.[124] The relatively clear "territorial" notion of *Polonia*, expressed several times, suggests an advanced idea of a territorial polity. It has been noted that the author uses this term in several different combinations in naming the country.[125] The "ethnic" parameter—Poles vs other peoples—is implicitly present, mainly in comparison to, usually negatively defined, neighbors. Among these—and in the "title" of the *GpP*—the rulers (and occasionally the country) are called those or that "of the Poles" (*Polonorum*). The author also calls Poland some thirty times *patria*, a usage not at all widespread in his times and perhaps charged with some emotion, and particularly interesting coming from the pen of a foreigner.[126]

A notion defining Poland's relations to her neighbors is the theme of "fighting the pagans." While the raids into Pomerania and the significant event of the Polish troops reaching the sea at one level represent no more than profitable campaigns of plunder or territorial expansion, the spreading of Christianity along

[123] On these in general, see Susan Reynolds, "Medieval *Origines gentium* and the community of the real," *History* 68 (1983): 375–90; in particular, Jacek Banaszkiewicz, "Slavonic *origines regni*: hero the lawgiver and founder of monarchy (introductory survey of problems)," *APH* 60 (1989): 97–131 (logically, not including the *GpP*).

[124] See Brygida Kürbis, "Kształtowanie się pojęć geograficznych o Słowiańszczyźnie w polskich kronikach przeddługoszowych" [The development of geographical notions concerning Slavic territories in the Polish chronicles before Długosz], *Slavia Antiqua* 4 (1953): 262–82.

[125] Kersken, *Geschichtsschreibung*, p. 562, n. 416; cf. Marek J. Karp, "Więź ogólnopolska i regionalna w średniowiecznych mitach początku" [The all-Polish and regional ties in the medieval myths of origin], *Przegląd Historyczny* 72 (1982): 211–27.

[126] See the overview of the use of *patria* in different writings of the region in Graus, *Nationenbildung*, pp. 224–7. Our author frequently employs classical formulae (*pater patriae, pro patria mori*, etc.).

the Baltic coast (Pomerania, Prussia) is an achievement claimed even for rulers who may have had merely temporary success in this. The reluctance of the heathen neighbors to accept the true faith and keep its commands is repeatedly quoted in justification of making war against these people. In this sense, it is quite justified to draw attention to the "crusader soul" of the anonymous.[127]

The author's view of history contains two conventional but opposed points of view, both simultaneously held. One is a movement of rise and fall, the first of the apogees being the conversion of Poland, the next the acknowledgement of Bolesław the Brave's royal standing by the emperor. The death of Bolesław I represents a break in the history of Poland. The golden era becomes one of lead under his successors, a decline only partially "restored" by Casimir. Here is introduced the classical and Christian concept of a continuous decline from a "golden age." However, the author does not follow this through consistently, because it would be contrary to his attempt to glorify the age of Bolesław III, who is predestined to return Poland to its "pristine state" in the days of the great Bolesław.[128] Bolesław III defeats the same enemies as his namesake, spreads Christianity by waging wars with the Pomeranians, and keeps good relations with the representatives of the Church. The earlier reign offers the standard for measuring the reign of his third namesake. Yet it retains a certain superiority, reflecting the medieval attitude to the past as a state "by definition" more perfect than the present.

---

[127] See A.F. Grabski, "Polska wobec idei wypraw krzyżowych na przełomie XI i XII w.: 'Duch krzyżowy' Anonima Galla" [Poland and the idea of crusade at the turn of the eleventh to the twelfth century: The 'crusading soul' of Gallus Anonymus], *Zapiski Historyczne* 26 (1961): 4, 49–64.

[128] II:20, p. 157.

THE INFLUENCE OF THE *GpP*
ON POLISH HISTORY-WRITING

While the manuscript evidence suggests a limited reception for the *GpP* in its own time, a hundred years later extensive use of it was made by Master Vincent Kadłubek (fl. 1207) as a source for Polish history up to the early twelfth century. Kadłubek "corrected" the shortcomings of the *GpP* by constructing a fanciful pre-history, beginning with the Tower of Babel and making a connection to the events of Roman history—the legendary Pumpil being identified as a member of the Pompilii clan—before continuing down to the times of the plowman Piast, after which he largely follows our author's account. Kadłubek's work surpassed the *GpP* in popularity for several centuries, as witnessed by the relative number of surviving manuscripts of the two works—three from the late Middle Ages for the *GpP*, twenty-nine from the fourteenth to the seventeenth centuries for Kadłubek.[129] Kadłubek's reworking became in turn the basis for the account of early Polish history in such fourteenth-century narratives as the chronicle of Dzierzwa[130] and the *Chronicle of Great Poland*,[131] and served, alongside the *GpP*, as one of the sources for the great historical synthesis of Jan Długosz.[132] It can be surmised that some other historians

---

[129] For a list of the Kadłubek MSS see Marian Plezia, "Wstęp" [Introduction], in *Magistri Vincentii dicti Kadłubek Chronica Polonorum*, ed. Marianus Plezia, MPH, n.s., 11 (Cracow: Secesja, 1994), pp. XII–XIV.

[130] Ed. August Bielowski, MPH 2 (Lvív, 1872). See Jacek Banaszkiewicz, *Kronika Dzierzwy: XIV-wieczne kompendium historii ojczystej* [The chronicle of Dzierzwa: a fourteenth-century compendium of national history] (Wrocław: Zakład Narodowy im. Ossolińskich, 1979).

[131] *Chronica Poloniae maioris*, ed. Brygida Kürbis, MPH, n.s., 8 (Warsaw: PWN, 1970).

[132] Aleksander Semkowicz, *Krytyczny rozbiór Dziejów polskich Jana Długosza (do roku 1384)* [A critical analysis of the History of Poland of John Długosz (up to the year 1384)] (Cracow: Akademia Umiejętności, 1887), pp. 26–8. On Długosz's copy of the *GpP*, see above, p. xx.

and annalists had also access to the text of the *GpP* which they utilised directly.[133]

The anonymous *Gesta*, for centuries under the shadow of Kadłubek, first came to be appreciated in the age of the Enlightment. What was earlier viewed as the anonymous's shortcomings now came to be regarded as strengths. The far fewer fantastic constructions, the less elaborate legendary motifs, and the absence of long moralizing inserts made eighteenth-century Polish savants more sympathetic to the *GpP*. The reticence of the anonymous about St. Stanislas, so different from the hagiographic accounts, was first appreciated by the antiquarian and historian Tadeusz Czacki (1765–1813). The *GpP* served as the basic source for the syntheses of Polish history by Adam Naruszewicz (1733–96) and Joachim Lelewel (1736–1861).

Books and articles containing critical studies and evaluations of the *GpP*, particularly since the late nineteenth century, run into the hundreds; many of them are still valuable, others dated.[134] For decades the reliability and the value of the chronicle as a historical source was the main focus of polemics, wherein views ranged from those idealizing the author's truthfulness to those that granted the work an exclusively polemical-political character.[135]

[133] On the use of the *GpP* by annalists, see Polak, "Uwagi" (as n. 88, above), pp. 449–53. On the traces of the *GpP* in the Lives of St. Stanislas, see Wiesołowski, *Kolekcje* (as p. xxii, n. 7 above), pp. 20–1. See also above, p. xxi, n. 6.

[134] Our bibliography (below, pp. 292–307) lists a limited selection of these.

[135] For the first position see Tadeusz Wojciechowski, *Szkice historyczne jedenastego wieku* [Historical sketches of the eleventh century] (Cracow: Akademia Umiejętności, 1904; reprint, with a foreword by A. Gieysztor, 1951); for the second, among others, Jan Adamus, *O monarchii Gallowej* [On the monarchy in Gallus] (Warsaw: Towarzystwo Naukowe Warszawskie, 1952).

While not questioning its essential credibility, Aleksander Brückner called the *GpP* "the first historical novel."[136]

Given its unique position, no student of these centuries can avoid taking a stand on "the Anonymus called Gallus."[137] Since there is now little hope of discovering new written sources, we can expect progress in the reconstruction of early Polish history to emerge mainly from comparative study and from the findings of archaeology. In the meanwhile, debates are likely to continue about the general character of the *GpP* and the details contained in it. However, the last decades have witnessed a shift in emphasis, with increasing awareness of the context of the writing and the background and "mentality" of its author and those whose outlook he is assumed to reflect. The focus of interest has moved to the elements of those traditions that found their way into the *GpP*, be they archaic, gentile, Christian, Biblical, or literary.[138] The publication of Maleczyński's critical edition and the ever-growing scholarly literature prove that the *GpP* continues to occupy a central position in Polish medieval studies in particular, and in the study of twelfth-century history writing in general.

---

[136] Aleksander Brückner, "Pierwsza powieść historyczna" [The first historical novel], *Przegląd Humanistyczny* 3 (1924): 116–36. Even though for his times this characterization was a rather ambiguous assessment, students of medieval *gesta* today are much more inclined to appreciate the literary (in contrast to "informative") character of such works.

[137] Symptomatic, perhaps, of this state of affairs is the polemical subtitle of Tadeusz Wasilewski's article "Zapomniane przekazy rocznikarskie o Bolesławie Mieszkowicu: O nie-Gallowe pojmowanie wczesnych dziejów Polski" [Forgotten chronicle accounts concerning Bolesław son of Mieszko: Towards a non-Gallus understanding of the earliest history of Poland], *Przegląd Historyczny* 80 (1989): 225–37.

[138] See, in particular, the writings of Marian Plezia, Czesław Deptuła, Jacek Banaszkiewicz, Norbert Kersken, Thomas N. Bisson and others, cited in the notes to this introduction and to the text.

EDITORIAL PRINCIPLES

According to the practice of the present series, the Latin parallel text in the present volume is reprinted from the most recent and reliable critical edition (with misprints and minor irregularities in punctuation tacitly corrected). The emendations of that edition are silently accepted; however, for reasons of economy the full listing of manuscript variants is omitted along with a good number of its references to literary sources. In a very few cases we have preferred variant readings or introduced our own emendations. In such cases we cite in footnotes to the Latin text the variant readings of the witnesses *Z* and/or *H* (ignoring the derivative *S*), as well as the readings of the edition (*Mal*); whichever witnesses then remain uncited can be assumed to agree with the text as printed. The reader should, however, be aware (as would be clear from a full listing of readings) that variation between the readings of the two principal witnesses is not uncommon, and that even where *Z* and *H* agree there are frequently difficulties and ambiguities in the text, so that the text in the critical edition is in many places based on conjecture. We endeavor to draw attention in our notes to the main instances of textual uncertainty.

In interpreting the text we have consulted earlier translations, particularly that of Grodecki with its extensive notes, and that in Marian Plezia's edition in the Biblioteka Narodowa volume. The complicated problems connected with the rendering of titles and designations of status (such as *comes, miles*),[139] terms for social groups or office-holders (*cives, castellani, oppidani*) and

---

[139] On *comes*, see below, I:1, p. 17. For an extensive bibliography on *miles* and development of this term, see, e.g., Maurice Keen, *Chivalry* (London: Yale UP, 1986); P. van Luyn, "Les 'milites' dans la France du XIe siècle: Examen des sources narratives," *Le moyen âge* 77 (1971): 5–51, 193–238; Josef Fleckenstein, "Über den engeren und breiteren Begriff von Ritter und Rittertum," in *Person und Gemeinschaft im Mittelalter: Karl Schmid zum 65. Geburtstage*, ed. Gerd Althoff et al. (Sigmaringen: Thorbecke, 1988), pp. 379–93.

settlements (*civitas, castrum/castellum*),[140] and so on, which remain the object of extensive ongoing discussion among historians and archaeologists, are taken up in some detail in the notes.

In our choice of wording we have tried as far as possible to keep close to the style and wording of the original while still offering a readable and idiomatic English version. Additionally, our translation attempts to reproduce some flavor of the poetic and rhetorical embellishments of the original. While we have been less willing than the critical edition to recognize shorter poetic elements as "verse," at the same time we have tried to do justice to the major poetic sections even to the point of attempting to reproduce—*stilo puerili*—both the original meter and rhyme. However, in several cases we took advantage of the more polished and freer translation renderings prepared for this edition by Dr. Barbara Reynolds (Cambridge), well known for her translations of, among others, Dante and Ariosto.

Regarding place names, our convention has been to print (and include in our map, reproduced on the front endpaper) forms according to present-day use as are to be found in a contemporary atlas. While this may occasionally sound anachronistic, it seems the only feasible solution to the complicated historical problems of toponyms in the region. Personal names are given in their modern Polish (or Czech, or other vernacular) forms if these are known, otherwise according to scholarly consensus; in cases of doubt, we follow Plezia's usage. An exception is made in the case of rulers, whose names are (as far as appropriate) anglicized according to accepted usage in English-language scholarship. Unfortunately, there is no consistent "rule" here

---

[140] Among the extensive literature we would draw the reader's attention in particular to the articles exploring the semantics of this issue in Hansjürgen Bachmann, ed., *Burg–Burgstadt–Stadt: Zur Genese mittelalterlicher nichtagrarischer Zentren in Ostmitteleuropa* (Berlin: Akademie, 1995).

either. For example, the Slavic name *Vladislav* usually appears as Władysław if the person in question is Polish, Vladislav if Czech, and Ladislas (in Magyar: László) or Wladislas (Ulászló) if Hungarian, even though the *GpP* has the same Latin form for all three. Biblical references are based on the *Nova Vulgata-Bibliorum Sacrorum Editio* (Vatican City, 1990) even though the author certainly had a different text of the Vulgate at hand.

The preparation of this book has been a team effort. The first round of English translation was prepared by Frank Schaer, CEMT Series Editor, and then revised by Paul Knoll from the University of Southern California, in both cases with the assistance of János Bak as the General Editor in charge of this volume. The contribution of graduate students in the translation seminars held at Central European University on the *GpP* in the academic years 1999–2001 was most valuable. Wojciech Polak from the Catholic University, Lublin, wrote the first draft of the Introduction, which was translated by Renata Mikołajczyk (doctoranda of CEU). For editorial reasons, many of his comments on scholarly debates had to be cut and the text revised by the other members of the team, so that the final version may not in all aspects reflect the views of Dr. Polak. All of the above worked on the annotations, in which they were assisted by very many friends and colleagues but especially by Grzegorz Żabiński and Krisztina Fügedi, doctoral candidates at CEU. The quality of the poetic inserts was greatly enhanced by the contributions of Dr. Reynolds. We also owe thanks to Jan Ziolkowski of Harvard University for his valuable comment on the poetic inserts. We are most grateful to Professor Thomas N. Bisson of Harvard University for having written a Preface to this work. Irina Kolbutova transcribed the Latin text into machine-readable form, which was then collated by Réka Forrai (both are Ph.D. candidates at CEU). The map and the genealogical table were drafted by Zbigniew Dalewski of the Historical Institute of the

Polish Academy of Sciences, who also helped us with further guidance regarding recent literature. Cosmin Popa-Gorjanu, doctorandus of CEU, prepared the indexes. Judith Rasson of CEU gave valuable assistance and advice in matters bibliographical.

The difficult task of typesetting was undertaken by Péter Tamási and his team; to him and the CEU Press go our thanks, which we hope the readers will endorse, for another handsome volume in the series.

At important stages of the preparation of this book, we received financial support from the Kosciuszko Foundation in New York, which we here gratefully acknowledge. For their permission and kind assistance in making available the title pages of the manuscripts of the *GpP*, we thank the Manuscript Department of the National Library, Warsaw.

GESTA PRINCIPUM POLONORUM

THE DEEDS OF THE PRINCES
OF THE POLES

(CRONICA ET GESTA DUCUM SIVE PRINCIPUM POLONORUM)[1]

(LIBER PRIMUS)

(EPISTOLA)[2]

Domino M(artino)[3] Dei gratia summo pontifici, simulque Symoni, Pavlo, Mauro, Syroslao, Deo dignis ac venerandis pontificibus Polonie regionis,[4] nec non etiam cooperatori[5] suo venerabili cancellario Michaeli, ceptique laboris opifici, subsequentis scriptor opusculi, *supra montem Syon* Domini *sanctum*[6] gregem commissum vigilanti studio speculari, ac *de virtute in virtutem* gradiendo *Deum Deorum facie ad faciem*[7] contemplari. Ni vestra auctoritate suffultus, patres pretitulati, vestraque opitulatione fretus fierem, meis viribus in vanum tanti ponderis onus subirem et cum fragili lembo periculose tantam equoris inmensitatem introirem. Sed securus nauta poterit in navicula residens per undas sevientis freti navigare, qui nauclerum habet peritum, qui scit eam certam ventorum et syderum moderamine gubernare. Nec valuissem quoquomodo tante caribdis naufragium evitare, ni libuisset vestre karitati meam naviculam vestri

---

[1] On the title of the work and the titles of the chapters, which seem to have been added later, see above, p. xxiv.

[2] For letters of dedication preceding historical works in general, and those addressed to influential and powerful persons whose protection the author requests in particular, see Simon, Topik I and II, esp. I:87–90, II:115–21.

[3] Martin, archbishop of Gniezno 1092–ca. 1115 (*PSB* 19:557–8).

[4] Simon was bishop of Płock ca.1102–29 (*SSS* 5:556); Paul was bishop of Poznań 1098–ca. 1112 (*SSS* 4:49); Maurus was bishop of Cracow 1110–8 (*PSB* 20:261–2); and Żyrosław bishop of Wrocław 1112–20 (*SSS* 7:276).

CHRONICLES AND DEEDS OF THE DUKES OR PRINCES OF THE POLES[1]

(FIRST BOOK)

(LETTER)[2]

To lord M(artin)[3] by the grace of God archbishop, likewise to Simon, Paul, Maurus, Żyrosław, bishops of the land of Poland venerable and pleasing to God,[4] as well as to his helper[5] the venerable chancellor Michael, the maker of the task embarked upon: the writer of the following work bids you watch over the flock entrusted *upon Zion the Lord's holy hill*[6] with vigilant zeal, and *striding from strength to strength* to gaze upon *the God of Gods face to face.*[7]

Honored fathers: were I not supported by your authority and able to rely on your assistance, it would be vain to take upon myself with my own strength a burden of such weight, and to venture upon the perils of such an immense sea in a fragile craft. But a sailor aboard a small boat can securely navigate the waters of the raging sea if he has a skilled pilot who knows how to steer the boat surely with the help of the winds and the stars. Amid such perils I would never have been able to escape shipwreck if

---

[5] 'His helper,' i.e. the writer's. The words *cooperator*, lit. 'co-worker,' and *opifex*, lit. 'creator, craftsman,' may of course simply be expressions of the medieval convention of affected humilty, the writer reducing himself to a mere 'scribe,' but probably hint at our author's having received much of his information from the churchmen addressed. Michael of the Awdańcy kindred was ducal chancellor and possibly bishop of Poznań 1113–4. His identification with an *episcopus Poloniae* mentioned in contemporary necrologies and other sources is debated (*PSB* 20:611–2). Plezia (Grodecki-Plezia, *Kronika*, xxii–iii) assumes that besides the chancellor Bishop Paul was also a major souce for the anonymous.

[6] Cf. Ps. 2:6.

[7] Cf. Ps. 83:8 and 1 Cor. 13:12.

remigii gubernaculis sublevare.[1] Nec de tanta silvarum densitate
ignarus vie potuissem exire, ni vestre benignitati placuisset certas
mihi metas interius aperire. Tantorum igitur rectorum ammini-
culis insignitus, portum subibo securus, ventorum turbinibus
expeditus, nec dubitabo lippis luminibus viam incognitam palpi-
tare, cum cognoverim rectorum oculos precedencium luce lu-
cidius choruscare. Et cum tales premiserim causidicos defensores, floccipendam quicquid mussitando murmurarent in-
vidiosi detractores.[2] Et quoniam fortuna voti compos vos
fautores obtulerit iuste rei, dignum duxi tantos viros inserere
quasi cronice seriei. Vestro namque tempore, vestrisque precibus
preciosis illustravit Deus Poloniam Bolezlaui tercii[3] gestis
memorialibus et famosis. Et cum multa et magnifica vobis gesta
degentibus pretermittam, quedam tamen suggerere subsequenter posteriorum memorie non dimittam. Sed ad presens
vos uno ore, una laude unanimiter unanimes uniamus, et quos
indissolubile karitatis vinculum annectit, nostris quoque preconiis adnectamus. Dignum est enim vestrum[a] eciam gesta an-
tistitum[4] prenotari, quos divina gratia facit donis carismatum
ipsis principibus principari,[5] uti quorum dispensatione subditorum quoque precatibus celestis alimonia fidelibus erogatur,
eorundem patrocinium nostre pusillanimitatis opusculum suf-
fragio tueatur. Nam quos Deus ordinavit tanto privilegio dignitatis hominibus ceteris preminere, oportet eosdem studiosius
singulorum utilitatibus et necessitatibus providere. Igitur ne
viles persone videamur vanitatis *fimbrias dilatare,*[6] codicellum

---

[a] veterum *Mal,* ut rerum *Z H*

---

[1] The metaphor of sailing in dangerous waters in reference to a literary effort
is a well-known topos from Antiquity through the Middle Ages, see Ernst
Robert Curtius, *European Literature and the Latin Middle Ages,* tr. Willard R.
Trask, Bollingen Series 36 (Princeton: Princeton University Press, 1953), pp.
128–30.

[2] On the author's real or imaginary *emuli,* see above, p. xxvi, and Simon, Topik,
I:91–3.

[3] Bolesław III Wrymouth (*Krzywousty*), b. 1085, duke of Poland 1102–38.

your graces had not seen fit to take the oars in aid of my little craft.[1] Nor could I, ignorant of the path, have ever found my way out from such a thick forest, had you in your goodness not assented to point out to me the correct markers therein. So when such helmsmen have honored me with their help I feel sure I will come safely to my harbor, escaping the raging whirlwinds, and will not feel hesitant to grope along this unknown path with my dim eyesight, knowing that the eyes of my guides who have gone before me blaze brighter than the day. With such advocates to plead my case I will disdain any mutterings and murmurings of envious detractors.[2] Having had the fortune to obtain your desired support in this worthy enterprise, I thought it fitting to introduce you into the text of this chronicle, so to speak, for it was in your time and through your precious prayers that God brought glory to Poland through the renowned and memorable deeds of Bolesław III.[3] Even if I omit many splendid deeds performed in your lifetimes, I will not fail to leave to the memory of posterity the record of at least a few in the pages to come. But for the present I would wish to unite you as one in concord, one in mind, one in my words and praise; whom the indissoluble bond of affection binds may we also bind in our glorious tale. For it is fitting that the deeds of you churchmen[4] also be recorded whom Divine Favor by the gifts of grace sets as princes over the princes themselves,[5] that as through their dispensation heavenly sustenance is obtained for the faithful prayers of their subjects, so my humble work should enjoy the protection of their patronage and favor. For those whom God has appointed to such a privileged rank over other persons should take studious care of the interests and needs of each single person. So then, as not to appear a low person *making long the fringes* of my vanity,[6]

---

[4] The exact sense is unclear, not only because of corruption in the manuscripts, but in particular because the *GpP* contains in fact relatively little about churchmen.

[5] Cf. Sidonius Apollinaris, *Carmina* 9.51.

[6] Cf. Matt. 23:5.

non nostro decrevimus sed vestris nominibus titulare.[1] Quocirca
laudem huius operis et honorem huius patrie principibus ascriba-
mus, nostrum vero laborem laborisque talionem vestre discrecionis arbitrio fiducialiter committamus. Spiritus sancti gratia,
que vos dominici gregis pastores ordinavit, tale suggerat consilium vestre menti, quatenus princeps digna det munera promer-
enti, unde vobis honor sibique gloria proferenti. Semper gaudete,
nobis operique favete.[2]

EXPLICIT EPISTOLA

INCIPIT EPYLOGUS[3]

> Bolezlauus dux inclitus
> Dei dono progenitus
> Hic per preces Egidij
> Sumpsit causam exordii.
> Qualiter istud fuerit,
> Si Deus hoc annuerit,
> Possumus vobis dicere,
> Si placeat addiscere.
> Relatum est parentibus
> Successore carentibus
> Conflent auri congeriem
> In humanam effigiem.
> Quam mittant sancto propere
> Fiat ut eis prospere,
> Votumque Deo voveant
> Atque firmam spem habeant.

---

[1] The convention of not mentioning one's own name but rather that of one's
sponsors (or persons to whom the work is addressed) was widespread among
medieval historians, and variously approved or disapproved by others; see
Simon, Topik, 1:87–90.

I have decided to put your names rather than mine at the head of this little book.[1] So let the praise and honor of this work fall to the princes of this country, and let our labour and its recompense be left with confidence to the discretion of your judgement. May the grace of the Holy Spirit who ordained you shepherds over the Lord's flock place such wise counsel in your minds that the prince may bestow fitting gifts on the deserving, and thus honor to yourselves and glory to the giver. Be happy for aye and forever, and favor this book and its author![2]

END OF THE LETTER

BEGINNING OF THE EPILOGUE[3]

> Duke Bolesław, the illustrious,
> By God's grace was engendered thus:
> His entry into life he made
> When prayers of St. Giles were said.
> And how and why this came to be,
> If God His favour grants to me,
> I'll now to you make plain and clear,
> So be it you are pleased to hear.
> A son and heir his parents lacked
> And they were counselled thus to act:
> A mass of gold they were to take,
> And thence a human likeness make
> And send it to St. Giles at speed,
> That he might help them in their need.
> And meanwhile they must pray to God
> With faith, as firm believers should.

[2] A Leonine hexameter in the original.

[3] The term *epilogus* was widely used in medieval literature to denote a summary of the argument (see *LexMA* 6:2066), though rarely at the beginning of a work. The story summarized here is detailed below, chs. 30–32.

Aurum illico funditur,
Effigies efficitur,
Quam pro futuro filio
Sancto mittunt Egidio.
Aurum, argentum, pallia
Donaque mittunt alia,
Vestes sacras et aureum
Calicem sat ydoneum.
Nec mora missi properant
Per terras, quas non noverant,
Pretereuntes Galliam
Pervenerunt Prouinciam.
Missi munera proferunt,
Monachi grates referunt,
Causam narrant itineris
Et qualitatem operis.
Tunc monachi continuo
Ieiunavere triduo
Et dum agunt ieiunium
Mater concepit filium.
Et pro vero pronunciant
Quod missi sic inveniant.
Monachi rem recipiunt,
Missi redire cupiunt.
Transeuntes Burgundiam
Remearunt Poloniam.
Ergo gravem inveniunt
Ducissam, quando veniunt.
Sic puer ille nascitur,
Qui Bolezlauus dicitur,
Quem Wladislaus[1] genuit
Dux, sicut Deus voluit.
Genitrix Iudith nomine,[2]

[1] Władysław Herman, duke of Poland, 1079–1102.

They melt the gold without delay
And pour the metal in the clay.
And to Saint Giles they send it fast
In hope a son to have at last.
And they send other presents too:
Gold, silver, mantles, not a few,
And holy robes for priests to wear,
A golden chalice fit and fair.
At once the messengers are gone.
Through unknown lands they travel on.
The whole of France is crossed and passed
When to Provence they come at last.
They take the presents from their trunks
And give them to the grateful monks.
They tell the reason for their trip
And praise the costly workmanship.
Forthwith the monks a three-day fast
Begin, and ere this time is past,
And while the fast is going on
The mother has conceived a son.
The messengers are told of this,
And true indeed the rumor is.
The monks their presents now receive.
The messengers are keen to leave,
And crossing the Burgundian land
They then returned to Poland.
And here the Duchess they behold
Now great with child, as they were told.
And so is born that longed-for son,
His name as Bolesław is known,
The offspring of Duke Wladislas,[1]
As God eternal willed for us.
And Judith was his mother's name[2]

[2] Judith, daughter of Duke Vladislav of Bohemia and Adelaide of Hungary, married Władysław Herman in 1080, d. 1085.

Fatali forsan omine,
Iudith salvavit populum
Per Olofernis iugulum.[1]
Ista peperit filium,
Triumphatorem hostium,
De cuius gestis scribere
Iam tempus est insistere.[2]

INCIPIUNT CRONICE ET GESTA DUCUM SIVE PRINCIPUM POLONORUM.

PRIMO PROHEMIUM

Quoniam orbis terrarum in universitate spaciosa a regibus ac ducibus plurimis plurima memorabilia geruntur, que fastidiosa negligentia philosophorum, forsitan inopia[3], silencio conteguntur, opere pretium duximus quasdam res gestas Polonicorum principum gratia cuiusdam gloriosissimi ducis ac victoriosissimi nomine Bolezlaui stilo puerili[4] pocius exarare, quam ex toto posterorum memorie nichil imitabile reservare.[5] Ob hoc etiam maxime, quod Dei dono precibusque sancti Egidij natus fuit, per quem, ut credimus, bene fortunatus, semperque victoriosus extitit. Sed quia regio Polonorum ab itineribus peregrinorum est remota, et nisi transeuntibus in Rusiam pro mercimonio paucis nota, [6] si breviter inde disseratur nulli videatur absurdum, et si

---

[1] Jth. 13:6–8.

[2] Translated by Dr. Barbara Reynolds.

[3] Boethius, *DCP*, 2 Prose 7, 13: *Sed quam multos clarissimos suis temporibus viros scriptorum delevit opinio?*

[4] Reference to artlessness, etc., of literary style is a commonplace in medieval literature, see Curtius, *European Literature*, pp. 407–10; Simon, *Topik*, I:108–18. A further contemporary parallel is Cosmas, *Chron. Boh.* I:Epist., Prefacio, pp. 1–3.

(A fateful sign?), as hers the same
Who Israel's salvation wrought
By cutting Holofernes' throat.[1]
A mighty son our Judith bore
Who conquered all our foes in war—
But now the time has come, I state,
His deeds of valor to narrate.[2]

HERE BEGIN THE CHRONICLES AND DEEDS OF THE DUKES, OR PRINCES, OF THE POLES.

FIRST: THE INTRODUCTION

Many a king and many a duke throughout this wide world performs deeds of note beyond counting, but for the neglect and scorn of the learned, or perhaps for the lack of them[3], these have been buried in silence. I have therefore thought it worth the while, for all my poor style,[4] to record something of the exploits of the Polish princes, in honor of one of the most glorious and victorious of dukes, by name Bolesław, rather than to leave posterity no record at all of deeds worth imitating.[5] In particular, too, because he was born by the gift of God and the prayers of St. Giles, thanks to whom, as we believe, he was blessed with good fortune and ever victorious. But as the country of the Poles is far from the routes of travelers, and known to few apart from persons crossing to Russia for the purposes of trade,[6] let no one think it out of place if this subject is briefly discussed, nor regard

[5] For the author's repeated reference to the past as an example to follow, see above, p. xxxiv. Many parallels are listed in Simon, Topik, I:81–3; II:103–6.

[6] Poland had extensive trade connections to both Scandinavia and Kievan Rus', see Charlotte Warnke, *Die Anfänge des Fernhandels in Polen* (Würzburg: Holzner, 1964), and Petr Charvát, "Bohemia, Moravia and Long-Distance Trade in the Tenth-Eleventh Centuries," *QMAeN* 5 (2000): 255–66.

pro parte describendo totum inducatur, nemo reputet onerosum.[1] Igitur ab aquilone Polonia septemtrionalis pars est Scla-
uonie, que habet ab oriente Rusiam, ab austro Vngariam, a sub-
solano[2] Morauiam et Bohemiam, ab occidente Daciam[3] et
Saxoniam[4] collaterales. Ad mare autem septemtrionale vel am-
phitrionale[5] tres habet affines barbarorum gentilium ferocissi-
mas naciones, Selenciam,[6] Pomoraniam[7] et Pruziam,[8] contra
quas regiones Polonorum dux assidue pugnat, ut eas ad fidem
convertat. Sed nec gladio predicacionis cor eorum a perfidia
potuit revocari, nec gladio iugulationis eorum penitus *vipperalis
progenies*[9] aboleri. Sepe tamen principes eorum a duce Poloniensi
prelio superati ad baptismum confugerunt, itemque collectis
viribus fidem christianam abnegantes contra christianos bellum
denuo paraverunt. Sunt etiam ultra eas et infra brachia am-
phitrionis alie barbare gentilium naciones et insule inhabitabiles,

[1] Such geographical overviews are typical for the *gesta* of the period, see Hans
Joachim Witzel, Der geographische Exkurs in den lateinischen Geschichtsquellen des Mittelalters, Diss. phil., Frankfurt am M., 1952.

[2] *Subsolanus*, lit. 'eastern' (or 'southern'), but here presumably in the sense
'southwest.'

[3] *Dacia* was often used by medieval authors in place of *Dania* for Denmark.
The two are, for example, explicitly equated (*Dacia que et Danamarchia*) by
William of Jumiège (*Gesta Normannorum ducum* I:2–3, ed. E. M. C. Van
Houts, pp. 12–15).

[4] The Elbian Slavs, between Poland and Saxony, seem to be disregarded by the
author, perhaps because in the times of Bolesław I they were at least formally
subject to Poland.

[5] As the Theban hero Amphitryon, son of the king of Tiryns, hardly fits the
context, the reference to the "Sea of Amphitryon" is best seen as a slip on the
part of the author. He presumably intended to refer to the Nereid Amphitrite,
daughter of Okeanos, whose name could stand for the sea in general (e.g., Ovid,
Met. 1.13), and 'her arms' (below) in this case to the northern Baltic.

[6] It is generally accepted that the author refers to some Baltic pagan state, but
to which one is unclear (*SSS* 5:127). Josef Bujnoch, in *Polens Anfänge: Gallus
Anonymus, Chronik und Taten der Herzöge und Fürsten von Polen* (Graz:
Styria, 1978), p. 212, n. 12, suggests that the reference is to Slavs west of the

it as burdensome if a description of the whole is given rather than the part.[1]

Starting from the north, then, Poland is the northernmost part of Slavonia; it borders to the east on Russia, to the south on Hungary, towards the east[2] on Moravia and Bohemia, and to the west on Denmark[3] and Saxony.[4] On the Northern Sea, or Sea of Amphitryon,[5] it has as neighbors three most savage nations of pagan barbarians, Selencia,[6] Pomerania,[7] and Prussia,[8] and the duke of the Poles is constantly at war with these countries, fighting to convert them to the faith. But neither has the sword of preaching been able to sway their hearts from faithlessness, nor the sword at their throats wipe out this *generation of vipers*[9] in its entirety. Yet often their leaders when defeated in battle by the Polish duke have taken refuge in baptism, only to deny the Christian faith when they recovered their strength and to take up arms afresh against the Christians. Even farther away and within the arms of Amphitryon are other barbarous pagan nations, as well as uninhabitable islands where there is perpetual

Oder, perhaps the Liutici, whereas Kossmann, 2: 80, speculates that Selencia was a distinct territory west of Pomerania, later absorbed by the latter.

[7] The name comes from Slavic *Pomorze* ('at the sea'), a typical Slavic topnym with the prefix 'po-' ('near to'); it spread through Polish transmission, appearing already around 1046 in imperial diplomas (see Piskorski, as below, pp. 18–29). The early medieval history of Pomerania is obscure and the relevant controversial literature in Polish and German extensive. An up-to-date bibliography appears in Jan M. Piskorski, *Pomorze plemenie: Historia – archeologia – językoznawstwo* [Tribal Pomerania: history, archaeology, linguistics] (Poznań: Sorus, 2002), pp. 235–75. A general overview based on an extensive study of written and archaeological sources (on at least one part of the region) is offered in Leopold Sobel, "Ruler and Society in Early Medieval Western Pomerania," *Antemurale* 25 (1981): 19–142, and by Lech Leciejewicz, "Die Pomoranen und der Piastenstaat im 10.–11. Jahrhundert," *Zeitschrift für Archäologie* 18 (1984): 107–16.

[8] By Prussia our author usually means the area between the lower Vistula and the river Niemen/Nemunas.

[9] Matt. 3:7, Luke 3:7.

ubi perpetua nix est et glacies.[1] Igitur terra Sclauonica ad
aquilonem hiis regionibus suis partialiter divisivis sive constitu-
tivis existens, a Sarmaticis, qui et Gete vocantur,[2] in Daciam et
Saxoniam terminatur, a Tracia autem per Ungariam ab Hunis,
qui et Ungari dicuntur,[3] quondam occupatam, descendendo per
Carinthiam in Bauariam diffinitur; ad austrum vero iuxta mare
mediterraneum ab Epyro derivando per Dalmatiam, Crouaciam
et Hystriam finibus maris Adriatici terminata, ubi Venetia et
Aquileia consistit, ab Hytalia sequestratur. Que regio quamvis
multum sit nemorosa, auro tamen et argento, pane et carne, pisce
et melle satis est copiosa, et in hoc plurimum aliis preferenda,
quod cum a tot supradictis gentibus et christianis et gentilibus
sit vallata et a cunctis insimul et a singulis multociens inpugnata,
nunquam tamen ab ullo fuit penitus subiugata.[4] Patria ubi aer
salubris, ager fertilis, silva melliflua, aqua piscosa, milites belli-
cosi, rustici laboriosi, equi durabiles, boves arabiles, vacce lac-
tose, oves lanose.[5] Sed ne digressionem nimium prolixam fecisse
videamur, ad intentionis nostre propositum revertamur. Est
autem intencio nostra de Polonia et duce principaliter Bolezlao
describere eiusque gratia quedam gesta predecessorum digna
memoria recitare. Nunc ergo sic ordiri materiam incipiamus, ut
per radicem ad ramum arboris ascendamus. Qualiter ergo ducatus honor generacioni huic acciderit, subsequens ordo narrationis intimabit.

---

[1] Other medieval authors also wrote about these northern islands (e.g.,
Honorius Augustodunensis, *De imagine mundi*, *MPL* 172:129), but place them
north of Britain.

[2] These names, taken from ancient geographers describing peoples of the
southern steppe and the lower Danube respectively, are presumed to have been
applied by the author to certain Baltic peoples, probably to the Jadzwings (see
SSS 5:70 s.v. "Jaćwież").

[3] The identification of these two peoples was a common feature in Western
European sources, see e.g., Jenő Szűcs, "Theoretical elements in Master Simon
of Kéza's *Gesta Hungarorum* 1282–1285," in Simon of Kéza, *The Deeds of the
Hungarians*, ed. and trans. L. Veszprémy and F. Schaer (Budapest: CEU Press,
1999), pp. XIV–XVI.

snow and ice.[1] So the Slavonian land is divided in the north into parts by or made up of these regions, and it runs from the Sarmatians, who are also known as Gets,[2] to Denmark and Saxony, and from Thrace through Hungary, which in past times was occupied by the Huns (who are also called Hungarians),[3] and passing down through Carinthia it ends at Bavaria. Toward the south, starting from Epirus on the Mediterranean Sea it includes Dalmatia, Croatia, and Istria, and ends on shores of the Adriatic Sea, where Venice and Aquileia stand, separating it from Italy. Although this land is thickly forested, yet it has ample resources of gold and silver, bread and meat, fish and honey; but in one respect it is especially to be preferred to all others, for in spite of being surrounded by all the many aforementioned peoples, Christian and pagan alike, and frequently attacked by all and sundry, it has never been completely subjugated by anyone.[4] A land where the air is healthy, the fields fertile, the woods full of honey, the water abounding in fish, the warriors warlike, the peasants hardworking, the horses hardy, the oxen strong at plowing, the cows give abundant milk and the sheep abundant wool.[5] But lest we seem to be extending our digression excessively, let us return to our first aim and purpose. Our intention is to tell of Poland and in particular of Duke Bolesław, and for his sake to recount some of the deeds of his forebears that are worthy of record. So let us now set about putting our matter in order in such a way that from the root of the tree we ascend to the crown. How, then, the honor of the duchy fell to this kindred will be explained in the next part of the narrative.

[4] This fairly precise overview of all western and southern (but not eastern!) Slavic lands, regarded as one *regio*, is a unique feature of this chronicle, as is its assertion of their never having been subjugated; see above, p. lvi. On the notion of *S(c)lavinia* and its ambiguous application to all or particular Slavic lands, see František Graus, *Die Nationenbildung der Westslawen im Mittelalter* (Sigmaringen: Thorbecke, 1980), pp. 151–3, 164, 186.

[5] This poetic praise of the Slavic "homeland" (*patria!*), recalling the vision of the Promised Land (Exod. 3:8 etc.), has even been termed the "first economic geography of Poland" by Kossmann (1:230–6), who argues that it is an accurate reflection of the conditions of the country in the early Middle Ages; in fact it is rather the familiar topos of a *laus terrae*.

(1) DE DUCE POPELONE DICTO CHOSISCO[1]

Erat namque in civitate Gneznensi, que nidus interpretatur sclauonice,[2] dux nomine Popel,[3] duos filios habens, qui more gentilitatis ad eorum tonsuram[4] grande convivium preparavit,[5] ubi plurimos suorum procerum[6] et amicorum invitavit. Contigit autem ex occulto Dei consilio duos illuc hospites advenisse,[7] qui non solum ad convivium non invitati, verum eciam a civitatis introitu cum iniuria sunt redacti. Qui statim civium[8] illorum

---

[1] This addition, and the one below (ch. 2) where Chościsko is—rather illogically—identified as the father of Piast, is seen by Grodecki-Plezia, *Kronika*, p.12, n.1, and other editors as a later insertion, as most of the rubrics seem to be added to the original narrative at a later date. Jacek Banaszkiewicz, *Podanie o Piaście i Popielu: studium porównawcze nad wczesnośredniowiecznymi tradycjami dynastycznymi* [The legend of Piast and Popiel: a comparative study on early-medieval dynastic traditions] (Warsaw: PWN, 1986), pp. 114–23, suggests that Chościsko goes back to an original form *Kosisko* derived from the word *kosa* 'braids,' and sees in this a local version of the *reges criniti* of Indo-European mythology.

[2] This etymology is accepted by modern historical and linguistic research, and may imply that the author knew some Polish.

[3] Two forms of this name appear in the text, *Popiel* and (below, I:3) *Pumpil*. Kadłubek, who constructed a classical origin for the dynasty, wanted to connect it with the Roman Pompilius; see *Magistri Vincentii dicti Kadłubek Chronica Polonorum*, ed. Marianus Plezia, MPH NS 11 (Cracow: Secesja, 1994), I:17, p. 23—henceforth: Kadłubek. Andrzej Bańkowski, "Imiona przodków Bolesław Chrobrego u Galla Anonima: rozważania etymologiczne" [The names of the ancestors of Bolesław Chrobry in Gallus Anonymus: etymological considerations], *Onomastica* 34 (1989): 109–11, sees in it a derivative of the Polish *papyl* 'blister on the skin'—symbolic of a bad ruler, as obnoxious for his subjects as a blister on the foot.

[4] For a detailed discussion of this "tonsure" see *SSS* 4:249–50, s.v. "Postrzyżyny," with bibliography. The cutting of hair as a *rite de passage* may have been originally connected with an offering to pagan godheads. It is, however, also known that in Kievan Rus' it marked the transfer of a young (two- or three-year-old) prince to the care of a tutor.

[5] Czesław Deptuła, *Galla Anonima mit genezy Polski: Studium z historiozofii i hermeneutyki symboli dziejopisarstwa średniowiecznego* [The myth of the origin of Poland of Gallus Anonymus: a study in historiosophy and the hermeneutics

1 OF DUKE POPIEL, CALLED CHOŚCISKO[1]

In the city of Gniezno (whose name means 'nest' in Slavic)[2] lived a duke named Popiel,[3] who had two sons. Now when the time came for the cutting of their hair—a custom among the pagans[4]—he prepared a great banquet[5] and invited large numbers of his nobles[6] and friends. But by God's secret plan it happened that two strangers arrived there.[7] However, not only were they not invited to join the banquet but they were treated injuriously and driven away from the entrance of the city. Disgusted by the rudeness of the townsmen,[8] they made their way forthwith down

of the symbols of medieval historiography] (Lublin: Instytut Europy Środkowo-Wschodniej, 2000), p. 27, draws a parallel between the author's choice of words for Popiel's feast and the description of Balthasar's in the Book of Daniel (Dan. 5:1). In both cases the sins of an old dynasty lead to its downfall, and the prophetic words are explained in the one case by Daniel and in the other by the travellers.

[6] Karol Modzelewski, "Comites, Principes, Nobiles: the structure of the ruling class as reflected in the terminology used by Gallus Anonymus," in *The Polish nobility in the Middle Ages: Anthologies*, ed. A. Gąsiorowski (Wrocław: Ossolineum-PAN, 1984), pp. 188–90, 192, has demonstrated that the author uses *proceres*, *principes*, and *nobiles* interchangeably to designate members of the "aristocracy," i.e. the great men of the kingdom. We therefore translate these terms by the word best fitting any given context, except for *comes*, which may mean both a 'companion,' or a 'member of the retinue' on the one hand, or a definite officeholder on the other, and is therefore usually left in Latin in the scholarly literature.

[7] Several Biblical parallels to this motif (discussed in Deptuła, *Galla mit*, pp. 234–38) include the visit of the "angels" to Abraham (Gen. 17:1 ff.) and to Lot (Gen. 18:1 ff.) and the one in which Gideon is called (Judg. 6:11). However, there are also classical ones, e.g., the visit of the strangers to Philemon and Baucis, Ovid, *Met.* 7.616. Late medieval Polish narratives, e.g., the *Chronica Poloniae Maioris*, ed. Brygida Kürbis, *MPH* n.s. (Warsaw: PWN, 1970), 8/7:13, regarded the two persons as SS. John and Paul.

[8] As far as we can judge the author uses *cives*, *castellani*, *oppidani* synonymously for the inhabitants (or frequently the defenders) of the towns, cities and castles mentioned in the *GpP*. Unless it is obvious that the narrative refers to a particular part of the populace with military duties (where we translate the term in question as 'garrison'), we decided to use the generic term 'townsmen,' since there is no clear evidence about the social and legal status of such persons.

inhumanitatem abhorrentes et in suburbium descendentes, ante domunculam aratoris[1] predicti ducis pro filiis[2] convivium facientis, forte fortuna devenerunt. Ille vero bone compassionis pauperculus hospites illos ad suam domunculam invitavit, suamque paupertatem eis benignissime presentavit. At illi pauperis invitationi gratanter inclinantes et hospitalitatis tugurium subeuntes: bene, inquiunt, nos advenisse gaudeatis et in nostro adventu bonorum copiam et de sobole honorem et gloriam habeatis.

(2) DE PAZT FILIO CHOSISCHONIS

Erant enim hospicii domestici Pazt filius Chossistconis et uxor eius Repca vocabulo nuncupati,[3] qui cum magno cordis affectu pro posse suo hospitum necessitati ministrare sathagebant, eorumque prudentiam intuentes, secretum, si quid erat, cum eorum consilio perficere disponebant.[4] Cumque de more residentes colloquerentur de plurimis et peregrini, an ibi potus aliquid habeatur, inquirerent, arator hospitalis respondit: est,

---

[1] The plowman as mythical ancestor (or first ruler) is a widespread motif. For Visigothic examples see Alexander Haggerty Krappe, "The Plowman King: A Comparative Study in Literature and Folklore," *Revue hispanique* 46 (1919): 516–46, and 56 (1922): 265–84; for a German one (the mythic Henry "with the golden plow") see Otto Gerhard Oexle, "Die 'sächsische Welfenquelle' als Zeugnis der welfischen Hausübelieferung," *Deutsches Archiv für Erforschung des Mittelalters* 24 (1968): 448–71. However, the closest parallel is the plowman Přemysl (Cosmas, *Chron. Boh.* 1:6, p. 16), ancestor of the dukes of Bohemia. See also Jacek Banaszkiewicz, "Königliche Karrieren von Hirten, Gärtnern und Pflügern," *Saeculum* 33 (1982): 265–86. The author may have known about a specific group of peasants who were the duke's plowmen; there is reference in the surviving sources of the early twelfth century to people who plowed another's land, using the tools and draft animals of the landowner, in return for their livelihood; see Karol Modzelewski, "*Ius aratorum* na tle praw grupowych ludności chłopskiej" [The *ius aratorum* in the context of group rights among the rural population], in *Społeczeństwo Polski średniowiecznej: zbiór studiów*, ed. S. K. Kuczyński (Warsaw: PWN, 1981), 1:86–127.

into the suburb, where by chance and by fortune they found themselves before a little cottage belonging to a plowman of the aforesaid duke,[1] who was about to make a banquet for his sons.[2] Although just a poor man, he was kind. He invited the strangers into his cottage and most warmly offered them his modest means. They accepted the poor man's invitation with pleasure and, as they entered the hut, they said: "May you truly be glad we have come, and may our arrival bring you abundance of good things, and honor and glory in your offspring!"

2 OF PAZT THE SON OF CHOŚCISKO

There were two domestics in the house, by name Pazt the son of Chościsko and Rzepka his wife,[3] who with heartfelt goodwill ministered to the needs of their guests, as best they might. When they saw how wise they were, they thought to bring about something secret, if such there was, with their advice.[4] So when they were seated and were talking about this and that as usually happens, the strangers asked if there was any drink to be had; then their good host the plowman said, "I have a jar of fermented

[2] The plural here is puzzling, as we read later (ch. 2, p. 21) about the only son of the plowman.

[3] The original form and etymology of the name Pazt has been a subject of much speculation. Most historians accept that it here represents a form of *Piast*. This could be connected with the root *pa*, which appears in the Old Church Slavonic *pasti* and the Old Polish *pastwiś* 'to nourish, feed,' as well as Latin *pascere*; see Banaszkiewicz, *Podanie*, p. 83. In fact, the name *Piast* does not appear in any other medieval source, and is applied to the dynasty only from the sixteenth century, apparently first by Bishop Martin Kromer; see Kossmann 2:124, n. 103. Rzepka, on the other hand, has the typical form of a nickname, and is most likely derived from the name of the vegetable (*rzepa* 'turnip').

[4] While this is a more or less the literal translation of the Latin sentence, the reference is quite obscure. Others render *secretum* as 'secret desires.'

inquit, mihi vasculum cervisie[1] fermentate, quam pro cesarie filii quem habeo unici tondenda preparavi. Sed quid prodest hoc tantillum, si libeat ebibatis. Decreverat enim rusticus ille pauper, quando dominus suus dux pro filiis convivium prepararet, nam in alio tempore pre nimia paupertate non posset,[2] aliquid obsonii pro suo tondendo parvulo preparare et quosdam amicorum et pauperum non ad prandium sed ad gentaculum invitare; qui etiam porcellum nutriebat, quem ad illud servitium reservabat. Mira dicturus sum, sed quis valet *Dei magnalia*[3] cogitare, vel quis audet de divinis beneficiis disputare; qui temporaliter *pauperum humilitatem* aliquociens *exaltat*[4] et hospitalitatem etiam gentilium remunerare non recusat. Imperant igitur cum hospites securi cervisiam propinari, quam bene noverant pitissando non deficere sed augeri. Usque adeo enim crevisse fertur cervisia,

> Donec vasa mutuata replerentur omnia
> Et que ducis convivantes invenere vacua.

Precipiunt et porcellum supradictum occidi, unde X situle, sclauonice cebri, mirabile dictu memorantur adimpleri.[5] Visis igitur Pazt et Repca miraculis que fiebant, aliquid magni presagii de puero sentiebant.

Iamque ducem et convivas invitare cogitabant sed non audebant, nisi prius peregrinos de hoc inquirant. Quid moramur? Consilio

---

[1] *Cervisium* refers to a drink produced by means of fermentation. In medieval Poland the seeds of various grains, often mixed with each other, were used in the production of ale; see Maria Dembińska, *Food and Drink in Medieval Poland: Rediscovering a Cuisine of the Past*, rev. and adapted by William Woys Weaver (Philadelphia: University of Pennsylvania Press, 1999), pp. 78–80.

[2] The connection drawn between the plowman's poverty and the timing of the ducal feast is not clear.

[3] Deut. 11:2; Sir 18:5, etc.

ale,[1] which I brewed for the cutting of my only son's hair. But what use is such a small amount? Drink it if you will." For this poor peasant had earlier decided to make ready a few dishes to celebrate his own boy's hair-cutting at the same time as his lord the duke was preparing a banquet in honor of his sons (for he could not do so at any other time because he was so poor).[2] He had been planning to invite some of his friends and poor people to dinner, or rather to share a breakfast. He had also been fattening a piglet and keeping it for the same occasion. What I am going to say will amaze you—but whose thoughts can encompass the *marvelous works of God*,[3] or who would venture to question His goodness? For at times He *exalts the poor and humble*[4] in this world and does not disdain to reward even pagans for their hospitality. Well, the guests had no qualms in ordering the ale to be served, for they well knew that the ale would not run out but go on increasing the more they sampled it. And indeed, we are told, the ale kept on increasing,

Till the cups that passed among them were all brimful every round
Even those the duke's companions earlier had empty found.

They ordered the piglet to be slaughtered too, whereupon—marvelous to relate—ten buckets (in Slavic, *cebri*) are reported to have been filled from it.[5] When Pazt and Rzepka saw these miraculous things happening, they realized that something of great significance was being foretold for the boy.

So the duke and all his fellows they were minded to invite, yet they did not dare to do so until they had asked the strangers'

---

[4] 1 Sam. 2:7–8; Luke 1:52.

[5] Deptuła (*Galla mit*, pp. 234–8) has drawn attention to the parallels for the multiplication of food in Scripture, e.g., the miracle of the prophet Elias in return for the hospitality of the widow of Zarephath (1 Kings 17:10–17), and of course to Christ's similar miracles in the Gospels, such as the miracle of the loaves and fishes (Matt. 14:13–21).

itaque hospitum et exhortatione dominus eorum dux et convive omnes ipsius ab agricola Pazt invitantur, neque rustico suo dux invitatus condescendere dedignatur. Nondum enim ducatus Polonie erat tantus, neque princeps urbis tanto fastu superbie tumescebat, nec tot cuneis clientele stipatus ita magnifice procedebat.[1] Inito de more convivio et habundanter omnibus apparatis, hospites illi puerum totonderunt, eique Semouith[2] vocabulum ex presagio futurorum indiderunt.

(3) DE DUCE SAMOUITHAY QUI DICITUR SEMOUITH, FILIO PAST

Hiis itaque peractis puer Semouith, filius Pazt Chossistconis[3] viribus et etate crevit et de die in diem in augmentum proficere probitatis incepit, eotenus quod rex regum[4] et dux ducum eum Polonie ducem concorditer[5] ordinavit et de regno Pumpil cum sobole radicitus exstirpavit.[6] Narrant etiam seniores antiqui, quod iste Pumpil a regno expulsus, tantam a muribus persecutionem paciebatur, quod ob hoc a suis consequentibus in insulam

---

[1] The simplicity and modesty of the "olden times" (cf. e.g., Ovid, *Met.* 1.89) is a commonplace usually implying a criticism of the author's own times.

[2] Siemowit was born probably around 845 and died around 900 *(PSB* 27:63–4). The etymology of the name is debated. The first part may come from the Old Slavonic *simuja* (servants, slaves, family); cf. Russian *sem'ia.* The part *-vit* is generally interpreted as 'a master, a noble', in which case the name would mean 'head of the family.' Aleksander Brückner, *Słownik etymologiczny języka polskiego* [Etymological dictionary of the Polish language] (Warsaw: Wiedza Powszechna, 1985), p. 489, links the name to those of Western Slavonic deities, which very often include the element *vit*; he thinks this name has a divine character and explains it as 'prosperity of the family.'

[3] The Latin genitive may reflect a Slavic patronymic. This time the reference to Chościsko is in the text and not the rubric, though it may still be an interpolation.

[4] Cf. Dan. 2:37; 1 Tim. 6:15; Apoc. 17:14, 19:16; but note the author's addition of *dux ducum* to accommodate non-royal lordship!

advice first. Well, to put it briefly, the two guests counseled and urged them to do so, and Pazt the farmer invited their lord the duke and all his guests, nor did the duke disdain to accept the invitation from his peasant. For the duchy of Poland had not yet grown so mighty, nor was the prince of the city so haughty and swollen with pride, strutting in pomp amid crowds of retainers.[1] So the feasting began as a feast should, with everything laid on in abundance, and the (two) guests cut the boy's hair, and in presage of the future they gave him the name Siemowit.[2]

3 OF THE DUKE SAMOUITHAY CALLED SIEMOWIT, THE SON OF PAZT

After the events described, the boy Siemowit, the son of Pazt Chościsko,[3] increased in age and strength, and his excellence grew ever day by day, until the King of Kings[4] and Duke of Dukes in harmony[5] made him duke of Poland, and he rid the kingdom once and for all of Pumpil and all his progeny.[6] Venerable persons of old tell a further story, that after this Pumpil was driven from the kingdom he was beset by a horde of rats, and so plagued that his followers ferried him over to an island. However, these horrible creatures even swam over there. For a while

[5] There is a long history of debate about the meaning of *concorditer*. Proponents of the ancient origin of popular consensus would read it as proof of common assent to Siemowit's rise to ducal office, but the sentence clearly refers to his being made ruler by divine will—though medieval political thought did not exclude divine will from the manifestation of popular assent (our author also uses the *vox populi vox Dei* adage, at III:12, p. 242). Others read it as referring to the prophecy with which the previous chapter ended, thus meaning 'in concert with that.'

[6] L. M. Popova, *Gall Anonim, Khronika u deianiia kniazei ili pravitelei polskikh* [Gallus Anonymus: Chronicle and Deeds of the Polish Princes or Dukes] (Moscow: Akad. Nauk SSSR, 1961), p. 145, n. 2 to ch. 3, would see this legend as the reflection of a struggle between two dynasties in early Poland, from which the "Piasts" emerged victorious.

transportatus et ab illis feris pessimis illuc transnatantibus in
turre lignea tam diu sit defensus, donec pre fetore pestifere
multitudinis interempte ab omnibus derelictus, morte turpis-
sima, monstris corrodentibus, expiravit.[1] Sed istorum gesta, quorum memoriam oblivio vetustatis abolevit et quos error et
ydolatria defedavit, memorare negligamus et ad ea recitanda, que
fidelis recordatio[2] meminit, istos succincte nominando transeamus. Semouith vero principatum adeptus non voluptuose vel
inepte iuventutem suam exercuit, sed usu laboris et militie probitatis famam et honoris gloriam acquisivit, atque sui principatus
fines ulterius quam aliquis antea dilatavit.[3] Cuius loco decedentis
Lestik[4] filius eius subintravit, qui paterne probitati et audacie
gestis sese militaribus adequavit. Lestik quoque morienti
Semimizl eius genitus successit, qui parentum memoriam et
genere et dignitate triplicavit.[5]

[1] A "punishment" of being devoured by mice is also recorded in Thietmar,
Chron. VI:82, ad a. 1012, p. 330, for a *miles* who failed to repent after damaging
the property of St. Clement. On this story see now Jacek Banaszkievicz, "Die
Mäusethurmsage—the symbolism of annihilation of an evil ruler," *APH* 51
(1985): 5–32. These "events" are believed to have happened around Kruszwica
in Kujawia at Lake Gopło (Grodecki-Plezia, *Kronika*, pp. 15–6, n. 4), which
might have been the center of a dynasty defeated by the "Piasts."

[2] The words "faithful record" have often been interpreted as an allusion to some
(now lost) annalistic works used by the author, but there is no proof for this.
While the names and deeds of the rulers before Mieszko are not known from
any other source, they are regarded as fairly authentic, see Kazimierz Jasiński,
Rodowód pierwszych Piastów [The genealogy of the first Piasts] (Warsaw and
Wrocław: Uniw. Wrocławski, 1993), 26–7.

[3] Nothing is known about these conquests. On the Polanian expansion into
the regions of both the upper and lower Vistula and Masovia, see now M. Kara,
"Anfänge der Bildung des Piastenstaates im Lichte neuer archäologischer
Ermittlungen," *QMAeN* 5 (2000): 57–85.

he kept himself safe in a wooden tower. But as the stench from the multitude of dead vermin grew, finally he was abandoned by all, and he died a vile and shameful death, gnawed to pieces by these monsters.[1] But let us pass over the story of the deeds of men stained by error and idolatry, lost to memory in the oblivion of ages, and turn to recount those whose memory has been preserved in faithful record,[2] and briefly list their names. So once Siemowit became prince he did not waste his youth foolishly in pleasure, but by his steady efforts won both fame for martial prowess and the glory of honor, and extended the boundaries of the realm farther than anyone previously.[3] And on his passing he was succeeded by his son Leszek,[4] whose prowess and boldness in martial deeds equaled his father's. And when Leszek died, his son Siemomysł succeeded him, who increased threefold the memory of his ancestors both in nobility and dignity.[5]

[4] The name Leszek (*Lestek*, *Lestik*) has been interpreted as a diminutive of Leścimir ('clever,' 'wise'); he may have lived in the first part of the tenth century (*SSS* 3:49). Whether his name is reflected in the name Licicavikii applied to the Polanians by Widukind of Corvey, *Res gestae Saxonicae*, III:66, *Quellen zur Geschichte der Sächsischen Kaiserzeit*, ed. A. Bauer and R. Rau, p. 170 (Darmstadt: Wiss. Buchges., 1977), FvS 8, and interpreted by Kossmann (2:59–60) as a variant of "Leszkoviki," i.e. the people of Leszek, is questionable. Constantine Porphyrogennetos mentions a Slavic prince Litzike in *De administrando imperio*, ch. 33, ed. Gyula Moravcsik, Engl. trans. R. I. H. Jenkins (Budapest: Pázmány Péter Tudományegyetem, 1949), p. 173, but the identification with this ruler is also problematic.

[5] For Siemomysł or Siemimysł see *SSS* 5:168. The name may mean 'he who thinks of his family'; for the etymology see Bańkowski, "Imiona," pp. 127–9. In the obscure threefold increase—more literally, 'triplication'—Kossmann (2:126) sees an implied reference to the notion of hereditary property in Polish customary law, which was acquired only by the third generation; on this see Piotr Górecki, "A Historian as a Source of Law: Abbot Peter of Henryków and the Invocation of Norms in Medieval Poland, c. 1200–1270," *Law & History Review* 18 (2000): 479–523, esp. pp. 482–3, 492–3. Thus Siemomysł as the third Piast would have established the dynasty's right to the realm.

(4) DE CECITATE MESCHONIS FILII ZEMIMIZL DUCIS

Hic autem Semimizl magnum et memorandum Meschonem progenuit, qui primus nomine vocatus illo[a,1] VII annis a nativitate cecus fuit. VII° vero recurrente nativitatis eius anniversario, pater pueri more solito convocata comitum aliorumque suorum principum concione, copiosam epulacionem et sollempnem celebrabat[2] et tantum inter epulas pro cecitate pueri, quasi doloris et verecundie memor, latenter ab imo pectore suspirabat.[3] Aliis equidem exultantibus et palmis ex consuetudine plaudentibus,[4] letitia alia aliam cumulavit, que visum recepisse cecum puerum indicavit. At pater nulli nuntianti hoc credidit, donec mater de convivio exsurgens ad puerum introivit, que patri nodum ambiguitatis amputavit, cunctisque residentibus videntem puerum presentavit. Tunc demum cunctis leticia plena fuit, cum puer illos, quos numquam viderat, recognovit, sueque cecitatis ignominiam in gaudium inextricabile commutavit. Tunc Semimizl dux seniores et discreciores, qui aderant, subtiliter sciscitatur, si quid prodigii per cecitatem et illuminacionem pueri designatur. Ipsi vero per cecitatem Poloniam sic antea fuisse quasi cecam indicabant, sed de cetero per Meschonem illuminandam et exaltandam super naciones contiguas prophetabant. Quod et ita se habuit, at aliter tamen interpretari potuit. Vere Polonia ceca prius erat, que nec culturam veri Dei nec doctrinam fidei cognoscebat,

---

[a] primus nomine vocatus illo] primus nomine vocatus alio *Z*, prius vocatus nomine alio *Mal*

---

[1] The readings of the Latin allow two interpretations. The commoner (so Mal. etc.) is that Mieszko 'had formerly another name'—which scholars have suggested may refer to his baptismal or confirmation name Dagome (Dagobert?), as in the famous text *"Dagome iudex"* referring to Poland being offered to the Holy See, see *LexMA* 7:54. A simpler one, which we (following *H*) here adopt, is that he was 'Mieszko the First.' Mieszko I, b. ca. 922, d. 992, is the first historically authentic Polish ruler.

4 THE BLINDNESS OF MIESZKO, SON OF DUKE SIEMOMYSŁ

Siemomysł's son was the great and memorable Mieszko, the first of that name,[1] who was blind for the first seven years of his life. But when his seventh birthday came around, the boy's father, following custom, called a gathering of his *comites* and other princes to celebrate a grand and lavish banquet.[2] Yet as they feasted, no one remarked how he did but sigh from the bottom of his heart[3] for the blindness of his son—thinking, it would seem, of the sadness and shame of it. But while the others rejoiced and clapped their hands, as the custom was,[4] a new joy augmented their joy, for it became clear that the blind boy had recovered his sight. But his father would not believe anyone who told him the news, until his mother rose from the feast and went to the boy's room, and cut the knot of his father's doubt when she presented the boy who now could see all the seated company. Then indeed everyone's happiness was complete when the boy recognized those whom he had never seen, turning the shame of his blindness to indescribable joy. Then Duke Siemomysł questioned the older and wiser among those present carefully, asking whether some portent was indicated by the boy's blindness and the recovery of his sight. Their explanation was that as he had once been blind, so too Poland had, as it were, been blind before; but in time to come, they prophesied, Poland would be illuminated by Mieszko and exalted over all the neighboring nations. And indeed, this is what came to pass. However, another interpretation could have been given. For Poland was indeed blind before, for she knew neither the worship of the true God nor the teachings of the Faith; but when Mieszko was enlightened Po-

[2] From this sentence it has been assumed that in Poland the seventh birthday of a boy was the usual time for his "tonsure" (on which see above, n. 4, p. 16).

[3] Cf. Ovid, *Met.* 10.402.

[4] Cf. *Vita Minor S. Stanislai*, ch. 9 (ed. Wojciech Kętrzyński, MPH 4, Lviv: Nakładem Własnym, 1884, p. 258), where the author regards the clapping of hands as a pagan habit.

sed per Meschonem illuminatum est et ipsa illuminata, quia eo credente Polonica gens de morte infidelitatis est exempta.[1] Ordine enim competenti Deus omnipotens visum prius Meschoni corporalem restituit, et postea spiritalem adhibuit, ut per *visibilia* ad *invisibilium*[2] agnicionem penetraret et per rerum noticiam ad artificis omnipotenciam suspicaret. Sed cur rota currum precurrit? Semimizl autem senio confectus extremum vale mundo fecit.

(5) QUOMODO MESCO RECEPIT DOBROWCAM SIBI IN UXOREM

At Mescho ducatum adeptus ingenium animi cepit et vires corporis exercere, ac nationes per circuitum bello sepius attemptare.[3] Adhuc tamen in tanto gentilitatis errore involvebatur, quod sua consuetudine VII uxoribus abutebatur.[4] Postremo unam christianissimam de Bohemia Dubroucam nomine in matrimonium requisivit.[5] At illa, ni pravam consuetudinem illam dimittat, seseque fieri christianum promittat, sibi nubere recusavit. Eo igitur collaudante se usum illum[a] paganismi dimissurum et fidei christiane sacramenta suscepturum, illa domina cum magno seculari et ecclesiastico religionis apparatu Poloniam in-

---

[a] illius *Z H Mal*

---

[1] A possible parallel to the author's Christian interpretation of this miraculous healing can be found in the legend of St. Volodimer (Vladimir) in the Russian Primary Chronicle, according to which the grand prince had lost his eyesight before baptism and regained it only upon the laying-on of hands by the bishop of Korsun; see Samuel Hazzard Cross and Olgert Sterbowitz-Wetzor, *The Russian Primary Chronicle–Laurentian Text* (Cambridge, MA: The Medieval Academy of America, 1953), p. 113.

[2] Heb. 11:3.

[3] According to Widukind, who is the first to mention him as ruler of the Poles (*Res gest. Sax.*, 3:66, pp. 170–1), Mieszko ascended to the duchy some time before 963; see Zygmunt Wojciechowski, *Mieszko I and the Rise of the Polish*

land was enlightened too, because when he came to believe, the people of Poland were saved from the death of unbelief.[1] For it was a fitting progression that Almighty God first restored to Mieszko his corporeal vision and then gave him spiritual sight, so that he might pass from *visible things* to the understanding of *invisible ones*,[2] and through knowledge of His works gain some inkling of the omnipotence of the Artisan. But why let the wheel run ahead of the cart? As it was, Siemomysł grew old and weak, and he bade the world a last farewell.

5 HOW MIESZKO TOOK DĄBRÓWKA AS HIS WIFE

But once he became duke, Mieszko began to put the quickness of his mind and strength of his body to use, and many times he went to war with the nations about.[3] Yet he was still so enmeshed in the error of paganism that following their custom he was wrongfully joined to seven wives.[4] But later he sought the hand of a most Christian woman from Bohemia called Dąbrówka.[5] However, she refused to marry him unless he gave up this wicked custom and promised to become a Christian. So when he assured her that he would give up that practice of paganism and receive the sacraments of the Christian faith, this lady came to Poland with a great retinue of Christian followers both secular and

---

State (Toruń: Baltic Inst., 1936). Mieszko waged wars with the Saxon lord Wichmann and also with the emperors Otto II and Otto III; a conflict with Kievan Rus' in 981 has also been assumed, see *CHP*, 16–20.

[4] Seven is a number frequent in myth and tale, often meaning simply "several." The same (*habebat septem uxores*) is said in St. Gerhard's *Legenda Maior*, ch. 8 (*SRH* 2:489) of the Hungarian chieftain Ajtony, who is depicted as an imperfect Christian.

[5] Dąbrówka—in Czech, Dubravka—daughter of Boleslav I, duke of Bohemia (ca. 929–67/73), born ca. 935, d. 977. The marriage is recorded also in Cosmas, *Chron. Boh.* I: 27, p. 49, ad a. 977, and in Thietmar, *Chron.* 4:55, pp. 170–3.

troivit, necdum tamen thoro sese maritali federavit, donec ille paulatim consuetudinem christianitatis et religionem ecclesiastici ordinis diligenter contemplans, errorem gentilium abnegavit, seque gremio matris ecclesie counivit.[1]

(6) DE PRIMO BOLEZLAUO QUI DICEBATUR GLORIOSUS SEU CHRABRI[2]

Primus igitur Polonorum dux Mescho per fidelem uxorem ad baptismi graciam pervenit,[3] cui ad laudem et gloriam satis habundanter sufficit, quod suo tempore et per eum *oriens ex alto* regnum Polonie *visitavit.*[4] De hac namque benedicta femina gloriosum Bolezlaum generavit, qui post ipsius obitum[5] regnum viriliter gubernavit et in tantam Deo favente virtutem et potentiam excrevit, quod, ut sic eloquar, sua probitate totam Poloniam deauravit. Quis enim eius gesta fortia vel certamina contra populos circumquaque commissa digne valeat enarrare, nedum etiam scriptis memorialibus commendare. Numquid non ipse Morauiam et Bohemiam subiugavit et in Praga ducalem sedem obtinuit, suisque eam suffraganeis deputavit.[6] Numquid non ipse Vngaros frequencius in certamine superavit, totamque terram

---

[1] For the commonplace of the devout wife converting her husband, cf. 1 Cor. 7:14, *sanctificabatur vir per mulierem fidelem*, which was applied, *inter alias*, to Chlotilde, wife of Chlovis of the Franks, and to Gisela, queen of Stephen of Hungary. It is explicitly quoted by the author of the *Chronicon Polono-Hungaricum*, ed. J. Deér (*SRH* 2:305), in regard to the (legendary) Queen Adelaide of Hungary. In fact Dąbrówka was related to the saints Wenceslas and Ludmilla, already then venerated, and two of her siblings took vows. See Jerzy Kłoczowski, *La Pologne dans l'Eglise médiévale* (Aldershot: Variorum, 1993), p. 10.

[2] Bolesław I Chrobry, born 967, duke of Poland from 992, crowned king 1025, d. 17 June 1025. The presently used form of the epithet, understood as meaning 'valiant,' is in fact of later origin, all MSS of *GpP* reading *Chrabri*; on this see Jasiński, *Rodowód,* p. 81.

[3] The Latin, however, may also be translated '... Mieszko I, duke of Poland, received....' Mieszko's baptism is usually dated to 966.

ecclesiastic. But she would not agree to marriage until he had taken time to consider carefully the observances of Christianity and the religion ordained by the church and set aside his pagan errors, and then laid himself in the bosom of the mother church.[1]

6 BOLESŁAW THE FIRST, WHO WAS CALLED THE GLORIOUS OR CHRABRI[2]

So, thanks to his devout wife, Mieszko was the first duke of Poland to receive the grace of baptism.[3] And it is fully enough to say to his praise and glory that in his days and through him the *dayspring from on high visited*[4] the kingdom of Poland. For the glorious Bolesław was born to him of that holy woman, and after his death[5] Bolesław governed the kingdom valiantly, and with God's favor so grew in courage and strength that, if I may put it so, his virtues gilded the whole of Poland. For who could do full justice in speaking of his brave deeds or his battles against the peoples all around, to say nothing of setting them down in written record? Did not he conquer Moravia and Bohemia and win the seat of the duchy in Prague and appointed his suffragans to it;[6] was it not he who time and again defeated the Hungarians in battle and made himself master of all their lands as far as the

---

[4] Luke 1:78.

[5] Mieszko died 25 May 992.

[6] Temporary Polish conquests in Bohemia around 1002 included the deposition and blinding of the Czech duke, Boleslav III the Redhaired; but after Bolesław Chrobry refused to do homage to the emperor for Bohemia, the Poles were expelled in 1004, see *CHP* pp. 25–6. However, there is no contemporary evidence that Bolesław established bishops (*suffragani*) of the Polish archdiocese in Bohemia. Grodecki proposed to translate the latter word as 'retainers,' referring to secular governors, possibly from among the Slavnikides. But Gerard Labuda ("Der 'Akt von Gnesen' vom Jahre 1000: Bericht über die Forschungsvorhaben und -ergebnisse," *QMAeN* 5, 2000: 174, 186) proposes that at the foundation of the archbishopric of Gniezno two Czech bishoprics (in Prague and in Moravia) may have been foreseen as suffragans.

eorum usque Danubium suo dominio mancipavit.[1] Indomitos
vero tanta virtute Saxones[2] edomuit, quod in flumine Sale in
medio terre eorum meta ferrea[3] fines Polonie terminavit.[4] Quid
igitur est necesse victorias et triumphos de gentibus incredulis
nominatim recitasse, quas constat eum quasi sub pedibus con-
culcasse.[5] Ipse namque Selenciam, Pomoraniam et Prusiam[6]
usque adeo vel in perfidia persistentes contrivit, vel conversas in
fide solidavit, quod ecclesias ibi multas et episcopos per apostoli-
cum, ymmo apostolicus per eum ordinavit.[7] Ipse etiam beatum
Adalbertum[8] in longa peregrinacione et a sua rebelli gente Bohemica multas iniurias perpessum ad se venientem cum magna
veneratione suscepit eiusque predicacionibus fideliter et insti-
tucionibus obedivit. Sanctus vero martir igne karitatis et zelo

[1] Regarding Bolesław's incursions into what is today Slovakia, see György
Györffy, *St Stephen of Hungary* (Boulder, CO: Social Science Monograph,
1994), pp. 107–8, who maintains that these were merely occasional forays
and that there is no evidence to suggest that parts of the region would have
been under Polish control for any length of time.

[2] Widukind *Res gest. Sax.* 1:10 (ed. Bauer-Rau, p. 36) also refers to: *insuperabiles
. . . Saxones.*

[3] The reference to a *meta ferrea* by or in the river is puzzling, since the River
Saale itself would have been a sufficient border. Hans-Jürgen Karp, *Grenzen
in Ostmitteleuropa während des Mittelalters* (Cologne: Böhlau, 1972), p. 115,
does not know of any parallel, save some *signa in medio rivuli* as border-signs
set up by King Ottokar I of Bohemia in 1219. Gotthold Rhode, "Die ehernen
Grenzsäulen Boleslaus des Tapferen von Polen: Wege einer Legende," *Jahrbücher für Geschichte Osteuropas*, NF 8 (1960): 331–53, has followed up the
history of this legend through the centuries.

[4] During the contested succession of Emperor Henry II following the murder
of Margrave Ekkehard of Meissen, Bolesław's father-in-law, the Polish duke
occupied the Lusatian Mark between the River Elbe and the River Saale and
adjacent territories, which led to continuous wars between Poland and the
Empire till 1018; see *CHP* 24–5.

[5] Cf. Dan. 7:14 etc.

[6] On Selencia see p. 12 above. It is assumed that Mieszko had some time before
967 defeated the Wolinians, who lived in Eastern Pomerania, but could not
conquer the estuary of the River Oder; no campaign of Bolesław I to that region
is known, see Jan M. Piskorski, *Pommern im Wandel der Zeiten* (Szczecin:

Danube?[1] The indomitable Saxons[2] were not a match for his valor: hence in the middle of their country an iron boundary sign[3] in the River Saale marked Poland's boundaries.[4] What need is there then to list by name his victories and triumphs over heathen nations, nations which, one may say, he trampled under his feet?[5] For when Selencia, Pomorania, and Prussia persisted in their perfidy he crushed them,[6] and when they converted he strengthened them in their faith, indeed he established through the pope many churches and bishops there, or rather the pope established them through him.[7] Moreover, when St. Adalbert came to him on his long wanderings after suffering many indignities through his rebellious Czech people, Bolesław received him with great veneration and paid faithful attention to his instructions and his sermons.[8] Then, once he saw that the faith

Zamek Książąt Pomorskich, 1999), pp. 31–2. Nor is there any record of a succeful campaign of Bolesław I in Prussia; however, he supported the missionary activity of Bruno of Querfurt, for which see Bruno's letter to Henry II (ed. J. Karwasińska, MPH, n.s. 4:3, pp. 97–103) and Reinhard Wenskus, *Studien zur historisch-politischen Gedankenwelt Brunos von Querfurt* (Münster-Köln: Böhlau, 1956), pp. 192–7. Recent excavations point to a major basilica near the Prussian border that may have been built as early as his time, see Wojciech Chudziak, "The Early Romanesque Building from Kałdus, Voivodeship of Toruń – Chronology and Functions," *Quaestiones Medii Aevi Novae* 4 (1999): 197–207.

[7] Regarding churches in these territories only the bishopric of Kołobrzeg/Kolberg is known to have been founded around 1000 (Thietmar, *Chron.* 4:45–6, pp. 161–3); however, it did not survive and had to be refounded later after the conversion of Pomerania. See Zofia Kurnatowska, "Die Christianisierung Polens im Lichte der archäologischen Quellen," in *Europeas Mitte* 1:490–4 (cf. *Europe's Centre*, pp. 317–9); and Jürgen Petersohn, *Der südliche Ostseeraum im kirchlich-politischen Kräftespiel des Reiches, Polens und Dänemarks vom 10. bis 13. Jahrhundert* (Köln: Böhlau, 1979), esp. pp. 42–8.

[8] On Adalbert/Wojciech, bishop of Prague, see Alexander Gieysztor, "*Sanctus et gloriosissimus martyr Christi Adalbertus*: un état et une église missionaires aux alentours de l'an mille," in *La conversione al christianismo nell'Europa dell'Alto Medioevo*, Settimane di Studio 14 (Spoleto: Centro di Studio, 1967), pp. 611–47. The most recent summary of his life is Ian Wood, *The Missionary Life: Saints and the Evangelisation of Europe 400–1050* (Turnholt: Brepols, 2001), pp. 207–25.

predicacionis accensus, ut aliquantulum iam in Polonia fidem pullulasse et sanctam ecclesiam excrevisse conspexit, intrepidus Prusiam intravit, ibique martirio suum agonem consumavit.[1] Postea vero corpus ipsius ab ipsis Prusis Bolezlauus auri pondere comparavit et in Gneznen metropoli condigno honore collocavit.[2] Illud quoque memorie commendandum estimamus, quod tempore ipsius Otto Rufus imperator ad sanctum Adalbertum orationis ac reconciliationis gratia simulque gloriosi Bolezlaui cognoscendi famam introivit,[3] sicut in libro de passione martiris potest propensius inveniri.[4] Quem Bolezlauus sic honorifice et magnifice suscepit, ut regem, imperatorem Romanum ac tantum hospitem suscipere decens fuit. Nam miracula mirifica Boleslaus in imperatoris adventu preostendit, acies inprimis militum multimodas, deinde principum in planitie spaciosa quasi choros ordinavit, singulasque separatim acies[5] diversitas indumentorum discolor variavit. Et non quelibet erat ibi vilis varietas ornamenti, sed quicquid potest usquam gencium preciosius reperiri. Quippe Bolezlaui tempore quique milites et queque femine curiales palliis pro lineis vestibus vel laneis utebantur, nec pelles quantum-

---

[1] St. Adalbert was murdered on 23 April 997.

[2] At the time Gniezno was not yet a metropolis; Adalbert's half-brother Gaudentius (Radzim/Radim) became its first archbishop in 1000, on which see below, n. 2, p. 80. Adalbert was first buried not in the cathedral, but in some smaller chapel. The phrase *condigno honore* recurs in the *Passio S. Adalberti martiris*, in MPH 1, ed. August Bielowski (Cracow: Nakładem Własnym, 1864), p.156.

[3] Otto III—the cognomen Rufus ('Red,' 'Red-haired') usually applied to Otto II is occasionally transferred to his son—was emperor 983–1002; see Karl Uhlirz, *Jahrbücher des Deutschen Reiches unter Otto II. und Otto III.*, ed. Margaret Uhlirz (Berlin: Duncker und Humbolt, 1902; reprint, 1967), 1:209, n. 68. The literature on the meeting in Gniezno A. D. 1000 would fill a library. The most recent summary is offered by Johannes Fried, *Otto III. und Bolesław Chrobry: das Widmungsbild des Aachener Evangeliars, der "Akt von Gnesen" und das frühe polnische und ungarische Königtum*, 2d ed. (Stuttgart: Steiner,

had begun to blossom in Poland and the holy church was growing, the holy martyr, alight with the fire of love and zeal for preaching, fearlessly entered Prussia; and there he met with martyrdom and brought his holy struggle to consummation.[1] Afterwards Bolesław obtained his body from the Prussians for a weight of gold and laid him to rest in the metropolitan see of Gniezno with all the honor befitting him.[2] One further matter seems to me worthy of record. In his time the emperor Otto Rufus went to visit St. Adalbert to pray and seek reconciliation,[3] and at the same time to learn more of what was reported of the glorious Bolesław (the story can be read at greater length in the book of his martyrdom),[4] and Bolesław received him with the honor and ceremony with which such a distinguished guest, a king and Roman emperor, should fittingly be received. Marvelous and wonderful sights Bolesław set before the emperor when he arrived: the ranks first of the knights in all their variety, and then of the princes, lined up on a spacious plain like choirs, each separate unit[5] set apart by the distinct and varied colors of its apparel, and no garment there was of inferior quality, but of the most precious stuff that might anywhere be found. For in Bolesław's time every knight and every lady of the court wore robes instead of garments of linen or wool, nor did they wear in

2001), pp. 82–125, and Gerd Althoff, *Otto III* (Darmstadt: Wissenschaftliche Buchgesellschaft, 1996), pp. 126–52. See also the critical comments by Labuda, "Der 'Akt von Gnesen,'" passim, with extensive bibliographical references.

[4] The *Passio S. Adalberti* has not come down to us. For a recent assessment of its role in the Adalbert-tradition, see Johannes Fried, "Gnesen-Aachen-Rom, Otto III. und der Kult des hl. Adalbert: Beobachtungen zum Älteren Adalbertsleben," in *Polen und Deutschland vor 1000 Jahren*, ed. M. Borgolte (Berlin: Akademie, 2002), pp. 267–9.

[5] The problematic term *miles* we translate as 'knight' or 'warrior' according to context, as far as it is possible to judge; see above p. lxii. *Acies* is traditionally translated 'battle line,' but here and elsewhere we have translated it *faute de mieux* as 'unit,' as there is no reliable evidence on the size of these detachments; see *Polska technika wojskowa do roku 1500* [Polish military technique up to A.D. 1500], ed. Andrzej Nadolski (Warsaw: Oficyna Naukowa, 1994), p. 39.

libet preciose, licet nove fuerint, in eius curia sine pallio[1] et aurifrisio portabantur. Aurum enim eius tempore commune quasi argentum ab omnibus habebatur, argentum vero vile quasi pro stramine tenebatur.[2] Cuius gloriam et potentiam et divitias imperator Romanus considerans, admirando dixit: Per coronam imperii mei, maiora sunt que video, quam fama percepi. Suorumque consultu magnatum coram omnibus adiecit: Non est dignum tantum ac virum talem sicut unum de principibus ducem aut comitem nominari, sed in regale solium glorianter redimitum diademate sublimari. Et accipiens imperiale diadema capitis sui, capiti Bolezlaui in amicicie fedus inposuit[3] et pro vexillo triumphali clavum ei de cruce Domini cum lancea sancti Mauritij dono dedit,[4] pro quibus illi Bolezlauus sancti Adalberti brachium redonavit.[5] Et tanta sunt illa die dileccione couniti, quod imperator eum fratrem et cooperatorem imperii constituit, et populi Romani amicum et socium appellavit.[6] Insuper etiam in ecclesiasticis honoribus quicquid ad imperium pertinebat in regno Polonorum, vel in aliis superatis ab eo vel superandis regionibus

---

[1] The meaning of *pallium* in the present context is unclear, though the many senses recorded—e.g., in J. F. Niermeyer, *Mediae latinitatis lexicon minus* (Leiden: Brill, 1997), s.v. *pallium*, 755–6—include 'precious fabric,' and 'ornamental tissue.' A later reference (II:23, p. 161) might suggest that precious robes lined with fur are meant.

[2] On the *topos* of the worthlessness of gold and silver in the "golden age" see e.g., Lucretius, *DRN*, 5.1269–75.

[3] The term *amicitia* has been shown to have had very important and technical meanings in the tenth–eleventh centuries, see Gerd Althoff, *Amicitiae und Pacta: Bündnis, Einung, Politik und Gebetsgedenken im beginnenden 10. Jh.*, MGH Schriften 37 (Hannover: Hahn, 1992), especially pp. 12–36. *Fedus* ('pledge') usually implies a contract or alliance. The significance of the placing of the crown on Bolesław's head is one of the central issues debated in the literature on this meeting.

[4] On the "Holy Lance" and its replica (now in Cracow), see P. E. Schramm, "Die 'Heilige Lanze,' Reliquie und Herrschaftszeichen des Reiches und ihre Replik in Krakau," in *Herrschaftszeichen und Staatssymbolik*, MGH Schriften 13 (Stuttgart: Hiersemann, 1955), 2:492–537, esp. 502, 517. See also Zbigniew Dalewski, "Die heilige Lanze und die polnischen Insignien," in *Europas Mitte*, 2:907–11; cf. *Europe's Centre*, pp. 602–5.

his court any precious furs, however new, without robes[1] and orphrey. For gold in his days was held by all to be as common as silver, and silver deemed as little worth as straw.[2] So when the Roman emperor beheld his glory and power and richness, he exclaimed in admiration, "By the crown of my empire, the things I behold are greater than I had been led to believe," and after taking counsel with his magnates he added before the whole company, "Such a great man does not deserve to be styled duke or count like any of the princes, but to be raised to a royal throne and adorned with a diadem in glory." And with these words he took the imperial diadem from his own head and laid it upon the head of Bolesław in pledge of friendship.[3] And as a triumphal banner he gave him as a gift one of the nails from the cross of our Lord with the lance of St. Maurice,[4] and in return Bolesław gave to him an arm of St. Adalbert.[5] And in such love were they united that day that the emperor declared him his brother and partner in the Empire, and called him a friend and ally of the Roman people.[6] And what is more, he granted him and his successors authority over whatever ecclesiastical honors belonged to the empire in any part of the kingdom of Poland or

[5] Otto III gave the arm of St. Adalbert to the Roman basilica founded by him and dedicated to St. Adalbert on the Isola Tibertina (since the twelfth century called the Island of St. Bartholomew, to whom the church was re-dedicated). In 1938 the reliquary with parts of St. Adalbert's arm was transferred to the cathedral of Gniezno. A part of the relics may have been given by Otto III to an Aachen church with St. Adalbert patrocinium. See M. Rokosz, "Inter duos pontes: O Ottońskiej fundacji ku czci św. Wojciecha na Wyspie Tybrowej" [Inter duos pontes: About the Ottonian foundation in honour of St. Adalbert on the Tiber Island], *Analecta Cracoviensia* 31/32 (1989–1990): 505–27; Aleksander Gieysztor, "Rzymska studzienka ze św. Wojciechem z roku około 1000" [A Roman fountain of St. Adalbert from ca. 1000 A.D.], in *Święty Wojciech w polskiej tradycji historiograficznej* [St. Adalbert in the tradition of Polish historiography] (Warsaw: Instytut Wydawniczy PAX, 1997), pp. 337–49.

[6] Cf. e.g., Sallust, *Jug.* 24.3.

barbarorum, sue suorumque successorum potestati concessit,[1] cuius paccionis decretum papa Siluester[2] sancte Romane ecclesie privilegio confirmavit.[3] Igitur Bolezlauus in regem ab imperatore tam gloriose sublimatus inditam sibi liberalitatem exercuit, cum tribus sue coronacionis[a,4] diebus convivium regaliter et imperialiter celebravit, singulisque diebus vasa omnia et supellectilia transmutavit, aliaque diversa multoque preciosiora presentavit. Finito namque convivio pincernas et dapiferos vasa aurea et argentea, nulla enim lignea ibi habebantur, cyphos videlicet et cuppas, lances et scutellas et cornua de mensis omnibus trium dierum congregare precepit et imperatori pro honore, non pro principali munere presentavit. A camerariis vero pallia extensa et cortinas, tapetia, strata, mantilia, manuteria et quecumque servicio presentata fuerunt, iussit similiter congregare et in cameram imperatoris comportare. Insuper etiam alia plura dedit vasa, scilicet aurea et argentea diversi operis, pallia vero diversi coloris, ornamenta generis ignoti, lapides preciosos et huiusmodi tot et tanta presentavit, quod imperator tanta munera pro miraculo reputavit.[5] Singulos vero principes eius ita magnifice muneravit,

---

[a] consecracionis Z Mal

---

[1] The meaning of 'honors' in this context is seen as a reference to imperial rights and properties (*Reichskirchengut*); the use of this expression points to Leuven/Louvain, where Sigebert of Gembloux was instrumental in working out the concepts of imperial regalia in the surroundings of Henry V; see Fried, "Gnesen – Aschen – Rom," pp. 265–6. On the problems connected with ecclesiastical foundations and in particular with the archbishopric of Gniezno, see Fried, *Otto*, pp. 92–99, where the contemporary sources (e.g., Thietmar, *Chron.* 4:45, p. 90) are critically reviewed. Fried's hypothesis about a change of plans from an archbishopric in Prague to one in Gniezno has been challenged by Knut Görich ("Ein Erzbistum in Prag oder in Gnesen," *Zeitschrift für Ostforschung* 40 (1991): 10–27) and by Labuda ("Der 'Akt von Gnesen,'" pp. 62–3 and 156–7); Fried's response is in "Gnesen – Aachen – Rom," pp. 273–9. The formula *superatis vel superandis* is frequently used by the papal chancellery, but whether the words here are taken from the bull allegedly issued for this occasion cannot be ascertained; see Kłoczowski, *La Pologne*, p. 13.

[2] Gerbert of Aurillac, Pope Sylvester II 999–1003.

other territories he had conquered or might conquer among the barbarians,[1] and a decree about this arrangement was confirmed by Pope Sylvester[2] in a privilege of the holy Church of Rome.[3] So Bolesław was thus gloriously raised to kingship by the emperor, and he gave an example of the liberality innate in him when for the three days following his coronation[4] he celebrated a feast in style fit for a king or emperor. Every day the plate and the tableware were new, and many different ones were given out, ever richer again. For at the end of the feast he ordered the waiters and the cupbearers to gather the gold and silver vessels—for there was nothing made of wood there—from all three days' courses, that is, the cups and goblets, the bowls and plates and the drinking-horns, and he presented them to the emperor as a token of honor, and not as a princely tribute. His servants were likewise told to collect the wall-hangings and the coverlets, the carpets and tablecloths and napkins and everything that had been provided for their needs and take them to the emperor's quarters. In addition he presented many other vessels, of gold and silver and of diverse workmanship, and robes of various hues and ornaments never seen before, precious stones and so many other marvelous things that the emperor regarded such presents as a miracle.[5] Each of his princes was given presents of such

[3] No copy of this privilege is known to have survived, but on 2 December 999 an *archiepiscopus Sancti Adalberti martyris* is listed as being in Rome (MGH DD OIII No. 339, p. 769); for the extensive literature on this bull, see Zofia Kozłowska-Budkowa, *Repertorjum polskich dokumentów doby piastowskiej* [Repertorium of Polish documents of the Piast age] (Cracow: PAU, 1937), pp. 5–6.

[4] Mal. accepts Z's reading *consecratio*, but Bolesław was not, even according to the author, consecrated (anointed, etc.) king. This took place only 25 years later, about which, strangely, the *GpP* says nothing. On the issue in general see Fried, *Otto*, pp. 70–81.

[5] Thietmar, *Chron.* IV. 45–6, pp. 203–9, adds the comment *dictu incredibile* in speaking of the Emperor's reception, and Gert Althoff, "Symbolische Kommunikation zwischen Piasten und Ottonen," in M. Borgolte, ed., *Polen und Deutschland vor 1000 Jahre* (Berlin: Akademie, 2002), pp. 305–6, puts forward the suggestion that our author's description is an ironical overstatement.

quod eos ex amicis amicissimos[1] acquisivit. Sed quis dinumerare poterit qualia et quanta maioribus dona dedit, cum nec unus quidem inquilinus de tanta multitudine sine munere recessit. Imperator autem letus magnis cum muneribus ad propria remeavit, Bolezlauus vero regnans in hostes iram veterem renovavit.

(7) QUOMODO TERRAM POTENTER BOLEZLAUS RUSSIE INTRAVIT

Igitur inprimis inserendum est seriei, quam gloriose et magnifice suam iniuriam de rege Ruthenorum[2] vindicavit, qui sibi sororem dare suam in matrimonium denegavit. Quod Bolezlauus rex indigne ferens, cum ingenti fortitudine Ruthenorum regnum invasit,[3] eosque primum armis resistere conantes, non ausos committere, sicut *ventus pulverem ante suam faciem*[4] profugavit. Nec statim tamen hostili more civitates capiendo, vel pecuniam congregando suum iter retardavit, sed ad Chyou caput regni, ut arcem regni simul et regem caperet, properavit. At Ruthenorum rex simplicitate gentis illius in navicula tunc forte cum hamo piscabatur, cum Bolezlauum adesse regem ex insperato nuntiant. Quod ille vix credere potuit, sed tandem aliis et aliis sibi nuntiantibus certificatus exhorruit. Tunc demum pollicem simul et indicem ori porrigens, hamumque sputo more piscatorum liniens,[5] in ignominiam sue gentis

---

[1] Cf. Sallust, *Jug.* 10.2.

[2] The king was Iaroslav the Wise, grand prince of Kiev 1015–6 and 1019–54, son of Vladimir the Great. His sister's name was Predyslava in Russian, Peredsława in Polish.

[3] On this campaign see the *PVL*, pp. 200–1, ad a. 1018. Since Bolesław's third wife Emnilde, daughter of Prince Dobrimir (on whom see *LexMA* 3:1150–1), died some time before 1017, and in February 1018 Bolesław was already married to Oda, daughter of Margrave Ekkehard of Meissen, the refusal of marriage, and the campaign, can be dated to the turn of 1017/8, cf. Thietmar, *Chron.* 8:31–3, pp. 472–7.

magnificence that from being friendly they now became closest friends.[1] But who could count what and how many presents he gave to all the lords, so that not a single servant out of all the multitude went away without a gift? The emperor returned home, delighted with the lavish gifts. Bolesław for his part returned to the business of the kingdom, and summoned up again his old anger against his foes.

7 HOW BOLESŁAW ENTERED THE LAND OF RUS' IN FORCE

A story specially worth including in our account is how gloriously and splendidly Bolesław avenged the injury done to him by the king of the Ruthenians when he refused to give him the hand of his sister in marriage.[2] Enraged at this, King Bolesław with boundless courage burst upon the kingdom of the Ruthenians.[3] At first they would have attempted resistance, but they did not dare to meet him in battle, and he scattered them before his face *as dust before the wind*.[4] Instead of slowing his advance in the usual way of armies by taking cities or exacting tribute, he sped directly to Kiev, the capital of the kingdom, so as to seize the citadel of the kingdom and its king at one and the same time. But at that particular time the king of the Ruthenians, with the simplicity of his nation, happened to be sitting in a little boat with a hook and line fishing, when out of nowhere came the news that King Bolesław was at hand. The king could scarcely believe his ears, but when report after report confirmed the story, at last horror seized him. Thereupon, the story goes, he brought his thumb and forefinger to his lips and spat on the fishhook the way fishermen do,[5] and to his people's shame he uttered the

[4] Ps. 17:43 (18:42).

[5] Ethnographers report that this is still a custom among fishermen, and similar recommendations are also to be found in medieval handbooks for fishermen; see Richard C. Hoffmann, *Fishers' Craft and Lettered Art: Tracts on Fishing from the End of the Middle Ages* (Toronto: University of Toronto Press, 1997), pp. 82–3, 160–1.

proverbium[1] protulisse fertur: Quia Bolezlauus huic arti non studuit, sed arma militaria baiolare consuevit, idcirco Deus in manum eius tradere civitatem istam regnumque Ruthenorum et divitias destinavit. Hec dixit, nec plura prosecutus fugam arripuit. At Bolezlauus nullo sibi resistente civitatem magnam et opulentam ingrediens[2] et evaginato gladio in auream portam percuciens,[3] risu satis iocoso suis admirantibus, cur hoc fecisset, enodavit: Sicut, inquit, in hac hora aurea porta civitatis ab isto ense percutitur, sic in nocte sequenti soror regis ignavissimi mihi dari prohibita corrumpetur; nec tamen Bolezlauo thoro maritali, sed concubinali singulari vice tantum coniungetur, quatinus hoc facto nostri generis iniuria vindicetur, et Ruthenis ad dedecus et ad ignominiam inputetur.[4] Sic dixit dictaque factis complevit. Igitur rex Bolezlauus urbe ditissima regnoque Ruthenorum potentissimo decem mensibus potitus, inde pecuniam in Poloniam transmittendo nunquam extitit otiosus; undecimo vero mense, quia regna quam plurima tenebat et puerum[5] ad regnandum Meschonem adhuc ydoneum non videbat, loco sui quodam ibi Rutheno sui generis[6] in dominum constituto, cum thezauro

[1] We chose this translation because the words *proverbium* or *proverbialiter*, used several times by the author, clearly do not refer to proverbs in the modern sense, nor to the genre of this name in medieval literature.

[2] 14 August 1018. See further Thietmar, *Chron.* 8:32, p. 530; Franklin-Shepard, *Rus*, pp. 186–7.

[3] As the Golden Gate of Kiev is believed to have been built in 1037, it is likely that the story (if not purely legendary) belongs rather to the capture of Kiev by Bolesław II in 1069 (see below, I:23, p. 89). A similar story of cutting a gate of a city is related by Simon of Kéza (*The Deeds*, ch. 42, pp. 97–100), in connection with a Hungarian expedition against Byzantium around 958; in this episode a Greek soldier challenges two Hungarians, and one of them, Botond, before starting to fight strikes the city gate with his axe, opening a great rent in it.

[4] According to Banaszkiewicz, Bolesław was not seeking to humiliate Predyslava and Rus'; rather, by entering into a relation with the daughter of the ruler he sought to confirm his right to that city and the state, and then took the lady together with her entourage to Poland; see Jacek Banaszkiewicz, "Bolesław i Peredsława: Uwagi o uroczystości stanowienia władcy w związku

memorable words:[1] "As Bolesław has not practiced this art but is used to bearing arms as a soldier, God has therefore ordained that this city and the kingdom of the Ruthenians and their wealth should pass into his hands." These were his only words, and without further ado he took to his heels. Bolesław thus met with no resistance when he entered this grand and rich city.[2] As he did, he drew his sword and struck it upon the Golden Gate, to his followers' amazement.[3] When they asked the reason for this, he laughed gleefully and explained: "Just as my sword pierces the Golden Gate of the city at this hour, so on the night to come the sister of this most cowardly king, whose hand had earlier been refused me, will be ravished. And she will not be joined to Bolesław as his lawful wife, but as his concubine and on one occasion only, that with this act the insult done to our people may be avenged, and shame and disgrace be brought upon the Ruthenians."[4] So said Bolesław, and what he said he did. Then for ten months the richest city of the Ruthenians and their powerful kingdom was in King Bolesław' hands, and he never rested from shipping money back to Poland. But by the eleventh month, as he was now lord of numerous realms and he had not seen the boy Mieszko,[5] who was now old enough to rule, he left a Ruthenian who was related to him as ruler in his place,[6] and

---

z wejściem Chrobrego do Kijowa" [Bolesław and Peredsława: Remarks on the ceremony of constituting the ruler with regard to Chrobry's entry into Kiev], *Kwartalnik Historyczny* 97, no. 3–4 (1990): 3–35. Moreover, it is possible that Poland was placed under interdict in the 1020s precisely because of the bigamy committed by Bolesław, who since 1018 had already been married to Oda.

[5] Since Mieszko II Lambert was born 990 (d. 1034), he was at the time of the Kievan campaign 28 years of age, so why the author refers to him as a boy (*puerum*) is unclear; indeed, the whole story may have been an invention to excuse Bolesław's forced retreat from Kiev. The following words in the Latin are also obscure; some translators understand them to mean that Mieszko was 'not old enough to rule,' which does not make much sense either.

[6] Sviatopolk the Cursed, born ca. 978, the son of Vladimir the Great, was grand prince of Kiev 1015–6, 1018–9, but then finally expelled by Iaroslav; he was married to a daughter of Bolesław I *Chrobry*. On these battles of succession and their background, see Franklin-Shepard, *Rus*, pp. 184–207.

residuo Poloniam remeabat. Illum itaque cum ingenti gaudio et pecunia remeantem iamque Polonie finibus propinquantem rex Ruthenorum fugitivus collectis viribus ducum Ruthenorum, cum Plaucis et Pincinaticis[1] a tergo subsequitur et ad fluvium Bugam committere certus de victoria conabatur.[2] Arbitrabatur namque Polonos more hominum de tanta victoria et preda gloriantes, unumquemque domum suam properare, utpote triumphatores terre sue finibus propinquantes et tam diu extra patriam sine filiis et uxoribus immorantes. Nec illud sine ratione cogitabat, quia magna pars iam Polonorum exercitus rege nesciente defluxerat. At rex Bolezlauus videns suos milites paucos esse, hostes vero quasi centies tantum fere, non sicut ignavus et timidus, sed ut audax et providus, suos milites sic affatur: Non est opus probos et expertos diu milites cohortari, nec triumphum sese nobis offerentem retardari sed est tempus vires corporis animique virtutem exercendi. Nam quid prodest tot et tantas prius victorias habuisse, vel quid prodest tanta regna nostro dominio subiugasse, tantasque divitias aliorum cumulasse, si forte nunc subactos nos contingat hec et nostra perdidisse. Sed de Dei misericordia vestraque probitate comperta confido, quod si viriliter in certamine resistatis, si more solito fortiter invadatis, si iactancias et promissiones in predis dividendis et in conviviis meis habitas ad memoriam reducatis, hodie victores finem laboris continui facietis et insuper famam perpetuam ac triumphalem victoriam acquiretis. Sin vero victi, quod non credo,

---

[1] All editors and translators agree that by *Plauci* are meant Cumans (*Polovci*); but their presence among the Ruthenian allies is questionable, as their arrival in Rus' is usually dated to 1062. They were Turkic (Kipčak) nomads, who since the tenth century had controlled the eastern steppes and became involved in events in East-Central Europe from the late eleventh century onwards; see *Cambridge History of Early Asia*, ed. D. Sinor (Cambridge: Cambridge UP, 1999), pp. 277–84; also Franklin-Shepard, *Rus*, pp. 252–75, passim. The Pechenegs were another nomadic people settled on the Pontic steppes and repeatedly mentioned sometimes as allies and sometimes as enemies of Rus', Hungary, and Poland; see *LexMA* 6:1845–6, also Thietmar, *Chron.* 8:32, p.474.

taking what treasure remained he set off back to Poland. But the king of the Ruthenians, the same who fled previously, had meanwhile gathered the forces of the Ruthenian dukes, including Cumans and Pechenegs,[1] and followed Bolesław from behind as he was marching home in great joy with all his money; and when Bolesław was nearly at the boundaries of Poland, the king sought to join battle with him at the river Bug, feeling certain of victory.[2] For he reasoned that after their great victory and with their plunder to boast of, the Poles like other men would be hurrying to return each to his own home, now that they were approaching the boundaries of their land in triumph and had been so long away from their country and separated from their wives and children. In fact, his thinking was not unreasonable, for a large part of the Polish army had indeed drifted away without the king's knowledge. Bolesław now realized how few his soldiers were, and the enemy a hundred times greater in number. It was not like Bolesław to be fearful or cowardly, but to be bold and foresightful. So he addressed his troops with the following words. "You, tried soldiers and true, need no long rousing speech, nor to make delay to seize a triumph that is present for our taking. What the hour calls for are strength of body and a courageous spirit. For what is the use of having won so many great victories or to have reduced so many realms to our rule or to have taken so much wealth from others if now we risk being defeated and losing what we won and even what we had before? But I have confidence in God's mercy and in your proven courage, and if you fight like men in this contest today, if you attack as bravely as you always have, if you call to mind the boasts and promises which you made at my banquets and when the booty was being divided, I have no doubt that you will carry the day and bring our long struggles to an end, and win a triumphant victory and undying renown. But on the other hand, should you

[2] Whether such a battle ever took place is debated, as it is assumed that Bolesław returned home on a southern route by way of Trembovla, and thus would not have crossed the River Bug.

fueritis, cum sitis domini, servi Ruthenorum et vos et filii vestri eritis et insuper penas pro illatis iniuriis turpissime rependetis. Hec et hiis similia rege Bolezlao proloquente, omnes sui milites hastas suas unanimiter protulerunt seque cum triumpho malle quam cum preda domum turpiter intrare responderunt. Tunc vero rex Bolezlauus suorum unumquemque nominatim exhortans, in hostes confertissimos sicut leo siciens penetravit. Nec est nostre facultatis recitare, quantas strages sibi resistentium ibi fecit, neque quisquam valet hostium peremptorum milia certo numero computare, quos constabat ad prelium sine numero convenisse, paucosque superstites fuga lapsos evasisse. Asserebant namque plurimi pro certo, qui post multos dies pro amicis vel propinquis inveniendis ad locum certaminis de longinquis regionibus veniebant, tantam ibi cruoris effusionem fuisse, quod nullus poterat nisi per sanguinem vel super cadavera per totam planiciem ambulare totumque Bugam fluvium plus cruoris speciem, quam fluminis retinere. Ex eo autem tempore Rusia Polonie vectigalis diu fuit.[1]

(8) DE MAGNIFICENCIA ET POTENCIA BOLEZLAUI GLORIOSI

Plura itaque sunt et maiora gesta Bolezlaui, quam a nobis possint describi, vel etiam nudis sermonibus enarrari. Nam quis arithmeticus satis certo numero ferratas eius acies valeat computare, nedum etiam describendo victorias et triumphos tante multitudinis recitare. De Poznan namque mille CCC° loricati milites cum IIII°ʳ milibus clipeatorum militum; de Gneznen mille quingenti loricati et quinque milia clipeatorum; de Wladislau castro octingenti loricati et duo milia clipeatorum; de Gdech CCC° loricati et duo milia clipeatorum. Hii omnes fortissimi et ad bella

be defeated—which I cannot believe—you and your sons will become the slaves of the Ruthenians you were masters of, and you will suffer the most humiliating penalties for the injuries you have done to them." Such and similar were the words Bolesław addressed to them. As he did so, all his men of one accord brandished their spears and answered that they would rather have the triumph than slink home in shame with the booty. Then, calling upon each of his followers by name and urging them on, King Bolesław plunged like a thirsting lion into the thickest of the foe. I have not the skill to relate the slaughter he made of those who barred his path, nor can anyone set a sure figure on how many thousands of the enemy were slain, but they say that of the untold numbers who joined the battle very few survived to slip away and escape. Many people, who days later came from far parts to look for friends and relatives on the battlefield, stated as a fact that there was such blood and gore that they could not walk anywhere over the whole field without stepping in blood or over bodies, and the whole course of the Bug looked more like a stream of blood than a river. Thereafter and for a long time to come Rus' was forced to pay tribute to Poland.[1]

8 THE POWER AND MAGNIFICENCE OF BOLESŁAW THE GLORIOUS

The deeds Bolesław performed are greater and more numerous than I can describe or tell in plain words. No clever arithmetrician could with any certainty set a figure on the numbers of his iron-clad ranks, let alone to set down in writing the victories or the triumphs won by so great a host. From Poznań, 1,300 mailed knights and 4,000 footsoldiers; from Gniezno, 1,500 mailed knights and 5,000 footsoldiers; from the stronghold of Włocławek, 800 mailed knights and 2,000 footsoldiers; from Giecz, 300 mailed knights and 2,000 footsoldiers—these were

[1] Nothing is known about any such regular tribute.

doctissimi magni Bolezlaui tempore procedebant.[1] De aliis vero civitatibus et castellis[2] et nobis longus et infinitus labor est enarrare et vobis forsitan fastidiosum fuerit hoc audire. Sed ut vobis fastidium numerandi pretermittam numerum vobis sine numero multitudinis anteponam. Plures namque habebat rex Bolezlaus milites loricatos, quam habet nostro tempore tota Polonia clipeatos; tempore Bolezlaui totidem in Polonia fere milites habebantur, quot homines cuiusque generis nostro tempore continentur.[3]

(9) DE VIRTUTE ET NOBILITATE GLORIOSI BOLEZLAY

Hec erat Bolezlaui regis magnificencia militaris, nec inferior ei erat virtus obediencie spiritalis. Episcopos quippe suosque capellanos in tanta veneratione retinebat, quod eis astantibus sedere non presumebat, nec eos aliter quam dominos appellabat. Deum vero summa pietate colebat, sanctam ecclesiam exaltabat, eamque donis regalibus adornabat. Habebat etiam preterea quiddam iustitie magnum et humilitatis insigne, quod si quando rusticus pauper vel muliercula quelibet de quovis duce videlicet vel comite quereretur, quamvis esset magnis negotiis occupatus, multisque cuneis et magnatum et militum constipatus, non prius se de loco dimovebat, donec causam ex ordine conquerentis auscultaret et pro illo, de quo querebatur, camerarium transmandaret. Interim vero ipsum conquerentem alicui fideli suo commendabat, qui eum procuraret sibique causam adversario

---

[1] *Loricati* (lit. 'warriors in chainmail') were members of the ruler's retinue, mounted knights maintained directly by him, whereas *clipeati* (lit. 'shield-bearers') were infantry, consisting of all free men capable of carrying arms; see *Polska technika*, pp. 37–70. See also n. 86, p. xlv, above.

[2] Here and in what follows we translate *civitates* and *castra* as 'cities,' 'towns' or 'castles' as far as can be determined by the context, but the author is in no way consistent enough in his choice of words to allow a differentiation between different types of strongholds and more or less fortified settlements. On this issue in general, see Bachmann, *Burg–Burgstadt–Stadt* (as n. 140, p. lxiii).

the forces mustered in the days of Bolesław the Great.[1] These were all the bravest of warriors, fully trained for war. How many came from other cities and castles[2] would be a long and endless labor for us to list, and perhaps tedious for you to listen to. But not to weary you with countless numbers, I shall recount the number of his forces without a count of numbers: King Bolesław had more knights in armor than all Poland now has men bearing shields; in his time there were almost as many knights in Poland as there are people of any kind in our time.[3]

9 THE VIRTUES AND NOBILITY OF THE GLORIOUS BOLESŁAW

Such was the military might of King Bolesław. But the king in no way fell short in the virtue of spiritual obedience. For he held his bishops and chaplains in such veneration that he would never presume to remain seated when they were standing, and he always addressed them as "My lords." He worshipped God with the greatest piety and promoted the holy Church and honored her with kingly gifts. Furthermore, he had such a great sense of justice and a special humility that if some poor peasant or some ordinary woman came with a complaint against any duke or count, no matter how important the matters he was engaged in, amid the throng and press of his lords and officers, he would not stir from the spot before he had heard the full account of the complaint and sent a chamberlain to fetch the lord against whom the complaint had been made. Meanwhile he left the aggrieved person in the care of one of his retainers, who would take his part and would help him with his plea while the adversary was

---

[3] The "good old days" commonplace apart, this comparison may have a basis in reality. In the mid-eleventh century the organization of military forces in Poland changed profoundly: the dukes no longer maintained a permanent retinue, but developed a system of land grants for warriors *iure militari*. The rulers were accompanied by a small unit of knights (*acies curialis*), while the majority of troops were called to arms only in case of necessity. See *Polska technika*, pp. 38–9.

adveniente suggereret, et sic rusticum quasi pater filium admone-
bat, ne absentem sine causa accusaret et ne iniuste conquerendo
iram, quam alteri conflabat, sibimet ipsi cumularet.[1] Nec accu-
satus citissime vocatus venire differebat, nec diem a rege constitutum qualibet occasione preteribat. Adveniente vero principe,
pro quo missum fuerat, non se illi maligne commotum ostende-
bat, sed alacri eum et affabili vultu recipiens ad mensam invitabat,
neque ea die, sed sequenti, vel tercia causam discutiebat. Sicque
diligenter rem pauperis, ut alicuius magni principis, pertractabat.
O magna discrecio magnaque perfeccio Bolezlaui. Qui personam
in iudicio non servabat, qui populum tanta iustitia gubernabat,
qui honorem ecclesie ac statum terre in summo culmine retinebat. Iustitia nimirum et equitate ad hanc Bolezlauus gloriam et
dignitatem ascendit, quibus virtutibus initio potentia Romanorum et imperium excrevit.[2] Tanta virtute, tanta potentia, tantaque victoria regem Bolezlauum Deus omnipotens decoravit,
quantam eius bonitatem et iustitiam erga se ipsum et homines
recognovit; tanta gloria Bolezlauum, tanta rerum copia, tantaque
letitia sequebatur, quantum eius probitas et liberalitas merebatur.

(10) DE PRELIO BOLEZLAUI CUM RUTHENIS

Sed ista memorare subsequenti pagina differamus et quoddam
eius prelium novitate facti satis memorabile referamus, ex cuius
rei consideracione humilitatem superbie preferamus. Contigit
namque uno eodemque tempore Bolezlauum regem Rusiam,
Ruthenorum vero regem Poloniam utroque de altero nesciente
hostiliter introisse,[3] eosque super fluvium alterum in alterius
termino regionis, interposito flumine, castra milicie posuisse.[4]

---

[1] There is ambiguity in the Latin of the terms of reference, so that what took place
between the persons involved in the dispute is open to other interpretations.

[2] Cf. Lucretius, *DRN* 2.610; Livy, *AUC* 7.2, 11; Tacitus, *Ann.* 6.2.

[3] The *PVL* ad a. 1022 (p. 202) records that Iaroslav undertook an expedition
to Brest' (Polish: Brześć), which may refer to this campaign.

coming. And so he would advise the peasant as a father would his son, so that he would not make a groundless accusation against the absent party, nor by complaining unjustly load upon himself the anger he was directing against the other.[1] Moreover, the accused would never fail to come with all speed when he was summoned and never for any reason neglect to appear on the day appointed by the king. When the great man who had been sent for arrived, Bolesław would never show him anger or ill-will, but would welcome him in a warm and friendly way and invite him to a meal, and wait till the second or even the third day before broaching the matter of contention. So he treated a poor man's problem with as much concern as if he had been a great prince. What great wisdom, what great accomplishment of Bolesław! He passed judgement regardless of person, he governed the people with such justice, and he set the dignity of the Church and the state of the country above all else. His sense of justice and fairness raised Bolesław to such glory and dignity—the virtues by which the Romans in the beginning rose to power and empire.[2] Such was the prowess, the power, and the victories which Almighty God bestowed on Bolesław in recognition of the goodness and justice which Bolesław showed to Him and to his fellow men! Bolesław enjoyed all the glory, abundance, and happiness that his worthiness and generosity deserved.

10 BOLESŁAW'S BATTLE WITH THE RUTHENIANS

But let us defer these themes to a later page, and turn to the story of a battle with some unusual features that make it quite memorable. From it we will be able draw a lesson that humility is better than pride. It came about that, unbeknown to each other, King Bolesław and the king of the Ruthenians invaded each other's countries at one and the same time.[3] The two armies camped on the banks of a river, each in the other's territory, with the river running between them.[4] The king of the Ruthenians had received

---

[4] In all likelihood the river Bug.

Cumque nunciatum esset Ruthenorum regi Bolezlauum ultra iam fluvium transivisse inque sui regni confinio cum exercitu consedisse, existimans rex insulsus se quasi feram in retibus eum sua multitudine conclusisse, proverbium ei magne superbie capiti suo retorquendum dicitur mandavisse: Noverit se Bolezlauus tamquam *suem in volutabro*[1] canibus meis et venatoribus circumclusum. Ad hoc rex Polonicus remandavit: Bene, inquam, suem in volutabro nominasti, quia in sanguine venatorum[a] canumque tuorum, id est ducum et militum, pedes equorum meorum inficiam et terram tuam et civitates ceu ferus singularis depascam. Hiis verbis utrimque renunciatis die sequenti sollempnitas imminebat, quam rex Bolezlauus celebraturus in diem tertium bellum committere differebat. Eo namque die animalia innumerabilia mactabantur, que sequenti sollempnitate ad mensam regis cum omnibus suis principibus comesturi more solito parabantur. Omnibus itaque cocis, inquilinis, apparitoribus, parasitis exercitus ad animalium carnes et exta purganda super ripam fluminis congregatis, ex altera ripa Ruthenorum clientes et armigeri clamosis vocibus insultabant, eosque probrosis iniuriis ad iracundiam lacessebant. Illi vero nichil iniurie e contrario respondebant, sed intestinorum sordes et inutilia contra eorum oculos pro iniuria iaciebant. Cumque Rutheni magis eos magisque contumeliis incitarent et sagittis etiam acrius infestarent, canibus que tenebant avibusque commissis, cum armis militum in meridiana dormiencium fluvio transnatato Bolezlaui parasitorum exercitus super tanta Ruthenorum multitudine triumphavit. Bolezlauus itaque rex et exercitus totus clamore simul et strepitu armorum excitatus, quidnam hoc esset sciscitantes, cognita rei causa, facta ex industria dubitantes,[b,2] cum ordinatis

---

[a] venatoris *Z Mal*
[b] cogitantes *H*

word that Bolesław had crossed the river and his army was
encamped within the boundaries of his own kingdom, and foolishly he imagined that he and his great host had Bolesław trapped
like a netted animal. It is said that the king sent a message
memorable in its pride, which was to redound upon his own
head: "Let Bolesław know that my dogs and my hunters have
caught him like *a pig wallowing in the mire*."[1] To this the Polish
king sent the following reply: "A pig in the mire? Well put,
indeed! The hoofs of my horses shall wallow in the blood of the
hunters and the dogs, that is, your captains and soldiers, and I
shall savage your land and your cities like a wild boar." So passed
this exchange between them. The next day a festival was due to
be held, and in order to celebrate it King Bolesław put off joining
battle till the third day. Now on that day great numbers of
animals were being slaughtered as usual in preparation for the
king's table at the coming holiday, when he was planning to eat
with all his princes. So all the army's cooks, kitchen-hands,
servants and camp-followers were gathered on the river-bank
cleaning the carcasses and purging the offal. Meanwhile on the
other bank the men-at-arms and retainers of the Ruthenians
jeered and hurled abuse, trying to provoke them to anger with
their gibes and mockery. They made no reply to the taunts, but
instead repaid the insults by hurling in their eyes offal and
excrement from the intestines. But when the Ruthenians grew
more and more provocative in their taunts, and even began to
harry them in earnest with arrows, they left what they were
handling to their dogs and birds. They borrowed the arms of the
soldiers sleeping in the midday heat, and swimming over the
river, Bolesław's army of camp-followers defeated the very size-
able host of the Ruthenians. The shouting and the din of the
fighting woke the king and the rest of the army, who wondered
what ever was going on. When they found out, they doubted[2]
that this had been intentional. So they drew up in battle array

---

[1] 2 Pet. 2:22.
[2] Or, following the reading of *H*, 'they imagined.'

aciebus in hostes undique fugientes irruerunt; sicque parasiti nec gloriam victorie soli nec sanguinum noxam soli habuerunt. Tanta vero fuit ibi militum flumen transeuntium multitudo, quod non aqua videbatur ab inferioribus, sed quedam itineris siccitudo. Hoc autem tantillum dixisse de bellis eius sufficiat, quatenus eius vite recordatio ab auditoribus[1] imitata proficiat.

(11) DE DISPOSICIONE ECCLESIARUM IN POLONIA ET VIRTUTE BOLEZLAI

Igitur rex Bolezlauus erga divinum cultum in ecclesiis construendis et episcopatibus ordinandis beneficiisque conferendis ita devotissimus existebat, quod suo tempore Polonia duos metropolitanos cum suis suffraganeis continebat.[2] Quibus ipse per omnia et in omnibus ita benivolus et obediens existebat, quod si forte aliquis principum contra quemlibet clericorum vel pontificum litigii causam inchoabat, vel si quidquam de rebus ecclesiasticis usurpabat, ipse cunctis manu silencium indicebat et sicut patronus et advocatus pontificum causam et ecclesie defendebat. Gentes vero barbarorum in circuitu, quas vincebat, non ad tributum pecunie persolvendum, sed ad vere religionis incrementum coercebat.[3] Insuper etiam ecclesias ibi de proprio construebat et episcopos honorifice clericosque canonice cum rebus necessariis

---

[1] Another reference to the fact that the author expected his work to be recited; see above, p. xxxiv.

[2] This mention of these two otherwise unknown archbishoprics has been seen by Karolina Lanckrońska, "A Cyrillo-Methodian See in Poland," in *Studies on the Roman-Slavonic Rite in Poland*, Orientalia Christinana Analecta, 161 (Rome: PIO, 1961), as proof of the existence of a Slavic rite metropolis in Cracow (assumed to have gone back to the Cyrillo-Methodian mission), besides the Latin one in Gniezno. There are several other hypotheses, including one that regards the missionary bishopric of Bruno of Querfurt as this alleged second metropolis. However, there is no other evidence for the highly doubtful existence of a double metropolitan constitution.

and went in pursuit of the enemy who were now fleeing in all directions. Thus in the end the glory of the victory did not go solely to the camp-followers, nor were they the sole ones to suffer bloodshed. But the number of soldiers who then crossed the river was so huge that from downstream the river did not seem to be water but a dry road. But let this little episode suffice on the subject of his wars, that the record of his life may serve as a model and be of benefit to the listeners.[1]

11 THE ARRANGEMENTS FOR THE CHURCHES IN POLAND, AND BOLESŁAW'S VIRTUES

King Bolesław was deeply devoted to religion, building churches and establishing episcopal sees and granting endowments; so much indeed, that in his days Poland had two metropolitans along with their suffragans.[2] He was always well-disposed towards them and he was so obedient to them in everything, that if, for example, one of the great men happened to open a lawsuit against a cleric or a bishop, or seized any ecclesiastical property, with a wave of his hand Bolesław would call for general silence, and then as patron and advocate he would defend the interests of the bishops and the church. With the neighboring barbarian peoples whom he defeated he was more concerned for the increase of the true faith than to force them to pay tribute.[3] Indeed, he even built churches there from his own means and appointed bishops with all honors and clerics canonically among

[3] This praise may imply a critique of missions bent more on profit than the spread of faith, a commonplace among clerical writers going back at least to Alcuin's *predicatores non predatores* in MGH Epp II, Ernst Dümmler et al., ed. (Hannover: Hahn, 1898), Nr. 111, p. 161. Mal. considers that the author may have wished to draw a contrast to Bolesław's action in imposing tribute on the Pomeranians in 1121—for which see *Herbordi Dialogus de Vita Ottonis episcopi Banbergensis*, ed. J. Wikavjak and K. Liman (Wrocław: PWN, 1974), p. 62—but that would contradict the assumed date of writing. However, tributes on conquered and converted populations may have been imposed earlier as well.

apud incredulos ordinabat.[1] Talibus ergo virtutibus, iusticia et equitate, timore scilicet et dilectione rex Bolezlauus precellebat, talique discretione regnum remque publicam procurabat. Virtutibus siquidem multis ac probitatibus longe lateque Bolezlauus emicuit, tribus tamen virtutibus: iusticia, equitate, pietate specialiter ad tantum culmen magnitudinis ascendit. Iusticia, quia sine respectu persone causam in iudicio discernebat, equitate, quia principes et populum cum discrecione diligebat, pietate, quia Christum eiusque sponsam modis omnibus honorabat. Et quia iusticiam exercebat et omnes equanimiter diligebat et matrem ecclesiam virosque ecclesiasticos exaltabat, sancte matris ecclesie precibus eiusque prelatorum intercessionibus *cornu eius in gloria* Dominus *exaltabat*[2] et in cunctis semper bene semperque prospere procedebat. Et cum sic esset Bolezlauus religiosus in divinis, multum tamen apparebat gloriosior in humanis.

(12) QUOMODO BOLEZLAUS PER SUAS TERRAS SINE LESIONE PAUPERUM TRANSIEBAT[3]

Eius namque tempore non solum comites, verum eciam quique nobiles torques aureas immensi ponderis baiolabant, tanta superfluitate pecunie redundabant. Mulieres vero curiales coronis aureis, monilibus, murenulis, brachialibus, aurifrisiis et gemmis ita onuste procedebant, quod ni sustentarentur ab aliis, pondus metalli sustinere non valebant.[4] Talem etiam gratiam ei Deus

---

[1] See above n. 7, p. 33.

[2] Ps. 111:9.

[3] On the ideals of "morally limited" lordship see Thomas N. Bisson, "Medieval lordship," *Speculum* 70 (1995): 751–2.

[4] It may be worth noting that among the archaeological finds surveyed by Witold Hensel, *La naissance de la Pologne* (Wrocław: Ossolineum-PAN,

the unbelievers, supplying them with all necessaries.[1] Such were the virtues which set Bolesław apart—justice, fairness, fear and affection, and such was the wisdom with which he managed the realm and the commonwealth. The light of Bolesław's many virtues and good qualities shone far and wide, but it was by three in particular—justice, fairness, and piety—that he attained the heights of greatness. Justice, in that he decided cases in law without respect to persons; fairness, for his concern and tact extended to both princes and commoners; and piety, for he honored Christ and His bride in every way. And since he exercised justice and respected all men equally and exalted the Mother Church and the men of the Church, the Lord in answer to the prayers of the holy Mother Church and the intercessions of his prelates *exalted his horn in honor,*[2] and all went well for him and all his ventures prospered. Yet for all Bolesław's piety in matters divine, it was in earthly affairs that he won even greater glory.

12 HOW BOLESŁAW WOULD TRAVEL ACROSS HIS LANDS WITHOUT CAUSING HARM TO THE POOR[3]

In Bolesław' time not only *comites*, but all the nobles used to wear enormously heavy gold necklaces, for they had money in such abundance and excess. The women of the court wore golden crowns, necklaces, chains, bracelets, gold brocade, and jewels, so heavy that without others to support them they were unable to walk under the weight of the metal.[4] Moreover, God endowed

1966), pp. 86–7, no gold objects of any type are listed, while silver of different origins has been found in abundance; cf. e.g., Zofia Kurnatowska, "The Organization of the Polish State: Possible Interpretations of Archaeological Evidence," *QMAeN* 1 (1996): 5–24, esp. pp. 15, 24; Lech Leciejewicz, "Zur Entwicklung der Frühstädte an der südlichen Ostseeküste," *Zeitschrift für Archäologie* 3 (1969), esp. p. 189. On the grotesque image of women overloaded with jewellery, see above, p. xliii.

contulerat et ita visu desiderabilis cunctis erat, quod si forte quemlibet a conspectu suo pro culpa veniali momentaneo removebat, quamvis ille rerum suique libertate frueretur, donec benivolencie eius ac conspectui redderetur, non se vivere, sed mori, nec se liberum, sed trusum carceri reputabat. Suos quoque rusticos non ut dominus in angariam coercebat, sed ut pius pater quiete eos vivere permittebat. Ubique enim suas staciones[1] suumque servitium determinatum habebat, nec libenter in tentoriis sicut Numida,[2] vel in campis, sed in civitatibus et castris frequentius habitabat. Et quotiens de civitate stationem in aliam transferebat, aliis in confinio dimissis, alios vastandiones et villicos[3] commutabat. Nec quisquam eo transeunte viator vel operator boves vel oves abscondebat, sed ei pretereunti pauper et dives arridebat, eumque cernere tota patria properabat.

(13) DE VIRTUTE ET PIETATE UXORIS BOLEZLAUI GLORIOSI

Duces vero suosque comites ac principes acsi fratres vel filios diligebat, eosque salva reverentia sicut sapiens dominus honorabat. Conquerentibus enim super illis inconsulte non credebat, contra lege condempnatis iudicium misericordia temperabat.

---

[1] The term *stationes* refers not merely to ducal strongholds but also to places with an obligation of the population to accommodate and supply the ruler, his entourage and/or his officials during their travels around the country—a part of the *ius ducale*, comparable to the *droit de gîte*. In general, see Karol Modzelewski, "The System of the *Ius Ducale* and the Idea of Feudalism (Comments on the Earliest Class Society in Medieval Poland)," *Quaestiones Medii Aevi* 1 (1977): 71–99; and, with a slightly different, comparative point of view, Barbara Krzemieńska and Dušán Třeštik, "Wirtschaftliche Grundlagen des frühmittelalterlichen Staates in Mitteleuropa," *APH* 40 (1979): 5–31.

[2] Classically the Numidians were a people of northern Africa (the word literally means 'nomad'); the most likely source of the author's familiarity with the name is Sallust.

[3] The readings of the MSS, *vastandiones*, is evidently a variant of *vastaldiones*, a term which seems to go back to the Lombard name for fiscal and urban office

Bolesław with such charm, and all were so attracted to the sight of him, that if ever he banished anyone from his presence even for a short time because of a minor transgression, even if the person continued to enjoy his possessions and liberty, he would feel as though he was dying rather than alive, and not free but cast into a dungeon until he was readmitted to the king's grace and presence. He did not treat his peasants like a lord and exact forced labor from them, but cared for them as a kind-hearted father and left them to live in peace. For everywhere he had his stations[1] and defined services, and did not like to live in tents like a Numidian[2] or in the open country but more commonly stayed in cities and in castles. And when he moved his station from one city to another he would dismiss some at the boundary and would replace others of his officers and stewards.[3] When he traveled by, no one on the road or at work would ever hide his sheep and cattle, but rich and poor alike would smile upon him as he passed and the whole country would come hurrying up to see him.

13 THE GOODNESS AND COMPASSION OF THE WIFE OF BOLESŁAW THE GLORIOUS

The king loved his dukes, *comites*, and princes as if they were his brothers or his sons, and as far his dignity permitted he honored them as a wise master would. If any complaint was made against them, he never would rashly believe it; while for those who had been sentenced he would temper judgement with mercy. For

holders (*guastaldiones*), originating in the Celtic *gwas* 'servant,' which is also the root of the word "vassal"; see Eduard Brinckmeier, *Glossarium diplomaticum* (Hamburg and Gotha: F.A. Perthes, 1856–63; reprint, Aalen: Scientia, 1961), 1:882. The use of this term, well documented for Northern Italy—see e.g., several Ottonian charters in MGH DD 1, see Index s.v. '*gastaldiones &c.*'—has been adduced as a possible evidence for the author's Italian origin. *Villici* may have been managers of royal estates, a term well-known from as early as Frankish times, widely used in France and elsewhere. In Central Europe it usually referred to local office-holders from village elders to small-town mayors.

Sepe namque uxor eius regina,[1] prudens mulier et discreta, plures
pro culpa morti deditos de manibus lictorum eripuit et ab imminenti mortis periculo liberavit, eosque in carcere, quandoque
rege nesciente quandoque vero dissimulante, sub custodia vite
misericorditer reservavit. Habebat autem rex amicos XII con-
siliarios,[2] cum quibus eorumque uxoribus omnibus curis et consiliis expeditis convivari multociens et cenare delectabatur et cum
eis regni familiarius et consilii misteria[a] pertractabat. Quibus
epulantibus pariter et exultantibus et inter alias locutiones in
memoriam ex occasione forte generis illorum dampnatorum
incidentibus, rex Bolezlauus illorum morti pro bonitate parentum condolebat, seque precepisse eos perimi penitebat. Tunc
regina venerabilis pium pectus regis blanda manu demulcens,
sciscitabatur ab eo, si carum ei fieret, si quis eos sanctus a morte
forsitan suscitaret. Cui rex respondebat, se nichil tam preciosum
possidere, quod non daret, si quis eos posset ad vitam de funere
revocare, eorumque progeniem ab infamie macula liberare. Hec
audiens regina sapiens et fidelis pii furti se ream et consciam
accusabat et cum amicis XII et uxoribus eorum ad pedes regis
pro sui dampnatorumque venia se prosternebat.[3] Quam rex
benigne complexans cum osculo de terra manibus sublevabat,
eiusque fidele furtum, ymmo pietatis opera collaudabat. Eadem

---

[a] ministeria H Mal

---

[1] As Bolesław's longest marriage was to Emnilde (987–1017), the reference
may be to her; however, if the author were (for once) consistent in his
chronology—the description is put after 1018—one would take it to be to Oda.
But at the same time, the fact that the author does not mention the name of
the lady in question turns the story into a sort of an *exemplum* depicting the
ideal wife of an ideal ruler.

[2] The number twelve is, of course, a widespread mythical and literary motif,
and it is hardly possible to determine which of the many precedents—from the
apostles to the knights of King Arthur—may have inspired the author or the
(oral, heroic?) tradition that reached him.

often his wife the queen,[1] a wise and discrete woman, would rescue those condemned to death for some crime from the hands of the executioners and save them at the last minute from the threat of death. She would leave them under guard in the prison, their lives preserved through her mercy. At times the king did not know of this, and at times he would pretend not to. The king had twelve friends as counselors,[2] and regularly, once free of all his cares and deliberations, he would enjoy their company, dining with them and their wives and discussing the secrets of the realm and council in a more intimate atmosphere. While they were feasting together and in high spirits, as the conversation turned to different matters it might chance that the occasion would arise to recall the family of those who had been condemned. Recalling their parents' goodness, King Bolesław would express sorrow at their deaths and regret having ordered their execution. Then the venerable queen, stroking the king's merciful breast with a gentle hand, would ask him if it would please him if some saint should raise them from the dead. To which the king would reply that he possessed nothing so precious that he would not give it if someone could call them back to life from the grave and save their offspring from the stain of infamy. Hearing this his wise and faithful queen would admit her guilt and her well-intentioned trickery, and then she and the twelve friends and their wives would all throw themselves at the king's feet and plead pardon for themselves and the condemned.[3] The king would embrace her fondly and kiss her and take her hands and raise her from the ground and speak in warm terms of her true-hearted trickery—indeed, of her works of mercy. So that

[3] On more formal but symbolically comparable acts of other queens, see John Carmi Parsons, "The Queen's Intercession in Thirteenth-Century England," in *The Power of the Weak: Studies on Medieval Women*, ed. J. Carpenter and S. B. Maclean (Urbana, IL: Univ. of Illinois Press, 1995), pp. 147–77, with extensive bibliography.

igitur hora pro captivis illis, per mulieris prudenciam vite reservatis cum equis plurimis mittebatur et euntibus redeundi terminus ponebatur. Tunc vero letitia multiplex illis residentibus accrescebat, cum regina regis honorem ac regni utilitatem sic sapienter observabat et rex eam cum amicorum consilio de suis petitionibus audiebat. Illi autem, pro quibus missum fuerat, venientes, non statim regi sed regine presentabantur, qui ab ea verbis asperis et lenibus castigati ad regis balneum ducebantur.[1] Quos rex Bolezlauus, sicut pater filios secum balneantes corrigebat, eorumque progeniem memorando collaudabat. Vos, inquit, tanta, vos tali prosapia exortos, talia committere non decebat. Etate quidem provecciores verbis tantum tam per se, quam per alios castigabat, minoribus vero verbera cum verbis adhibebat. Sicque paterne commonitos ac indumentis regalibus adornatos, datis muneribus collatisque honoribus, ire domum cum gaudio dimittebat. Talem igitur sese rex Bolezlaus erga populum et principes exhibebat, sic sapienter et timeri et amari se a cunctis sibi subditis faciebat.

(14) DE MAGNITATE MENSE ET LARGITATE BOLEZLAY

Mensam vero suam sic ordinate, sic honorifice retinebat, quod omni die privato[2] XL[a] mensas principales, exceptis minoribus, erigi faciebat et nichil tamen de alienis, sed de propriis, in hiis omnibus expendebat. Habebat etiam aucupes et venatores omnium fere nationum, qui suis artibus capiebant omne genus volatilium et ferarum, de quibus singulis, tam quadrupedibus quam pennatis, cottidie singula apponebantur fercula suis mensis.[3]

---

[1] Cf. Einhard, *Vita Caroli Magni*, ch. 22, p. 60. Charlemagne was in the practice of taking a number of his courtiers with him to the baths at Aachen; see Pierre Riché, *Daily Life in the World of Charlemagne*, trans. Jo Ann McNamara (Philadelphia: University of Pennsylvania Press, 1992), pp. 42–3, 95, 167–8. For the place of the bath in Slavic cultures, see *SSS* 3:114–5, s.v. "Łaźnia."

very hour messengers and a team of horses would be sent to fetch the prisoners whose lives had been spared thanks to a woman's wit, and a time would be set for their return. Then the guests at the banquet would burst into joy and delight that the queen had shown such wisdom in guarding the interests of the country while respecting the king's honor, and that the king had taken the advice of his friends and listened to her and her petitions. When those who had been sent for arrived, they were not presented to the king first but to the queen. She would rebuke them with both sharp and mild words, and then have them taken to the king's bath.[1] There King Bolesław would bathe with them as a father would with his children, berating them and dwelling on the praises of their forebears. "It was unworthy of you, who are descended from such a distinguished family, to stoop to such things." The older ones he would merely rebuke either personally or through others, while for the younger ones the words would be accompanied by the switch. After this paternal reprimand he would dress them in royal garments, give them presents and honors, and send them home with joy. Such was King Bolesław's way of treating the people and the princes, and thus through his wise ways he caused himself to be both feared and loved by all who were subject to him.

14 BOLESŁAW'S LAVISH TABLE AND HIS LIBERALITY

His table was maintained in such magnificent array that every non-festal day[2] there were forty main courses laid out (not counting the minor ones)—all supplied not at other persons' expense, but at his own. He had fowlers and hunters from all nations who by their special skills could catch birds and animals of every kind, and at his table there would be at least one dish served every day with each kind of animal and bird.[3]

[2] For *die privato* see *Benedicti Regula*, ch. 13.

[3] Cf. Einhard, *Vita Caroli Magni,* ch. 24, pp. 70–2.

(15) DE DISPOSICIONE CASTRORUM ET CIVITATUM SUI REGNI PER BOLEZLAUM[1]

Solebat quoque magnus Bolezlauus in finibus regionis ab hostibus conservandis multociens occupatus, suis villicis ac vicedominis,[2] quid de indumentis in festis annualibus preparatis, quidve de cibis et potibus in singulis civitatibus fieret interrogantibus, proverbium posteris in exemplum commemorare, sic inquiens: Satius et honestius est hic michi galline pullum ab inimicis conservare, quam in illis vel illis civitatibus desidiose convivanti insultantibus michi meis hostibus locum dare. Nam pullum perdere per virtutem non pullum reputo, sed castrum vel amittere civitatem. Et advocans de suis familiaribus, quos volebat, singulos singulis civitatibus vel castellis deputabat, qui loco sui castellis et civitatibus convivia celebrarent ac indumenta aliaque dona regalia, que rex dare consueverat, suis fidelibus presentarent. Talibus dictis et factis admirabantur universi prudentiam et ingenium tanti viri, conferentes ad invicem: Hic est vere pater patrie, hic defensor, hic est dominus, non aliene pecunie dissipator, sed honestus rei publice dispensator, qui dampnum rustici violenter ab hostibus illatum castello reputat vel civitati perdite conferendum. Quid multis moramur? Si singula facta vel dicta magni Bolezlaui memoranda carptim voluerimus scriptitare, quasi stilo laboremus guttatim pelagus exsiccare. Sed quid nocet ociosis lectoribus hoc audire, quod vix potest cum labore hystoriographus invenire.

---

[1] On the government of early medieval Poland in general see Tadeusz Wasilewski, "Poland's administrative structure in early Piast times: *Castra* ruled by *comites* as centres of territorial administration," *APH* 44 (1981): 5–31; Ambroży Bogucki, "The administrative structure of Poland in the eleventh and twelfth century," *APH* 72 (1995): 5–32.

15 BOLESŁAW'S ARRANGEMENTS CONCERNING THE CASTLES AND CITIES IN HIS REALM[1]

Also, when the great Bolesław, who was many times occupied with the defense of his borders against enemies about, was asked by his stewards and governors[2] what should be done about the garments or about the food and drink prepared for the annual festivals in the different cities, he used to say something memorable that would go down as an example to posterity. He would say: "For me it is better and more honorable to safeguard a single chicken here from the enemy than to feast idly in one city or another while my enemies get a chance to do me injury. For I do not regard losing a chicken in a brave fight as the loss of a chicken but as the loss of a castle or a city." And he would summon those of his companions whom he pleased to, and send them each to a city or castle, and have them hold in his stead banquets in the castle or city, and present his faithful men with clothes and other royal gifts which the king was in the habit of giving. When they heard or saw him do such things everyone expressed admiration for the wisdom and intelligence of this great man. They would confer among themselves and say: "He is truly the father of our country, our defender, our lord—not the squanderer of other people's money but the honest steward of the commonwealth. He treats the violence and damage inflicted on a peasant by the enemy as equal to the loss of a castle or the city." What need is there to go on? If we wished to write down separately every memorable deed or saying of the great Bolesław, it would be as great a task for my pen as draining the ocean drop by drop. But what does it hurt my leisured readers to hear this, which the writer of history could only laboiously find out?

[2] For *villici* see above, n. 3, p. 59; *vicedomini* do not feature elsewhere in the *GpP* and the terms is not a widely used in the region. However, it is well known in France (hence the French *vidame*) as the name for a lord's agent.

(16) DE MORTE BOLEZLAUI GLORIOSI LAMENTABILI

Cum igitur tot et tantis rex Bolezlauus diviciis probisque militibus, ut dictum est, plus quam rex alius habundaret, querebatur tamen semper, quia solis militibus indigeret. Et quicumque probus hospes[1] apud eum in militia probabatur, non miles ille, sed regis filius vocabatur; et si quandoque, ut assolet, eorum quemlibet infelicem in equis[2] vel in aliis audiebat, infinita dando ei circumstantibus alludebat. Si possem sic hunc probum militem a morte divitiis liberare, sicut possum eius infortunium et paupertatem mea copia superare, ipsam mortem avidam diviciis honerarem, ut hunc talem, tam audacem in milicia reservarem. Quocirca talem ac tantum virum successores debent virtutibus imitari, ut valeant ad tantam gloriam et potentiam sublimari. Qui cupit post vitam acquirere tantam famam, acquirat, dum vivit, in virtutibus tantam palmam. Si quis captat Bolezlauo memoriali titulo comparari, elaboret suam vitam eius vite venerabili conformari. Tunc erit virtus in gestis militaribus collaudanda, cum fuerit vita multis honestis moribus adornata. Hec erat magni Bolezlaui gloria memoranda, talis virtus recitetur posterorum memorie imitanda. Non enim in vacuum Deus illi *gratiam super gratiam*[3] cumulavit, nec sic eum sine causa tot regibus ac ducibus antefecit, sed quia Deum in omnibus et super omnia diligebat et quoniam erga suos, sicut pater erga filios caritatis visceribus affluebat.[4] Unde cuncti, sed specialiter quos venerabatur archiepiscopi, episcopi, abbates, monachi, clerici, sedule eum suis precibus Domino commendabant; duces vero, comites, aliique

---

[1] *Hospes* was a technical term for foreigners (though more for urban or rural settlers than for knights) who came to Central Europe mainly from the western parts of the continent; on the different types of "foreign experts," see Tomasz Jurek, "Fremde Ritter im mittelalterlichen Polen," *QMAeN* 3 (1998): 19–49.

[2] Lit. 'in regard to horses.' Others translate: 'had suffered a lack of horses.' Either interpretation seems to fit the context, though the reference to death supports our interpretation.

16 THE TRAGIC DEATH OF THE GLORIOUS BOLESŁAW

So, as mentioned, King Bolesław had abundance of wealth and fine warriors in numbers beyond any other king. And yet he was always lamenting that knights were the one thing he lacked. If any doughty foreigner[1] was at his court proving his worth in martial skills, he would be not be called a warrior but the king's son. And if the king ever heard that any of them had suffered some mishap on horseback[2] or otherwise, as happens on occasion, he would give him endless gifts and confide in the bystanders: "If I could save this fine warrior from death by my wealth, just as I can relieve his misfortunes or his poverty by my resources, then I would ply greedy death with riches to preserve this fine, brave warrior in my service." The successors of such a great man should therefore strive to copy his qualities, so that they might rise to the heights of glory and power that he did. Any man, who seeks to win such fame after his life, let him win such a palm for his virtues while he is alive. If anyone wants to equal Bolesław in memory and renown, let him strive to pattern his life on that man's venerable life. Valor in warlike deeds will find due praise when a man's life is graced by many honorable qualities. Such was the glory of the great Bolesław, worthy to be remembered; let his valor be told and remembered, and imitated by those who come after him. For it was not for naught that God heaped on him *grace upon grace*,[3] nor without reason did He set him before so many dukes and kings, but because he loved God in everything and above all else, and because love for his people abounded within him,[4] as in a father towards his sons. Because of this everyone, but especially the archbishops and bishops, abbots, monks, and clerks whom he venerated, never ceased to commend him to God in their prayers; while his dukes, *comites*,

---

[3] Sir. 26:19.

[4] Cf. *Vita minor S. Stanislai, MPH* 4:258: *pietatis visceribus affluebat.*

proceres hunc semper victorem, hunc sibi fore superstitem exoptabant. Gloriosus itaque Bolezlauus felicem vitam laudabili fine concludens,[1] cum sciret se debitum carnis universe completurum, tum omnibus suis ad se principibus et amicis undique congregatis, de regni gubernacione et statu secrecius ordinavit, eisque multa post se mala futura voce prophetica nuntiavit. O utinam, fratres mei, inquit, quos delicate tanquam mater filios enutrivi, que *positus in agone*[2] nocitura video, vobis in prospera convertantur et utinam ignem sedicionis accendentes *Deum et hominem vereantur.*[3] Heu, heu, iam quasi *per speculum in enigmate video*[4] regalem prosapiam exulantem et oberrantem et hostibus, quos sub pedibus conculcavi, misericorditer supplicantem. Video etiam de longinquo *de lumbis meis procedere*[5] quasi carbunculum emicantem, qui gladii mei capulo connexus, suo splendore Poloniam totam efficit relucentem. Tunc vero luctus et meror ibi astantium et hoc audientium cordis viscera penetravit et pre dolore nimio mentes omnium stupor vehemens occupavit. Cumque paulisper dolore represso Bolezlauum inquirerent, quanto tempore funus ipsius habitu cultuque lugubri celebrarent, voce veridica respondit: Nec mensibus, nec annis doloris terminum vobis pono, sed quicumque me cognovit, meamque gratiam acquisivit, memor mei die cottidie me plorabit. Et non solum, qui me noverunt, meamque benivolentiam habuerunt, sed etiam eorum filii filiique filiorum Bolezlaui regis obitum narrantibus aliis condolebunt. Bolezlauo igitur rege de mundana conversacione decedente, etas aurea in plumbeam est conversa.[6] Polonia prius regina, auro radiante cum gemmis coro-

---

[1] Bolesław died on 17 June 1025.

[2] 2 Macc. 3:21.

[3] Luke 18:2, 4.

[4] 1 Cor. 13:12.

and other great nobles ever wished and prayed that he would survive them and be victorious for ever. So the glorious Bolesław brought a felicitous life to a praiseworthy end.[1] For when he realized that he was due to render the debt that all flesh must pay, he summoned to him all his princes and friends from all parts, and gave instructions in private for the governance and disposition of the realm. And with the voice of prophecy he foretold that many woes were to befall them after he had gone. "O my brothers," he said, "whom I have fostered and spoilt as a mother her sons, if only the harm that I foresee *in my great anguish*[2] might turn to good for you, and that those who light the fire of sedition might *have regard for God and man*![3] Alas, alas, now *as through a glass darkly*[4] I see our line of kings in exile, wandering afar and begging piteously from those very foes that I have trodden beneath my feet. I see, too, afar that *from my loins comes*[5] as it were a glowing ruby attached to the hilt of my sword, that makes all of Poland ablaze with its light." Then indeed grief and woe gripped to the very hearts those who stood about and heard these words, and their pain was so great that the minds of all were quite numb. When they had contained their grief for a moment, they asked Bolesław how long should they commemorate his passing and wear mourning. He told them in truth: "I set you no limits of months and years to your grief; but let every one who knew me and enjoyed my favor weep every single day in memory of me. And not only those who knew me and have gained my goodwill, but their sons and their sons' sons shall hear the story from others and lament King Bolesław's passing." So Bolesław passed from the company of this world, and the age of gold became an age of lead.[6] Poland, once queen and crowned

[5] Gen. 35:11.

[6] The decline of the world expressed in terms of ever baser metals is a commonplace (see, e.g., Ovid, *Met.* 1.80–131). However, lead does not seem to feature among them, unless we see it implied in Juvenal, *Sat.* 13.28, where the poet speaks about an age worse than iron: *nunc aetas agitur peioraque saecula ferri. Plumbeus* is otherwise often applied to the poor quality of, for example, coins or arms or even persons; see *Thesaurus linguae latinae*, s.v. "plumbeus."

nata, sedet in pulvere *viduitatis vestibus*[1] involuta. *In luctum cythara*, gaudium in merorem, *organum* in suspiria convertuntur.[2] Illo nimirum anno continuo nullus in Polonia convivium publice celebravit, nullus nobilis vir vel femina vestimentis-se sollempnibus adornavit, nullus plausus, nullus cythare sonus audiebatur in tabernis, nulla cantilena puellaris, nulla vox letitie resonabat in plateis. Hoc per annum est a cunctis universaliter observatum, sed viris nobilibus et feminis plorare Bolezlauum est cum vite termino terminatum. Rege itaque Bolezlauo inter homines exeunte, pax et letitia rerumque copia videntur simul de Polonia commeasse. Hactenus Bolezlaui magni laudibus termini metam inponamus, eiusque funus aliquantulum carmine lugubri lugeamus.

DE MORTE BOLEZLAUI CARMINA

Omnis etas, omnis sexus, omnis ordo currite,
Bolezlaui regis funus condolentes cernite,
Atque mortem tanti viri simul mecum plangite.
Heu, heu Bolezlaue, ubi tua gloria,
Ubi virtus, ubi decus, ubi rerum copia?
Satis restat ad plorandum, ve michi Polonia.
Sustentate me cadentem pre dolore comites
Viduate[3] mihi queso[a] condolete milites,
Desolati respondete: heu nobis hospites!
Quantus dolor, quantus luctus erat pontificibus,
Nullus vigor, nullus sensus, nulla mens in ducibus,
Heu, heu capellanis, heu ipsis omnibus.

[a] quesco *Mal*

---

[1] Gen. 38:19. Cosmas, *Chron. Boh.* II:2, p. 83, also calls Poland "widowed" after Casimir's death (*suo viduatam principe*).

[2] Job 30:31.

with radiant gold and gems, sits in the dust wrapped in the *garments of her widowhood.*[1] Her *harp is turned to mourning,* her joy to sorrow, and her *organ music to* sighs.[2] For all through that year no one celebrated a public feast in Poland, no noble man or woman dressed in formal attire, no clapping or sound of stringed instruments was heard in the taverns, no girls sang songs, nor did any voice of happiness echo in the streets. This year of mourning was universally observed by all, but noble men and women never ceased to weep for Bolesław till the day of their death. So when King Bolesław passed from the world of men, it seemed as if peace and happiness and abundance departed from Poland at the same time. At this point let us bring to an end our praises of the great Bolesław, and mourn his passing with a few sad verses.

VERSES ON THE DEATH OF BOLESŁAW

Come, men, women of all ages, of all stations, run to me;
Lo! King Bolesław is dead and passed from us; come grieve with me.
Come and join with me and mourn, so great a man has passed away.
Ah Bolesław, ah Bolesław, where is all your glory gone?
All your valor, all your splendor, and the treasures you had won?
Woe to me, O Poland, there is much too much for us to mourn.
Hold me up, good lords, sustain me, for I may collapse for grief.
Widowed I am,[3] mourn you with me knights and warriors, join me
    please,
You, our foreign guests abandoned, answer with your voice in grief!
Oh how great the pain and sorrow that the bishops felt at heart;
All the dukes lost strength, sense, thought, and mindless are they
    for their part.
Woe, oh woe, too for the chaplains, woe to all, all none apart.

---

[3] While the Latin is not unequivocal, it would seem to fit the author's intentions to see the "speaker" as a personification of the community of the realm.

Vos, qui torques portabatis in signum militie
Et qui vestes mutabatis regales cottidie,
Simul omnes resonate, ve, ve nobis hodie.
Vos matrone, que coronas gestabatis aureas
Et que vestes habebatis totas aurifriseas
His exute vestiatis lugubres et laneas.
Heu, heu Bolezlaue, cur nos pater deseris,
Deus talem virum umquam mori cur permiseris,
Cur non prius nobis unam simul mortem dederis.
Tota terra desolatur tali rege vidua,
Sicut suo possessore facta domus vacua,
Tua morte lugens, merens, nutans et ambigua.
Tanti viri funus mecum omnis homo recole,
Dives, pauper, miles, clerus, insuper agricole.
Latinorum et Slauorum[1] quotquot estis incole
Et tu lector bone mentis, hec quicumque legeris,
Queso motus pietate lacrimas effuderis
Multum eris inhumanus, nisi mecum fleveris.

(17) DE SUCCESIONE MESCHONIS II BOLEZLAYDES GLORIOSI

Postquam ergo magnus Bolezlauus de mundo decessit, secundus Mescho, filius eius in regnum successit, qui iam vivente patre sororem tertii Ottonis imperatoris uxorem acceperat, de qua Kazimirum, id est Karolum, restauratorem Polonie, procrearet.[2]

---

[1] The reference may be either to Christians of Roman and Slavic liturgy, or to Western settlers (*hospites*) and Poles.

[2] Mieszko II Lambert, king of Poland 1025–31, married in 1013 Richeza, b. ca. 995, d. 21 March 1063, the daughter of Ezzo of Lorraine and Mathilda, daughter of the sister of Otto III—and thus Otto's grand-niece, not his sister; on the problematic genealogy of this queen, see now Eduard Hlawitscka, "Königin Richenza von Polen–Enkelin Herzog Konrads von Schwaben, nicht Kaiser

Those of you who used to bear the badge of knighthood fair, I say,
Those of you who helped the king to change his garments every day,
All of you, resound and cry out, woe oh woe for us today.
And you matrons, used to wearing crowns of gold upon your heads,
Rich brocaded dresses gleaming light and bright with golden threads,
Set aside these splendid garments, change to mourning, woolen
    vests.
Bolesław, oh our dear father, you desert us now, but why?
Why, O God, did you permit that such a man as this should die?
Why not sooner give to all of us a single death, oh why?
All the land is desolated, widowed of its noble king,
Like a house made void and empty when its owner is missing,
Grieving, mourning, staggering, and lost in doubt by your passing.
Every person join with me and call to mind this great man's fall:
Rich men, poor men, soldiers, clergy, peasants, too, and plain folk
    all,
Latin people, Slavic people,[1] settlers in this realm withall,
And whoever reads these verses, gentle reader, I pray you,
Let your heart be moved by pity, let your tears burst forth anew.
Hard of heart you are and churlish if you all do not weep too!

17 HOW MIESZKO II SUCCEEDED THE GLORIOUS BOLESŁAW

So Bolesław the Great passed from this world, and his son
Mieszko II succeeded to the realm. Mieszko had already married
the sister of Emperor Otto III during his father's lifetime, and
begotten a son by her, Casimir (that is, Charles), the restorer of
Poland.[2] This Mieszko was a fine warrior and performed many

Ottos II," in L. Fenske, W. Rösener, and T. Zotz, ed., *Institution, Kultur und Gesellschaft im Mittelalter: Festschrift für Josef Fleckenstein* (Sigmaringen: Thorbecke, 1984), pp. 221–44. Their son Casimir the Restorer, born 25 July 1016, was duke of Poland 1034–58, d. 28 November 1058. The insertion of the name Charles has been seen as a later addition (Mal. p. 40, n. 4), but may very well have been his confirmation name, as Lambert was of Mieszko II or Herman of Władysław I, though not as widely used.

Hic vero Mescho miles probus fuit, multaque gesta militaria, que longum est dicere, perpetravit. Hic etiam propter patris invidiam vicinis omnibus extitit odiosus, nec sicut pater eius vita, vel moribus, vel divitiis copiosus. Dicitur etiam a Bohemicis in colloquio per traditionem captus et genitalia, ne gignere posset, corrigiis astrictus, quia rex Bolezlauus, pater eius, similem eis iniuriam fecerat, quoniam eorum ducem suumque avunculum excecaverat.[1] Qui de captione quidem exivit, sed uxorem ulterius non cognovit. Sed de Meschone sileamus et ad Kazimirum restauratorem Polonie descendamus.

(18) DE SUCCESSIONE ET DEIECCIONE KAZIMIRI POST MORTEM PATRIS

Mortuo igitur Meschone, qui post obitum regis Bolezlaui parum vixit, Kazimirus cum matre imperiali puer parvulus remansit.[2] Que cum libere filium educaret et pro modo femineo regnum honorifice gubernaret, traditores eam de regno propter invidiam eiecerunt,[3] puerumque suum secum in regno quasi decepcionis obumbraculum tenuerunt. Qui cum esset adultus etate et regnare cepisset, maliciosi veriti, ne matris iniuriam vindicaret, in eum insurrexerunt, eumque in Vngariam secedere coegerunt. Eo namque tempore sanctus Stephanus Vngariam gubernabat, eamque tunc primum ad fidem minis et blanditiis convertebat; qui cum Bohemicis, Polonorum infestissimis inimicis, pacem et amicitiam retinebat, nec eum liberum, quoadusque vixit, eorum

---

[1] Bolesław had indeed blinded Boleslav III Rufus, duke of Bohemia 999–1003; see Cosmas, *Chron. Boh.* I:34, p. 61, and p. 31, n. 6, above.

[2] In fact Mieszko died 10 May 1034, thus nine years after Bolesław's death; moreover, his son Casimir was already about 19 years of age at the time. However, the definition of age groups (*puer, iuvenis,* etc.) was rather fluid in the Middle Ages, depending on which of the authorities, such as Isidore of Seville or legal definitions, was respected; see Isidore, *Etym.* xi. 2.

martial exploits, which it would take long to narrate. He also attracted the hatred of the neighboring peoples because of the ill-will they bore his father, but he was not distinguished like his father for his life, character, or wealth. It is also said that he was treacherously seized at a parley by the Czechs, and had straps tied around his genitals to prevent him from procreating, for his father King Bolesław had done them a like injury when he blinded their duke, who was his uncle.[1] He finally escaped their hands, but never had relations with his wife again. But enough of Mieszko; let us pass on to Casimir, the Restorer of Poland.

18 HOW CASIMIR SUCCEEDED HIS FATHER BUT WAS DEPOSED

After Mieszko died—and he lived for only a short time after Bolesław's death—Casimir, a small boy, remained with his imperial mother.[2] Though she gave her son a liberal upbringing, and governed the kingdom as honorably as a woman could, she was driven out of the kingdom by traitors who bore her ill will.[3] But they kept her son with them in Poland, as if to disguise their perfidy. When the boy had grown to adulthood and began to rule, his enemies were afraid that he would take revenge for the wrong his mother had suffered, so they rose up against him and forced him to quit the kingdom for Hungary. Now at that time Hungary was ruled by St. Stephen, who by inducements or threats was converting the country to the faith for the first time. He had maintained peace and friendship with the Czechs, the bitterest enemies of the Poles, and for their sake he would not

[3] The education of Casimir in the liberal arts is referred to several times in the chronicle, e.g., chs. 19 and 21 (the latter reference, however, being to sacred letters). Richeza may have left for Germany as early as 1031; thus Casimir's rule without his mother could have started soon thereafter.

gratia dimittebat.[1] Quo de hac vita migrante, Petrus Ueneticus[2] Vngarie regnum recepit, qui ecclesiam sancti Petri de Bazoario[3] inchoavit, quam nullus rex ad modum inchoationis usque hodie consumavit. Hic Petrus etiam rogatus a Bohemicis, ne Kazimirum dimitteret, si cum eis amicitiam ab antecessoribus receptam retinere vellet, voce regali respondisse fertur: Si lex antiqua diffinierit, quod Vngarorum rex Bohemicorum ducis carcerarius fuerit, faciam que rogatis. Et sic Bohemorum legationi cum indignacione respondens, eorumque amicitiam vel inimiciciam parvipendens, datis Kazimiro C equis totidemque militibus, qui eum secuti fuerant, armis et vestibus preparatis eum honorifice dimisit, nec iter ei, quocumque vellet ire, denegavit. Kazimirus vero gratanter iter arripiens, ac in regionem festinanter Theutonicorum perveniens, apud matrem et imperatorem,[4] quanto tempore nescio,[5] fuerit conversatus, sed in actu militari miles audacissimus extitit comprobatus. Sed paulisper eum cum matre requiescere permittamus et ad desolationem et devastacionem Polonie redeamus.

---

[1] King (St.) Stephen I of Hungary (grand prince from 997, king 1000–38) was in fact rather on hostile terms with Bohemia and Moravia; indeed Cosmas, *Chron. Boh.* I:41 (ad a. 1030, but probably wrongly dated), p. 76, even mentions a war between them. Moreover, there is no other evidence for Casimir's stay in Hungary; indeed, it is not very likely that a brother of the wife of Béla, one of the Árpádian princes who had been exiled by Stephen (or fled from his wrath) and whom Casimir's father had welcomed in Poland, would have been given asylum in Stephen's Hungary. On the other hand, the son of Bolesław I, Bezprym, had spent some time in exile in Hungary after being expelled from Poland—see Györffy, *St. Stephen*, p.140; now also Gyula Kristó, "Les relations des Hongrois et des Polonais au Xe-XIIe siècles d'après les sources," *QMAeN* 7 (2002):127–44. However, neither his exile, nor his short rule in Poland in 1031–2, is mentioned in *GpP*.

[2] Peter Orseolo, son of King Stephen's sister and the doge of Venice, king of Hungary 1038–41 and 1042–46.

let Casimir go as long as he was alive.[1] But when Stephen passed away, Peter the Venetian received the kingdom of Hungary.[2] It was Peter who began the church of St. Peter of Bazoarium, which no king has to this day succeeded in completing after the original plan.[3] When the Czechs asked Peter not to release Casimir if he wished to retain the friendship with them that he had inherited from his predecessors, Peter is reported to have replied in a tone worthy of a king: "If ancient laws had stipulated that the king of Hungary was to act as jailer for the duke of Bohemia, I would do as you request." With this indignant answer to the Czech envoys, and little caring whether they remained his friends or his foes, he gave Casimir a hundred horses as well as arms and clothing for the hundred knights who had followed him, and sent him on his way with all honor, and did not deny him passage whichever way he wished to journey. Casimir set out with great joy and hastened to the land of the Germans, where he joined his mother and the emperor.[4] How long he stayed with them I do not know,[5] but he proved himself the boldest of knights in martial deeds. But let us now leave Casimir to relax with his mother for a while, and return to ravaged and desolate Poland.

[3] The name (de) Bazoario has not been explained. It has often been assumed to be a form of "Budavár," but Buda had no castle (vár) before the later twelfth century. Most recently Gerard Labuda, "Bazoar Anonymus Gallus krónikájában" [Bazoar in the Chronicle of Gallus Anonymus], Századok 104 (1970): 173–7, suggested that Vác, at the bend of the Danube, is meant, but this is hardly convincing. Other proposals include Vasvár in western Hungary, but no church is known there before the end of the twelfth century (see KMTL p.721). The word could even be a personal or family name.

[4] Conrad II (1024–39). Harry Bresslau, Jahrbücher des Deutschen Reiches unter Konrad II. (Leipzig: Duncker & Humblot, 1884), 2:494–97, devotes a long excursus to the contradictory evidence regarding Richeza's and her son's arrival and stay in Germany.

[5] It has been suggested that Casimir's exile ended in 1037 or 1038, but that does not fit with the story of the assistance given by King Peter, who came to the throne of Hungary only in the fall of 1038.

(19) DE REHABICIONE REGNI POLONIE PER KAZIMIRUM QUI FUIT MONACHUS[a,1]

Interea reges et duces in circuitu Poloniam quisque de parte sua conculcabat, suoque dominio civitates quisque castellaque contigua vel applicabat, vel vincendo terre coequabat. Et cum tantam iniuriam et calamitatem ab extraneis Polonia pateretur, absurdius tamen adhuc et abhominabilius a propriis habitatoribus vexabatur. Nam in dominos servi, contra nobiles liberati[2] se ipsos in dominium extulerunt, aliis in servicio versa vice detentis, aliis peremptis, uxores eorum incestuose honoresque sceleratissime rapuerunt. Insuper etiam a fide katholica deviantes, quod sine voce lacrimabili dicere non valemus, adversus episcopos et sacerdotes Dei seditionem inceperunt, eorumque quosdam gladio quasi dignos peremerunt, quosdam vero quasi morte dignos viliori lapidibus obruerunt. Ad extremum autem tam ab extraneis, quam ab indigenis ad tantam Polonia desolationem est redacta, quod ex toto pene diviciis et hominibus est exuta. Eo tempore Bohemi Gneznen et Poznan destruxerunt, sanctique corpus Adalberti abstulerunt.[3] Illi vero, qui de manibus hostium

---

[a] qui fuit monachus *om. Mal*

---

[1] The bracketed words, though omitted in Mal., appears in all the manuscripts. Casimir's period of study in a monastery is mentioned below (ch. 21), but his having been a monk is first reported in the *Vita Maior S. Stanislai* (pp. 380–1). In the fifteenth century an assumed papal dispensation for the monk Casimir to become ruler was adduced to explain the origin of the "Peter's penny" tax, paid by all Polish subjects to Rome; see Jacek Banaszkiewicz, "L'affabulation de l'espace: l'exemple médiéval des frontières," *APH* 45 (1982): 26–7.

[2] As there is no evidence for any class of 'freedmen,' some emend *liberati* to *foederati*; others, forcing the Latin, translate 'serfs having freed themselves into lords against the nobles (seized power...).' Bisson, "On not eating," p. 286, offers another reading, that some men claimed to be lords and imposed services on others, and compares the events with rebellions in, for example, France and Catalonia; see also Aleksander Gieysztor, "Récherches sur les fondements de

19 THE RECOVERY OF THE REALM OF POLAND BY CASIMIR (WHO HAD BEEN A MONK)[1]

In the meantime, the neighboring kings and dukes had been riding roughshod over the portion of Poland nearest each of them, adding the cities and castles near the borders to their dominions or capturing them and leveling them to the ground. Yet at the same time as Poland was suffering this devastation and ruin at the hands of foreigners, her own inhabitants were doing even more senseless and ghastly things to her. For serfs rose against their masters, and freedmen against nobles,[2] seizing power for themselves, reducing some in turn to servitude, killing others, and raping their wives and appropriating their offices in most wicked fashion. Furthermore—and I can barely say it without tears in my voice—they turned aside from the Catholic faith and rose up against their bishops and the priests of God; some they deemed worthy to be put to death by the sword, some by the baser death of stoning. In the end foreigners and her own people had between them reduced Poland to such desolation that she was stripped of almost all her wealth and population. At the same time the Czechs sacked Gniezno and Poznań and made off with the body of St. Adalbert.[3] Such as were able to escape the

---

la Pologne médiévale: état actuel des problèmes," *APH* 4 (1961): 7–33, esp. 28–9, and for the comparative scene see Thomas N. Bisson, "The 'feudal revolution,'" *Past & Present* 142 (February 1994): 6–42. This rebellion of the 1030s is also recorded in the *PVL*, p. 203 ad a. 1030, as well as in the *Annales Hildesheimenses* ad a. 1031 (*MGH SSrG* 8:99) and in Cosmas ad a. 1022 (*Chron. Boh.* I:40, p. 75); see also Kossmann, 1:267–9, with extended literature. If we see the events in terms of a rebellion against the new and Christian order, we may compare them with "pagan" uprisings in Hungary in 1046; see e.g., Pál Engel, *The Realm of St. Stephen: A History of Medieval Hungary 895–1526* (London: Tauris, 2001), pp. 29, 31, 45–7, and Chr. Lübke, "Das 'junge Europa' in der Krise: Gentilreligiöse Herausforderung um 1000," *Zeitschrift für Ostmitteleuropaforschung* 50 (2001): 475–96.

[3] This Czech incursion is dated to 1038 or 1039, cf. Cosmas, *Chron. Boh.* II:2,3,5, p. 83.

evadebant, vel qui suorum sedicionem devitabant, ultra flumen Wysla in Mazouiam fugiebant. Et tam diu civitates predicte in solitudine permanserunt, quod in ecclesia sancti Adalberti martiris sanctique Petri apostoli *sua* fere *cubilia posuerunt*.[1] Que plaga creditur eo toti terre communiter evenisse, quia Gaudentius, sancti Adalberti frater et successor, occasione qua nescio, dicitur eam anathemate percussisse.[2] Hec autem dixisse de Polonie destruccione sufficiat et eis, qui dominis naturalibus fidem non servaverunt, ad correccionem proficiat. Kazimirus igitur apud Theutunicos aliquantulum conversatus, magnamque famam ibi militaris glorie consecutus, Poloniam se redire disposuit, illudque matri secretius indicavit. Quem cum mater dehortaretur, ne ad gentem perfidam et nondum bene christianam rediret, sed hereditatem maternam pacifice possideret et cum etiam imperator eum remanere secum rogaret, eique ducatum satis magnificum dare vellet, proverbialiter, ut pote homo literatus, respondit: Nulla hereditas avunculorum vel materna iustius vel honestius possidebitur quam paterna. Et assumptis secum militibus quingentis Polonie fines introivit, ulteriusque progrediens, castrum quoddam a suis sibi redditum acquisivit, de quo paulatim virtute cum ingenio totam Poloniam a Pomoranis et Bohemicis aliisque finitimis gentibus occupatam liberavit, eamque suo dominio mancipavit. Postea vero de Rusia nobilem cum magnis divitiis uxorem accepit, de qua filios IIII[or] unamque filiam, regi Bohemie desponsandam, generavit. Nomina autem filiorum eius hec sunt: Bolezlaus, Wladislauus, Mescho et Otto.

---

[1] Prov. 30:26; cf. also Vergil, *Georg.* 2.471, *Aen.* 3.646. The two churches were in Gniezno and Poznań.

[2] Gaudentius was made "archbishop of St. Adalbert" by Pope Sylvester II in 999, but possibly on account of the resistance of Bishop Unger of Poznań was unable to enter office. The subsequent movements of Gaudentius are un-

clutches of the foe or their rebellious fellow-countrymen fled over the river Vistula into Mazovia. The cities aforementioned remained so long deserted and wasted that wild beasts *set* their *beds* in the church of St. Adalbert the holy martyr and St. Peter the Apostle.[1] It is believed that this disaster struck the whole land in common because Gaudentius, St. Adalbert's brother and successor, is said—for reasons unknown to me—to have placed the whole land under anathema.[2] But let this suffice on the subject of Poland's ruin, and may it serve in correction of those who failed to keep faith with their natural masters. Casimir remained some time among the Germans, acquiring a great name there in military glory. Then he decided to return to Poland, and told this to his mother in private. His mother tried to dissuade him: the people were not yet fully Christian and not to be trusted, and rather than returning there he should stay and possess his maternal inheritance in peace. The emperor added his plea, begging him to stay with him and offering him a quite splendid duchy. But Casimir as a man of learning answered with these well-chosen words: No inheritance from a maternal uncle or mother is possessed as rightly or as properly as the one from one's father. Thereupon he chose five hundred knights to accompany him and crossed over into Poland. As he advanced his people surrendered to him a certain castle, whence, using his wits as well as his courage he proceeded little by little to free the whole of Poland from the occupation of the Pomeranians, Czechs, and other neighboring peoples and to make himself master of it. Subsequently, he took as wife a Russian woman of noble family and great wealth, by whom he had four sons and a daughter who was to become the bride of the king of Bohemia. The names of his sons are Bolesław, Władysław, Mieszko, and Otto. But let us

known, except that evidently he managed to enter upon his office in the end. The date of his death is not known either; it is supposed to have occurred around 1016. If the ban was imposed because of Bolesław's assumed bigamy (see p. 42, n. 4, above), this would have been done by Gaudentius's successor. However, there is no other evidence for all this outside our text.

Sed de Kazimiro, quid egerit primitus pertractando finiamus et postea de filiis, quis eorum prius, quisve posterius regnaverit ordinabilius edicamus.[1]

(20) DE PRELIO CUM MECZZLAUO ET CUM MAZOUITIS

Igitur eliberata patria et expugnata, profugatisque gentibus exterorum, non minor Kazimiro restabat hostilis profugatio sue gentis suorumque iure proprio subditorum. Erat namque quidam Meczzlauus nomine,[2] pincerna patris sui Meschonis et minister, post mortem ipsius Mazouie gentis sua presumptione princeps existebat et signifer. Erat enim eo tempore Mazouia Polonis illuc antea fugientibus, ut dictum, in tantum populosa, quod agricolis rura, animalibus pascua, habitatoribus loca non satis erant spaciosa. Unde Meczlauus in audacia sue milicie confisus, ymmo ambicione perniciose cupiditatis excecatus, nisus est obtinere per presumptionis audaciam, quod sibi non cedebat per ius aliquod vel naturam. Inde etiam in tantum superbie fastum conscenderat, quod obedire Kazimiro renuebat; insuper eciam ei armis et insidiis resistebat. At Kazimirus indignans servum patris ac suum Mazouiam violenter obtinere, sibique grave dampnum existimans et periculum, ni se vindicet, imminere, collecta pauca quidem numero manu bellatorum sed assueta bellis, armis congressus, Meczzlauo perempto, victoriam et pacem totamque patriam triumphaliter est adeptus. Ibi namque tanta cedes Mazouitarum facta fuisse memoratur, sicut adhuc

---

[1] In 1041 Casimir married Maria Dobronega, a daughter of Vladimir the Great of Kiev. Their daughter, Świętosława/Swatawa (b. 1046/8, d. 1126), in 1062 married Vratislav II of Bohemia. Of the four sons, Bolesław II (b. 1039) and Władysław Herman (b. 1040) became rulers of Poland; Mieszko (b. 1045) may have held a part of the realm for a few years after the expulsion of Bolesław II; and Otto (b. 1047) died as a child.

first finish our account of Casimir's achievements, and at a later point we will tell of his sons, who reigned first and who reigned after, all in proper order.[1]

20 THE BATTLE WITH MIECŁAW AND THE MAZOVIANS

Having freed his country by force of arms and driven out the foreign peoples, now no less a struggle remained for Casimir in driving out the enemy from within his own people and those by rights subject to him. For there was a man called Miecław[2] who had been his father Mieszko's butler and servitor, who after his master's death had had the presumption to become the leader and standard-bearer of the Mazovian people. At that time the population of Mazovia had grown so great from the number of Poles who had been fleeing there (as we said previously) that the farmers were short of land, the animals of pasture, and the inhabitants of space. Thereupon Miecław, relying on the boldness of his army, or rather blinded by ambition and a fatal greed, had the audacity and presumption to attempt to seize what belonged to him neither by any right or by nature. At length his pride reached such bounds that he refused to obey Casimir, and indeed took up arms and began plotting against him. Furious that a servant of his father's and a servant of his should possess Mazovia through violent means, and believing that he was threatened by grave peril and loss unless he retaliated, Casimir gathered a force of knights, small in number but experienced in combat. In the ensuing battle Casimir was victorious, Miecław was slain, and Casimir in triumph restored peace and extended his control over the whole of his country. For it is related that an enormous number of Mazovians were slaughtered there, as the battlefield

[2] Miecław was in all probability a leading magnate of the kingdom who took advantage of the disturbed time after Mieszko II's death to establish sovereign power in Mazovia, and may have even attempted to rule all of Poland; see Jan Bieniak, *Państwo Miecława: Studium analityczne* [The dominion of Miecław: An analytical study] (Warsaw: PWN, 1963), pp. 67–107.

locus certaminis et precipitium ripe fluminis protestatur.[1] Ipse
etiam ibi Kazimirus ense cedendo nimis extitit fatigatus, brachia
totumque pectus et faciem effuso sanguine cruentatus, et in
tantum fugientes hostes solus est persecutus, quod mori debuit
a suis hominibus non adiutus. Sed quidam non de nobilium
genere, sed de gregariis militibus nobiliter opem tulit morituro,
quod bene Kazimirus sibi restituit in futuro; nam et civitatem ei
contulit et eum dignitate inter nobiliores extulit.[2] In illo enim
certamine XXXª acies ordinatas Mazouienses habuerunt, Kazimirus vero vix tres acies bellatorum plenas habebat, quoniam,
ut dictum est, tota Polonia pene deserta iacebat.

(21) DE PRELIO KAZIMIRI CUM POMORANIS

Hoc itaque prelio memorabiliter superato, Pomoranorum exer-
citui in auxilium Meczzlao venienti, Kazimirus cum paucis indubitanter obviam properavit.[3] Nuntiatum namque prius illud ei
fuerat, ipsosque in auxilium inimicis advenire presciebat. Unde
prudenter disposuit singulariter prius cum Mazouiensibus dif-
finire, postea facilius cum Pomoranis campum certaminis introire. Illa enim vice Pomorani IIIIᵒʳ legiones[4] militum in arma
ducebant, Kazimiri vero milites nec unam dimidiam adimple-
bant. Sed quid tamen? Cum perventum esset ad locum certaminis, Kazimirus, ut vir eloquens et peritus, in hunc modum
suos milites cohortabatur:

---

[1] The place of the battle is debated, see Mal. p. 46, n. 2.

[2] While the Latin is not entirely clear, this most likely comes down to saying
that he, a commoner, was ennobled.

[3] The details of this campaign are unclear. However, a passage in the Hungarian
chronicle, assumed to be written in mid-eleventh century, records a fight
between Duke Béla, at that time in exile in Poland (thus before 1046), and a

and the steep river-banks bear witness to this day.[1] Casimir himself grew weary from wielding the sword, his arms and his whole chest and his face were covered in blood from the slaughter, and he advanced so far on his own in pursuit of the fleeing foe that he would surely have met his death if his men had not come to his rescue. But one of them, not a man of noble birth but a soldier from the rank and file, showed a noble spirit in coming to his aid when his life was in peril, and Casimir rewarded him fittingly in due course when he bestowed a city upon him and raised him in dignity among the more noble.[2] The Mazovians had thirty units drawn up on the battlefield, whereas Casimir had barely three full units of warriors, because, as has been said, Poland was in ruins and almost deserted.

21 CASIMIR'S BATTLE WITH THE POMERANIANS

After his memorable success in this battle, Casimir and a small number of his men marched unhesitatingly to meet a force of Pomeranians coming to the aid of Miecław.[3] He had previously had word of this, so he knew beforehand that they were on their way to aid the enemy. He therefore wisely decided to take care of matters one by one, first to finish the matter with the Mazovians, so that afterwards he could more easily take on the Pomeranians in battle. For the Pomeranians this time had four legions[4] in arms, while Casimir could not even raise half a one. But what of it? When they reached the battlefield, Casimir, a man of experience skilled in speech, roused his soldiers with words like these:

Pomeranian leader (*SRH* 1:334–5). This tradition may be connected with this campaign of Casimir. That Miecław had built an alliance with Pomeranians and Prussians is argued by Jan Bieniak, *Państwo Miecława*, pp. 152–3.

[4] The size of a legion—an expression not used elsewhere in *GpP*—is not known; Grodecki-Plezia, *Kronika*, pp. 47–8, n. 1, suggest that it may have contained 1000 warriors.

Ecce dies expectata primitus,
Ecce finis de labore penitus,
Superatis tot falsis christicolis
Iam securi pugnate cum discolis.
Multitudo non facit victoriam
Sed cui Deus dedit suam gratiam.[1]
Mementote virtutis preterite
Et labori vestro finem ponite.[2]

Hiis dictis cum adiutorio Dei prelium introivit, magnamque victoriam acquisivit. Dicitur quoque sanctam ecclesiam affectu magno pietatis honorasse, sed precipue monachos sanctarumque monialium congregaciones augmentasse,[3] quoniam monasterio parvulus a parentibus est oblatus, ibique sacris litteris liberaliter eruditus.

(22) DE SUCCESSIONE SECUNDI BOLEZLAY DICTI LARGI KAZIMIRIDIS[4]

Hiis igitur Kazimiri gestis memorialibus prelibatis, aliisque compluribus sub silencio pre festinancia reservatis, vite terminum finienti, finem terminemus et scribendi. Postquam itaque extremum vale Kazimirus mundo fecit, Bolezlauus eius primogenitus, vir largus et bellicosus, Polonorum regnum rexit. Qui sua satis gesta gestis predecessorum coequavit, nisi quod quedam eum ambicionis vel vanitatis superfluitas agitavit. Nam cum in principio sui regiminis et Polonis et Pomoranis imperaret, eorumque

---

[1] Cf. 1 Macc. 3:19; Gen. 39:21. On victory as divine judgement, see Paul Rousset, "La croyance en la justice imminente à l'époque féodale," *Le Moyen âge* 54 (1948): 225–48; also Kurt-Georg Cram, *Judicium belli: Zum Rechtscharakter des Krieges im deutschen Mittelalter*, Beihefte des Archivs für Kulturgeschichte, 5 (München: Böhlau, 1955), esp. pp. 5–7.

[2] Translated by Dr. Barbara Reynolds.

[3] Little is known about early monasteries in Poland. See Jerzy Kłoczowski, "La vie monastique en Pologne et en Bohème aux Xe-XIIe siècles," in *La Pologne*

Now is the dawn of the awaited day,
Now comes the very end of toil and fray.
So many heretics you put to rout,
These pagans you will vanquish, have no doubt.
Numbers do not secure a victory,
God gives the victor grace, and only He.[1]
Remember all our former fortitude.
In triumph now your valiant deeds conclude.[2]

With these words and God's help he joined battle and won a great victory. It is said, too, that he honored holy church with great affection and piety, but in particular increased the (numbers of) monks and the congregations of holy nuns.[3] This was because when he was a child his parents had offered him to a monastery, and there he had received a broad education in the Scriptures.

22 THE SUCCESSION OF BOLESŁAW II, SON OF CASIMIR, CALLED THE BOUNTIFUL[4]

After the memorable deeds of Casimir recounted above as well as many others, which for want of time we must pass over in silence, Casimir's life came to end, and with this we must end our story of him, too. So after Casimir bade the world his last farewell, his first-born son Bolesław, a generous and warlike man, ruled over the realm of the Poles. His successes equaled those of his predecessors, albeit he was driven by a certain excess of ambition or vanity. For although he began his reign as overlord of both the Poles and the Pomeranians, and he gathered a multitude of them beyond number to besiege the fortress of

dans l'Eglise mediévale, pp. 157, 162; and Marek Derwich, "Die ersten Klöster auf dem polnischen Gebiet," in *Europas Mitte*, 1:515–8; cf. *Europe's Centre*, pp. 332–4.

[4] Usually called Bolesław *Smiały* 'the Bold', b. 1039, duke 1058–76, king 1076–9, d. 1081/2. On his life and reign see Tadeusz Grudziński, *Boleslaus the Bold Called Also the Bountiful and Bishop Stanislaus: The Story of a Conflict* (Warsaw: Interpress, 1985), pp. 15–88.

multitudinem ad castrum Gradec[1] obsidendum innumerabilem congregaret, sue contumacie negligencia non solum castrum non habuit, verum etiam Bohemorum insidias vix evasit, ac Pomoranorum dominium sic amisit.[2] Sed non est mirum aliquantulum per ignoranciam oberrare, si contigerit postea per sapientiam, que neglecta fuerint, emendare.

(23) DE CONVENCIONE BOLEZLAUI CUM DUCE RUTHENORUM

Non est igitur dignum probitatem multimodam et liberalitatem Bolezlaui secundi regis silencio preterire, sed pauca de multis in exemplum regni gubernatoribus aperire. Igitur rex Bolezlauus secundus audax fuit miles et strennuus, hospitum susceptor benignus, datorque largorum largissimus. Ipse quoque sicut primus Bolezlauus magnus Ruthenorum regni caput, urbem Kygow precipuam hostiliter intravit, ictumque sui ensis in porta aurea signum memorie dereliquit.[3] Ibi etiam quendam sui generis Ruthenum, cui pertinebat regnum, in sede regali constituit, cunctosque sibi rebelles a potestate destituit.[4] O pompa glorie temporalis, o audacia fiducie militaris, o maiestas regie potestatis. Rogatus itaque Bolezlauus largus a rege, quem fecerat, ut obviam ad se veniret, sibique pacis osculum ob reverentiam sue gentis exhiberet, Polonus quidem hoc annuit, sed Ruthenus dedit, quod voluit[a]. Computatis namque Largi Bolezlaui passibus equinis de statione ad locum convencionis, totidem auri marcas Ruthenus

[a] noluit Z

---

[1] Today, Hradec u Opavy in the Czech Republic, close to the Polish (Silesian) border.

[2] Nothing else is known about the connection between these two events; nor is the implication of the following sentence particularly clear.

Hradec,[1] through his obstinate negligence he not only failed to capture the fortress but barely evaded an ambush set by the Czechs; and so he lost the dominion over the Pomeranians.[2] Still, it is no surprise if ignorance sometimes leads to error, as long as the neglect can be repaired by wise behavior later.

23 BOLESŁAW'S MEETING WITH THE DUKE OF THE RUTHENIANS

So it would not be fitting to pass over in silence the many-sided virtues and the liberality of King Bolesław II, and we will reveal a few examples among many as a lesson for the governors of the realm. King Bolesław II was a bold and energetic knight, hospitable and warm-hearted to guests, and in giving the most generous among the generous. Also, like Bolesław I the Great, he marched on the great city of Kiev, the capital of the Ruthenians, and drove his sword into its Golden Gate as a sign to remember.[3] He set on the royal throne a Ruthenian he was related to, to whom the kingdom belonged, and removed from power all those who had rebelled against him.[4] What worldly pomp and glory; what boldness and confidence in battle; what royal power and majesty! When Bolesław the Bountiful was asked by the king whom he had made to come to meet him, and to give him publicly the kiss of peace to show respect for his people, the Polish king, indeed, agreed, but the Ruthenian gave him what he wished. For a count was made of how many steps Bolesław the Bountiful's horse had made from his residence to the meeting place, and the Ruthenian laid out the same number of gold marks.

---

[3] According to the *PVL* ad a. 1069, pp. 212–3, Bolesław entered Kiev on 2 May 1069. On the legend regarding the Golden Gate see above n. 3, p. 42.

[4] Iziaslav (b. 1025, d. 1078), son of Iaroslav the Wise and thus an uncle of Bolesław II, ruled Kievan Rus' during most of the time between 1054–78, though several times expelled; see Franklin-Shepard, *Rus*, pp. 245–61.

posuit. Nec tamen equo descendens, sed barbam eius subridendo divellens, osculum ei satis preciosum exhibuit.[1]

(24) DE DELUSIONE BOHEMORUM CONTRA BOLEZLAUM LARGUM

Contigit eodem tempore Bohemorum ducem[2] cum tota suorum virtute militum Poloniam introisse, eumque transactis silvarum condensis in quadam planicie, satis apta certamini consedisse. Quo audito Largus Bolezlauus impiger hostibus obviam properavit, eosque properanter transgyrando viam, qua venerant, obsidens interclusit. Et quia plurima pars diei preterierat, suosque properando fatigaverat, sequenti die se venturum ad prelium per legatos Bohemis intimavit, eosdem ibidem residere, nec se diucius fatigare, magnis precibus exoravit. Antea quidem exeuntes, inquit, de silva sicut lupi capta preda famelici, silvarum latebras absente pastore inpune solebatis penetrare, modo vero presente cum venabulis venatore, canibusque post vestigia dissolutis, non fuga nec insidiis, sed virtute poteritis extensa retiacula devitare.[3] At contra Bohemorum dux versuta calliditate Bolezlauo remandavit: indignum esse tantum regem ad inferiorem declinare, sed die crastina, si filius est Kazimiri, sit paratus ibidem Bohemorum servitium expectare. Bolezlauus vero, ut se filium ostenderet Kazimiri, ibi stando Bohemorum fallacie satisfecit. Sed die iam postera mediante, Polonorum castris ab exploratoribus nuntiatur, quod a Bohemis nocte precedenti fuga non prelium ineatur. In eadem hora Bolezlauus delusum se dolens, acriter eos per Morauiam fugientes persequitur, captis-

---

[1] While the Latin text is not without ambiguity, the meaning is clear enough. The hierarchical symbolism of the exchange of the kiss of peace between two men, both on horseback, implies equality, but tugging the beard is an obvious gesture of derision. Here the two are combined in comic antithesis, while the price exacted by the Polish duke adds tangible humiliation for the one and profit for the other.

[2] Vratislav II, duke of Bohemia from 1061, king 1085–92, and Bolesław II's brother-in-law.

Nor yet did he dismount from his horse, but smiling he tugged his beard and gave him the dearly purchased kiss.[1]

24 BOLESŁAW'S DECEPTION BY THE CZECHS

At the same time it happened that the duke of Bohemia[2] entered Poland with his warriors in full strength. After crossing the thick forests he came into a plain which was quite suitable for battle and camped there. When Bolesław heard the news he lost no time in hastening to meet the foe. He swiftly circled around the enemy, seized the road they had come by, and cut them off. The best part of the day was past, and the hasty march had left his men exhausted, so he gave the Czechs to understand through messengers that he would come to fight them the next day, and entreated them earnestly to remain there and not to tire him further. "For before," he said, "you would come out of the forest like wolves, and hungry after capturing your prey you would make your way into the forest hiding-places with impunity while the shepherd was absent. But now the hunter is here with his hunting spears, and the hounds are set loose upon your trail, and it will not be by flight or by trickery but by courage that you will succeed in avoiding the nets that have been stretched out for you!"[3] But the duke of the Czechs with practiced cunning sent Bolesław back the following answer: it was not fitting that so great a king should go out of his way to meet with a lesser one, but on the next day, if he was the son of Casimir, he should be in the same place ready to await the Czechs at his service. Bolesław, wishing to show that he was Casimir's son, fulfilled the deceitful request of the Czechs by remaining there. But by the middle of the next day word was brought by scouts to the Polish camp that the Czechs had slipped away during the previous night rather than join battle. Bolesław felt bitter about having been tricked, but the very same hour set off in hot pursuit of the Czechs as they fled through Moravia. Though many were

[3] Cf. 1 Sam. 2:5.

que pluribus ac peremptis, quia sic evaserant sibimet ipsi dedignando, revertitur. Adnectendum est etiam rationi,[a,1] que causa fere totum de Polonia loricarum usum abolevit, quas antiquitus magni Bolezlaui regis exercitus ingenti studio frequentavit.

(25) DE VICTORIA BOLEZLAUI LARGI CONTRA POMORANOS

Contigit namque Pomoranos ex subito Poloniam invasisse,[2] regemque Bolezlauum ab illis remotum partibus hoc audisse. Qui cupiens animo ferventi de manu gentilium patriam liberare, collecto nondum exercitu decrevit antecedens inconsulte nimium properare. Cumque ventum esset ad fluvium,[3] ultra quem turme gentilium residebant, non ponti requisito vel vado loricati milites et armati sed profundo gurgiti se credebant. Pluribus itaque loricatorum ibi presumptuose submersis, loricas reliqui superstites abiecerunt, transmeatoque flumine, quamvis dampnose victoriam habuerunt. Ex eo tempore loricis Polonia dissuevit et sic expeditior hostem quisque invasit, tutiorque flumen obiectum sine pondere ferri transmeavit.

(26) DE LIBERALITATE ET LARGITATE BOLEZLAUI. DE QUODAM PAUPERE CLERICO

Item unum memorabile secundi Bolezlaui factum liberalitatis eximie non celabo, sed ad imitacionis exemplum successoribus intimabo. In civitate Cracouiensi quadam die Largus Bolezlauus

---

[a] romani *H*, rationem *Mal*

---

[1] The Latin is corrupt in the MSS, and Mal. *rationem* is grammatically impossible, but the sense is probably not materially affected.

[2] The date of this attack is debated, and both 1068–71 and 1075 have been argued for; see Gerard Labuda, "Zatargi z Czechami i Pomorzanami w pierwszym okresie rządów Bolesława Śmiałego (1058–1073)" [Battles with Czechs and Pomeranians in the first period of the reign of Boleslaw the Bold (1058–73)], *Zapiski Historyczne* 50 (1985): 33–49.

seized and cut down, Bolesław turned back, still angry at himself that they had succeeded in escaping in this way. It remains to add the reason[1] that almost totally ended the practice of wearing armor in Poland, which had been studiously observed from past times in the army of the great King Bolesław.

25 THE VICTORY OF BOLESŁAW THE BOUNTIFUL OVER THE POMERANIANS

For it chanced that the Pomeranians made a sudden attack on Poland,[2] and King Bolesław was in a distant region when he heard the news. Burning with eagerness to free his country from the hands of the pagans, he decided to hurry on ahead all too rashly before his army had even assembled. On reaching the river where the bands of pagans were encamped on the farther side,[3] his armored knights in full gear attempted to cross through the depths of the stream rather than looking for a bridge or ford. A great many of the mailed warriors who were foolish enough to do so were drowned, so their companions who were left alive cast aside their chainmail, and once they had succeeded in crossing the river they were victorious, for all their losses. From that time on, such armor went out of use in Poland, so each soldier came to grips with his foe less encumbered, and if there was river in their path they ran less risk crossing it when not weighed down with iron.

26 BOLESŁAW'S GENEROSITY AND OPEN-HANDEDNESS—A POOR CLERIC

Likewise, there is one memorable act of the extraordinary generosity of Bolesław II that I cannot omit, but will set it forth as an example for his successors to imitate. One day in the city of Cracow Bolesław the Bountiful was seated in his court in front

[3] Probably the river Parsęta or the Warta.

ante palacium in curia residebat, ibique tributa Ruthenorum aliorumque vectigalium in tapetis strata prospectabat. Contigit ibidem clericum quendam pauperem et extraneum affuisse,[1] tantique thesauri magnitudinem prospexisse. Qui cum ammiratione tante pecunie illuc oculis inhiaret,[a] suamque miseriam cogitaret, cum ingenti gemitu suspiravit. Bolezlauus autem rex, ut erat ferus, audiens hominem miserabiliter gemuisse et existimans aliquem camerarios percussisse, iratus sciscitatur, qui fuerit ausus sic gemere, vel quis presumpserit ibi quempiam verberare. Tunc ille miser clericus tremefactus maluisset nunquam pecuniam se vidisse, quam ea de causa regis curiam introisse. Sed cur miser clericelle latitas? Cur indicare gemuisse te dubitas? Gemitus iste totam tristiciam conculcabit, suspirium istud magnam tibi letitiam generabit. Noli, Large rex, noli, miserum clericellum pre timore diutius anhelare, sed festina tuo thezauro eius humeros honerare. Igitur interrogatus a rege clericus, quid cogitasset, cum sic lacrimabiliter suspirasset, cum tremore respondit: Domine rex, meam miseriam, meamque paupertatem, vestram gloriam vestramque maiestatem considerans, felicitatem infortunio dispariliter comparando, pre doloris magnitudine suspiravi. Tunc rex Largus ait: Si propter inopiam suspirasti, Bolezlauum regem paupertatis solacium invenisti. Accede itaque ad pecuniam, quam miraris, et sit tuum quantumcumque uno honere[b] †conaris. Et accedens ille pauperculus auro et argento cappam suam tantum implevit, quod ex nimio pondere rupta fuit et eadem pecunia †visum cepit.†[2] Tunc rex Largus de collo suo pallium extraxit, illudque clerico pauperi pro sacco pecunie porrexit, eumque iuvans melioribus honeravit. In tantum enim clericum auro et argento rex Largus honeravit, quod sibi collum

---

[a] iniaret Z, inhixeret (*i.e.* inhisceret) H, inhereret *Mal*
[b] *add* plus Z H, *add* deportare plus *Mal*

---

[1] It has been suggested that the clerk in the story is the author himself, but chronologically this would be problematic.

of the palace, surveying the tribute from the Ruthenians and other tributaries which was spread out on carpets. It happened that a poor clerk from a foreign country[1] was there and was looking at this vast and rich treasure. He was so awed at the sight of such wealth that he could not tear his eyes away, and contemplating his own poverty, he sighed with a loud groan. Then King Bolesław, fierce man that he was, hearing a man give a groan of pain, and thinking that his chamberlains had struck someone, angrily demanded to know who had dared to groan like that, or who had presumed to strike anyone there. The poor clerk was trembling all over, and at this point wished rather that he had never set eyes on the money, instead of coming into the king's court for this very reason. But poor little clerk, why do you hide? Why do you hesitate to say it's you who sighed? That groan of yours will dispel all your sadness, that sigh will be the source of great happiness to you. Don't, Bountiful King, don't leave your poor clerk panting with terror any longer, be quick to load his shoulders with your treasure. So when the king asked him what he had been thinking about when he sighed so tearfully, the clerk replied trembling, "My lord king, it was my poverty, my wretched state, and your glory and your majesty that I was thinking of. I compared fortune and misfortune, and seeing the difference, for the greatness of my sorrow I sighed." Then said the Bountiful King, "If you sighed because of your need, then in King Bolesław you have found solace for your poverty. So approach the money that you marvel at, and as much as what you can manage in one load shall be yours." So the poor clerk went and filled his cloak with gold and silver, so much that it tore under the weight and the money caught the eye of the king.[2] At this the Bountiful King took the mantle from around his own shoulders and handed it to the poor clerk to use as a money-sack, and helping him he loaded it with better things. For the Bountiful King piled so much gold and silver upon him that the clerk

---

[2] The general sense of these two sentences is clear enough, but owing to corruption in the Latin the translation is at times guesswork.

dissolvi clericus, si plus poneret, exclamavit. Rex fama vivit, ditatus pauper abivit.[1]

(27) DE EXILIO BOLEZLAUI LARGI IN VNGARIAM

Ipse quoque Salomonem regem de Vngaria suis viribus effugavit, et in sede Wladislauum, sicut eminentem corpore, sic affluentem pietate collocavit. Qui Wladislauus ab infancia nutritus in Polonia fuerat et quasi moribus et vita Polonus factus fuerat.[2]

> Dicunt talem nunquam regem Vngariam habuisse,
> Neque terram iam post eum fructuosam sic fuisse.

Qualiter autem rex Bolezlauus de Polonia sit eiectus longum existit enarrare, sed hoc dicere licet, quia non debuit christus in christum peccatum quodlibet corporaliter vindicare.[3] Illud enim multum sibi nocuit, cum peccato peccatum adhibuit, cum pro traditione pontificem truncacioni membrorum adhibuit.[4] Neque enim traditorem episcopum excusamus, neque regem vindicantem sic se turpiter commendamus, sed hoc in medio deseramus et ut in Vngaria receptus fuerit disseramus.

---

[1] A hexameter in the original. In the chronicle of Kadłubek (II: 16–7, ed. M. Plezia, pp. 50–52) the story ends with the poor man's neck being broken under the weight, thus combining in one *exemplum* the praise of magnanimity with the punishment of avarice. See also Grzegorz Żabiński, "Polish Economic Thought Before Physiocracy," in *Physiocracy Yesterday and Today: Economy—Philosophy—Politics*, ed. Janina Rosicka (Cracow: Academy of Economics, 1996), pp. 153–4.

[2] King Andrew I's son Solomon, king of Hungary 1063–71, d. 1087, was driven out of the country by his cousins Ladislas (in Hungarian, László; here called *Wladislauus*), Géza, and Lambert, with Polish support. In fact, it was first Géza who became king (Géza II, 1071–7) after Solomon's expulsion, and subsequently Ladislas (Ladislas I, 1077–95). However, it is true that Ladislas spent the first two decades of his life in Poland, and note of his stature appears also in his legend (*SRH* 2:517).

[3] The reference is to the punishment meted out by a king, presumably anointed at his coronation, on an anointed bishop. Stanislas of Cracow (1072–9, canon-

exclaimed that his neck would break if he put any more in. The fame of the king lives on, the clerk with his treasure went off.[1]

27 THE EXILE OF BOLESŁAW THE BOUNTIFUL TO HUNGARY

Bolesław himself also drove out King Solomon from Hungary with his forces, and placed Ladislas on the throne, who was conspicuous for his piety as he was tall in stature. Ladislas had been raised from childhood in Poland and had almost become a Pole in his ways and life.[2]

> Hungary had never had as great a king, so they repute
> And the land thereafter never bore that much and splendid fruit.

How King Bolesław came to be driven out of Poland is a long story, but this may be said, that no anointed man must take bodily retribution on another anointed man for any wrong whatever.[3] For this harmed him much, when he added sin to sin, when for treason he subjected[4] a bishop to mutilation of limbs. For neither do we forgive a traitor bishop, nor do we commend a king for taking vengeance in such a shameful way. Still, let us leave this question open, and tell how he was received in Hungary.

ized 1253) was sentenced to mutilation of limbs and executed on 11 April 1079. The exact reason of the conflict between him and King Bolesław is unclear; Grudziński, *Boleslaus the Bold*, pp. 167–207, presumes from the meager evidence that the bishop was involved in some kind of ecclesiastical conflict, which was augmented by aristocratic opposition to the ruler.

[4] Presumably some such sense attaches to the second *adhibuit* ('put,' 'ordered,' 'condemned'?); however, the uncharacteristic repetition of the verb at the end of the parallel clause leads one to suspect that the reading is not original. What exactly this "treason" amounted to has been much debated, but it is unlikely that it involved treasonable cooperation with an external power. The author of the *GpP* uses the word *traditio* at least as often for rebellion against higher authority as for siding with an enemy or other breach of loyalty (Grudziński, *Boleslaus the Bold*, pp. 137–41), so that the implication is rather that the bishop betrayed his due fidelity towards the ruler.

(28) DE SUSCEPCIONE BOLEZLAUI PER WLADISLAVUM REGEM VNGARORUM

Cum audisset Wladislauus Bolezlauum advenire,
Partim gaudet ex amico, partim restat locus ire,
Partim ex recepto quidem fratre gaudet et amico
Sed de fratre[a] Wladislauo facto dolet inimico.[1]

Non eum recipit velud extraneum vel hospitem, vel par parem
recipere quisque solet, sed quasi miles principem, vel dux regem,
vel rex imperatorem recipere iure debet.

Bolezlauus Wladislauum suum regem appellabat,
Wladislauus se per eum regem factum cognoscebat.

In Bolezlauo tamen unum ascribendum est vanitati, quod eius
pristine multum obfuit probitati.

Nam cum regnum alienum fugitivus introiret,
Cumque nullus rusticorum fugitivo obediret,

obviam ire Bolezlauo Wladislauus ut vir humilis properabat,
eumque propinquantem eminus equo descendens ob reverentiam expectabat. At contra Bolezlauus humilitatem regis man-
sueti non respexit, sed *in* pestifere fastum *superbie cor erexit.*[2]
Hunc, inquit, alumpnum in Polonia educavi, hunc regem in
Vngaria collocavi. Non decet eum me ut equalem venerari, sed

---

[a] de fratre] deferre Z

---

[1] The Latin transmits two quite different readings. With *H*'s reading *de fratre*
(accepted by Mal. and here) one must assume that *Wladislauo* refers to
Bolesław II's brother Władysław Herman, whom the author by implication
charges with having driven Bolesław into exile. However, this accusation
against Władysław Herman (who would thus by implication have belonged to
the martyred bishop's party) is not mentioned anywhere else. With *Z*'s reading
deferre, the sentence could be translated as follows: 'but it grieves (him, i.e.

28 THE RECEPTION OF BOLESŁAW BY LADISLAS THE KING OF THE HUNGARIANS

When Ladislas heard Bolesław was about him to approach,
As his friend he welcomed him, but there remained still some
   reproach;
For as a friend and a brother he was glad he did him see,
But he grieved his brother Władysław had become an enemy.[1]

He did not welcome him as a stranger and a guest or as a man welcomes an equal, but in the manner appropriate for a knight receiving a prince, or a duke a king, or a king an emperor.

When he spoke of Ladislas, King Bolesław called him "his king";
Ladislas admitted, too, becoming king through his making.

Yet there is one incident that must be set down to Bolesław's vanity, which detracted much from his former decency.

For, when he came to a kingdom not his own, as fugitive,
And not even a poor peasant would obedience him give,

Ladislas in all humility made haste to meet Bolesław and when he saw him coming in the distance, out of respect he got off his horse and waited for him. But Bolesław showed no regard the mild king's humility, and *lifted up his heart in* the bane of *boastfulness.*[2] "I was this person's guardian in Poland," he said, "I raised him, I installed him as king in Hungary. It is not fit that

Ladislas) (that Bolesław) shows hommage to (him, i.e. Ladislas) because of a hostile act (i.e. Bolesław's banishment); see Gerard Labuda, *Święty Stanisław biskup krakowski, patron Polski: Śladami zabójstwa – męczeństwa – kanonizacji* [St. Stanislas, bishop of Cracow, patron of Poland: Evidence on his murder, martyrdom, and canonisation] (Poznań: Instytut Historii UAM, 2000), pp. 50–76. For other proposed emendations, see Mal. p. 53, n. x.

[2] Cf. 2 Chron. 25:19.

equo sedentem ut quemlibet de principibus osculari.[1] Quod
intendens Wladislauus aliquantulum egre tulit et ab itinere declinavit, ei tamen servicium per totam terram fieri satis magnifice
commendavit. Postea vero concorditer et amicabiliter inter se
sicut fratres convenerunt, Vngari tamen illud altius et profundius
in corde notaverunt. Unde magnam sibi Ungarorum invidiam
cumulavit, indeque cicius extrema dies eum, ut aiunt, occupavit.[2]

(29) DE FILIO EIUSDEM BOLEZLAUI MESCONE III

Habuit autem unum filium rex Bolezlauus nomine Meschonem,[3]
qui maioribus non esset inferior probitate, ni Parcarum invidia
puero vitale filum interrumperet, pubescenti iam etate. Illum
enim puerum rex Ungarorum Wladislauus mortuo patre nutriebat, eumque loco filii parentis gratia diligebat. Ipse nimirum puer
coetaneos omnes et Vngaros et Polonos honestis moribus et
pulcritudine superabat, omniumque mentes in se futuri spe
dominii signis evidentibus provocabat. Unde placuit patruo suo
Wladislauo duci puerum in Poloniam sinistro alite revocare,
eumque Ruthena puella fatis invidentibus uxorare.[4] Uxoratus
igitur adolescens inberbis et formosus, sic morose, sic sapienter
se habebat, sic antiquum morem antecessorum gerebat, quod
affectu mirabili toti patrie complacebat. Sed fortuna rebus secun-

---

[1] The Latin text is ambiguous, but considering the symbolic meaning of the
higher ranking person's being on horseback, we decided to follow Bujnoch's
translation (*Polens Anfänge*, p. 93). The whole scene is, however, somewhat
unclear, as we do not learn whether the Hungarian Ladislas expected his guest
and senior to dismount in turn (cf. the Kievan incident, p. 90 , n. 1). It may be
that the text is corrupt, or the author's information was inaccurate.

[2] Bolesław's death is dated between 1079–81. As he died outside his country a
number of legends emerged regarding his end (see e. g. Długoss, *Ann.* 4:144
ad a. 1081). According to one, based on a reference to him in an inscription in
the Carinthian monastery of Ossiach (*Boleslaw Rex Poloniae occisor S. Stanislai
episcopi*), he became a penitent monk, see Richard Roeppel, *Geschichte Polens*
(Hamburg: Friedrich Perthes, 1840), p. 204, n. 23; but Gotthold Rhode, *Kleine*

I should do him honor as an equal, I can kiss him from on horseback as I would any other of the princes."[1] When Ladislas noted this he was somewhat put out and turned aside from the road; still, he gave instructions that fully honorable hospitality should be offered to him throughout the land. Later they were reconciled and would meet each other on friendly terms like brothers. However, the Hungarians took all this deeply to heart, and from this time on he attracted great ill will with the Hungarians, and so, they say, his last day came upon him all the more swiftly.[2]

29 THE SAME BOLESŁAW'S SON, MIESZKO III

Now King Bolesław had one son named Mieszko, whose fine qualities would have been in no way inferior to his forefathers', had the Fates in envy not snapped the thread of his life when he was still growing up.[3] For King Ladislas of Hungary had been looking after the boy after his father died, and for his father's sake treated him as if he were his own son. Certainly none of the Polish and Hungarian friends of his own age could match him in honest character and good looks, and by these evident signs he drew everybody's attention to him with good hope for his future rule. For this reason his uncle Duke Władysław made an ill-omened decision to call the boy back to Poland and to marry him, in spite of fate's envy, to a girl from Ruthenia.[4] So the young man was married before his beard had grown, a handsome lad who was so well-bred and so wise and so followed his forefathers' ancient ways that he was held in marvelous affection by the entire

Geschichte Polens (Darmstadt: Wissenschaftliche Buchgesellschaft, 1965), p. 25, n. 1, maintains that the inscription is late and can hardly be authentic.

[3] Bolesław's son Mieszko was born 1069 and died in 1089. He is usually not counted among the princes with this name, Mieszko III being the standard appellation of Mieszko the Old, son of Bolesław III (b. ca. 1126, d. 1202).

[4] In 1088.

dis mortalium inimica in dolorem gaudium commutavit et spem probitatis et florem etatis amputavit. Aiunt enim quosdam emulos timentes, ne patris iniuriam vindicaret, veneno puerum bone indolis peremisse;[1] quosdam vero, qui cum eo biberunt, vix mortis periculum evasisse. Mortuo autem puero Meschone tota Polonia sic lugebat, sicut mater unici mortem filii. Nec illi solummodo, quibus notus erat, lamentabantur, verum etiam illi, qui nunquam eum viderant, lamentando feretrum mortui sequebantur. Rustici quippe aratra, pastores pecora deserebant, artifices studia, operatores opera pre dolore Meschonis postponebat. Parvi quoque pueri et puelle, servi insuper et ancille Meschonis exequias lacrimis et suspiriis celebrabant.[2] Ad extremum misera mater,[3] cum in urna puer plorandus conderetur, una hora quasi mortua sine vitali spiritu tenebatur, vixque post exequias ab episcopis ventilabris et aqua frigida suscitatur. Nullius enim regis vel principis exitium apud etiam barbaras nationes tam diutino merore legitur conclamatum, nec exequie tethrarcharum magnificorum[4] ita lugubres celebrantur, nec anniversarium cesaris[5] ita fuerit cantu lugubri celebratum. Sed de mestitia pueri sepulti sileamus et ad letitiam regnaturi pueri[6] veniamus.

---

[1] The circumstances of young Mieszko's death are controversial; see *PSB* 5:38. Moreover, the author's extended eulogy of him, comparable only to the *laudatio* of major rulers such as Bolesław *Chrobry*, raises questions. It has even been suggested that he knew the young man personally and was an eyewitness at the funeral (Mal. 56, n. 2), and so may have come with him to Poland from Hungary.

[2] A similar list of mourners appears in the *Chronici Hungarici compositio saeculi XIV* (*SRH* 1:322) in the description of the passing of King Saint Stephen.

country. But fortune, ever hostile to mortal happiness, turned their joy to sorrow, and cut off the hopes of his worth and the flower of his youth. They say it was certain jealous persons, who feared that he would take revenge for the wrongs done to his father, who did away with this boy of fine promise by poison.[1] Indeed, some of those who were drinking with him barely escaped death themselves. The death of the boy Mieszko threw the whole of Poland into mourning like a mother mourning for her only son. Not only did those who knew him lamented but even those who had never set eyes on him followed the dead boy's bier with lamentation. The peasants left their plows, the shepherds their flocks, the craftsmen neglected their workshops, the workmen their work for grief at the death of Mieszko. Young girls and boys, even servants and maids attended Mieszko's funeral with tears and groans.[2] At the last his poor mother,[3] when her son's remains were laid to rest in the sarcophagus, remained for an hour almost lifeless without signs of breathing, and was barely revived after the ceremony by the bishops with fans and cold water. No king or prince's passing even among barbarous nations is said to have been celebrated with such protracted mourning, the funerals of splendid tetrarchs[4] were not accompanied by such displays of grief, nor the anniversary of the death of an emperor[5] celebrated with such doleful songs. But let us cease our talk of grief for the boy buried and pass to the joy for the boy who was to reign.[6]

[3] The name of Mieszko's mother, married to Bolesław II before 1069, is not known.

[4] This classical word the author may have picked up from his school readings, as Cicero uses the phrase "kings and tetrarchs" quite frequently (e.g., *Phil.* 11.13).

[5] Sometimes assumed (e.g., Mal. 56 n.4) to be a reference to the funeral of Emperor Henry IV in 1111.

[6] I.e. Bolesław III.

(30) DE UXORACIONE WLADYSLAUI PATRIS TERTII BOLEZLAUI

Mortuo itaque rege Bolezlauo aliisque fratribus defunctis,[1] Wladislauus dux solus regnavit, qui filiam Wratislaui Bohemici regis, nomine Juditham, uxorem accepit,[2] que filium ei tercium Bolezlauum peperit, de quo nostra intencio titulavit, ut tractatio que sequitur intimabit. Nunc vero, quia succincte per arborem a radice derivando transivimus, ad inserendum cathalogo ramum pomiferum et stilum et animum applicemus. Erant enim futuri pueri parentes adhuc carentes sobole, ieiuniis et orationi instantes, largas pauperibus elemosinas facientes, quatenus omnipotens Deus, qui steriles matres facit in filiis letantes, qui Baptistam contulit Zacharie et *wlvam aperuit Sare,*[3] ut *in semine* Abrahe *benediceret omnes gentes,*[4] talem filium daret eis in heredem, qui Deum timeret, sanctam ecclesiam exaltaret, iustitiam exerceret, ad honorem Dei et salutem populi regnum Polonie detineret. Hec incessanter illis agentibus, accessit ad eos Franco Poloniensis episcopus,[5] consilium salutare donans, eis sic inquiens: Si que dixero vobis devotissime compleatis, vestrum desiderium procul dubio fiet vobis. Illi vero libentissime de tali causa pontificem audientes, atque magna se facturos spe sobolis promittentes rem dicere pontificem quantocicius exorabant. Ad hec presul: Est, inquit, quidam sanctus in Gallie finibus contra austrum iuxta Massiliam, ubi Rodanus intrat mare, terra Prouincia et sanctus Egidius nominatur, qui tanti meriti apud Deum existit, quod omnis, qui in eo devotionem suam ponit et memoriam eius agit, si quid ab eo petierit, indubitanter obtinebit. Ad modum ergo

---

[1] Mieszko and Otto, see above, p. 82, n. 1.

[2] Władysław I Herman married Judith of Bohemia ca. 1080.

[3] Gen. 21:1–2, cf. Gen. 29:31.

30 THE MARRIAGE OF WŁADYSŁAW THE FATHER OF BOLESŁAW III

After King Bolesław died and his other brothers[1] passed away, Duke Władysław ruled alone. He took to wife a daughter of King Vratislav of Bohemia called Judith,[2] and she bore him a son, Bolesław III, who is the chief subject of our enterprise, as the following treatment will show. As we have passed swiftly from the root of the tree upwards let me now turn my mind and pen to setting a fruitful branch into our catalogue. The parents of the future son, as yet lacking offspring, gave themselves to fasting and prayer, giving alms generously to the poor, in order that Almighty God, who makes sterile mothers to rejoice in sons and who granted John the Baptist to Zachary and *opened* Sarah's *womb*,[3] that *in the seed of* Abraham he might *bless all peoples,*[4] might give them such an heir who should fear God, exalt holy Church, exercise justice, and hold the kingdom of Poland to the honor of God and the salvation of the people. While they performed these devotions tirelessly, a Polish bishop called Franco[5] came to them and gave good counsel, saying to them, "If you do what I say with full devotion, without doubt your desires will be granted you." They listened to the bishop with great delight as he told them this, and making great promises in the hope of getting offspring, they begged the bishop as quickly as possible to explain. In reply the bishop told them, "There is a saint in the south of France near Marseilles, where the Rhone enters the sea, in a land called Provence. His name is St. Giles, and he has found such merit with God that those who show him their devotion and remember him will unquestionably obtain whatever they seek from him. So have an image of gold fashioned

---

[4] Gen. 22:18, 26:4, etc.

[5] The precise identity of Bishop Franco is debated; G. Sappok, *Die Anfänge des Bistums Posen und die Liste ihrer ersten Bischöfe* (Leipzig: Hirzel, 1937), p. 81, lists him as a bishop of Poznań.

pueri ymaginem auream fabricate,[1] regalia munera preparate, eaque sancto Egidio mittere festinate. Nec mora puerilis ymago cum calice de auro purissimo fabricatur. Aurum, argentum, pallia, sacre vestes preparantur, que per legatos fideles[2] in Prouinciam cum huiusmodi litteris deferentur:

EPISTOLA WLADISLAUI AD SANCTUM EGIDIUM ET AD MONACHOS

Wladislauus Dei gratia dux Poloniensis et Juditha, legitima coniunx eius O(diloni)[3] venerabili abbati sancti Egidij cunctisque fratribus humillime devotionis obsequium. Audita fama, quod sanctus Egidius prerogativa pietatis premineat dignitate et quod promptus sit adiutor, sibi data divinitus potestate, pro spe sobolis munera sibi nostre devocionis offerimus, vestrasque sanctas orationes in auxilium nostre petitionis humiliter imploramus.

(31) DE IEIUNIIS ET ORATIONIBUS PRO NATIVITATE TERTII BOLEZLAUI

Perlectis itaque litteris et muneribus receptis abbas et fratres grates[a],[4] mittenti munera retulerunt et triduanum ieiunium cum letaniis et orationibus peregerunt, divine maiestatis omnipoten-

---

[a] *om. Z H.*

---

[1] The description of the altar of St. Giles (dated to ca. 1116) in the famous pilgrims' guide from the twelfth century, the *Liber S. Jacobi: Codex Calixtinus*, bk. 5, ch. 8—recent edition by Klaus Herbers and Manuel Santos Noia (Santiago de Compostella: Xunta de Galicia, 1999)—mentions that *quidam inclytus suam imaginem auream ... clavis affixit* ('a certain famous person attached with nails a golden image of himself'). This may refer—by a faulty identification—to this *ex voto* statue. See also Richard Hamann, "Der Schrein des heiligen Aegidius," *Marburger Zeitschrift für Kunstwissenschaft* 6 (1931): 124, who, however, assumed the image to have been that of a local donor or a distinguished abbot.

in the shape of a boy,[1] and prepare gifts worthy of a king, and send them in haste to St. Giles. Without delay an image of a child as well as a cup was fashioned from the purest gold. Gold, silver, robes, and holy garments were made ready, which faithful messengers were to bear to Provence,[2] along with the following letter:

THE LETTER OF WŁADYSŁAW TO ST. GILES AND THE MONKS

"Władysław, by the grace of God duke of Poland, and Judith his lawful wife, to O(dilo)[3] the venerable abbot of St. Giles and to all the brothers: our obedience and most humble devotion. Having heard the report that St. Giles stands above all in piety and is ever swift to help, through the power he has been given from God, we offer to you these gifts in token of our devotion to him, in hope of offspring, and humbly beg your holy prayers in aid of our petition."

31 THE FASTING AND PRAYERS FOR THE BIRTH OF BOLESŁAW III

When they had read the letter and received the gifts, the abbot and the brothers gave thanks[4] to the one who sent them and performed a three-day fast with supplications and prayers, im-

---

[2] Cosmas, *Chron. Boh.* II, 36, pp. 133–4, records that the embassy was headed by Queen Judith's chaplain, Peter.

[3] The initial O is expanded by all editors to Odilo. Actually the abbot of St. Gilles in 1084 was Benedict (1071–91), and Odilo was his successor (1091–99). Cf. Etienne Goiffon, *Bullaire de l' abbay de St Gilles* (Nimes: Comité de l' art chrétienne, 1882), p. 45f. However, this minor mistake does not invalidate the assumption of the author's close connection to St. Gilles.

[4] The MSS omit *grates*, but without some such word the text makes little sense.

tiam obsecrantes, quatenus devotionem fidelium presentialiter sibi tanta mittentium, multoque plura voventium, adimpleret, unde gloriam sui nominis apud gentes incognitas exaltaret, atque famam Egidii sui famuli longe lateque dilataret.

> *Euge, serve* Dei,[1] caput huius materiei
> Perfice servorum que poscunt vota tuorum,
> Pro puero puerum, pro falso perfice verum
> Confice carnalem, retinens tibi materialem.[2]

Quid plura? Necdum ieiunium a monachis in Prouintia complebatur et iam mater in Polonia de concepto filio letabatur. Nondum inde legati discedebant et iam monachi dominam eorum concepisse predicebant. Unde missi domum citius et alacrius remeantes et presagium monachorum certum esse probantes, de concepto filio fiunt leti, sed de nato leciores erunt facti.

EXPLICIT PRIMUS LIBER

ploring God's omnipotent majesty to reward the devotion of the faithful who had already sent such gifts to Him and who had vowed to give many more, that the glory of His name might be exalted among peoples unknown, and the fame of his servant St. Giles be spread far and wide.

> Rise, *faithful servant* of God,[1] this matter's head and chief,
> And let your servants' prayers a miracle achieve
> In place of this child-form, please grant a living boy
> A real one for its sponsors, for yourself of alloy.[2]

In short, the monks had not yet completed their fast in Provence when the mother in Poland was rejoicing to conceive a son. Before the ambassadors had even left the monks were predicting that their lady had conceived. So they were sent home and returned swiftly and joyfully and proved the monks' prediction to be true. They were delighted that a son had been conceived and were even happier at the birth of the boy.

END OF THE FIRST BOOK

[1] Matt. 25:21 and 23.

[2] Translated by Dr. Barbara Reynolds.

(LIBER SECUNDUS)

INCIPIT EPISTOLA

Domino Paulo, Dei gratia Poloniensi reverende discretionis episcopo, suoque cooperatori[1] imitande[a] religionis Michaeli cancellario, modici dispensator obsonii[2] paterne venerationis ac debite servitutis obsequium. Meditanti mihi de plurimis iniecit se vestre recordatio largissime karitatis, vestraque fama longe lateque diffusa vobis collate divinitus sapientie ac humanitus probitatis. Sed quia plerumque capax mentis intentio concipit que tarda loquendi facultas non exprimit, bone voluntatis intencio sufficiat pro loquela.

Nam cum facit quis quod potest, tunc iniuste fit querela.

Verum tamen ne tantorum virorum gloriam, tamque religiosorum memoriam prelatorum silencio preterire videamur, eorum laudibus insistendo quasi guttam de fonticulo comportare Tyberinis gurgitibus innitamur.[3] Licet enim quod perfectum est non possit naturaliter[4] augmentari, ratio tamen non prohibet

---

[a] imittende Z

[1] 'His helper,' i.e. the author's, as at p. 1, n. 5. But in place of Mal.'s reading *imitande* (*pietatis*) some authorities (e.g. David, *Les sources*, p. 41) prefer Z's reading *i(m)mittende* (qs. 'his helper in the spread of religion'), interpreting this as a reference to Bishop Paul's and Chancellor Michael's missionary efforts among the Pomeranians. On the bishop of Poznań and the chancellor, see the same note.

[2] The word *dispensator* is commonly applied to officials (*villici*, etc.) charged with distributing royal bounty, while *obsonium* in medieval texts describes a

(SECOND BOOK)

BEGINNING OF THE LETTER

To lord Paul, by the grace of God Polish bishop of reverend
discretion, and his helper[1] the chancellor Michael of exemplary
piety, this dispenser of modest fare[2] offers filial obedience and
due submission. As I pondered upon all manner of things there
came into my mind the memory of your most open-handed
charity and your reputation spread far and wide for wisdom
granted by God and uprightness with man. But as generally the
intention of the mind is quicker to conceive than speech is to
express, let my good will and good intention suffice in place of
eloquence.

For when someone's done his best it's hardly fair to quarrel with it.

All the same, lest we seem to be passing over in silence the glory
of men so great, or the memory of such devout churchmen, let
us press on with their praises, adding, as it were, our drop from
the fountain to the Tiber's flood.[3] For though what is perfect
cannot be improved in a natural way,[4] yet reason does not forbid

---

(usually small) meal; whence the phrase could be interpreted to refer to the
author's holding of a minor prebend, for which, however, there is no other
evidence. More commonly the phrase is seen as an expression of affected
humility regarding literary abilities (cf. the parallel *subsequentis scriptor opusculi*
at p. 1).

[3] Persius 11:15.

[4] This assertion may go back to Aristotle's *perfectum enim naturaliter precedit
imperfectum* (*De Coelo* 1 c. 4, n. 9), but more likely to its paraphrase by
Boethius (*In topica Ciceronis*, MPL 64, col. 175). It may imply that a perfect
thing can be improved only by grace or *caritas*, which are supernatural.

illud scriptis laudumque preconiis venerari. Nec indecens in picturis aliquando iudicatur si preciosis coloribus pro varietate operis niger color inseratur. In mensa quoque regum sepe quoddam vile presentatur edulium, quo deliciarum propellatur cottidianarum fastidium. Insuper etiam formica, cum sit camelo quantitate corporis animal inequale, opus tamen suum exercet studiose, suis viribus coequale.[1] Quarum exemplo rerum inductus, balbutientis more puerilia verba formare conor in laudem virorum per se laudabilium adhibita sine laude,[2] vel in preconium Israhelitarum veraciter sine fraude.[3] Quorum vita laudabilis, doctrina perspicabilis, mores imitabiles, predicacio salutaris, quorum sapientia, bicipiti philosophie monte[4] derivata, condensa silvarum Polonie sic sagaciter illustrat, ne prius triticeum fidei semen in terram humani cordis incultam spargant, donec inde *spinas et tribulos*[5] verbi divini ligonibus radicitus expellant, similes existentes etiam *homini patri familias* scienti *de thesauro proferre nova et vetera*,[6] vel Samaritano wlnerato *plagas alliganti, vinum*que desuper *et oleum infundenti*.[7] Qui triticum quoque conservis fideliter distribuunt ad mensuram, et *talentum* non *abscondunt* sed dividunt ad usuram.[8]

Sed cur mutus fari nititur de facundis, vel ingenii puer parvi cur implicat se tam profundis.

> Parcat tamen ignorantie,
> Parcat et benivolentie.[9]

---

[1] A nice poem that may have been known to the author about the ant's ability to perform heavy duties is preserved in the Codex Salmasianus; see Alexander Riese, ed., *Anthologiae partes selectae* (Leipzig: Teubner 1894), fasc. 1, *Libri Salmasiani aliorumque carmina*, 104, 3.

[2] Cf. Cicero *De Fin.* 2.15.50: *ipsum per se, sua vi, sua natura, sua sponte laudabile*.

[3] See John 1:47 (where Jesus greets Nathanael with the words *ecce vere Israhelita in quo dolus non est* 'Behold, an Israelite indeed, in whom is no guile!').

[4] Traditionally, commentators have seen here an allusion to Parnassus (cf. Persius, *Prol.*); but Plezia, *Kronika Galla* (p. 128), argues convincingly that the

us venerating such a thing by proclaiming its praises in our writings. At times pictures are deemed not unpleasing if elements of black are inserted into the bright colors for the sake of variety. So, too, at kings' tables some plain dish is often served as a welcome relief from daily delicacies. Moreover, the ant, a creature in size no equal to the camel, nevertheless performs diligently that work to which is her strength is equal.[1] Moved by these examples, in stuttering manner I shall try to frame childish words in praise of men praiseworthy of themselves when no praise is added,[2] and laud the *men of Israel truthfully without deceit*.[3] Their praiseworthy life, their conspicuous learning, exemplary morals, wholesome preaching, and their wisdom stemming from the twin peaks of philosophy[4] so sagaciously illuminates the dense forests of Poland that they do not allow a single wheat-grain of faith to fall upon the untilled soil of the human heart until they have uprooted and cleared away its *thorns and thistles*[5] with the hoes of the divine word; like, too, to the *paterfamilias* who knows how to *bring out of his treasure what is new and what is old*,[6] or the Samaritan who *bound up the wounds* of the injured man, *pouring oil and wine on* them.[7] So, too, they distribute the grain faithfully in measure to their fellow-servants, and they do not *hide their talent*, but they portion it for profit.[8]

But why does a mute try to speak of matters of eloquence, or a boy of few gifts involve himself in such profound matters?

> Yet let him pardon ignorance
> As well as pardoning goodwill.[9]

twin peaks refer to Plato and Aristotle, the two philosophers *par excellence* in medieval tradition.

[5] Gen. 3:18, Heb. 6:8.

[6] Matt. 13:52.

[7] Luke 10:34.

[8] Matt. 25:25. The second part of the sentence can be scanned as two trochaic octosyllables.

[9] This is a literal translation of the verse, but the Latin is clearly unsound.

Magni patres, vestre discrecio sanctitatis nec perpendat, quid vel quantumlibet sui laboris offerat, sed quid captet nostre desiderium facultatis. Nam cum potenti pauper amicus quantumlibet sui laboris minimum amministrat, non donum sed dantis affectum perpendens, illud recipere magno pro munere non recusat. Igitur opusculum, almi patres, stilo nostre pusillanimitatis ad laudem principum et patrie vestre pueriliter exaratum suscipiat et commendet excellens auctoritas et benivolentia vestre mentis, quatenus Deus omnipotens bonorum temporalium et eternorum vos amplificet incrementis.

EXPLICIT EPISTOLA

INCIPIT EPYLOGUS

Nobis astate, nobis hoc opus recitate,
Per vos, si vultis, opus est laudabile multis.[1]

Non est mirum a labore si parum quievimus,
Tempus erat quiescendi, tot terras transivimus
Neque ceptum iter bene cognitum habuimus,
Sed per illos, qui noverunt paulatim inquirimus.
Exurgamus iam *de sompno*,[2] nam satis dormivimus
Vel unius iam diei viam inquisivimus;
Hac expleta de futura satis cogitabimus.
Duce Deo prosequamur quod interposuimus
Persolvamus, quod frequenter supra titulavimus
Et addamus, si quid minus ignoranter diximus.[3]

---

[1] The first two lines of the poem, distinct in meter (hexameter in the original) and otherwise from those that follow, perhaps belong rather with the Epistola.

Great fathers, the discretion of your holinesses should not weigh what or how much labor our ability's desire can offer, but what it aims at. For when a poor friend offers a part of his labor, however small, to a powerful one, he does not refuse to accept it as a great present, weighing not the gift but the giver's affection. Therefore, bountiful fathers, though this modest work in praise of your country and its princes is childishly written in my feeble style, may your lofty authority and the goodwill of your mind accept and commend it, that Almighty God may grant you increase of all good things temporal and eternal.

END OF THE LETTER

BEGINNING OF THE EPILOG

Stand with us and read this work out loud for us;
Thus, if you so desire, the work will fame acquire.[1]

It is no marvel if a pause awhile we made.
We needed rest, so many lands we'd visited.
When we set out we knew not where the road would lead,
But step by step we learn from those who know indeed.
Now let us *rise from sleep*,[2] enough have we delayed.
Already for one day we have our route surveyed,
With that behind us will our future plans be laid.
God willing let us now take up our broken thread
And finish what we forecast in our title-head,
Adding whatever by mistake we left unsaid.[3]

[2] Rom. 13: 11.

[3] Translated by Dr. Barbara Reynolds.

INCIPIT SECUNDUS LIBER TERTII BOLEZLAUI

(1) PRIMO DE NATIVITATE

Natus igitur puer Bolezlaus in die festo sancti Stephani regis[1] fuit, mater eius vero subsequenter infirmata nocte dominice nativitatis occubuit.[2] Que mulier in pauperes et captivos ante diem precipue sui obitus opera pietatis exercebat et multos christianos de servitute Iudeorum suis facultatibus redimebat.[3] Illa mortua Wladislauus dux, quia homo gravis egerque pedibus erat, et etate parvulum habebat, sororem imperatoris tertii Henrici, uxorem prius Salemonis Vngarie regis[4] in matrimonium desponsavit, de qua nullum filium, sed tres filias procreavit. Una quarum in Rusia viro nupsit, una vero suum sacro velamine caput texit, unam autem sue gentis quidam sibi counivit.[5] Sed ne tanti pueri parentem nudo sermone transeamus, aliquo eum ornamento militie vestiamus. Igitur Polonorum dux Wladislauus, Romanorum imperatori maritali connubio counitus, de Pomoranis succurrentibus suis castrum eorum obsidendo triumphavit, eorumque contumaciam suis sub pedibus annullavit, eiusque victorie gaudium Dei Genitricis assumptio geminavit.[6] Quibus victis civitates eorum et municipia infra terram et circa maritima violenter occupavit, suosque vastaldiones[7] et comites in locis principalioribus et munitioribus ordinavit. Et quia perfidie pa-

---

[1] 20 August 1085, in fact only two years after the canonization of King Stephen I of Hungary.

[2] Judith's death is dated Christmas 1085 by Cosmas, *Chron. Boh.* II:36, p. 133.

[3] The reference is evidently to slaves to be sold abroad by Jewish traders; on this see Dmitrij Mishin, "*Ṣaqlabī* servants in Islamic Spain and North Africa in the Early Middle Ages" (Ph.D. diss., Central European University, 1999), pp. 76–9. It is also the earliest mention of the presence of Jews in Poland.

[4] Judith Maria, in fact daughter of the German King Henry IV (Emperor Henry III), born ca. 1047, was engaged in 1058 and later married to Solomon of Hungary till the king's death in exile in 1087; she married Władysław Herman in 1088 or 1089.

BEGINNING OF THE SECOND BOOK OF BOLESŁAW THE THIRD

1 FIRST, ABOUT HIS BIRTH

The boy Bolesław was born on the feast of St. Stephen the king[1]; but his mother subsequently fell ill and on the night of our Lord's birth she passed away.[2] She was a woman who had always performed acts of charity towards the poor and those in captivity, especially preceding the day of her death, and she had redeemed many Christians with her resources from the servitude of the Jews.[3] After her death Duke Władysław, a heavy man suffering from pain in his feet, now had charge of this young boy. So he took to wife the sister of Emperor Henry III, who had formerly been the wife of King Solomon of Hungary,[4] of whom he begot no son, but three daughters. One of these married a husband in Rus'; one took the holy veil; and the last, one of her own people married.[5] But, not to pass over the father of a boy so distinguished with these bare words, let us clothe them with some military distinction. Władysław duke of the Poles, through bonds of matrimony related to the Roman emperor, triumphed over the Pomeranians when they came to the aid of their people whose castle he was besieging. He trampled their pride beneath his feet, the celebration of the Assumption of the Mother of God doubling the joy of the victory.[6] After their defeat he forcibly seized their cities and towns both inland and along the coast, and installed his retainers[7] and *comites* in the more important and better-fortified places. And since he desired to remove from the

[5] One daughter, name unknown, married a duke of Rus'; the one who took the veil might have been Agnes, abbess of Gandersheim (d. 1126/27); the third, name unknown, married—on our author's statement—a Polish nobleman; on the controversial literature, see Mal. 64, nn. 1–3.

[6] The battle probably took place near Drzycim in Northern Kujawia on 15 August 1090.

[7] On the term *vastaldio*, see above, p. 58, n. 3.

ganorum omnino voluit insurgendi fiduciam amputare, suosmet
prelatos[1] iussit nominato die in hora constituta omnes in medi-
tullio regni municiones concremare. Quod ita factum fuit. Nec
sic tamen gens rebellis edomari potuit. Nam quos Setheus eis
prefecerat, qui tunc milicie princeps erat,[2] partim pro eorum
noxa peremerunt, nobiliores vero discretius et honestius se ha-
bentes, vix amicorum assensu fugaverunt.

(2)[3]

At Wladislauus dux, illate suis iniurie reminiscens, cum forti
manu terram eorum ante quadragesimam introivit, ibique ieiunii
plurimum adimplevit.[4] Expleta itaque ibi ieiunii parte quam
plurima sinum[a] terre populosiorem et opulenciorem[5] ex inpro-
viso intravit, indeque predam inmensam et captivos innumer-
abiles congregavit. Cumque iam cum sua preda nichil dubitans
remearet, iamque securus sui regni finibus propinquaret, Pomorani subito subsequentes eum super fluvium Unda invaserunt,
bellumque cum eo pridie Palmas[6] cruentum et luctuosum partibus utrisque[b] commiserunt. Illud enim prelium hora quasi diei
tercia[7] est inceptum, vespertino vero crepusculo diffinitum. Po-

---

[a] summi Z, urbem H, (populosiores) sinus *Kadłubek*
[b] utrisque Z, utrique *Mal*

---

[1] The word *prelati* cannot here mean, as usual, churchmen. The author does
not use it any other place in its secular meaning, but elsewhere (I:6, p. 30) it
seems he calls non-ecclesiastical officials by the clerical term *suffragani*. Moreover, no less an authority than St. Gregory the Great uses *prelati* and *praepositi*
for both secular and ecclesiastical leaders; see *The Cambridge History of
Political Thought c. 350–c. 1450*, ed. J. H. Burns (Cambridge: Cambridge UP,
1988), pp. 119–20.

[2] Sieciech of the Topór kindred was count palatine of Poland in the late eleventh
century (*SSS* 5:155–6).

perfidious pagans all spirit to revolt, he ordered his officers[1] to burn down on a certain day at an agreed hour all the fortresses in their land. And so it was done. Yet even with this it proved impossible to wholly tame this rebel race. For of those whom Sieciech, the military commander at the time,[2] set over them, some were murdered for their abuses, while the better sort who had behaved with discretion and honor barely managed to escape with the connivance of friends.

2 [WAR WITH THE POMERANIANS][3]

But Duke Władysław did not forget the injury done to his representatives. He marched into their land with a strong force before Lent, and spent there most of time of the fast.[4] Then once the better part of the fast was passed, he invaded by surprise the richer and more populous heartland[5] and collected enormous quantities of booty from it and captives beyond counting. As he was returning home quite unsuspectingly with his plunder, and feeling safe as he was approaching the boundaries of his kingdom, the Pomeranians, who had been trailing him, suddenly fell upon him by the river Unda on the day before Palm Sunday.[6] The battle was grievous and bloody for both sides. For it began around the third hour of the day,[7] and only ended as twilight fell

[3] Certain chapters in this book and the next have no headings in the critical edition. Those that appear within square brackets in the English have been added by the present editors, usually following earlier editions and translations.

[4] 25 February to 6 April, if the usual dating of the campaign to spring 1091 is correct.

[5] Where the campaign was conducted is unclear. It may have been in the region of Gdańsk, or near Białogard, at the River Wiezyca. The reading *sinum*, a conjecture based on the text of Kadłubek, has ambiguous implications, while an alternative proposal *Stetin* (i.e. Szczecin) does not seem to fit the context; see Mal. p. 65, n. v.

[6] April 5. The river could be the Noteć, the Drawa, or the Wda lub Bda (today, Czarna Woda), a tributary of the lower Vistula; see Mal. p. 66, n. 2.

[7] Equivalent to 9 a.m.

morani tandem pro municione noctis caliginem induerunt, Poloni vero campum victorie Drzu[1] vocabulo tenuerunt. In dubio enim pependit, utrum christianorum lues an paganorum ibi extiterit.[2] Quod flagellum Deus, ut credimus, omnipotens in transgressoribus observancie quadragesimalis ad correccionem exercuit, sicut quibusdam postea de ipso liberatis periculo revelavit. Et quia luctuosa et dampnosa, sicut dictum est, victoria multis erat, diesque dominice resurreccionis inminebat, vicit racio redeundi consilium dantium persequendi.[3]

(3)

Itemque de Bohemia tribus aciebus in auxilium evocatis,[5] Pomoraniam invadit Wladislauus circa sancti sollempnia Michaelis.[4] Ibique castrum Nakel[6] obsidentibus inaudita mirabilia contingebant, que singulis eos noctibus armatos et quasi in hostes pugnaturos terroribus agitabant. Cumque talem delusionem diutius paterentur, et quidnam illud esset vehementius mirarentur, una nocte pavore solito concitati longius a castris exeuntes, nocturnas umbras quasi palpitantes delusi hostium vicissitudine sequebantur; interim vero oppidani properanter de propugnaculis descenderunt, eorumque machinas partemque stationis combusserunt. Itaque Poloni, cum se nichil profecisse nec se bellum invenisse conspicerent, et cum magna pars exercitus, presertimque Bohemi, victualia non haberent, incassum labore consumpto redierunt. Sicque Pomorani contra Poloniam paulatim in superbiam sunt erecti, per puerum Martis, quem calamo

---

[1] The identification of this location is also debated. Bielowski (MPH 1, p. 430) suggests Drezdenko, Gumplowicz (Zbigniew, p. 29) Raciąż, and Grodecki-Plezia (*Kronika*, p. 66, n. 6) Drzycim.

[2] This may mean that the losses were so great on both sides that neither could count it as a victory, or it may be a veiled admission of a Polish defeat.

[3] The Latin as it stands is not entirely grammatical, but the general sense seems clear.

[4] 29 September 1091.

that evening. Finally at night the Pomeranians escaped under the cloak of the darkness, and the Poles had possession of the battlefield, which was called Drzu.[1] For it hung in doubt whether the Christians or the pagans were smitten there.[2] But we believe Almighty God here wielded his scourge in correction of those who had violated the observance of Lent, as He afterwards revealed to certain persons who were rescued from this peril. And since this victory was purchased at the price of sorrow and suffering of many, as has been said, and the day of the Lord's resurrection was at hand, the arguments for returning prevailed over that of those who counseled pursuit.[3]

3 [THE SIEGE OF NAKŁO]

Then Władysław invaded Pomerania around Michaelmas[4] after calling upon three units of reinforcements from Bohemia.[5] There at the castle of Nakło[6] unheard-of wonders befell the besiegers who, though armed and as good as ready to fight the enemy, were stricken every night by terrors. After enduring these delusions for much time, and wondering greatly what they could possibly be, one night, roused by the usual terror, they wandered further from their camp, and in their delusion they followed what seemed flickering night shadows as if they were the enemy. In the meantime, the townspeople speedily descended from the battlements and burnt their siege engines and part of their encampment. So when the Poles realized that their efforts were frustrated and there was no battle coming, and as a large part of the army, in particular the Czechs, had run out of provisions, they went back, their efforts spent in vain. And so the Pomeranians little by little grew lofty in pride against Poland—to be eradicated by the son of Mars whom our pen is

[5] I.e. from Vratislav, 1061–92 duke, from 1086 king of Bohemia, and married to a sister of Władysław; the Polish rulers were intermittently on good terms with him, even though he took the title of "king of Poland."

[6] By the river Noteć, on the borders of Pomerania.

pingimus,[1] exstirpandi. Sed ne letam exenterare materiam videamur, malorum invidiam potius quam detraccionis infamiam patiamur.[2] Nec absurdum ullatenus ulli discreto videatur, si in hac historia cum legitimo concubine filius inducatur.[3] Nam in historia principali[4] duo filii Abrahe memorantur, sed ab in vicem a patre pro discordia separantur. Ambo quidem de patriarche semine procreati, sed non ambo iure patrimonii coequati.

(4)

Igitur Zbigneuus a Wladislauo duce de concubina progenitus, in Cracouiensi civitate adultus iam etate litteris datus fuit,[5] eumque noverca sua in Saxoniam docendum monasterio monialium transmandavit.[6] Eo tempore Setheus palatinus comes vir quidem sapiens, nobilis et formosus erat, sed avaricia excecatus, multa crudelia et inportabilia exercebat. Alios scilicet vili occasione transvendebat, alios de patria propellebat, ignobiles vero nobilibus preponebat.

Unde multi sua sponte non coacti fugiebant
Quia idem sese pati sine culpa metuebant.
Sed, qui prius fugitivi per diversa vagabantur,

---

[1] I.e. Bolesław III; his struggles against the Pomeranians occupy much of this and the third book. Here and in the following chapters the author applies to the young Bolesław such classical epithets as *puer Martis* (ch. 11), *Martis filius* (ch. 17) and *Martis prole progenitus* (ch. 14), etc.

[2] While the precise meaning of this sentence is far from clear, it seems to include yet another reference to the real or fictitious enemies of the author.

[3] I.e. Bolesław and Zbigniew. The latter was born ca. 1073 to Duke Władysław. His mother might have been a Polish woman or a (pagan?) Pomeranian princess (so Gumplowicz, Zbigniew, p. 10; other hypotheses are listed in Mal. p. 68, n. 1). She is evidently regarded a "concubine" by the author because she was not married to Władysław according to ecclesiastical rites, whereas the duke seems to have treated their child as the legitimate firstborn son. It should also be noted that our author wrote after the "Gregorian" reform, which made ecclesiastical marriage a much more strict requirement than it had been in the

depicting.[1] But lest we seem to exhaust a happy theme, we would rather suffer the spite of the ill-willed than the shame of detraction.[2] And let no thoughtful person think it inappropriate at all if we introduce into our history besides the legitimate son the son of the concubine as well.[3] For in the account of the beginnings[4] two sons of Abraham are spoken of, but because of discord they were separated from each other by their father. Both sprang from the patriarch's seed, but they were not both equal in their birthright.

4 [ON ZBIGNIEW THE REBEL]

So Zbigniew was born to Duke Władysław of a concubine, and when he was grown up he was put to learn letters in the city of Cracow,[5] and then his stepmother sent him to Saxony to be taught in a convent of nuns.[6] At that time Sieciech was the count palatine, a wise, noble, and handsome man, but blinded by greed he perpetrated many cruel and intolerable deeds. He would sell people into servitude on the slightest pretext, drive others from their country, and promote non-nobles over the nobility.

So that many of their freewill fled their country while not guilty
For they feared that if they didn't they would suffer from his cruelty
But those who had earlier fled and wandered through parts far
    and near

late eleventh century. In fact Zbigniew's status, which may have changed over the years, cannot be ascertained with any accuracy.

[4] The book of Genesis (see Gen. 25:5–6, 21:1–14).

[5] While there is no other direct evidence of a (cathedral) school in Cracow in late eleventh century, a list of books from the early twelfth century suggests its existence; see Marian Plezia, "Księgozbiór katedry krakowskiej wedle inwentarza z r. 1110" [The library of the cathedral of Cracow according to an inventory from 1110], *Silva Rerum*, n.s., 1 (1981): 16–29.

[6] Zbigniew may have studied in Quedlinburg, where his sister Agnes was abbess at that time. It has been assumed that he was consecrated as priest during that time, see ch. II:17, p. 153 below.

Brethizlaui ducis[1] consilio in Bohemia congregantur. Sicque Bohemorum calliditate quosdam precio conduxerunt, qui Zbigneum furtim de claustro monialium extraxerunt. Recepto igitur Zbigneuo in Bohemia fugitivi legationem in hec verba comiti mittunt nomine Magno Wrotislauensi:[2] Nos quidem, comes Magne, quoquomodo Zethei contumelias in exilio positi toleramus, sed tibi Magne, cui nomen ducatus est plus dedecoris quam honoris, lacrimabiliter condolemus, cum laborem honoris nec honorem[3] habeas, cum pristaldis Zethei dominari non audeas; sed si iugum servitutis de cervice volueris excutere, festina puerum, quem habemus, in clipeum defensionis recipere. Et hoc totum dux Bohemicus suggerebat, qui libenter discordiam inter Polonos seminabat. Hoc audito Magnus diu imprimis hesitavit, sed communicato consilio maioribus[4] et laudato, verbis eorum eum recipiens acquievit.

Pro quo facto Wladislauus pater eius contristatur,
Sed Zetheus cum regina[5] multo magis conturbatur.

---

[1] Břetislav II, duke of Bohemia 1092–1100, son of Duke Vratislav II and Adelaide of Hungary.

[2] The identity and legal status of Magnus is debated; he may have been the same person as the *comes* of Mazovia mentioned in ch. 49 below, or a member of the Powała kindred, or of the Turzynit clan, which would make him a relative of Bishop St. Stanislas; see Fedor von Heydebrand u. d. Lasa, "Die staatsrechtliche Stellung des comes nomine Magnus Wratislawensis," *Zeitschrift des Vereins für Geschichte Schlesiens* 74 (1940): 14–68. There are hypotheses about his being a descendant of the Anglo-Saxon King Harold II Godwinson, which might explain the use of the title *dux* in the *GpP*, not elsewhere applied to someone not of princely blood; see Tomasz Jurek, "Kim był komes wrocławski Magnus" [Who was Magnus the *comes* of Wrocław], in *Venerabiles, nobiles et honesti, Studia z dziejów Polski średniowiecznej: Prace ofiarowane Profesorowi Januszowi Bieniakowi w siedemdziesiątą rocznicę urodzin i czterdziestopięciolecie pracy naukowej* [*Venerabiles, nobiles et honesti*—studies on the history of medieval Poland: Works offered to Prof. Janus Bieniak on his 60th birthday and the 40th year of his scholarly activities], ed. A. Radzimiński, A. Supruniuk and J. Wroniszewski (Toruń: Uniwersytet Mikołaja Kopernika, 1997), pp. 181–92.

gathered together in Bohemia on the advice of Duke Břetislav.[1] And so by a cunning ruse of the Czechs they hired some men who abducted Zbigniew secretly from the nuns' convent. Once they had Zbigniew back in Bohemia the exiles sent a delegation to the *comes* of Wrocław, named Magnus,[2] with the following message: "*Comes* Magnus, we in exile endure indignities of every kind from Sieciech. But for you, Magnus, we weep heartfelt tears, for the princely title is more a source of shame than honor for you. You have all the burden of the honor without any of the honor,[3] as you do not dare to be lord over Sieciech's bailiffs. But if you wish to throw the yoke of servitude from your neck, hurry to take the boy we have in our charge as a shield in your defense." Now all this had been put to them by the duke of Bohemia, who was glad to sow discord among the Poles. When Magnus had heard this, he first hesitated for a long while, but when he consulted with the elders[4] and they approved the plan, he acquiesced to the proposal and received the boy.

Grieved was his father's spirit when he heard that this had happened. Sieciech and the queen,[5] however, were much more alarmed and frightened.

[3] *Honor* is used here in two meanings: as the office itself and the honor going with it. In the neighboring kingdom of Hungary the *pristaldi* were officers of the court in charge of summons and legal acts; see J. M. Bak *et al.* ed., *The Laws of the Medieval Kingdom of Hungary/Decreta Regni Mediaevalis Hungariae*, vol. 1 [1000–1301], 2d ed. (Idyllwild: Schlacks, 1999), p. 139. The term occurs rarely in the *GpP* (cf. II:16, p. 142), and it is not known from Polish legal documents otherwise. We settled on the translation 'bailiff,' a word elsewhere describing judicial officeholders.

[4] The author uses the term *maiores* in reference to the leading men of the city or the duchy; in the next paragraph they are called *magnates*.

[5] The role of Queen Judith Maria in these conflicts is unclear; the author mentions her only twice. Kossmann (1:263) assumes that the animosity towards Queen Judith had anti-German implications and Sieciech was also close to imperial circles. On similar, but more explicit accusations against "foreign" queens in neighboring Hungary (including the murder of one), see J. M. Bak, "Queens as Scapegoats in Medieval Hungary," in *Queens and Queenship in Medieval Europe*, ed. A. Duggan (London: Boydell, 1997), pp. 223–34.

Igitur legatum Magno Wratislauensisque magnatibus regionis transmiserunt sciscitantes, quid hoc esset, quod Zbigneuum cum fugitivis sine patris imperio recepissent, si rebelles existere, vel obedire sibi vellent. Ad hec Wratislauienses unanimiter responderunt, non se patriam Bohemicis vel alienis nacionibus tradidisse, sed dominum ducis filium suosque fugitivos recepisse, seseque velle domino duci legitimoque filio suo Bolezlauuo in omnibus et per omnia fideliter obedire, sed Setheo suisque malis operibus modis omnibus contraire. Populus autem legatum lapidare volebat, quia Sethei partes falsis ambagibus defendebat. Unde multum Wladislauus indignatus et Setheus ira nimis inflammatus Wladislauum Vngarie regem contra Wratislauenses et Brethizlauum Bohemie ducem in auxilium sibi mandaverunt,[a,1] unde plus dedecoris et dampni quam honoris et proficui habuerunt. Nam Setheum rex Wladislauus vinctum secum in Vngariam transportasset, ni pro salute cum parvulo Bolezlauo transfugisset. Cumque nichil virtute contra Wratislauienses proficere potuissent, quia sui contra suos bellum gerere noluissent, pacem invitus cum filio pater fecit, eumque tunc primum suum filium appellavit. Reversus interim de Polonia,[2] quo fugerat, Setheus maiores inter eos callide promissis et muneribus attemptabat, eosque paulatim in partem aliam inflectebat. Ad extremum vero pluribus inflexis cum exercitu dux Wladislauus ad urbem Wratislauiensem accedebat, iamque castra sibi reddita per circuitum obtinebat. Zbigneus vero videns sibi proceres intus et extra defecisse, *durum* intelligens *se contra*

[a] Wladislauum Vngarie regem et Brethizlauum Bohemie ducem in auxilium sibi contra Wratislauenses mandaverunt *Z H Mal*

---

[1] The Latin as printed in Mal. p. 70, 14–15, does not really make sense, since the Bohemian duke was, as described in the previous chapter, the main supporter of the young princes; we have therefore emended the text on the basis of a rearrangement proposed by Gumplowicz (Zbigniew, p. 35) and others. Cosmas, *Chron. Boh.* III:1, p. 161, records that Břetislav led a campaign into Poland in 1012/3; it is, however, also possible that our author conflated information on Bohemian alliances and enmities during these years. For

Consequently they sent an emissary to Magnus and the magnates of the Wrocław region demanding to know what they were
about in harboring Zbigniew as well as the exiles without his
father's orders: did they intend to be rebels, or to obey him? To
this those in Wrocław unanimously replied that they had not
surrendered their country to the Czechs or to foreign nations
but had received the lord the duke's son and the fugitives with
him, and that they would obey faithfully their lord the duke and
his legitimate son Bolesław in all matters and circumstances, but
they would oppose Sieciech and his evil deeds by all means
possible. The people, however, wanted to stone the emissary for
defending Sieciech's role with deceitful arguments. At this
Władysław was outraged, and Lord Sieciech very angry indeed.
Accordingly they decided to enlist the help of King Ladislas of
Hungary against Wrocław and Duke Břetislav of Bohemia.[1] But
this action brought them more loss and disgrace than honor or
advantage. For Sieciech would have been taken away in chains to
Hungary by King Ladislas had he not for his safety fled the
country together with young Bolesław. Failing to make any
headway against the people of Wrocław by force of arms, as his
men had no desire to fight against their own people, the father
reluctantly made peace with his son; and it was then that for the
first time the father called him his son. Meanwhile, returning
from Poland[2] to where he had fled, Sieciech slyly tempted the
leading townsmen with gifts and promises and slowly began
to win them over. When he finally managed to win the greater
part of them round, Duke Władysław marched on the city of
Wrocław with an army, receiving the surrounding castles that
had been returned to him. Seeing himself deserted by the leaders
inside the city as well as without, Zbigniew realized that *it was*

Ladislas of Hungary, see above p. 96, n. 2; his position in these events is unclear,
but enmity between Ladislas and Sieciech (as well as Władysław Herman) may
have existed as a result of the suspicion that they were accomplices in the death
of young Mieszko (see I:29, and further Gumplowicz, Zbigniew, p. 22, and
Grodecki-Plezia, *Kronika*, p. 70, n. 12).

[2] I.e. Greater Poland.

stimulum calcitrasse,[1] vulgi fidei[a] viteque sue diffidens, de nocte fugit, fugiensque castrum Crusuicz[2] militibus opulentum ab oppidanis receptus introivit.

(5)

At pater dolens eum inpune sic evasisse, eumque Crusuicienses contra se ipsum recepisse, cum eodem exercitu Zbigneuum fugientem persequitur, totisque viribus Crusuiciense castrum aggreditur. Zbigneuus vero convocata multitudine paganorum,[3] habensque VII acies Crusuiciensium, exiens de castro cum patre dimicavit, sed *iustus iudex*[4] inter patrem et filium iudicavit. Ibi namque bellum plus quam civile[5] factum fuit, ubi filius adversus patrem et frater contra fratrem arma nefanda tulit.[6] Ibi spero, miser Zbigneuus paterna malediccione, quod futurum erat, promeruit; ibi vero Deus omnipotens Wladislauo duci misericordiam tantam fecit, quod innumerabilem de hostibus multitudinem interfecit et de suis sibi paucissimos mors ademit. Tantum enim humani cruoris ibi sparsum fuit, tantumque cadaverum in lacum castello contiguum corruit, quod ex eo tempore piscem illius aque comedere quisque bonus christianus exhorruit. Sicque Crusuicz, diviciis prius et militibus opulentum, ad instar pene desolacionis est redactum. Igitur Zbigneus in castrum fugiens cum paucissimis liberatus, utrum vitam perdat an membrorum aliquid est incertus. At pater, iuventutis stulticiam non ulciscens, ne paganis dubitans, vel alienis gentibus adhereret, unde maius

---

[a] vulgi, fidei, *Mal*

---

[1] Acts 26:14.

[2] For Kruszwica, see above, p. 24, n. 1.

[3] Evidently referring to Pomeranian allies.

[4] Ps. 7:12. For God deciding victory, see above, p. 86, n. 1.

[5] Lucan, *Bell. Civ.* 1.1: *Bella per Emathios plus quam ciuilia campos.*

[6] This conflict can be dated to 1096: Duke Władysław Herman asked the support of the Hungarian duke Álmos in a letter of August of that year,

hard to have been kicking against the goad.[1] He no longer trusted the loyalty of the common people and feared for his life. So he fled by night, and as he did so he reached the well-garrisoned town of Kruszwica,[2] where he was taken in by the townsmen.

5 [SIEGE AND DESTRUCTION OF KRUSZWICA]

But his father was grieved that Zbigniew had thus escaped unpunished, and that the people of Kruszwica had defied him by taking Zbigniew in. So with the same army he went in pursuit of the fleeing Zbigniew and put all his forces to attack the fortress of Kruszwica. Zbigniew, however, got together a force of pagans,[3] and with seven units raised from Kruszwica he marched out from the fortress and took the field against his father. But the *righteous Judge*[4] decided between father and son. For this was a "more than civil war,"[5] with son in arms against father and brother against brother in a cursed contest.[6] There, I trust, the wretched Zbigniew earned by his father's curse what was later to happen. And there indeed Almighty God showed such mercy to Duke Władysław that he slew countless numbers of the enemy while among his own forces very few were snatched from him by death. Indeed, so much human blood was spilt there, and so many dead bodies fell into the lake next to the castle, that henceforth every good Christian would shrink from eating fish from its waters. And thus Kruszwica, previously a wealthy and populous town, was reduced almost to the likeness of a desolation. Meanwhile, Zbigniew was still at large, having fled to the fortress with his few last followers; but he could only contemplate whether his life or some limb would be forfeit. Yet his father was prepared to overlook his youthful stupidity. However, he had misgivings that Zbigniew might go over to the

promising the same support should an occasion arise for him to prove his gratitude. The editor of the letter in the *MGH*, Carl Erdmann, dated it on the basis of the analysis of the extant letter collection of Henry IV; see Franz-Josef Schmale, ed., *Quellen zur Geschichte Kaiser Heinrichs IV: Die Briefe Heinrichs IV.* (Darmstadt: Wissenschaftliche Buchgesellschaft, 1963), pp. 90–3.

periculum immineret, pro vite membrorumque salute quesita fide et concessa, secum illum in Mazouiam transportavit, eumque carcere in castro Sethei[1] aliquanto tempore maceravit. Postea vero in consecracione Gneznensis ecclesie interventu episcoporum eum et principum advocavit, eorumque precibus gratiam, quam perdiderat, acquisivit.

(6) MIRACULUM DE SANCTO ADALBERTO

Et quoniam ecclesie mencio Gneznensis in hoc fieri forte contigerit, non est dignum preterire miraculum, quod in vigilia dedicacionis[2] preciosus martir Adalbertus et paganis et christianis ostenderit. Accidit autem eadem nocte in quoddam castrum Polonorum quosdam traditores eiusdem castri Pomoranos sursum funibus recepisse,[3] eosque receptos in propugnaculis diem crastinum ad oppidanorum perniciem expectasse. Sed ille, qui semper vigilat, *nunquam dormitabit*, oppidanos dormientes sui militis Adalberti vigilantia *custodivit*[4] et paganos in insidiis christianorum vigilantes armorum terror spiritualium agitavit. Apparuit namque quidam super album equum Pomoranis armatus, qui gladio eos extracto territabat, eosque per gradus et solium castri precipites agitabat.[5] Sicque procul dubio castellani, clamoribus paganorum et tumultibus excitati, defensione gloriosi martiris Adalberti ab imminenti sunt mortis periculo liberati. Hec ad presens de sancto dixisse sufficiat et ad intervallum superius nostre stilus intentionis incipiat.

---

[1] Sieciechów on the Vistula was the principal seat of the count palatine (*SSS* 5:156–7), and later (perhaps as early as the late eleventh century) the site of a Benedictine monastery founded by him.

[2] 30 April 1097.

[3] This castle has not been identified.

[4] Ps. 120:4–5.

pagans or some foreign nations, which would have posed a greater danger. So when he was asked to promise to exempt his son from death or maiming, he acquiesced and had him taken with him to Mazovia, and left him for a while to grow lean in the prison of the fortress of Sieciechów.[1] Subsequently, however, the bishops and princes at the consecration of the church of Gniezno intervened with him, so he had him summoned, and thanks to their entreaties he recovered the good graces he had lost.

6 A MIRACLE OF ST. ADALBERT

Since by chance we have had occasion to mention here the church of Gniezno, it is hardly proper not to recount the miracle which the precious martyr Adalbert showed to Christian and pagan alike on the vigil of the dedication.[2] It happened that on that same night certain traitors in one of the Polish castles had let the Pomeranians up into the castle with the help of ropes.[3] Concealed in the battlements they waited for the next day to fall upon the townsfolk. But He who is ever watchful, who *will never slumber*, set the vigilance of his soldier Adalbert to *watch over* the townsfolk as they slept,[4] and unearthly arms struck terror in the pagans lying awake to ambush the Christians. For there appeared to the Pomeranians an armed figure mounted on a white horse, who with drawn sword struck terror in them and drove them headlong down the castle steps and across the grounds.[5] The townsmen were roused by the cries of the pagans and the tumult, yet it was without a doubt the protection of the glorious martyr Adalbert that thus rescued them from imminent peril and death. For the present, let this suffice on the subject of the saint, and in the meantime let the pen of our intention take up at the previous paragraph.

[5] Cf. (though without reference to this episode) František Graus, "Der Heilige als Schlachtenhelfer: Zur Nationalisierung einer Wundererzählung in der mittelalterlichen Chronistik," in *Festschrift für Helmut Beumann zum 65. Geburtstag*, ed. Kurt-Ulrich Jäschke and Reinhard Wenskus (Sigmaringen: Thorbecke, 1977), pp. 330–48.

(7) DE DIVISIONE REGNI INTER UTRUMQUE FILIUM

Igitur Gneznensi basilica consecrata et Zbigneuo gratia patris impetrata, Wladislauus dux ambobus filiis suum exercitum commendavit et in Pomoraniam eos in expedicionem delegavit. Illi autem abeuntes et quale nescio consilium capientes, inperfecto negocio ex itinere redierunt. Unde pater, nescio quid suspicans, confestim inter eos regnum divisit,[1] sed de manu tamen sua sedes regni principales non dimisit.[2] Sed quid in divisione cuique contigerit, enumerare nobis inminet onerosum, neque multum hoc audire vobis fuerit fructuosum.

(8)

Interrogatus autem pater a principibus, quis eorum excellencius emineret in legacionibus mittendis et suscipiendis, in exercitu convocando et conducendo et in tanti regni dispensacione multimoda, sic respondisse fertur: Meum quidem est, ut hominis senis et infirmi, regnum inter eos dividere,[3] ac de presentibus iudicare, sed alterum alteri prerogare vel probitatem et sapientiam eis dare, non est mee facultatis, sed divine potestatis. Hoc autem unum cordis mei desiderium vobis possum aperire, quod discreciori ac probiori in terre defensione et hostium inpugnacione volo vos omnes post mortem meam unanimiter obedire. Interim vero, sicut divisum eis regnum partem suam quisque retineat. Post obitum quidem meum Zbigneus cum hoc, quod habet, Mazouiam simul habeat, Bolezlauus vero, legitimus filius

---

[1] It has been suggested that what lies behind these movements was less a campaign against Pomerania than the conflict between the young princes and their father; see J. Powierski et al., ed., *Studia z dziejów Pomorza w XII wieku* [Studies on the history of Pomerania in the twelfth century] (Słupsk: Polskie Towarzystwo Historyczne, Oddział w Słupsku, 1993), p. 25.

[2] Among these were Wrocław, Cracow, and Sandomierz (as below, ch. 8, p. 135), and probably others such as Gniezno and Poznań as well.

7 THE DIVISION OF THE KINGDOM BETWEEN THE TWO SONS

So after the cathedral of Gniezno had been consecrated and Zbigniew had been pardoned by his father, Duke Władysław entrusted his army to both his sons and sent them on an expedition into Pomerania. They set out, following some unknown plan, but they turned back without finishing the business. Thereupon their father, suspecting I know not what, immediately divided the kingdom between them.[1] Nevertheless he kept the chief seats of the realm in his own hands.[2] However, it would be burdensome for us to detail what fell to each of them in the division, nor would it be greatly profitable for you to hear it.

8 [MORE ON THE DIVISION]

Now when their father was asked by the magnates which of his sons more distinguished himself in sending and receiving embassies, in calling up and levying an army and in the manifold affairs of so great a kingdom, he is said to have replied: As an old and infirm man it is my duty to divide the realm between them and to judge matters for the present.[3] However, to set the one before the other, or to grant them excellence and wisdom, is not something in my power, it belongs to God Almighty. Still, I can reveal to you the one desire of my heart: that after my death I would have you all with one accord obey the one who is wiser and better in defending the land and striking the foe. But in the meantime, let each of them keep the part of the realm as it has been divided between them. When I am gone, Zbigniew, in addition to what he now has, should also have Mazovia; while Bolesław, my legitimate son, should have the principal seats of

---

[3] The division was most likely made in 1099, when Władysław Herman was only 56 years old.

meus, in Wratislaw et in Cracou et in Sudomir sedes regni principales obtineat.[1] Ad extremum autem, si ambo probi non fuerint, vel si forte discordiam habuerint, ille qui exteris nationibus adheserit et eas in regni destruccionem induxerit, privatus regno patrimonii iure careat; ille vero solium regni lege perhenni possideat, qui honori terre melius et utilitati provideat. Facta autem, ut dictum est, regni divisione, habitaque patris luculenta satis oratione,[2] puerorum quisque suam regni porcionem visitavit, eorum vero pater semper in sua Mazouia libentius habitavit.

(9)

Interim ne sit alicui aliquatenus admirandum, si quid scripserimus de Bolezlaui puericia memorandum. Non enim, sicut assolet plerumque lascivia puerilis, ludos inanes sectabatur, sed imitari strennuos actus ac militares, in quantum puer poterat, nitebatur. Et quamvis sit puerorum nobilium in canibus et in volucribus delectari, plus tamen solebat Bolezlauus adhuc puerulus in milicia gratulari. Nondum enim equum ascendere vel descendere suis viribus prevalebat et iam invito patre vel aliquotiens nesciente, super hostes in expeditionem dux militie precedebat.

(10) ZECZECH ET BOLEZLAUS MORAUIAM VASTAVERUNT

Nunc vero quoddam eius initium puerilis militie depingamus et sic paulatim de minoribus ad maiora transcendamus. Sicut notum est, dux Wladislauus, senio gravis et etate, Setheo palatino comiti suum exercitum committebat, eumque pugnaturum vel terras hostium vastaturum delegabat. Unde cum esset Morauiam

---

[1] Judging by the reference in II:17 (p. 151, below), Zbigniew had been granted Greater Poland and perhaps also Kujawia, which he held ca. 1098–1102, and Bolesław (see below, II:13, p. 139) Silesia.

the realm—in Wrocław, in Cracow, and in Sandomierz.[1] But in the last resort, if both of them prove unfit, or if they should happen to fall out with each other, he who sides with foreign nations and brings them in to the destruction of the realm, should be deprived of rule and forfeit his right of inheritance. And let him possess the throne of the kingdom by perpetual right who better provides for the honor and advantage of the land." So the kingdom was divided, as has been told, and the father delivered this quite fine speech,[2] and each of the boys visited his own part of the realm, but their father always preferred to stay in his own Mazovia.

9 [ON BOLESŁAW'S CHILDHOOD]

In the meantime, let no one in any way be surprised if we write something about matters memorable in Bolesław's childhood. For he did not indulge in silly games, the way children usually like to play, but he did his best as much as a boy could to imitate vigorous and martial deeds. And although the sons of the nobles commonly take delight in hounds and hunting-birds, Bolesław, even as a young lad, always had more pleasure in things martial. Even before he was able to mount or get off a horse by himself, he would march against the enemy at the head of knights, against the wishes of his father or at times without his knowledge.

10 SIECIECH AND BOLESŁAW PLUNDER MORAVIA

Now let us depict something of the beginning of his boyhood career as a warrior, and so pass by stages from lesser matters to greater ones. As is known, Duke Władysław, now heavy with age and years, usually entrusted his army to the Count Palatine, Sieciech, and sent him to fight or ravage the lands of the enemy.

---

[2] For *luculenta oratione*, cf. Sallust *Cat.* 31:6 (the orator being Cicero). Micipsa's deathbed speech to his sons (idem *Jug.* 10) also exhibits parallels.

invasurus, ivit cum eo puerulus solo nomine pugnaturus.[1] Illa vice partem Morauie maximam destruxerunt, indeque predam multam et captivos adduxerunt, ac sine belli discrimine vel itineris redierunt.[2]

(11) BOLESLAUS PUER INTERFECIT APRUM

Multa possem de audacia huius pueri scriptitare, nisi tempus iam instaret ad summam operis properare.

> Tamen quoddam in oculto non permittam latitare,
> Cum sit dignum ad exemplum probitatis rutilare.

Quadam vice puer Martis ad gentaculum in silva residens, aprum immanem transeuntem, ac densitatem silve subeuntem, vidit, quem statim de mensa surgens, assumpto venabulo subsecutus, sine comite vel cane presumptuosus invasit. Cumque fere silvestri propinquasset et iam ictum in eius gutture vibrare voluisset, ex adverso quidam miles eius occurrit, qui vibratum ictum retinuit et venabulum ei auferre voluit. Tum vero Boleslauus ira, immo audacia stimulatus, geminum duellum mirabiliter, humanum scilicet et ferinum, singulariter superavit. Nam et illi venabulum abstulit et aprum occidit. Ille vero miles postea, cur hoc fecerit requisitus, se nescivisse, quid egerit, est professus et ob hoc tamen est ab eius gratia longo tempore sequestratus. Ille vero puer inde rediit fatigatus et vix tandem vires obtinuit ventilatus.

---

[1] Or, by pairing the words differently, the Latin could be understood to mean that the boy intended to fight 'only nominally'; cf. Sulpicius Severus, *Vita Sancti Martini* 3: *solo licet nomine militavit.*

So when he was planning a campaign against Moravia the boy went with him to fight—in name alone a boy.[1] On that occasion they wasted the greatest part of Moravia, brought back much plunder and captives, and came home without suffering losses in battle or on the way.[2]

11 AS A BOY BOLESŁAW KILLED A WILD BOAR

I could keep writing much about this intrepid boy, if time were not pressing me to hasten to the main part of the story.

> Yet there is a thing, which cannot rightly be consigned to silence
> For a worthy deed of valor should shine bright for others' guidance.

On one occasion, the son of Mars was in the forest, sitting down to breakfast, when he saw a huge boar crossing his path and disappearing into the dense woods. He immediately left his meal, seized a hunting spear and went after it, boldly rushing in without any companion or hound. He was closing upon the savage creature of the woods and was leveling his spear at its throat, when one of his warriors burst in from the side, blocked the intended blow and tried to wrest the spear from him. Then Bolesław in fury, or rather in boldness, won single-handed an amazing double duel, against the man and against the beast. For he managed both to wrench back the spear and kill the boar. Afterwards, when asked why he did this, the man maintained that he had not known what he was doing; all the same, for a long time he was out of favor with the prince. The boy returned exhausted and only after much fanning did he finally recover his strength.

[2] According to Cosmas, *Chron. Boh.* II:43, p.148, this campaign took place in 1091.

(12)

Aliud quoque factum eius puerile, huic simile non tacebo, quamvis noverim quia emulis non per omnia complacebo. Idem puer cum paucis in silva deambulans, in eminenciori loco forte constitit, ac deorsum huc illucque contemplans, ursum ingentem cum ursa colludere prospexit. Quo viso statim aliis prohibitis in planiciem descendit, ac solus et intrepidus equo sedens cruentas feras adivit, ursumque contra se conversum brachiis erectis venabulo perforavit. Quod factum satis fuit illic astantibus ammirandum, et non videntibus pro tanta audacia pueri recitandum.

(13)

Interea Bolezlauus, Martialis puer, viribus et etate crescebat, nec ut assolet etas puerilis luxui vel vanitatibus intendebat, sed ubicumque hostes predas agere sentiebat, illuc inpiger cum coequevis iuvenibus properabat et plerumque furtim cum paucis terram hostium introibat, villisque combustis captivos et predam adducebat. Iam enim ducatum Wratislauensem puer etate, senex probitate retinebat, necdum tamen militarem gradum attingebat.[1] Unde quia spes in eo iuvenis bone indolis pullulabat iamque magnum in eo glorie signum militaris apparebat, omnes eum principes diligebant, quia futurum in eo magnum aliquid perpendebant.

---

[1] On the significance of knighting, see Zbigniew Dalewski, "The Knighting of Polish Dukes in the Early Middle Ages: Ideological and Political Significance," *APH* 80 (1999): 15–43.

12 [BOLESŁAW KILLS A BEAR]

Another of his boyhood exploits was not dissimilar, and I will not keep silent about it, though I know that there are jealous persons whom I will not in all respects please. The boy was strolling in the woods with a few companions, and they happened to stop on a little rise, and as he looked from above this way and that, he caught sight of a huge male bear playing with a she-bear. At the sight he rushed down to the level, waving his friends back, and alone upon his horse and without fear he approached the bloodthirsty beasts. The male bear turned upon him with its arms raised, but Bolesław ran him through with his spear. Those at hand found this deed quite astounding, and a tale to tell to those who had not seen it, as a example of the boy's enormous courage.

13 [BOLESŁAW ATTACKS ENEMY COUNTRIES]

Meanwhile Bolesław, this boy-Mars, was growing in years and strength. However, he took no interest in luxury and vanities as lads of that age are wont, but whenever he got wind that the enemy were raiding, restless as ever he would rush to the area with his young friends. Then, usually in stealth, he would cross into enemy territory with a few companions, burn down their villages, and carry off captives and plunder. A boy by age, an old man in capability, he already held the duchy of Wrocław, yet he had still not attained the rank of knighthood.[1] So there was great hope in a boy of such good qualities, and clear signs of martial glory were already apparent in him, so that all the magnates held him in great affection, for they sensed there was something great in store for him.

(14)

Idem vero puerulus, Martis prole progenitus, quadam vice super Pomoraniam equitavit, ubi iam evidencius famam sui nominis propalavit. Namque castrum Meczirecze[1] tantis viribus obsedit tantoque impetu assultavit, quod paucis diebus oppidanos dedicionem facere coartavit. Ibi quoque dapifer Woyslauus[2] in vertice tale signum audacie comparavit, quo vix eum extractis ossibus operatio sagax medici liberavit.

(15)

Inde regressus quieti militum aliquantulum indulsit,[3] eosque statim illuc puer laboriosus reduxit. Qui regionem barbarorum subiugare concupiscens, predas agere prius vel incendia facere non conatur, sed eorum municiones vel civitates obtinere vel destruere meditatur. Igitur gressu concito quoddam nobile satis ac forte castrum[4] obsessurus invasit, quod tamen eius primum impetum non evasit. Unde predam multam et captivos egit, bellatores vero sentencie bellice redegit. Et quo magis amari debuit, eo sibi maiorem invidiam cumulavit, et inimicorum insidias ad suum interitum provocavit.

(16)

Interea namque Zetheus multas, ut ferunt, ipsis pueris insidias pretendebat, ac paternum animum ab affectu filiorum multis machinationibus avertebat. In castellis etiam puerorum partibus deputatis aut sui generis, aut inferioris, quibus dominarentur,

---

[1] West of Poznań on the river Obra. It seems the town had been captured by the Pomeranians during the dynastic conflicts of the previous years.

[2] Wojsław, who later became Bolesław's tutor, may have been a relative of Sieciech on the female line. He is regarded as the ancestor of the Powała-Ogończycy kindred. However, his identity with persons of the same name

14 [BOLESŁAW FIGHTS IN POMERANIA]

One time the same young scion of the offspring of Mars was riding against Pomerania, where he broadcast his name and reputation even more clearly. For he besieged the stronghold of Międzyrzecz[1] in such strength and mounted so fierce an attack that he forced the townsmen into surrender after a few days. There, too, the chief steward Wojsław[2] received such a sign of courage on his head that only the skilled ministration of the surgeon removing the bones could free him of it.

15 [WAR IN POMERANIA]

Having returned from there, he indulged in a little rest with his men.[3] Then the tireless lad at once led them back there. As he was eager to subjugate the barbarian region, he wasted no efforts in first burning and plundering, but purposed to seize or destroy their fortifications or cities. He therefore swiftly marched on a quite famous and strong castle,[4] planning to lay siege to it, but it was unable to resist his first assault. He won captives and much plunder from it, and dealt with the fighting men according to the law of war. And yet the more he deserved to be loved, the more he attracted envy, and provoked his enemies to plot his destruction.

16 [SIECIECH'S PLOTTING]

For, as they tell, Sieciech in the meantime was weaving plots against the boys and using all manner of wiles to turn the father's feelings from love of his sons. He even installed his *comites* or bailiffs, either from his own clan or an inferior, to take control

mentioned in sources of the early twelfth century is disputed; see Bieniak, "Polska elita," 2:19–25.

[3] Or: 'he conceded a little rest to his warriors.'

[4] Gumplowicz (Zbigniew, p. 41) suggests this was the castle of Rzecino near Białogard.

comites vel pristaldos preponebat, eosque pueris inobedientes
existere versuta calliditate commovebat. Ambobus siquidem fratribus infestus insidiator existebat, sed magis tamen Bolezlauum,
legitimum et acrem animo,[1] post patrem regnaturum suo infortunio metuebat. Ipsi vero fratres iureiurando se coniunxerant et
inter se signum fecerant, quod si Zetheus eorum alteri machi-
naretur insidias, alter alteri subvenire cum totis viribus suis
nullius more pateretur inducias.[2] Contigit autem, nescio vel
calliditate, vel rei veritate, ducem Wladizlauum Bolezlauo puero
mandavisse se Bohemos in Poloniam intraturos, predam facturos
ab exploratoribus audivisse; quapropter oporteret eum ad locum
citissime determinatum properare et comites sui ducatus, quos
Zetheus prefecerat et in quibus puer nullatenus confidebat, in
auxilium advocare. Puer vero paternis iussionibus credulus ad
locum constitutum cum suis collateralibus festinus, nichilque
dubitans incedebat, sed cum eo tamen comes Woyslauus, cui
commissus erat, non pergebat. Unde unus ad alium in vicem
susurrantes, utpote signum traditionis suspicantes: Non es, inquiunt, sine causa periculi, quod pater tuus te precepit ad locum
solitudinis ambulare et insidiantes vite tue Zethei familiares et
amicos illuc in auxilium advocare. Scimus enim et certi sumus,
quia Zetheus totam tuam progeniem teque maxime nititur, ut
heredem regni, modis omnibus abolere, solusque totam sub
manu sua captam Poloniam retinere. Insuper etiam Woyslauus
comes, cui commissi sumus, qui propinquus est Zetheo, nobis-
cum procul dubio advenisset, ni machinamentum aliquod nobis
fieri cognovisset. Unde necesse est citissime nos consilium
aliquod invenire, quo possimus istud periculum nobis imminens
preterire. Hiis dictis puer Bolezlauus vehementissime metuebat,
totusque sudore et lacrimis manantibus affluebat. Accepto

---

[1] Sallust *Jug.* 7.4: *ut erat impigro atque acri ingenio.*

of the castles in the boys' assigned areas, and by skilful cunning
he encouraged them not to pay heed to the boys. His hostile
plots were in fact directed against both brothers, but most he
feared Bolesław: he was the legitimate heir and a strong personality,[1] and should he become king after his father Sieciech knew
it would be to his misfortune. The brothers, however, had bound
themselves together by oath. They agreed upon a sign, so that if
Sieciech attempted to plot against either of them, the other
would come to his aid with all his forces and suffer no delay or
truce.[2] Now it happened—whether as a trick or because of how
things really stood I do not know—that Duke Władysław sent
word to the boy that he had heard from spies that the Czechs
were about to invade Poland in search of plunder. Bolesław
should therefore hasten with all speed to a specified location and
call to his aid the *comites* of his duchy—appointees of Sieciech
in whom the boy had not the least confidence. The boy, however,
in good faith obeyed his father's orders and hastened to the
designated place with his companions. He had no doubts about
setting out, even though *comes* Wojsław, who had been entrusted
with his care, was not going along. Suspecting in this a sign of
treachery, they whispered one to another: "You have reason to
fear danger. Your father has ordered you to proceed to a lonely
place, and to summon Sieciech's friends and henchmen there to
your aid. But these people have designs on your life. We know,
we are certain that Sieciech will stop at nothing to eliminate your
whole family and you in particular as the heir to the kingdom,
and to seize the whole of Poland and keep it in his hands alone.
What is more, *comes* Wojsław, in whose charge we are entrusted,
is related to Sieciech and would undoubtedly have come with us
had he not discovered that there was some intrigue afoot against
us. So now we must come up very quickly with some idea so we
can get around the danger which threatens us." These words
struck very deep fear into young Bolesław, tears flowed and his
body ran with sweat. A plan was agreed on—one which for

[2] The exact sense is unclear, and the text may be faulty.

itaque convenienti satis consilio secundum ingenium puerile,[1]
velociter ad Zbigneuum, ut ad se cum suis quantotius in auxilium
properaret, cum signo constituto transmiserunt, ipsique statim
ad urbem Wratislauiensem, ne preocuparetur ab insidiatoribus,
emuli[2] redierunt. Regressus[3] igitur puer Bolezlauus inprimis
maiores et seniores civitatis deinde totum populum in con-
cionem advocavit[4] eisque, quas a Zetheo paciebatur insidias ex
ordine sicut puer cum lacrimis enarravit. Illis econtra pre pietate
pueri lacrimantibus et iram indignacionis in Zetheum absentem
verbis ignominiosis iactantibus, Zbigneuus cum paucis, nondum
collecta multitudine, properanter adveniens, orationem fratris,
ut litteratus et maior etate, rethorice coloravit, ac populum
tumultuantem ad fidelitatem fratris et contrarietatem Zethei
luculenta oratione sequenti vehementer animavit:[5] Ni vestre
fidei, cives, stabilitas inviolabilis nostris antecessoribus nobisque, licet parvulis, nota fuisset et experta, nequaquam puerilis
etatis inbecillitas tantis calamitatibus attentata, totque faccionibus inimicorum agitata, totam refugii spem in vobis et
consilii posuisset. Sed notum constat exteris nationibus et
propinquis vos multa perpessos pro insidiis vite nostre machi-
nantibus ab hiis, qui successionem nostri generis nituntur penitus abolere, dominorumque naturalium hereditatem ordine
prepostero distorquere. Quapropter, quia senio iam confectus ge-

---

[1] The more than usually ambiguous phrase *secundum ingenium puerile* is here
taken with the preceding words, as referring to a plan conceived by Bolesław's
young companions (Bolesław himself evidently being in no state to think
clearly). However, others take it as an allusion to the signal agreed upon
'according to the boys' [i.e. the two brothers'] clever design,' or (so Plezia)
together with *velociter*, to mean 'with boyish haste.' Yet another possibility is
that it is a veiled illusion to the fact that because of his good relations with
Břetislav II (see n. 3, below) Bolesław did not wish to fight against the Czechs;
in which case the phrase could simply be translated 'as the boy intended.'

[2] "Equally fast," *emuli* taken to mean lit. '(as) rivals,' 'competing.' Others take
this word with *insidiatoribus*, as referring to (the plotters) 'of [his] enemy.'

[3] According to Cosmas, *Chron. Boh.* III:9, p. 170, Bolesław was Břetislav's
guest at Christmas dinner at Žatec (Saaz) in Bohemia in 1099, and he was made
sword-bearer of his uncle the duke.

young minds was quite well-conceived[1]—and they sent to Zbigniew the agreed signal that he and his men should come to their
aid as soon as possible, and they themselves hurried back equally
fast[2] to the city of Wrocław before the plotters could seize
control of it. So young Bolesław returned,[3] and on arrival called
a meeting, first of the leading townsmen and elders, and then of
the people as a whole.[4] In tears, as a boy would be, he told them
point by point of the plot that Sieciech had set for him. They in
turn wept out of affection for the boy. Angry and indignant, they
cried out against Sieciech, reviling him in his absence. Then
Zbigniew arrived in haste with a small band of followers, not
having had time to gather more. Being older and versed in letters,
he was able to add rhetorical color to his brother's speech, and
now that the people were in uproar, his fine oration roused them
further to protest their loyalty to his brother and opposition to
Sieciech. These were his words.[5] "Citizens, your constant and
unbroken loyalty has been known and proved to our forefathers
and to us as well, young as we are. If it were not so, we would
never have placed in you all our hope for protection and counsel
at this hour. Young and weak, we have been the victims of
terrible events, and find ourselves hard-pressed by enemies on
all sides. But our own people and foreigners alike know full well
how much you have suffered for the plots that are directed
against our lives by persons whose aim it is utterly to abolish the
succession of our kindred and by turning order upside down to
distort the inheritance of natural lords. Our father is old and

[4] Klaus Zernack, *Die burgstädtischen Volksversammlungen bei den Ost- und
Westslawen: Studien zur verfassungsgeschichtlichen Bedeutung des Veče* (Wiesbaden: Harrasowitz, 1967), pp. 249–52, discusses this meeting as the unique
reference to general popular assemblies in early medieval Poland, as an example
of the urban assemblies in Slavic cities, the origin and development of which
is highly debated.

[5] This speech owes much to Sallust, *Cat.* 20, especially the opening words.

nitor noster et infirmitate sibi nobisque vel patrie minus prevalet
providere, necessarium est nos in nostro[a,1] fretos presidio, gladiis
ambitiosorum vel maleficiis interire, vel in exilium fugientes
fines Polonie transilire. Unde vestrum dignemini nobis animum
aperire, si manere liceat, vel de patria nos exire. Ad hec multitudo
tota Wratislauiensium dolore cordis intrinsecus tacta, paulisper
conquievit, erumpensque statim in vocem, intentionem mente
conceptam unanimiter cum affectu pietatis aperuit. Nos quidem,
inquientes, fidem servare volumus domino nostro naturali, patri
vestro, dum vixerit, nec eius soboli deficiemus, quamdiu nobis
flatus vitalis affuerit. Igitur de nobis nullam diffidentiam habe-
tote, sed exercitu congregato ad curiam patris armati properate,
ibique salva reverentia paterna vestram iniuriam vindicate. Que
dum adhuc dicebantur et iureiurando a civibus firmabantur,
Woyslauus comes, qui puerum Bolezlauum nutriebat, de servitio
suo veniebat et que fiebant ignorabat. Qui suspectus prodicionis
ob Zethei consanguinitatem est habitus et civitatem introire
rebusque pueri providere prohibitus. Illo autem satisfaccionem
proferente se, si quid controversie contigerit, nescivisse, satis-
facere volentem,[2] eosque subsequentem, nequaquam pueri tunc
temporis receperunt, sed obviam patri collecta multitudine proc-
esserunt. Igitur dux Wladislauus eiusque filii in loco, qui dicitur
Sarnouecz,[3] seiunctis filiis a patre, cum exercitibus consederunt,
ibique diucius inter se legacionibus altercantes, vix tandem consiliis procerum minisque iuvenum Zetheum dimittere senem
pueri coegerunt. Aiunt etiam patrem ibi filiis iurasse, numquam
se deinceps eum ad honorem pristinum revocare. Ad castrum
itaque sui nominis[4] Zetheo fugiente, ad patrem fratres humiliter

---

[a] nostro Z, vestro *Mal*

---

[1] The reading *vestro* (so Mal.) is less satisfactory, but would perhaps mean 'even
though relying on your help.'

[2] The offer of *satisfactio*, twice referred to in this sentence, suggests some
formal procedure of pardon, explanation, even penance (see Niermeyer, *Lexicon Minus*, s.v. *satisfactio*, p. 940; also below, III:25, p. 276, n. 1).

infirm, and is less able to see to his own needs and ours or to the needs of our country. Thus with no one but ourselves to protect us,[1] we have no chance: either we fall by the swords or the wicked deeds of upstarts, or we flee beyond the borders of Poland into exile. So we beg you, open your hearts to us, tell us your feelings: may we stay, or must we leave our country?" At these words the whole multitude of the people of Wrocław were touched to the heart with grief. For a brief moment they were dumbstruck, then at once they burst into speech and with one accord revealed the thoughts that rose in their minds along with their feelings of loyalty. "We indeed intend to keep our faith to our natural lord," they declared, "to your father while he lives, nor will we fail his children as long as we draw breath. So have no lack of faith in us. Gather a force, take arms, hasten to your father's court, and there—with all due respect for your father—get satisfaction for the injury you have suffered." The townsmen were still speaking and protesting their loyalties on oath, when *comes* Wojsław, who was bringing up the boy Bolesław, arrived from his service and was unaware of what was going on. But as he was related to Sieciech, he was suspected of treachery and kept from entering the city and attending to the boy's needs. He insisted he could set their minds at rest, and that if there had been a falling out he had been unaware of it. He kept following them and asking for pardon,[2] but at that point the boys would not have anything to do with him, but gathered troops and set out to confront their father. Their armies met at a place called Żarnowiec,[3] Duke Władysław and his sons camping separately. Protracted wrangling through envoys from both sides followed, but in the end, with the counsel of the magnates and the threats of the young men, the boys managed to force the old man to dismiss Sieciech. They say the father even took an oath never again to recall him to his former position of honor. Then Sieciech fled towards the fortress that bore his name,[4] and the brothers went to the father

[3] North of Cracow.

[4] Sieciechów; see n. 1, p. 130 above.

inermes et pacifici perrexerunt, eique non ut domini, sed ut
milites vel servi suum obsequium pronis mentibus et cervicibus
obtulerunt. Sicque pater et filii cunctique proceres couniti,
Zetheum fugientem ad castellum, quod fecerat, cum toto exercitu sunt secuti. Quem dum persequi et extra terram expellere
conarentur, ipse dux noctu, cum lectulo suo requiescere putaretur, nemine suorum conscio, cum tribus exceptis familiaribus
exercitum latenter exiens, ad Zetheum ex altera parte Wysle
fluminis cum navicula transmeavit. Unde cuncti proceres indignati asserebant, quia deserere filios totque principes cum exercitu
non sapientis, sed consilium delirantis, statimque facto consilio
decreverunt, quatenus Bolezlauus Sudomir et Cracow, sedes
regni principales et proximas, occuparet, easque fidelitate recepta in dominium possideret; Zbigneuus autem contra Mazouiam properaret et urbem Plocensem illamque plagam
contiguam obtineret. Bolezlauus quidem sedes predictas occupavit et tenuit, Zbigneuus vero, preventus a patre, suum ceptum
explicare non potuit. Sed quid tam diu finalem causam Zethei
faccionis prolongamus; si labores singulos et dissensiones Zethei
describamus, gesta Zethei procul dubio Iugurtino volumini co-
equamus.[1] Et ne tamen insulsi vel desidiosi videamur, ceptum
iter adhuc aliquantulum gradiamur. Item alio tempore pueri
principes et exercitum asciverunt et contra Plocensem urbem ex
altera parte Wysle fluminis castra militie posuerunt; ubi etiam
Martinus archiepiscopus,[2] senex fidelis, magno labore magnaque
cautela iram et discordiam inter patrem et filios mitigavit. Ibi
quoque dux Wladislauus, ut aiunt, iureiurando se Zetheum re-
tenturum numquam amplius confirmavit. Tunc Bolezlauus patri
sedes occupatas restituit, nec pater cum filiis paccionem factam
obtinuit. Ad extremum in tantum senem pueri coegerunt, quod
Zetheum de Polonia propellendo suum desiderium im-

---

[1] This is the author's only explicit allusion to Sallust, although textual and
stylistic borrowings from this classical writer are extensive throughout the
work. See also p. xxxviii, n. 59.

[2] Martin of Gniezno seems to have mediated both between the young dukes
themselves and between them and their father. However, it may be that he

humbly, unarmed and in peace, and not as lords but as his knights or servants offered their obedience with bowed necks and meek hearts. So the father and his sons and all the magnates united pursued Sieciech with their whole army as he fled to the castle he had built. As they were pursuing him and doing their best to drive him from the land, the duke himself slipped out of the camp at night when he was believed to be sleeping in his bed, and without the knowledge of his entourage, boarded a small boat with only three close retainers and crossed to Sieciech on the other side of the Vistula. At this the magnates were outraged. It was not the action of a wise person, they said, it was the decision of a madman to forsake his sons and all the nobles as well as the army. They called a council on the spot and decreed that Bolesław was to seize Sandomierz and Cracow, the nearest main seats of the kingdom, extract assurances of their loyalty, and rule them as lord, while Zbigniew was to hasten against Mazovia and secure Płock and the adjoining region. Bolesław did in fact seize and hold the aforesaid cities, but Zbigniew failed in his mission as his father got there first. But why draw out excessively the end of the case of Sieciech's faction? For if I were to describe every single trouble and dissension he caused, the history of Sieciech would undoubtedly be as long as the book on Jugurtha.[1] Nevertheless, lest we appear inept or idle, let us proceed a little further on the journey we have undertaken. On another occasion, the boys gathered the army and the princes and set up an armed camp before Płock on the other side of the river Vistula. There the loyal old man, Archbishop Martin,[2] with great pains and tact diffused the anger and discord between the father and the sons. This time, too, they say, Duke Władysław affirmed on oath that he would never more retain Sieciech. Then Bolesław restored to his father the cities he had occupied, but the father did not observe the agreement made with the sons. Finally the boys pressured the old man to the point that they fulfilled their wishes

favored Zbigniew, which would explain his later incarceration by Bolesław (below, II:38, p. 189); see *PSB* 19:557-8.

pleverunt.[1] Qualiter autem hoc contigerit, vel qualiter de exilio redierit, prolixum et tediosum est edocere, sed hoc dixisse sufficiat, quia postea non sibi licuit ullum dominium exercere.

(17)

Hactenus de Zetheo et regina[2] dixisse sufficiat, nunc vero penna temperata de puero Marti dedito cepte studium intentionis proficiat. Hiis ita peractis, ecce nuntiatum est eis Pomoranos exivisse, eosque contra Zutok,[3] regni custodiam et clavem castrum oppositum erexisse. Erat enim castrum novum ita altum et ita proximum christianis, quod ea, que dicebantur et fiebant in Zutok et audiri et videri bene poterant a paganis. Igitur Zbigneuus, quoniam etate maior erat, partemque regni Pomoranis patrique proximam retinebat, cum exercitu patris atque suo contra Pomoranos sine fratre parvulo properavit, minusque tamen laudis maior cum multis antecedens, quam iunior frater cum paucis subsequens, acquisivit. Nam maior illuc properans neque castrum illud novum viriliter assultavit, nec hostes cum tanta multitudine in prelium irritavit, sed timens inde magis quam timendus, ut aiunt, ad propria remeavit. At puer Bolezlauus, Martis filius, fratre maiore discedente, ut advenit, quamvis nondum cinctus gladio, plus preripiens,[a,4] quam frater maior tenens gladium, ibi fecit.

Nam et pontem invadendo castellanis abstulit
Et in portam persequendo suos enses intulit.[5]

[a] preripiens *Mal*, precipiens *Z H*

---

[1] Sieciech was expelled in 1100.

[2] On the queen's possible implication in Sieciech's regime, see above, n. 5, p. 125.

[3] At the confluence of the Warta and the Noteć. See Albert Brackmann, ed., *Zantoch, eine Burg im deutschen Osten* (Leipzig: Hirzel, 1936).

[4] It is unclear how Bolesław did so, as neither the readings of the Latin MSS nor the edition yield much sense. Note also how, characteristically, the author has made no previous mention of Zbigniew's knighting.

of expelling Sieciech from Poland.[1] But how this came about, and how he returned from exile, would be long and tiresome to explain; suffice it to say that thereafter he was no longer allowed to exercise any authority.

17 [ON THE FORT OF THE POMERANIANS DESTROYED BY THEIR OWN HAND]

Enough, then, on the subject of Sieciech and the queen;[2] let our poised pen proceed with the story we intended about the boy devoted to Mars. After these events had thus transpired, suddenly news came to them that the Pomeranians had burst out and had raised a castle opposite Santok,[3] the linchpin in the country's defenses. This new fort was so high and so close to the Christians that the pagans could quite easily see and hear anything that was been done or said in Santok. So Zbigniew, being the elder and the one who held the part of the kingdom closest to the Pomeranians and to his father, hastened with his and his fathers' army against the Pomeranians, without his young brother. However, though he went ahead with a large force he won less praise than his younger brother who came after with fewer forces. For instead of resolutely attacking the newly constructed castle when he arrived, the older brother avoided provoking the enemy to battle, in spite of his superior forces. He returned to his own lands, as they say, more fearing than feared. But young Bolesław, the son of Mars, arriving after his brother's departure, though not yet girded with the sword, achieved more[4] than his brother who had been girded.

> For he stormed the bridge and took it from the garrison on wait
> And he turned his swords against them as he chased them through the gate.[5]

[5] Some understand the Latin as describing another act of "gate-striking" (compare I:7, p. 43), a possible, but not necessary interpretation.

Hoc initium militie Bolezlaui magnum future probitatis indicium extitit christianis, magnumque signum sue destructionis,
magnum terrorem intulit ipsis etiam Pomoranis. Zbigneo autem
cum multitudine venienti, nichilque virile facienti, insultantes
ignaviam ascribebant, Bolezlauum vero cum paucis postea venientem et audacter suos hostes usque ad portas invadentem, lupi
filium appellabant. Zbigneus, inquientes, debet ut clericus ecclesiam gubernare,[1] istum vero decet puerulum, ut apparet, stren-
nuis actibus militare. Sicque iunior frater cum paucis paulatim
incedens plus honoris et laudis acquisivit, quam maior, qui cum
magno impetu et cum magna multitudine properavit. Videntes
igitur pagani puerum, quia paucos habebat, revertentem,
metuentes interitum, si cum multis redierit, imminentem, castellum suum, quod fecerant, ipsimet destruxerunt, cassoque
labore securitatis latibula pecierunt.

(18)

Videns igitur Wladizlauus, quia puer etate florebat, gestisque
militaribus prepollebat, cunctisque regni sapientibus complacebat, eum accingi gladio in assumptione sancte Marie[2] disposuit,
apparatumque magnificum in civitate Plocensi preparavit. Iam
enim etate et infirmitate continua senescebat et in illo puero
successionis fidutiam expectabat. Dum se cuncti prepararent et
ad festum properarent nunciatum est Pomoranos Zutok castrum
obsedisse, nec audebat quisquam eis de principibus contraire.
Igitur invito patre multisque prohibentibus puer Martis illuc
irruens de Pomoranis triumphavit, sicque rediens armiger victor,
a patre gladio precinctus cum ingenti tripudio[3] sollempnitatem
celebravit. Neque solus illa die balteo militari cinctus fuit, sed ob
amorem et honorem filii multis pater coetaneis arma dedit.

[1] For the notion that Zbigniew had been ordained, see p. 123, n. 6 above.
[2] 15 August, 1100.
[3] Or perhaps: 'a great war dance.' On the significance of knighting, see
Dalewski, "Knighting," as p. 138, n. 1, above.

This first campaign of Bolesław's was a great indication to the Christians of his future valor, and also to the Pomeranians a clear sign of their own destruction, and it struck great terror into them. When Zbigniew had come with a large force and took no manly initiative they jeered and called it cowardice, but when Bolesław arrived subsequently with a few men and fought his foes boldly up to their gates, they nicknamed him "the wolf's son." Zbigniew, they remarked, should rather as a cleric be in charge of a church,[1] but this young lad, it seems, is cut out for valiant deeds of arms. So the younger brother, advancing steadily with a few knights, acquired more respect and praise than his elder brother who hastened there with large numbers and great show. So when the pagans saw the boy retiring (for his forces were limited), fearing that their end was in sight if he came back with more, they themselves pulled down the castle they had constructed and, their labor wasted, returned to the security of their hiding-places.

18 [ON THE KNIGHTING OF BOLESŁAW]

Władysław, seeing that the boy was in the prime of his life and had a special gift for soldiering, and that he had won the approval of all the wise men of the kingdom, decided that he should be girded with the sword on the feast of the Assumption of Saint Mary,[2] and prepared a great celebration in the city of Płock. For he was now old and in constant ill-health, and placed in the boy his hope for the succession. But while everyone made ready and hurried to the celebrations, news came that the Pomeranians had laid siege to the castle of Santok and none of the princes dared to march against them. So against his father's wishes and in spite of protests from many others the boy Mars sped to that place, and there he triumphed over the Pomeranians. Returning as a victorious esquire, he was girded with the sword by his father and celebrated the festivity with great joy.[3] Nor was he the only one that day to receive the sword-belt of knighthood, but out of love and honor for his son the father gave arms to many of his young companions.

(19)

Bolezlauo itaque milite noviter constituto, *in* Plaucis Deus *reve-lavit*,[1] quanta per eum operari debeat in futuro. Contigit namque noviter eo militari balteo precincto, Plaucos in unum innumer-abiles convenisse, seseque more solito per Poloniam discursuros, in partes seiunctos tres vel IIII[or] ab invicem remotius Wyslam fluvium nocturno tempore natavisse. Qui sequentis diei diluculo cursu rapido discurrentes et predam innumerabilem capientes, onerati spoliis circa vesperam ultra retro fluvium redierunt, ibique securi ac fatigati nocturne quietis tuguria posuerunt; sed non ita securi quieverunt, sicut antiquitus sueverunt. Namque Deus, christianorum conservator, sueque vigilie vindicator, paucorum fidelium audaciam in multorum perniciem paganorum suscitavit, quibus irruentibus dominice diei in gloria *sue potencie brachio* triumphavit.[2] Ex eo tempore Plauci adeo sunt stupefacti, quod regnante Bolezlauo videre Poloniam non sunt ausi.

(20)

Contigit quoque quoddam a quodam fieri verbum in militaris consilio cinccionis, quod dignum est inseri nostre titulo inten-tionis. Domine dux, inquit ille quidam, Wladislaue, pius Deus hodie regnum Polonie visitavit, tuamque senectutem et infirmi-tatem totamque patriam per hunc hodie factum militem exalta-vit. Beata mater, que talem puerum educavit. Usque modo Polonia fuit ab hostibus conculcata, sed per istum puerulum erit ut antiquitus restaurata. Ad hec verba omnes, qui aderant, stu-puerunt et, ut sileret pro reverencia ducis innuerunt. Nos tamen non credimus hoc verbum de vanitate processise, sed *prophecie spiritu*[3] advenisse, quia iam in factis eius puerilibus compro-

---

[1] Rom. 1:17. For the Cumans see above p. 44, n. 1.

[2] Isa. 62:8, Gps 88:11, Luke 1:51, etc. Gumplowicz (Zbigniew, p. 47) dates the victory to a Sunday in the fall of 1101.

[3] Rev. 19:10.

19 [ON THE VICTORY OVER THE CUMANS]

So Bolesław had just been made a knight when God *revealed in the case of* the Cumans what great exploits He was to perform through him in the future.[1] For it came about when he had just been girded with the swordbelt of knighthood that vast numbers of Cumans assembled, planning in their wonted manner to raid Poland. Dividing into three or four groups they swam by night across the Vistula at quite separate points, and at the break of the next day broke off in different directions. Moving at speed, they seized booty beyond measure, and around evening returned laden with their spoils to the other side of the river. There, tired but feeling safe, they put up their huts for a night of rest. But it was not to be the safe rest they were used to from days of old. For God, protector of Christians and avenger of His vigil, roused the courage of a few of the faithful to the destruction of a vast number of pagans, and triumphed as they fell upon them in the glory of the Lord's day and *in might of His arm*.[2] From that time forth the Cumans were struck with awe and did not dare to set eyes on Poland again during Bolesław's reign.

20 [PROPHECIES ABOUT BOLESŁAW]

It also happened at the council of the knightly girding that something was said by a certain person which deserves to be included in the text of our work. "My lord Duke Władysław," said that certain person, "today the good Lord has visited the kingdom of Poland, and has exalted your old age and your infirmity and our whole country by his knighting today. Blessed is the mother who raised such a son. Until now Poland was trodden down by her enemies, but this young lad will restore her as she was in times of old." Everyone present was struck with amazement at these words, and signaled to him out of respect for the duke to hold his tongue. But we do not believe that these words were uttered idly, but from *the spirit of prophecy*,[3] for

batur, quod Polonia quandoque per eum *in statum pristinum*[1] restauratur.

(21)

Sed ad presens se puer aliquantulum a labore reficiat, dum ducem Wladizlauum pium et mansuetum virum, in pace nostra penna sepeliat. Dux igitur Wladizlauus pristine sedicionis reminiscens, quoniam Zetheum de Polonia profugavit, quamvis etate debilis et infirmitate fuerit, nullum tamen in curia sua palatinum vel palatini vicarium prefecit. Omnia namque per se ipsum vel suo consilio sagaciter ordinabat, vel cuilibet comiti, cuius provinciam visitabat, curie responsionem et sollicitudinem commendabat. Et sic per se patriam sine palatino comite rexit, donec spiritus eius corporea mole solutus, ad locum debite mansionis perrexit, eternaliter permansurus. Mortuus est ergo dux Wladizlaus etate plenus et infirmitate longa detentus,[2] cuius exequias quinque diebus in urbe Plocensi cum capellanis celebrando, Martinus archiepiscopus expectando filios sepelire non est ausus. Advenientes autem ambo fratres, adhuc insepulto patre magnum inter se pene de divisione thesaurorum et regni discidium habuerunt, sed divina gratia inspirante et archiepiscopo sene fideli mediante, preceptum viventis in presencia mortui tenuerunt. Wladislao igitur duce in ecclesia Plocensi honorifice satis ac magnifice tumulato, thesaurorumque patris inter filios facta divisione regnoque Polonie vivente patre designato, sortem uterque sue divisionis habuit, Bolezlauus tamen legitimus duas sedes regni principales[3] partemque terre populosiorem obtinuit. Puer autem Bolezlauus adepta parte patrimonii, militibus et consilio confor-

---

[1] 2 Chron. 24:13.
[2] On 4 June 1102.

already the exploits of his boyhood proved that Poland would one day be restored by him *to her pristine state*.[1]

21 [ON THE DEATH OF WŁADYSŁAW]

But for the moment let the boy take some rest from his labors, while our pen brings Duke Władysław, that good and gentle man, to his grave in peace. For the duke, mindful of the earlier uprising, since he had banished Sieciech from Poland, would not appoint a palatine or vice-palatine to his court, even though he was now weak with age and ill-health. Instead, he either made wise provision for everything personally or by his council, or gave over the care and responsibility for his court to some *comes* whose province he was visiting. Thus he ruled his country alone without any count palatine, until his spirit was set free from the burden of his body, and passed on to its deserved dwelling-place, there to abide for eternity. So Duke Władysław died in the fullness of age and after a long illness.[2] And for five days Archbishop Martin with the chaplains celebrated the funeral rites in the city of Płock, not daring to bury him because he was waiting for the sons. When they came, before their father was even in his grave a bitter quarrel nearly broke out between the two brothers about the division of the treasury and the kingdom. But by grace of God and the faithful old archbishop's mediation, they kept the instructions their father had given in life while he lay dead before them. So Duke Władysław was laid to rest with great pomp and honor in the church of Płock, and the king's treasury was divided between his sons, and each received his portion of the kingdom of Poland that their father had assigned them while alive. However, Bolesław as the legitimate son kept the two principal seats of the kingdom[3] and the more populous part of the land. Now that he had his share of the patrimony and supported by his council and knights, the young Bolesław set

---

[3] Presumably Cracow and Sandomierz, as he already held Wrocław.

tatus, cepit animi virtutem viresque corporis exercere, cepitque fama simul et etate iuvenis bone indolis adolescere.[a]

(22) BOLESLAUS EXPUGNAT ALBAM URBEM REGIAM

Novus igitur nova bella miles incipit renovare, hostesque suos cogitat acrius et frequentius provocare. Convocata itaque multitudine bellatorum cum paucis electis penetravit meditullium patrie paganorum. Cumque ad urbem regiam et egregiam, Albam nomine,[1] pervenisset, neque partem terciam sui exercitus habuisset, equo descendens, nullum instrumentum expugnandi vel machinamentum adaptavit, sed violenter ac mirabiliter urbem opulentam et populosam die qua venerat expugnavit. Dicunt etiam quidam eum primum omnium invasisse, eumque primum propugnacula conscendisse. Ex quo facto terribilis per nimium extitit Pomoranis, suisque laudabilis et amabilis omnibus christianis. De civitate autem predam innumerabilem asportavit, munitionem vero planitiei coequavit.

(23)

Sed pretermissis pluribus suo loco retractandis, de nupciis referamus eiusque donis Bolezlaui magni regis muneribus comparandis.[2] Quatenus autem hoc a Paschali papa secundo[3] concessum fuerit, quod nuptias istas de consanguinitate licuerit, Balduinus Cracouiensis episcopus,[4] ab eodem papa Rome consecratus, fidei

---

[a] adolere *Z H Mal*

---

[1] Białogard (in Polish Białogród), near the river Parsęta, which may have been a kind of cultic centre of Pomerania, or at least of a part of it. This otherwise unusual Latin place-name may have been influenced by the Hungarian Alba Regia (Fehérvár).

about developing his courage and his bodily strength, and in repute and years began to grow into a youth of fine character.

22 BOLESŁAW STORMS THE ROYAL CITY OF ALBA

So the new knight began to launch new campaigns, and planned to challenge his foes harder and more often. So he called together a large number of fighters and with a chosen few penetrated into the very heartland of the pagans. Reaching their great royal city named Alba[1] with not even a third of his army, he dismounted from his horse and without setting up any siege engines or equipment, in a wondrous way he stormed that rich and populous city on the very same day as he arrived. Some even say that he was at the forefront of the assault and the first to scale the battlements. Through this exploit he became exceedingly dreaded by the Pomeranians, but praised by his men and loved among all Christians. He took away booty beyond reckoning from the city and leveled its defenses to the earth.

23 [ON THE WEDDING OF BOLESŁAW]

But let us now leave aside a number of events which will be recounted in their due place, and let us tell of his wedding and the gifts and presents which bear comparison with those of King Bolesław the Great.[2] Now in order that Pope Pascal the Second[3] might grant a dispensation to allow the marriage in view of the closeness of kinship, Bishop Baldwin of Cracow,[4] who had been consecrated by the same pope in Rome, drew attention to the

[2] On 25 March 1103 Bolesław married Zbysława, the daughter of Sviatopolk, grand prince of Kiev (1093–1113).

[3] 1099–1118. As Sviatopolk's father, Iziaslav, had married the sister of Casimir the Restorer, the bride was related to Bolesław in the third degree, and hence canonical exemption was necessary.

[4] 1102/3–9.

ruditatem et patrie necessitatem intimavit,[1] sicque Romane sedis
auctoritas, ut fertur, hoc coniugium misericorditer, non canonice nec usualiter, sed singulariter collaudavit. Nos autem de
peccato tractare vel iustitia materiam non habemus, sed res gestas
regum ducumque Polonie sermone tenui[2] recitamus. Octo
siquidem diebus ante nuptias totidemque post nupciarum oc-
tavas belliger Bolezlauus dare munera non quievit, aliis scilicet
renones et pelles palliis coopertas et aurifrisiis delimbatas, principibus pallia, vasa aurea et argentea, aliis civitates et castella, aliis
villas et predia.

(24)

Interea Zbigneuus frater eius, qui vocatus ad nuptias fratris
venire refutavit, cum Pomoranis et Bohemis amicitias federavit
et dum nuptie fierent, ut ferunt, intrare Poloniam Bohemos
animavit.[3] Qui Bohemi per provinciam Wratislauiensem discurrentes et predas captivosque colligentes et incendia facientes,
pluribus annis dampnum illi regioni nocuum[a] intulerunt. Quo
audito inpiger[4] Bolezlauus, licet magis de violata fraternitate,
quam de regni depopulatione doluerit, misit tamen legationem
fratri, cur hoc sibi fecerit, vel in quibus eum offenderit. Zbigneus
contra se tale quid nescivisse respondebat, seque innoxium talis
flagitii quibusdam circumlocucionibus asserebat. Cumque
Bolezlauus assidue cum hostibus et Bohemis et Pomoranis dimi-
caret, sueque divisionis porcionem ab invasoribus viriliter expug-
naret, Zbigneuus fratri suo laboranti nec invitatus auxilium

---

[a] et nocuum *Mal*

---

[1] The implication seems to be that the papacy—mildly disapproved of by our
author—was moved to grant dispensation by two arguments: on the one hand,
the slow progress of Christianisation of the realm, and on the other, the need
for a diplomatic tie to neighboring Rus'.

[2] Vergil uses this word to describe the modest style of his eclogues (*Ecl.* 1:2,
6:8).

primitive state of the Faith and pressing needs of his homeland,[1] so that, as they say, the authority of the Holy See gave its blessing to this marriage compassionately, as an exception, according neither to canon law nor custom. It is not our brief to discuss the question of sin or justice but to narrate in our lowly[2] style the exploits of the kings and dukes of Poland. So for eight days before the wedding and as many after the octave of the wedding the warlike Bolesław did not cease handing out gifts, to some pelts and cloaks lined with furs and worked with orphrey, to the magnates mantels and gold and silver vessels, to some cities and castles, to others villages and estates.

24 [ON THE PLOTTINGS OF ZBIGNIEW]

Meanwhile his brother Zbigniew, who had been invited to the wedding but had refused to attend, allied himself with the Pomeranians and Czechs, and, as they say, encouraged the Czechs to march into Poland while the nuptials were being celebrated.[3] The Czechs overran the province of Wrocław, looting, burning and rounding up captives, and causing grievous damage to the region for many years to come. On hearing this Bolesław, energetic as ever,[4] and more distressed for the violation of brotherly ties than the wasting of the country, nevertheless sent an embassy to his brother asking why he had acted so or in what way he had caused him offence. However Zbigniew in reply denied any knowledge of such things, asserting in a roundabout way that he was blameless of such wrong-doing. Indeed, while Bolesław was fighting without cease against his foes, both the Czechs and the Pomeranians, battling valiantly to reclaim his part of the kingdom from the invaders, Zbigniew even when invited never lent a hand to

[3] Cosmas, *Chron. Boh.* III:16, p.179, mentions this campaign, probably of 1103 (Gumplowicz, Zbigniew, p. 47).

[4] Here as elsewhere (e.g. Book II, chs. 14; 24; 28; 29; 32; 44; Book III, chs. 1; 4; 17; 24) the author applies the adjective *inpiger* 'active, energetic, restless' to Bolesław as an *epitheton ornans* in the classical manner. In other cases *belliger*, 'the warlike,' is added to his name in a similar way.

impendebat, insuper etiam cum hostibus fratris occulte fedus et amiciciam coniungebat et pecuniam illis pro militibus in subsidium transmittebat. Et cum frequenter eum belliger Bolezlauus et legatis et colloquiis conveniret, fraterna karitate commonendo, ne familiaritatem et amicitiam cum hostibus paterne hereditatis palam vel clanculo iniret, unde magnum regno Polonie discidium eveniret, ille econtra sapienter et pacifice respondebat et sic fratris iram et principum invidiam temperabat. Sed de hoc plenius in alio loco subsequenter disseramus et interim gestis Bolezlaui militaribus alludamus.

(25) POLONI VASTAVERUNT MORAUIAM

Igitur belliger Bolezlauus, iniurie Bohemorum vindicator, tres acies militum in Morauiam transmisit, qui in ipsa ebdomada dominice resurrectionis[1] euntes et predam et incendia facientes, dignam pene suis factis recompensationem invenerunt, quia tante sollempnitatis reverenciam infregerunt. Nam Suantopolc[2] dux Morauiensis cum acri militum acie persecutus est eos, cum redirent, et abstulisset eis predam, ut aiunt, ni cum ea pedites anteirent. Videntes autem Poloni Morauienses ad bellum preparatos fiducialiter propinquare, non cogitant in fuga sed in armis suam fiduciam collocare. Igitur utrimque bellum acerrimum inchoatur, quod non sine dampno gravissimo partibus singulis terminatur. In primo namque conflictu Suatopolc, dux Morauiensis, sicut aper molosis[3] indagatus, scilicet undique curvo dente percuciens, alios perimit, aliis viscera fundit, nec prius gradum figit, vel facere dampnum desistit, donec venator anhelus cum alia turba canum suis laborantibus occurrit. Sic primum Suatopolc Polonos onustos preda circumflexo tramite precedens

---

[1] 22–28 March 1103.

[2] Prince of Olomouc 1090–1107, duke of Bohemia 1107–9.

help his hard-pressed brother, but actually concluded a secret treaty of friendship with his brother's enemies and sent them money to help them pay troops. Warlike Bolesław treated with him frequently through embassies or parleys, urging him out of brotherly affection not to have dealings or to keep friendship either secretly or openly with the foes of their father's legacy, which would cause great dissension in the kingdom of Poland. But his brother would reply with well-chosen and conciliatory words, and so mollified his brother's anger as well as the ill-will of the magnates. But let us discuss this more fully at a subsequent point, and in the meantime make mention of Bolesław's martial exploits.

25 THE POLES PILLAGED MORAVIA

So the warlike Bolesław, avenger of the wrongs done by the Czechs, sent three units of troops into Moravia. They marched in during the very week of the Lord's resurrection,[1] burning and looting, and nearly earned just retribution for their actions in infringing the reverence due to such a solemn festival. For the duke of Moravia, Svatopluk,[2] pursued them with a unit of keen warriors as they were returning and, they say, would have taken their plunder off them had the foot-soldiers not been marching in front with it. Seeing the Moravians approaching confidently and ready for battle, the Poles did not consider trusting to flight but placed their confidence in their arms. So battle was joined most fiercely on both sides, and only ended when both sides had suffered the most severe losses. For in the first fray Svatopluk fought like a boar beset by Molossian hounds,[3] lashing on all sides with its curved tusks, slaying some and slashing open the guts of others, and not staying his steps or ceasing to wreak havoc until the breathless hunter raced up with another pack of hounds to help the sorely beset ones. So at the outset Svatopluk

[3] Molossian hounds are quite frequently mentioned in classical literature, e.g. Vergil, *Georg.* 3.405; Lucretius, *De rerum nat.* 5.1063.

pene triumphaliter oppressisset, ni militaris acies totis viribus glomerata iram instantis pariter et audaciam repressisset. Tunc quidem tinnitus de galeis percussis per concava montium condensaque silvarum resonant. Ignis scintille de ferro per aera micant, haste clipeis collise crepant, pectora scinduntur, manus et cervices corporaque truncata per campum palpitant. Ibi campus martialis, ibi fortuna ludit.[1] Ad extremum adeo sunt utrimque fatigati et in dampno peremptorum militum coequati, quod nec Morauienses letam victoriam habuerunt, nec Poloni notam infamie incurrerunt.[2] Ibi quoque Zelislauus comes manum, qua clipeo corpus tegebat, amisit, quam amissam statim viriliter abscisorem interimens vindicavit. Dux vero Bolezlauus ob honorem sibi pro carnea manum auream restauravit.[3]

(26)

Item ipse Morauiam intravit, sed cunctis rusticis audita fama in municionibus cum preda receptis, licet Bohemis et Morauiensibus congregatis, incendio maiori, quam alio dampno ibi facto, tamen inpugnatus remeavit, in quo facto tamen difficultate rei perpensa non parvam gloriam acquisivit. Nam de parte Polonie Morauia arduitate moncium ac densitate silvarum adeo est obstrusa, quod et pacificis viatoribus itinera ac peditibus expeditis[4] periculosa videntur ac per nimium onerosa. Ipsi etiam Morauienses adventum eius longe ante prescientes, non sunt ausi cum

---

[1] Cf. Statius *Theb.* 12.35. On the role of "chance" in battle, see Hans F. Haefele, *Fortuna Heinrici IV. imperatoris: Untersuchungen zur Lebensbeschreibung des dritten Saliers* (Vienna: Institut für Österreichische Geschichtsforschung 1954), pp. 49–86.

[2] Cf. Cosmas, *Chron. Boh.* III:16, p. 179.

[3] We know nothing of Żelisław from other sources. On the complex symbolic meaning of this reward, the problem of the handicapped warrior, and the significance of the hand in heroic narratives, see Jacek Banaszkiewicz, "Złota

overtook the plunder-laden Poles by a circuitous path and nearly crushed them triumphantly, had the unit of warriors not gathered their whole strength together and withstood the attacker's fury and boldness. The din of blows on helmets rang through the mountain passes and the depths of the forests, fiery sparks flew through the air from metal, spears crashed and clattered on shields, chests were pierced open, severed arms and necks and bodies quivered upon the field. That was the field of Mars—the playground of Fortune![1] In the end both sides were so exhausted and so equal in the number of slain warriors that neither could the Moravians rejoice in victory nor could the Poles be accused of having suffered disgrace.[2] In the battle *Comes* Żelisław had his shield-holding hand cut off but immediately avenged the loss by manfully striking down his maimer. To honor him Duke Bolesław gave him a golden hand in place of the one of flesh he had lost.[3]

26 [BOLESŁAW WASTES MORAVIA]

Then Bolesław himself entered Moravia. But on hearing the news the peasants all retreated behind their fortifications with their cattle, and although the Czechs and the Moravians gathered their forces, Bolesław retired without fighting, causing more damage by fire than otherwise. Yet considering the difficulty of the undertaking, he acquired not a little glory from this. For Moravia is walled with such high mountains and thick forests on the Polish side that the roads are regarded as dangerous and very difficult even for peaceful travelers or light-armed foot-soldiers.[4] Yet the Moravians, though they knew well in advance of his

ręka komesa Żelisława" [The golden hand of *comes* Żelisław], in *Imagines potestatis: Rytuały, symbole i konteksty fabularne władzy zwierzchniej, Polska X–XV w.* [*Imagines potestatis*: rituals, symbols and narrative contexts of supreme power—Poland, the tenth to the fifteenth centuries], ed. Jacek Banaszkiewicz (Warsaw: PAN, 1994), pp. 228–48.

[4] Or: 'people on foot with little baggage.'

eo prelium campestre committere, nec in itineris difficultate
saltem insidiis intranti vel exeunti resistere.[1]

(27)

Eo itaque de Morauia satis glorianter redeunte, Romane sedis
legatus Walo nomine, Beluacensis episcopus,[2] Poloniam advenit,
qui cum virtute Bolezlaui, zelo iustitie tantum canonice district-
cionis rigorem exercuit, quod duos episcopos ibi nullo vel prece
vel pretio subveniente deposuit.[3] Sedis itaque Romane legato
reverenter honorato, concilioque canonice celebrato, missus
apostolica data benedictione, Romam rediit, belliger vero
Bolezlauus hostes suos inpugnaturus adiit.

(28)

Igitur in Glogou[4] exercitu convocato, nullum peditem, sed
milites tantum electos, equosque precipuos duxit secum; nec
eundo per deserta die noctuque labori vel esuriei continuis quinque diebus sufficienter indulsit. Sexta die tandem sextaque feria
communicati sunt eucharistia, refecti pariter victu corporeo,
Cholbreg veniunt ductu sidereo.[5] Precedenti nocte Bolezlauus

---

[1] The date of this expedition is debated. Gumplowicz, Zbigniew, p. 52, argues
for 1104, while on the other hand Cosmas, *Chron. Boh.* III:16, p. 178, records
a Czech campaign in Silesia in April 1103 that may be related to the present
conflict.

[2] 1100–4. The date of this legatine mission is debated, but was most likely
April-May 1103; see T. de Morembert, ed., *Dictionnaire d'histoire et de géo-
graphie ecclésiastiques* (Paris: Letouzey & Ané, 1981), s.v. "Walo" (vol. 19, col.
911).

[3] No contemporary source records the identity of these bishops, while Długosz
Ann. 2:217, ad a. 1104, speaks of two suffragans of the archdiocese of Gniezno,
and suggests that one of them was Czasław of Cracow. On different recon-
structions, see Mal. p. 91, n. 2.

coming, did not dare to engage him in battle on the open field nor even to try to ambush him on the difficult stretches of road as he marched in or out.[1]

27 [VISIT OF THE PAPAL LEGATE]

So Bolesław returned not ingloriously from Moravia, to find that a legate of the see of Rome named Walo, the bishop of Beauvais,[2] had arrived in Poland. With Bolesław's backing and with a passion for justice he exercised his canonical jurisdiction so rigorously that he deposed two bishops without anyone presenting pleas or money on their behalf.[3] After due honor and reverence was shown to the Roman legate and a canonical council held, Walo gave the apostolic blessing and returned to Rome, while Bolesław turned again to do battle against his enemies.

28 [CAMPAIGN AGAINST THE CITY OF KOŁOBRZEG]

He therefore gathered an army in Głogów,[4] but took with him chosen knights only, with the best horses, and no infantry, and for five days on end marched day and night through wilderness, making no concession to satisfy tiredness or hunger. At last on the sixth day, a Friday, they took communion and some bodily refreshment as well, and reached Kołobrzeg by the guidance of the stars.[5] The night before Bolesław had mass celebrated in

---

[4] In Silesia. Gumplowicz, Zbigniew, p. 50, argues that this expedition took place in 1105; Mal. p. 95, n. 2, however, proposes the fall of 1103.

[5] Kołobrzeg was probably the most important center of eastern Pomerania, and an early episcopal see (see above, p. 33, n. 7); on its history see Winfried Schich, "Die pommersche Frühstadt im 11. und frühen 12. Jahrhundert am Beispiel von Kolberg (Kołobrzeg)," in *Die Frühgeschichte der europäischen Stadt im 11. Jahrhundert*, ed. J. Jarnut and P. Johanek (Cologne: Böhlau, 1998), pp. 273–304. As Kołobrzeg is 280 km from Głogów the army would have had to march 55 km daily, which is, however, not impossible for mounted knights.

officium fieri sancte Marie constituit, quod postea usu pro devotione retinuit. Die sabbato, aurora lucescente, ad urbem Cholbreg propinquantes, fluviumque[1] proximum sine ponte vel vado,
ne prescirentur a paganis, cum periculo transeuntes, agminibus
ordinatis, aciebusque retro duabus in subsidio collocatis, ne forte
Pomorani hoc prescirent, eosque incautos adirent, urbem opulentam divitiis, munitamque presidiis unanimiter invadere con-
cupiscunt. Tunc quidam comes ad Bolezlauum accessit, datoque
consilio revertendi cum derisione recessit. At Bolezlauus suos
breviter adhortatur, unde quisque satis ad audaciam provocatur.
Ni vestram, inquit, milites expertam probitatem et audatiam
habuissem, nequaquam retro tantam meorum multitudinem
dimisissem, nec cum paucis usque ad maritima pervenissem.
Nunc vero de nostris auxilium non speramus. Hostes retro, fuga
longa, si de fuga cogitamus,[2] in Deo tantum et in armis iam securi
confidamus. Hiis dictis ad urbem potius volare quam currere
videbantur, quidam tantum predam, quidam urbem capere medi-
tantur. Et si cuncti sicut quidam unanimiter invasissent, illa die
procul dubio gloriosam Pomoranorum urbem et precipuam
habuissent. Sed copia diviciarum predaque suburbii militum
audaciam excecavit, sicque fortuna civitatem suam a Polonis
liberavit. Pauci tantum probi milites gloriam divitiis preferentes,
emissis lanceis, pontem extractis gladiis transierunt, portamque
civitatis intraverunt, sed a civium multitudine coartati, vix tandem retrocedere sunt coacti. Ipse dux etiam Pomoranus[3] illis
advenientibus intus erat, timensque totum exercitum advenire,
per aliam portam effugerat. At Bolezlauus inpiger non in uno
loco consistebat, sed officium simul probi militis ac strennui
ducis exercebat; suis videlicet laborantibus occurrebat, simulque

[1] Probably the river Parsęta.
[2] Cf. Regino, *Chron.* ad a. 860, p. 79.

honor of the holy Mary, which afterwards he kept as his normal practice in devotion. On the Saturday as dawn was breaking they drew near the city of Kołobrzeg. So as not to alert the pagans they made a perilous crossing of the nearby river without using bridge or ford,[1] and drew up their lines, leaving two units behind as reinforcements in case the Pomeranians found out and attacked them by surprise. They were eager to burst upon this rich and well-garrisoned town all together. At this point a certain *comes* approached Bolesław, advising him scornfully to retire, and turned away. But Bolesław made a short speech to his men, which roused each of them to boldness. "My warriors," he said, "if I did not have past experience of your mettle and your boldness, I would certainly not have left such a large part of my forces behind nor advanced as far as the sea-coast with so few. But we have no hope of help from our people now. The foe are behind us, we've a long way to run if flight's our intention.[2] Just trust in God and in your weapons, and have no care." He spoke these words, and it seemed they flew rather than ran against the town. Some only thought of plunder while others sought to capture the town. And if they had all stormed the town with one accord as these few did, there is no question that they would that day have had this great and glorious city of the Pomeranians. But the vast wealth and booty of the suburbs blinded the ardor of the soldiers, and so Fortune saved their city from the Poles. Only a few stalwart knights set glory above riches. Casting their lances aside and seizing their swords they crossed the bridge and entered the city gate, but they were boxed in by a great mass of townsfolk and finally with difficulty forced to retreat. The duke of the Pomeranians[3] himself was inside when they arrived, but fearing that the whole army was on the way he fled out the other gate. However, restless Bolesław would not stay in one spot, but playing the role of the doughty warrior and good commander at once, he rushed to help his men wherever they were in difficulty,

[3] This is assumed to be the same duke as is mentioned below, ch. 39, p. 192. While the details are debated, it is supposed that there were several dukes in Pomerania in this time.

nocitura vel profutura providebat. Interea alii aliam portam et alii aliam invadebant, alii captivos ligabant, alii marinas divicias colligebant, alii pueros et puellas educebant. Igitur Bolezlauus milites suos, quamvis tota die fatigatos assultando, vix tandem eos circa vesperam revocare potuit comminando. Militibus itaque revocatis ac suburbio spoliato, recessit inde Bolezlauus magni Michaelis[1] consilio extra muros, omni prius edificio concremato. Ex quo facto nacio tota barbarorum concussa vehementer exhorruit, famaque Bolezlaui longe lateque dilatata percrebruit. Unde etiam in proverbium cantilena componitur, ubi satis illa probitas et audacia convenienter extollitur, in hec verba.

> Pisces salsos et fetentes apportabant alii,
> Palpitantes et recentes nunc apportant filii.
> Civitates invadebant patres nostri primitus,
> Hii procellas non verentur, neque maris sonitus.
> Agitabant patres nostri cervos, apros, capreas,
> Hii venantur monstra maris et opes equoreas.[2]

(29)

Labore tanto militibus ex itinere fatigatis et iam aliquantula quiete concessa recreatis, ad expedicionem Bolezlauus cohortes iterum revocavit et Pomoranos ad bellum denuo provocavit. Huius vero expedicionis Suatobor,[3] eius consanguineus, causam excitavit, cuius progenies nunquam fidelitatem Polonis dominis observavit. Erat enim ipse Suatobor in Pomorania carceratus et a quibusdam a regno suo traditoribus supplantatus. Inpiger autem Bolezlaus suum cupiens consanguineum liberare, terram

---

[1] Michael of the Awdańcy kindred, a relative or the father of the palatine Skarbimir (see p. 174, n. 4).

[2] Translated by Dr. Barbara Reynolds.

[3] A duke of the Pomoranians, who may have been connected to the Piasts by marriage.

as mindful of advantage as of peril. Meanwhile some assailed one gate, others the other, some were tying up prisoners, some were collecting the wealth from the sea, others were leading off young boys and girls. So by evening, although the soldiers had exhausted themselves in the assault all that day, Bolesław could in the end call them back only with difficulty and by threats. Once they had come back and the suburbs had been looted, Bolesław, on the advice of Michael the Old,[1] withdrew outside the walls, after every building was first burnt down. This dealt a heavy blow to the whole barbarian nation and filled them with horror, and Bolesław' reputation spread far and wide and became well-known among them. About which a memorable little song is composed, extolling in fitting words this valor and boldness, which runs as follows:

Salted fish and stinking fish in days gone by were all we'd get,
Now the sons bring fish aplenty, fresh and quivering from the net.
Once our fathers conquered cities, threw themselves at tower
    and wall,
But neither roaring seas nor tempests daunt these boys today at all.
Once our fathers drove before them deer, boar, and the goats
    that leap,
Now the boys can hunt sea monsters and the riches of the deep.[2]

29 [A FRESH CAMPAIGN AGAINST THE POMERIANS AND A PARLEY WITH COLOMAN]

The men, exhausted from their journey, were given some rest to recover from these great labors. Then Bolesław again called up his troops for a campaign and challenged the Pomeranians once more to war. His kinsman Świętobór[3] was the reason for this campaign. For his progeny never remained loyal to their Polish masters, and Świętobór himself had been imprisoned in Pomerania and ousted by certain traitors from his realm. Restless Bolesław, anxious to free his kinsman, made plans to invade the

Pomoranorum meditatur totis viribus expugnare.[1] Sed Pomorani metuentes audaciam Bolezlaui, callidum consilium inierunt; namque sibi consanguineum reddiderunt et sic eius iram et impetum intollerandum evaserunt. Inde rediens Bolezlauus cum rege Vngarorum Colomanno, super reges universos suo tempore degentes litterali scientia erudito,[2] diem et locum colloquii collocavit, ad quem rex Vngarorum venire, timens insidias, dubitavit. Erat enim Almus, Vngarorum dux, tunc temporis de Vngaria profugatus et a duce Bolezlauo hospitalitatis gratia sustentatus.[3] Postea tamen aliis inter se legationibus transmandatis, insimul convenerunt et ab invicem discesserunt, perpetuis fraternitatibus et amiciciis confirmatis.

(30)

Interea Scarbimirus comes Polonie palatinus,[4] cum suis commilitonibus Pomoraniam introivit, ubi non parvam gloriam Polonis acquisivit, hostibusque suis dampnum et contumeliam dereliquit. Qui castellorum vel civitatum nominari maluit expugnator, quam villarum multarum fieri vel armentorum depredator. Igitur audaci violentia unum castellum expugnavit,[5] unde quibusdam modo captivatis, eductaque preda totum radicitus concremavit.

---

[1] Gumplowicz, Zbigniew, p. 51, puts the date of the incursion to 1106, but if Bolesław met Coloman in the same year, the date is more probably 1105, because Álmos returned to Hungary in 1106 (see n. 3, below).

[2] Coloman, called "the Bookman," probably originally trained as a cleric, was king of Hungary 1095–1111.

[3] Coloman's younger brother Álmos, designated as heir by King Ladislas I, challenged his brother's right to rule and enlisted the help of Poles, Germans, and Byzantines in no less than five attempts to gain the throne. In 1106 he managed to capture a castle with Polish help; but Coloman made peace with

land of the Pomeranians with all his forces.[1] But the Pomeranians, fearing Bolesław's boldness, thought up a clever idea: they surrendered to him his kinsman and thus escaped his anger and his irresistible onslaught. On his return Bolesław arranged a time and a place to meet with Coloman, the king of the Hungarians, who was the most well-versed in the science of letters among all the kings of his day.[2] However, the king of the Hungarians hesitated to come to the meeting, fearing treachery. For Álmos, duke of the Hungarians, was at the time an exile from Hungary and was enjoying the hospitality of Duke Bolesław.[3] Subsequently, however, after other embassies had passed between them, the two kings met and vowed perpetual friendship and brotherhood before they departed.

30 [THE CAMPAIGNS OF SKARBIMIR IN POMERANIA]

Meanwhile Skarbimir, the count palatine of Poland,[4] entered Pomerania with his fellow knights, where he won no little glory for the Poles, while his foes were left with loss and shame. He wanted rather to be known as a stormer of castles and cities than to be a raider of numerous villages or cattle. So with daring force he stormed one castle,[5] taking from it some prisoners and removing the spoils before burning it all to the ground.

Bolesław and Álmos had to submit. Deprived of his duchy, he was finally (in 1113 or earlier) blinded together with his son, an act designed to incapacitate them for rule. See *Chron. Hung. comp. saec. xiv*, ch. 150, *SRH*, pp. 429–30; Engel, *Realm*, pp. 33–6.

[4] Skarbimir of the Awdańcy kindred, Bolesław's tutor and later his palatine (*PSB* 38: 27–31).

[5] The castle cannot be identified. Gumplowicz (Zbigniew, p. 51) speculates about some stronghold by lake Lubczesko, or the castle of Tuczno on the shore of the same lake.

(31)

Alia vice similiter aliud castrum nomine Bitom[1] expugnavit, unde non minus laudis et utilitatis quam ex alio reportavit. Nam inde predam multam et captivos expulit et locum illum ad instar desolationis retulit. Sed hoc non ideo de Scarbimiro recitamus, ut eum in aliquo suo domino conferamus, sed ut veritatem hystorie teneamus.

(32)

Belliger itaque Bolezlauus postquam de colloquio Vngarorum est reversus, cum Zbigneo fratre suo colloquium aliud ordinavit,[2] ubi simul ambo fratres in hec verba alter alteri coniuravit, quod alter scilicet non sine altero de pace vel bello cum hostibus conveniret, nec ullum fedus alter sine altero cum aliquibus communiret et quod alter alteri super hostes et in omnibus necessariis subveniret. Hiis itaque confirmatis, sub eodem iuramento diem et locum ubi cum exercitibus convenirent, indixerunt et sic a colloquio discesserunt. Inpiger autem Bolezlauus cum paucis ad locum venire determinatum in die nominato, fidem servaturus, festinavit, Zbigneuus vero non solum fidem et iusiurandum non veniendo violavit, verum eciam fratris exercitum ad se declinantem ab itinere revocavit. Unde pene regno Polonie tale debuit dampnum et dedecus evenire, quod nec Zbigneus potuisset nec alius postea subvenire.[3] Nunc qualiter Deo iuvante Bolezlauus illud periculum evitaverit, subsequens statim pagina propalabit.

---

[1] This Latin form of the name may refer to Bytyń (Gumplowicz, Zbigniew, p. 51), but more likely to Bytów in Pomerania (Grodecki-Plezia, *Kronika polska*, p. 98, n. 1).

[2] Perhaps in the autumn of 1105 or in the next year.

31 [THE STORMING OF THE CASTLE OF *BITOM*]

On another occasion he similarly stormed another castle called *Bitom*,[1] winning no less glory and profit than from the other. For he took away much plunder and captives and reduced the place to the likeness of a desolation. However, I am telling this about Skarbimir not in order to compare him in any respect with his master, but to keep to the facts of history.

32 [A TREATY WITH ZBIGNIEW AND SUBSEQUENT BETRAYAL]

So the warlike Bolesław after returning from the meeting with the Hungarians arranged a further parley with his brother Zbigniew.[2] At this meeting the two brothers swore an oath each to the other to the effect that neither without the other would come to any arrangement with the foe on matters of peace or war, nor make any treaty without the other with any other persons, and that either would come to the help of the other against enemies and in all matters of need. Having confirmed these arrangements, and under the same oath, they appointed a day and a place where they should meet with their armies, and therewith they left the meeting. Restless Bolesław, anxious to keep faith, came in all speed with a few men on the appointed day to the designated place, whereas Zbigniew not only broke his faith and his oath by not coming, but ordered back his brother's army from its route as it was turning toward him. From this was to come such harm and shame to the kingdom of Poland that neither Zbigniew nor anyone else was hardly able to make it good afterwards.[3] Now how with God's help Bolesław avoided this danger the pages that follow immediately will make clear.

---

[3] Another obscure passage, as it is left quite unclear what was done that afterwards caused such harm to Poland, or how Bolesław's subsequent efforts "avoided this danger."

(33)

Forte quidam nobilis in confinio terre[1] ecclesiam construxit, ad cuius consecracionem Bolezlauum ducem, adhuc satis puerum cum suis iuvenibus invitavit. Expleta est itaque consecracio spiritalis et subsequenter adhibita desponsacio maritalis. Sed utrum Deo displicuerit cum divinis nupciis carnales celebrari, facile potest per discrimina, que sepius inde contingunt, comprobari; sepe namque cernimus, ubi simul ecclesie consecracio ac nupcialis desponsacio fiunt, seditiones et homicidia comitari. Unde constat, quia nec bonum est nec honestum talem consuetudinem imitari. Nec istud dicimus tamen, ut nuptias condempnemus, sed ut singula suis locis suisque temporibus reservemus.[2] Cuius rei manifestum indicium in consecracione Rudensis ecclesie[3] Deus omnipotens revelavit, nam et homicidium ibi et unum de ministris ad insaniam redactum constat evenisse et ipsos etiam desponsatos infelici connubio, sicut notum est, convenisse, nec anniversarium desponsacionis implevisse. Sed de miraculis sileamus, nostramque materiam teneamus. Igitur belliger Bolezlauus, convivio vel potationi militiam vel venacionem anteponens, senioribus cum tota multitudine in convivio derelictis, paucis comitantibus silvas venaturus adivit, sed contrarius venatoribus obviavit. Pomorani namque per Poloniam discurrentes, predas et captivos agebant et incendia faciebant. At Bolezlauus belliger, sicut leo caude stimulis iracundia concitatus,[4] nec principes, nec exercitum expectavit, sed sicut leena raptis catulis sitibunda sanguinis, depredatores eorum et cursores *in ore gladii*[5] momen-

---

[1] It is debated which "borderlands" of the part of the kingdom held at that time by Bolesław are meant here: Gumplowicz (Zbigniew, p. 60) thinks it was the Lubusz-land or some other western part of Greater Poland.

[2] The basis for the author's disapproval of a wedding at a church dedication is unclear. A vaguely similar tale about an unhappy marriage connected to the dedication of a church to St. Sebastian is told in Jacobus de Voragine, *The Golden Legend: Readings on the Saints*, trans. William G. Ryan (Princeton: Princeton UP, 1993), 1:101.

33 [BOLESŁAW FALLS INTO THE TRAP OF THE POMERANIANS]

It happened that a certain noble had built a church in the borderlands,[1] and invited Duke Bolesław and his young companions to the consecration, though he was still little more than a boy. So the spiritual consecration was performed, and afterwards a betrothal of marriage took place. But whether the celebration of a marriage in the flesh at the same time as divine nuptials has displeased God can easily be demonstrated by the troubles which often arise thereupon. For often we observe that when the consecration of a church and a marriage betrothal take place at the same time, it is accompanied by riots and murder. Hence it is clear that it is neither good nor proper to imitate such a custom. Not that we are saying this to condemn weddings, but to keep each thing in its proper place and time.[2] Manifest proof of this fact Almighty God revealed in the case of the consecration of the church at Ruda,[3] for it is known that there was a murder there and one of the attendants went mad, and, as is well-known, even the marriage between the betrothed turned out unhappily and did not even last till the first anniversary of the betrothal. But let us say no more about miraculous events, and keep to our theme. Bolesław the warrior, who set soldiering and hunting above feasting and drinking, had left the older persons with the main crowd at the feast, and went with a few companions into the forest to hunt. But instead he ran into the hunters: for the Pomeranians had been raiding through Poland, burning and taking away captives and plunder. But warlike Bolesław like a lion driven to fury with the beating of its tail,[4] waited neither for the princes nor the army, but like a lioness thirsting for blood when her cubs are snatched away, scattered the raiders and plunderers in an instant *with the edge of the sword*.[5] As he pursued them

[3] In the south-eastern part of Greater Poland.

[4] Cf. e.g. Lucan, *Bell. Civ.* 1.205–12, and also Gen. 49:9.

[5] Exod. 17:13.

taneo dissipavit. Cumque magis eos magisque persequi et patrie dampnum ulcisci niteretur, incidit inscius in insidias,[1] ubi dampnum inreparabile pateretur. Ipse tamen, licet paucos, octoginta scilicet, inter pueros et iuvenes habuisset, illi vero tria milia, non fugam petivit, nec tantam multitudinem dubitavit, sed prima vice cum sua parva acie tantam hostium congeriem penetravit. Mira dicturus sum, multisque forsitan incredibilia, utrum presumpcioni vel audacie, nescio, si fuerint ascribenda. Cum suos pene perdidisset, aliis interemptis, aliis dispersis, se quinto solummodo remansisset, hostes confertissimos vice secunda transforavit. Cumque tertiario regirare voluisset, quidam de suis, viscera equi sui per terram cadere cernens, exclamavit: Noli, inquit, domine, noli iterum prelium introire, parce tibi, parce patrie, equum ascende meum, melius est hic me mori, quam te ipsum, Polonie salutem interire. Hoc audito vix equo cadente consilio militis acquievit et sic tandem aliquantulum a campo certaminis declinavit. Videnssque se multum attenuatum, nec Scarbimirum, milicie principem, residuis interesse, iam recuperare victoriam desperavit. Erat enim Scarbimirus seorsum alibi gravi wlnere sauciatus et, quod nec siccis oculis est dicendum, dextro lumine mutilatus. Illi autem, qui in convivio residebant, audito, quod contigerat, exsurgentes subsidio suis laborantibus properabant. Advenientes vero Bolezlauum invenerunt cum paucis, admodum XXX[ta] non tamen de loco certaminis fugientem, sed paulatim hostium fugientium vestigia subsequentem. Sed nec hostes subsistendo pugnandi copiam dabant, nec nostri fatigati eos amplius infestabant. Erant enim pagani de tanta audacia iuvenis stupefacti, quod plus laudabant eum tam parva manu talia presumpsisse, sicque mordaciter institisse, quam se ipsos tanto mortis dispendio tristem victoriam habuisse. Quis, inquientes, puer iste erit, si enim diu vixerit et si plures secum habuerit, quis ei bello resistere poterit. Sicque pagani de dampno

---

[1] The alliteration in the Latin—*incidit inscius in insidias*—is remarkable.

further and further in desire to avenge the harm done to his country, he unwittingly fell into an ambush[1] in which he could have suffered irreparable loss. He had only a small number of companions, eighty boys and young men in all, while they were three thousand. Nevertheless, he did not take to flight or shy before such a multitude, but right away penetrated the great mass of enemy with his small band. What I am going to tell is amazing, and many perhaps will not believe it; whether it should be regarded as presumption or boldness I know not. He had lost almost all his men, some killed and some scattered, and he remained alone with four comrades, when he charged for a second time through the densest ranks of the enemy. And when he prepared to wheel for a third time, one of his comrades, seeing the entrails of his horse spilling on the ground, cried out, "Don't, my lord, don't join battle a further time. Spare yourself, spare your country, mount my horse, it is better that I die here than for you, the salvation of Poland, to perish." When he heard this, with his horse sinking beneath him he reluctantly took the advice of his man and so finally withdrew a little from the battlefield. Seeing how his numbers were diminished, and that Skarbimir, the leader of his knights, was not among those left, he now lost hope of rescuing victory. In fact Skarbimir had been badly wounded, somewhere else, and—it cannot be told without tears—had lost his right eye. When those who were at the banquet heard what had happened they rose up and hastened to the help of their comrades in trouble. When they reached them, they found Bolesław with a few men—barely thirty—yet not in retreat from the battlefield but following step by step upon the tracks of the fleeing enemy. But the enemy would not stop and give battle, and our men were exhausted and had ceased to harry them further. The pagans were stunned by the audacity of the young man, so that they rather praised him for daring such things with so small a band and for fighting on so tenaciously than themselves for their bitter victory purchased at such mortal cost. "What will this boy be?" they said. "If he lives longer and has more men beside him, who will be able to resist him in war?" So

presenti conquerentes, simulque timore probitatis experte mur-
murantes, plus honerati tristicia quam preda redierunt. De suis vero
Bolezlauo sequenti die plurimi solacio iam magis quam auxilio
occurrerunt. Advenientes autem illuc proceres dolorem de dampno
tante nobilitatis habuerunt et Bolezlauum de audacia tante presumptionis reverenter increpuerunt. Filius vero Martis Bolezlauus
non solum aurem correctoribus non adhibuit, nec se talia presumpsisse penituit, sed per eos se iuvandum et de hostibus vindicandum sub testatione fidelitatis ammonuit. Ibi vero Bolezlaus tot
ictus super loricam habuit et super galeam lanceis gladiisque
sustinuit, quod caro eius trita multis diebus testimonium lesionis
exhibuit. Inde quoque de sua iuventute minus aliquantulum[1] tam
glorianter perempta condoluit, quia tantam stragem hostium sibi
pro lucro proposuit. Etenim pro uno de peremptis vel sauciatis
Bolezlaui de Pomoranis poterant plures mortui computari.

(34) BOLEZLAUS BOHEMOS PROFUGAVIT ET POMORANOS SUBIUGAVIT

Hoc eventu Bolezlauus cum eodem exercitu de Pomoranis se
vindicare disposuit, iamque cepta via Bohemos in Poloniam exire
fama precurrens innotuit.[2] Tum vero Bolezlauus in dubio magno
pependit, utrum prius de recenti contumelia se debeat continuo
vindicare, an ab invasoribus suam patriam liberare. Tandem sicut
Machabeorum imitator,[3] diviso exercitu et patrie defensor extitit
et iniurie vindicator. Nam partem exercitus in Pomoraniam
delegavit, que depredando et comburendo satis eos turpiter
conculcavit; ipse vero cum expeditis militibus Bohemis obviam
properavit, eosque de silvis exituros diutius expectavit; sed eos
audita fama Bolezlaui timor animi revocavit.

[1] Or: 'grieved less for the loss of some of...'

[2] This Czech invasion is dated to 1106 (Mal, p.103, n. 1) or 1107 (Gumplowicz,
Zbigniew, pp. 58–9). Since Cosmas, *Chron. Boh.* III:20, p. 185, records that
Duke Svatopluk of Bohemia was in Germany in 1105, the campaign and the
retreat of the Czechs may have been connected with the conflict between him
and Bořivoj in 1106.

the pagans, lamenting their present loss, and muttering in fear of the valor they had experienced, returned laden more with grief than plunder. The great number of his men who met him next day offered Bolesław consolation rather than help. When the leaders arrived they grieved for the loss of so many noble dead, and with due respect rebuked Bolesław for his daring and presumption. But Bolesław the son of Mars turned a deaf ear to those who admonished him, and he had no regret for his actions, instead reminding them of their obligation of loyalty to aid him and take vengeance on the enemy. Bolesław had there received so many blows on his chainmail and on his helmet from swords and lances that his bruised flesh bore witness to his injuries for many days. As well, he grieved a little less for[1] his young men who had perished so gloriously, because he counted as a gain the enormous slaughter of the enemy. For many dead Pomeranians could be reckoned for every one of Bolesław's men killed or wounded.

34 BOLESŁAW SCATTERS THE CZECHS AND SUBJUGATES THE POMERANIANS

Hereupon Bolesław determined to revenge himself on the Pomeranians with the same army. But he had no sooner set out than word overtook them that the Czechs were marching into Poland.[2] Bolesław then was in great doubt whether to take vengeance immediately for the recent humiliation or whether to deliver his country from the invaders. At last, imitating the Maccabees,[3] he divided his host so as to be able both to defend his country and avenge his injury. For he sent part of his army into Pomerania, which looting and burning it crushed quite ignominiously. Meanwhile he himself hastened against the Czechs with his light-armed troops, and for a long time waited for them to come out of the forests. But having heard of Bolesław's reputation, the Czechs withdrew with fear in their hearts.

[3] See 1 Macc. 5:17–21.

(35)

Non solum autem exterorum discordia vel bellum hostium Bolezlauum aggravabat, verum etiam sedicio civilis ymmo fraterna invidia modis omnibus infestabat. Eo namque bello superiori aliquantulum inclinato plus gaudebat Zbigneuus, quam eo victoria[1] multociens exaltato. Cuius rei manifestum indicium apparebat, cum a paganis[2] de victoria pro signo munuscula capiebat et legatis magna pro parvis munera rependebat. Et si Poloniam depredantes de sorte Bolezlaui captivos adducebant, statim eos venumdandos ad barbarorum insulas[3] transportabant; si quid vero, vel predam, vel homines ignoranter de parte Zbigneui capiebant, illud sine precio vel dilacione remittebant. Unde cuncti Polonie sapientes indignati ad odium Zbigneui ex amicicia sunt redacti, sic ad invicem inquientes, de tali consilium capientes: Usque modo patrie nostre discidium et detrimentum vel negligentes, vel dissimulantes per nimium sustinuimus patienter, nunc vero hostes latentes manifestos et insidias occultas detectas cernimus evidenter. Scimus enim et certi sumus, quia frequenter Zbigneus Bolezlauo nobis presentibus hoc iuravit, unde non semel, vel tercio, sed multotiens peieravit, quoniam nec cum amicis fratris amiciciam retinebat, nec cum inimicis inimiciciam exercebat, ymmo per contrarium hostium fratris amicus et amicorum inimicus existebat. Et non solum ei sufficiebat fidem promissam violare, vel iuratum auxilium non prestare, verum etiam, si fratrem ire super hostes sentiebat, ex altera parte Poloniam intrare hostes alios incitabat et sic eum a proposito revocabat. Qui satis puerile consilium et nociturum audiebat, cum propter paucorum odium totam patriam offendebat,[4] ac pater-

---

[1] Presumably referring to Bolesław; but the whole sentence is rather unclear.

[2] I.e. the Pomeranians.

[3] Most likely to the island of Rügen, on which Ralswiek was a center of long-distance trade; see Joachim Herrmann, *Ralswiek auf Rügen: Die slawisch-wendischen Siedlungen und deren Hinterland*, 2 vols. (Lübstorf: Archäologisches Landesmuseum für Mecklenburg-Vorpommern, 1997–8).

35 [ZBIGNIEW'S HOSTILE INTENTIONS AGAINST HIS BROTHER]

However, Bolesław was not only troubled by discord or war with foreign enemies, but plagued with civil strife, or rather his brother's jealousy, in every form. For Zbigniew was happier with that earlier war which was somewhat undecided, than with his[1] being glorified by manifold victories. This was clearly shown when after the victory he received from the pagans[2] some small presents in token, and repaid the ambassadors with lavish gifts for these small trifles. And when they raided Bolesław's part of Poland and took captives, they would immediately ship them for sale to the islands of the barbarians,[3] whereas if they inadvertently captured anything, whether plunder or people, in Zbigniew's part, they sent it back without delay or cost. So all the wise men of Poland were angry and their friendship with Zbigniew turned to hatred. They took counsel over his behavior and said to each other, "Up to now we have ignored or turned a blind eye to the damage and division of our country and borne it all too patiently, but now we plainly see the hidden enemy in the open and the secret plots uncovered. For we know and are certain that Zbigniew on many occasions gave his oath about this to Bolesław in our presence, which means he has perjured himself not once or thrice but many times. For he has not kept his friendship with his brother's friends, nor enmity with his enemies, on the contrary he has proved to be the friend of his brother's enemies and the enemy of his friends. It was not enough to him merely to break his word and his promise, and to fail to give the help he had sworn to, but if he discovered his brother's plans to march against his enemies, he would incite other foes to enter Poland from the other side and so force him to abandon his plans. He listened to quite childish and harmful counsel, offending the whole country for the hatred of a few,[4]

[4] The Latin is open to various interpretations—for example, that Zbigniew hated a few men of his brother's side, or a few of his own people hated Bolesław; Grodecki-Plezia, *Kronika*, p. 104, n. 5 prefer the latter.

nam hereditatem conculcandam hostibus exponebat.[1] Et
quoniam Zbigneuus malo consilio suggerente, neque fidem fratri, neque iusiurandum observabat, nec honorem patrie nec
paternam hereditatem defendebat, neque dampnum vel detrimentum imminens perpendebat, heu, cecidit inde gravius, unde
voluit[a] exaltari et unde non poterit amplius a suis malis consul-
toribus relevari.[2] Unde posteri sibi caveant vel presentes, ne sint
in regno pares socii dissidentes.[3]

<h2 style="text-align:center">(36)</h2>

Bolezlauus autem hec omnia soli Domino commendabat, ini-
uriamque fraternam adhuc equanimiter tolerabat, semperque
laboriosus Poloniam *sicut leo rugiens* metuendus *circuibat*.[4] Cui
forte fuit interim nunciatum Kosle castrum in confinio Bohemorum a se ipso tamen non ab hostibus concrematum.[5] Qui
reputans aliquem per tradicionem hoc fecisse, dubitansque Bohemos ad illud muniendum properare, illuc statim cum paucissimis transvolavit, ibique laborem propriis manibus inchoavit.
Iam enim tantum tamque diu huc illucque cursitando suos ita
fatigatos reddiderat, quod tam subito revocare iniuriosum visum
erat. Tamen et suos ad auxilium advocavit et fratrem per nuncios
satis ydoneos invitavit, eique verba subsequentia delegavit:
Quoniam quidem frater, inquit, cum sis maior etate, parque
beneficio regnique divisione, me solum iuniorem laborem totum
subire permittis, nec te de bellis vel de regni consiliis intromittis,

---

[a] noluit *Z H*

---

[1] In fact, since the Latin text does not mark where the direct speech ends, it is
debatable whether the words that follow are delivered as authorial comment,
or whether they continue the commentary of the previous speakers.

[2] Or, if one follows the reading of the MSS, the author may imply that Zbigniew
did not even want to "rise" from his "fall," i.e., his final defeat in 1111–2. The
repeated reference to "evil counselors" (also below, ch. 41) may be to actual
opponents of Bolesław and the Awdańcy, but is also a familiar *topos* serving to
exonerate rulers.

and leaving their father's inheritance open to be trampled by the foe."[1] And since Zbigniew through evil counsel would neither keep his word to his brother nor his oath nor defend the honor of his country nor his paternal inheritance, nor take account of the harm or injury threatening it, alas, he has fallen grievously where he sought advancement, and from where he will not afterwards be able to be raised by his evil counselors.[2] So let those today and in the future beware lest partners equal in rule fall out.[3]

36 [ZBIGNIEW'S HOSTILITY BREAKS OUT OPENLY]

But Bolesław entrusted all these things to the Lord alone. He continued to bear with equanimity his brother's injurious behavior, and ever toiled, *ranging* through Poland fearsome *as a roaring lion*.[4] Meanwhile by chance news came to him that the fortress of Koźle on the Czech border had been burnt down not by the enemy but by its own people.[5] Imagining that someone had done this by treachery and fearing that the Czechs were hurrying to fortify the position, he immediately sped to the place with a very small force and began the work there with his own hands. For with his many long campaigns hither and thither he had so worn out his men that it seemed hard on them to call them up again immediately. Nevertheless, he summoned his men to his aid and invited his brother with quite appropriate messages and sent to him the following words: "My brother, although you are older than me and have benefited equally from the division of the kingdom, you leave me, the younger, to endure all the travail alone, and do not involve yourself in the battles or the decisions of the kingdom. So, you should either assume the whole care and

---

[3] By these words the author seems to concede that Zbigniew and Bolesław were at some point regarded as equals.

[4] 1 Pet. 5:8, also Thietmar, *Chron.* VI, ch.10, p. 254.

[5] Koźle, on the river Oder in Silesia, was burnt down most probably in the summer of 1106.

aut totam regni curam ac sollicitudinem, sicut maior esse vis,[1] obtineas, aut mihi legitimo, licet etate minori, onus terre sufferenti, totumque laborem patienti, si non prosis, saltem non noceas. Quodsi curam istam susceperis et in vera fraternitate perstiteris, quocumque me pro communi consilio vel utilitate regni vocaveris, me promptum ibi cooperatorem habueris. Aut si forte quiete vivere, quam laborem tantum subire malueris, michi totum committe et sic Deo propicio tutus eris. Ad hec Zbigneus convenientem nequaquam responsionem remandavit, sed legatos pene vinculis et carceri mancipavit. Iam enim totum suum exercitum fratrem invasurus collegerat, simulque Pomoranos ac Bohemos ad eum de Polonia propellendum asciverat. At Bolezlauus castro munito, horum inscius, in loco vocabulo Lapis[2] residebat, ibique iacens more solito vicinius et rumores et legationes audiebat, ac velocius ex improviso suis hostibus occurrebat. Legati tandem vix amicorum subsidio liberati ad Bolezlauum nunciantes, que viderant et audierant, sunt reversi. Quo audito Bolezlauus, an resistat, an desistat[3] diu dubitans hesitavit, sed reversus ad cor suum quantocius suum exercitum congregavit et ad regem Ruthenorum Vngarorumque pro auxilio delegavit.[4] Sed si per se vel per ipsos nichil agere potuisset, ipsum regnum et spem regni expectando perdidisset.[5]

(37)

Igitur belliger Bolezlauus tribus exercitibus circumdatus, quos prius expectet, vel in quos irruat, meditatur, sicut leo vel aper molosis canibus indagatus latratibus canum tubisque venatorum

[1] The Latin *maior* may imply that the author believed that Bolesław was ready under circumstances to grant Zbigniew the senior position, which indeed their father may have designated for him.

[2] According to Bielowski *MPH* I:452, the town of Kamień in Pomerania; however, Mal. p. 106, n. 6, suggests Kamieniec in Silesia.

[3] The Latin plays on 'resisting' or 'desisting.'

[4] Sviatopolk, grand prince of Kiev and father-in-law of Bolesław III (see above p. 159, n. 3).

responsibility for the realm, inasmuch as you wish to be the greater;[1] or if you cannot help me, the legitimate though younger one, bearing the land's burdens and enduring all the travail, then at least do me no harm. If you take over this task and remain in true brotherhood, wherever you summon me for common counsel or the good of the realm you will have in me a ready helper. Or should you prefer to live a quiet life rather than taking on such a task, entrust the whole thing to me and so, God willing, you will be safe." To this Zbigniew sent no satisfactory reply at all, but nearly threw the ambassadors into prison and chains. For by now he had gathered his whole army in order to invade his brother, and at the same time he had called on the Pomeranians and Czechs in order to drive him out of Poland. But Bolesław, unaware of all this, had fortified the fortress and was in residence at a place called "The Stone."[2] Encamped there close by in his usual way he could listen to rumors and messengers and could mount an unexpected attack on his enemies the more swiftly. Finally with difficulty his ambassadors regained their freedom with the help of friends and returned to Bolesław, reporting what they had seen and heard. At his news Bolesław for a long time hesitated, unsure whether he should fight back or back off.[3] But taking heart again he gathered his army as swiftly as possible and sent messages for help to the king of the Ruthenians[4] and the king of the Hungarians. But if he had been unable to succeed either by himself or with their help, the kingdom and the hope of ruling would have vanished while he waited.[5]

37 [ALLIANCE MADE WITH THE CZECHS AND THE FLIGHT OF ZBIGNIEW]

So Bolesław the warrior, surrounded by three armies, pondered whom he should first await, or whom attack—like a lion or a boar who, harassed by Molossian hounds, is roused to fury by

[5] The second part of the Latin sentence can be scanned two trochaic halflines.

ad iracundiam provocatur.[1] Sed omnes tantum Bolezlauum metuebant, quod eo stante medio, ad locum determinatum convenire non audebant. Interim autem Zbigneui littere capte cum nuntiis sunt allate, quibus multe tradiciones et insidie sunt prolate.[2] Quibus lectis, quisque sapiens admiratur, totusque populus pro periculo lamentatur. Ad extremum vero Bolezlauus sapienter satis ac convenienter pro tempore pacem cum Bohemis federavit,[3] ac exercitu concitato Zbigneum eliminare disposuit. Zbigneus vero non fratris adventum eadem facturus vel bellum commissurus expectavit, nec castris securus, nec civitatibus retardavit, sed fugiens velud cervus Wyslam fluvium transnatavit.

(38) ZBIGNEUS REDIIT IN GRACIAM FRATRIS

At Bolezlauus festinanter Calis[4] adveniens, ibique quosdam fideles Zbigneui sibi resistentes inveniens, paucis diebus et illud castrum obtinuit et accepta legatione suum comitem in Gnezdensi civitate constituit. Inde progrediens in Spitimir[5] senem fidelem inclusit,[6] quem audita fama sue sedis reddite vix exclusit. Quo secum assumpto ad Lucic sedem translatam properavit, ibique vetus castellum contra Mazouiam reparavit. Tum primum Ruthenorum auxilium et Vngarorum commeavit, cum quibus iter arripiens, Wyslam fluvium transmeavit. Tum vero Zbigneuus in desperacionem est redactus, ac Yaroslauo duce Rutheno[7] simulque Balduino Cracouiensi episcopo[8] mediantibus, ante fratrem satisfacturus et obediturus est adductus. Tunc primum

---

[1] For Molossian hounds, see above p. 163, n. 3.

[2] According to Budkowa, *Repertorjum*, Nr. 18, this occurred in the fall of 1106.

[3] Cosmas, *Chron. Boh.* III:20, p. 185, dates this truce to the years 1106/7.

[4] South-east of Poznań, in Greater Poland.

[5] On the river Warta.

[6] I.e. Archbishop Martin of Gniezno. However, the whole sentence, with the apparent play on *inclusit/exclusit*, is quite obscure, as is the subsequent reference to the transferred see. Łęczyca on the river Bzura in Masovia may have been some kind of principal seat of Kujawia.

the barking of the dogs and the horns of the hunters.[1] But all were so afraid of Bolesław that as long as he stood in the middle they did not dare to meet him at the determined place. In the meanwhile, letters of Zbigniew were seized, together with their bearers, revealing evidence of much plotting and treason.[2] When these letters were read out, those of sound counsel were astonished, and the whole people bewailed their danger. But in the end Bolesław wisely and appropriately enough arranged a temporary peace with the Czechs,[3] and rousing his army decided to dispose of Zbigniew. Zbigniew, however, not planning to do the same or make war, did not wait for his brother's arrival. Not tarrying in the security of castles or cities, he fled like a stag, swimming across the river Vistula.

38 ZBIGNIEW IS RESTORED TO HIS BROTHER'S FAVOUR

But Bolesław, arriving in haste at Kalisz,[4] discovered resistance from certain adherents of Zbigniew. However, in few days he took the castle, and after receiving their emissaries installed his *comes* in the city of Gniezno. From there he advanced to Spicymierz[5] and imprisoned the loyal old man,[6] whom he only just managed to remove, after he learnt that he had surrendered his see. He took him with him and hastened to his transferred see of Łęczyca, and there repaired an old fort facing Mazovia. Only then did aid arrive from the Ruthenians and the Hungarians, and with them Bolesław set out across the Vistula. Then indeed Zbigniew was reduced to despair. Through the mediation of the Ruthenian duke Iaroslav[7] as well as Bishop Baldwin of Cracow[8] he was brought before his brother to proffer satisfaction and pledge obedience. Then he recognized for the first time that he

[7] Most likely Prince Iaroslav, son of Sviatopolk, who may have been a brother-in-law of Bolesław, and died in 1123.

[8] See p. 159, n. 4.

inferiorem se fratre reputavit, tunc iterum se numquam fratri
fore contrarium, sed in cunctis obediturum et castrum Galli[1]
destructurum, coram omnibus adiuravit. Tunc a fratre Mazouiam retinere sicut miles, non ut dominus impetravit. Pacifi-
catis itaque fratribus Ruthenorum exercitus et Vngarorum ad
propria remeavit, Bolezlauus vero per Poloniam quocumque sibi
placuit, ambulavit.

(39) ZBIGNEI PERFIDIA ERGA FRATREM

Rursus hiemali tempore Pomoraniam invasuri Poloni congregantur, ut facilius municiones congelatis paludibus capiantur.
Tunc quoque Bolezlauus Zbigneui perfidiam est expertus, quia
in hiis omnibus periurus manifeste, que iuraverat, est repertus.
Qui propere castrum, quod Gallus fecerat, non destruxit, nec in
fratris auxilium invitatus, unam solam aciem vel instruxit. Dux
vero septentrionalis[2] conturbatus aliquantulum ex hac arte,
suum tamen non dimisit propositum, cor habens in Domino non
in fratre. Igitur sicut draco flammivomus solo flatu vicina com-
burens, non combusta flexa cauda percuciens, terras transvolat
nociturus, sic Bolezlauus Pomoraniam impetit, ferro rebelles,
igne municiones destructurus. Sed quid eundo per terram vel
transeundo egerit obmittamus et in medio terre civitatem Albam[3] obsidendam adeamus. Adveniens itaque Bolezlauus ad
urbem, que quasi centrum terre medium reputatur, castra ponit,
instrumenta parat, quibus levius et minori periculo capiatur.
Quibus paratis assidue armis et ingeniis laboravit, quod paucis
diebus urbem cives reddere coartavit. Qua recepta suos ibi
milites collocavit, signoque dato motisque castris, ad maritima

---

[1] The identity of Gallus and his castle is uncertain and debated; see Mal. p.108,
n. 9.

[2] In the following chapters the author several times styles Bolesław "the
northern duke."

was no match for his brother, then again he gave his oath in the presence of all that he would never oppose his brother, but would obey him in all matters, and would destroy Gallus's fortress.[1] He was then allowed by his brother to retain Mazovia, but as a knight not as lord. So peace was made between the brothers, the Ruthenian and Hungarian armies went home, and Bolesław could now move about in Poland wherever he pleased.

39 ZBIGNIEW'S TREACHERY TOWARDS HIS BROTHER

It was winter when the Poles gathered again to invade Pomerania, for they could more easily seize the strongholds once the marshes had frozen. Then again Bolesław discovered Zbigniew's treachery when it was revealed openly that he had broken his oath in all matters he had sworn to. He did not promptly pull down the castle that Gallus had built, nor did he gather even a single unit when bidden to help his brother. The northern duke[2] was somewhat troubled by this deviousness, but did not abandon his plans, having set his trust in God and not in his brother. So like a fire-breathing dragon that burns down everything nearby by its breath alone and demolishes what is not burnt with the sweep of its tail and flies across the lands bringing destruction, so Bolesław threw himself against Pomerania, destroying the rebels with the sword and their strongholds with fire. But let us pass over what he did as he crossed and re-crossed their land, and proceed to the siege of Alba,[3] a city in the middle of the land. When Bolesław reached the city, held to be the very center of the land, he pitched camp and made ready siege-engines, in order to capture the city the more easily and with the less danger. When they were ready, he plied arms and engines without cease, so that in a few days he forced the townsmen to surrender the city. Having received it, he installed his troops there. He then raised his banners, struck camp, and set off towards the coast. He had

[3] Białogard (as at ch. 22, p. 158 above).

properavit. Cumque iam ad urbem Cholbreg declinaret et castrum mari proximum expugnare, priusquam ad urbem accederet, cogitaret, ecce cives et oppidani pronis cervicibus obviam Bolezlauo procedentes, semet ipsos et fidem et servicium proferentes, ipse quoque dux Pomoranorum[1] adveniens Bolezlauo se inclinavit, eiusque residentis[a] equo se servicio et milicie deputavit.[2] Quinque autem Bolezlaus ebdomadis expectando bellum vel querendo per Pomoraniam equitavit, ac totum pene regnum illud sine prelio subiugavit. Talibus ergo Bolezlauus preconiorum titulis est laudandus, talibusque bellorum ac victoriarum triumphis coronandus.

(40)

Sed cum isto gaudio de victoria triumphali exortum est maius gaudium orto sibi filio progenie de regali.[3] Puer autem etate crescat, probitate proficiat, probis moribus augeatur,[4] de patre autem nobis sufficiat, si cepta materia teneatur.

(41)

Videns igitur Bolezlauus, quia frater in omnibus et promissis et iuramentis fidei nullius existebat et quoniam toti terre noxius et obnoxius[5] obsistebat, eum de toto regno Polonie profugavit,

---

[a] residens *Z H*

---

[1] The duke may be the same person as in ch. 28 (p. 169, above). The word *inclinavit* may imply a gesture of submission, though this sense is not explicitly listed in in the *Thesaurus Linguae Latinae* (7: 941–3, s.v. *inclino*). However, Du Cange, *Glossarium* (4:327, s.v. *inclino*) quotes a passage from a letter of the archbishop of Bulgaria to Pope Innocent III where it is used as expression of devotion; perhaps there, too, we have a reflection of a Slavic rite. For a more explicit description of this gesture, see below III:23, p. 263, n. 2.

[2] This is a more or less literal rendering of a problematic passage. The reading of the MSS, *residens*, would imply that the one pledging homage was on horseback, which is unlikely considering the hierarchical symbology of being

turned off towards the city of Kołobrzeg and was considering
storming its fortress by the sea before approaching the city,
when lo, the citizens and the townsmen came out to meet him
with necks bowed, surrendering their persons and vowing their
loyalty and service, and the duke of the Pomeranians himself
came to Bolesław and bowed before him,[1] and pledged to serve
and fight for him who sat on horseback.[2] For five weeks Bolesław
rode through Pomerania expecting or seeking battle, and
brought almost the whole of the kingdom under his sway without a fight. With such titles of glory is Bolesław to be praised,
with such triumphs of war and victories to be crowned!

40 [A SON IS BORN]

However, at the same time as this joy from the triumph of
victory another greater joy arose when a son was born to him of
royal stock.[3] But let us leave the boy to grow and increase in
virtue and good ways,[4] and as to his father suffice it us if we keep
to the theme we began.

41 [ZBIGNIEW DEFEATED AGAIN]

So Bolesław, on seeing that his brother had shown himself
faithless in every promise and every oath, and since he set himself
ever against the whole land, harmful and liable to harm,[5] he
banished him from the entire realm of Poland, and when resis-

on horseback as opposed to dismounted, as in the previous episode involving
Bolesław II and Ladislas of Hungary (I: 28, p. 99). It may be, however, that the
duke was regarded by Bolesław as a "grand duke" in Pomerania and thus more
or less his equal. Of course, it may be another example of where only fragmentary information reached our author, or of scribal error.

[3] This is the sole reference in the work to a son of Bolesław (most probably
Władysław II, his successor, born 1105).

[4] Cf. Luke 2:40.

[5] The wordplay *noxius-obnoxius* is difficult to reproduce.

sibique resistentes et castellum[1] in terre confinio defendentes, cum auxilio Ruthenorum et Vngarorum expugnavit. Sicque dominium Zbigneui malis consiliariis est finitum, totumque regnum Polonie sub Bolezlaui dominio counitum. Et cum ista brumali tempore peregisse multis sufficeret ad laborem, Bolezlauus tamen nichil grave reputat, ubi regni proficuum[2] augmentari noverit vel honorem.

(42) SAXONES NAVIGIO VENERUNT IN PRUSSIAM[3]

Igitur in Prusiam, terram satis barbaram, est ingresus, unde cum preda multa factis incendiis, pluribusque captivis, querens bellum nec inveniens, est reversus.[4] Sed cum forte contigerit regionem istam in mencionem incidisse, non est inconveniens aliquid ex relatione maiorum addidisse. Tempore namque Karoli Magni, Francorum regis, cum Saxonia sibi rebellis existeret, nec dominacionis iugum nec fidei christiane susciperet, populus iste cum navibus de Saxonia transmeavit et regionem istam et regionis nomen occupavit. Adhuc ita sine rege, sine lege persistunt, nec a prima perfidia vel ferocitate desistunt. Terra enim illa lacubus et paludibus est adeo communita, quod non esset vel castellis vel civitatibus sic munita; unde non potuit adhuc ab aliquo subiugari, quia nullus valuit cum exercitu tot lacubus et paludibus transportari.

---

[1] The name of this castle is unknown.

[2] The unusual word *proficuum* has been taken as evidence of the author's French origin (Plezia, *Kronika Galla*, p. 104).

[3] According to their *origo gentis* legend the Saxons reached their medieval homeland by boat, see Widukind, *Res gest. Sax.* 1:3 (ed. Bauer–Rau, p. 22). While not mentioned in the latter source, "Prussia and the island of Rügen" are

tance was offered by the defenders of a castle on the borders of the country,[1] he seized the castle with the help of the Ruthenians and the Hungarians. Thus was brought to end the lordship of Zbigniew's evil counselors, and the whole realm of Poland was united under Bolesław's lordship. And whereas for many to achieve this much in the winter season would have been labor enough, Bolesław thought nothing too arduous where he knew the profit[2] or the honor of his kingdom was being increased.

42 THE SAXONS CAME BY SHIP TO PRUSSIA[3]

So he entered Prussia, a quite barbarous country, from where after burning he returned with much plunder and many captives, having sought battle but found none.[4] But as mention happens to have been made of this region, it is not out of place to add some facts which tradition has passed down. For in the time of Charlemagne, king of the Franks, when Saxony rose in revolt against him, and would accept neither the yoke of lordship nor the Christian faith, this people migrated with their ships from Saxony and took over this land and the name of the land. They still remain so, without king and without religion, and have not abandoned their ancient faithlessness and ferocity. For their land is so well protected by lakes and marshes that castles and cities would not protect it better. So the land has never been subdued by anyone, for no one has ever been able to ferry themselves and an army across so many lakes and marshes.

mentioned in a later law book, the *Sachsenspiegel* (Book III, ch. 45)—see Maria Dobozy, ed. and trans., *Saxon Mirror* (Philadelphia: University of Pennsylvania Press, 1999), p. 126. Our author seems to have known a less fabulous version connected to Charlemagne's wars.

[4] Gumplowicz, Zbigniew, p. 66, dates this campaign to 1108.

(43) MIRACULUM DE POMORANIS

Nunc autem Pruzos cum brutis animalibus relinquamus et quandam relationem rationis capacibus, ymmo Dei miraculum referamus. Contigit forte Pomoranos de Pomorania prosilisse, eosque more solito predam capturos per Poloniam discurrisse. Quibus dispersis et discurrentibus per diversa, cunctisque mala facientibus et perversa, quidam tamen eorum ad maiora scelera proruperunt, quod metropolitanum ipsum et sanctam ecclesiam invaserunt.[1] Igitur Martinus, archiepiscopus Gneznensis senex fidelis Spitimir in ecclesia sua confessionem cum sacerdote missam auditurus faciebat, suamque viam insellatis iam equis alias iturus disponebat. Sicque procul dubio simul omnes ibidem aut fuissent iugulati, aut pariter dominus sicut servus captivitatis vinculis mancipati, nisi quidam de ministris foris astantibus, armis eorum recognitis, ad ecclesie ianuam properaret, iamque presentes adesse Pomoranos exclamaret. Tum vero presul, sacerdos, archidiaconus[2] tremefacti de vita temporali iam desperare sunt coacti. Quid consilii caperent, vel quid agerent, vel quo fugerent? Arma nulla, clientes pauci, hostes in ianuis, et quod periculosius videbatur, ecclesia lignea ad comburendum eos paratior habebatur. Tandem archidiaconus per ostium exiens, per solarium coopertum ad equos ire volebat et sic evadere se putabat. Sed salutem deserens et salutem querens,[3] a salute deviavit, quia Pomoranis illuc irruentibus obviavit. Quo capto, pagani putantes archiepiscopum esse gavisi sunt vehementer, quem positum in vehiculo non ligant, non verberant, sed custo-

---

[1] Gumplowicz, Zbigniew, p. 66, dates this to 1108.

[2] This is the first mention of an archdeacon in Poland. Długosz *Ann.* 2:231, ad a. 1107, names this person Nicholas.

43 A MIRACLE REGARDING
THE POMERANIANS

But let us leave the Prussians among the brute beasts and tell a story, or rather a divine miracle, to those endowed with reason. It chanced once that the Pomeranians had sallied forth from Pomerania and in their customary manner were ranging through Poland in search of plunder. As they scattered and ranged far and wide, all doing harm and wicked deeds, certain of them, however, dared to commit even greater misdeeds, when they went after the metropolitan himself and broke into a holy church.[1] The loyal old archbishop Martin of Gniezno was in his church at Spicymierz making his confession with the priest before hearing mass. He was planning to leave for elsewhere and was making ready for his journey and his horses were already saddled. Thus there is no doubt that all of them there would either have been slaughtered together or cast into chains and captivity, lord and servant alike, had not one of the ministers standing outside recognized their arms and rushed to the door of the church, crying out that the Pomeranians had arrived and were upon them. Then indeed the bishop, priest, and archdeacon[2] were terrified and driven to despair for their temporal life. What plan could they follow? What were they to do? Where flee to? They had no arms, their retainers were few, the enemy were at the doors, and what seemed most perilous, the timber church would more easily serve to burn them all. At last the archdeacon slipped out a door and tried to make it to the horses by a covered porchway, thinking thus to escape. But as he abandoned sanctuary and sought safety he missed his chance for salvation,[3] for he ran into the Pomeranians as they burst in by that way. The pagans were exceedingly delighted to have seized him, for they thought he was the archbishop. They did not tie him up or maltreat him, but placed him in a vehicle and guarded him with reverence.

[3] The original play on the different senses of *salus* ('sanctuary,' 'safety,' 'salvation') cannot be exactly reproduced.

diunt veneranter. Interim autem archiepiscopus Deo se votis et
precibus commendavit, seque crucis sacro signaculo consignavit
nec, ubi nisi iuvenis[a] dubitaret, illuc scandere senex tremulus
dubitavit.[1] Mirabile dictu, vires, quas etas senilis denegavit, periculum mortis timorque subitaneus ministravit. Presbiter vero,
sicut erat paratus,[2] se post altarium reclinavit et sic uterque presul
et sacerdos Deo iuvante manus hostium evitavit. Nam paganos
in ecclesiam irrumpentes ita divina maiestas excecavit, quod
nullus eorum vel sursum ascendere, vel post altare respicere ad
memoriam revocavit. Qui tamen archiepiscopi altaria viatica,
ecclesieque reliquias abstulerunt, statimque cum eis et cum archidiacono, quem ceperant, abierunt. Sed Deus omnipotens
sicut presulem, sacerdotem et ecclesiam liberavit, sic reliquias
postea totumque sanctuarium incontaminatum et inviolatum
archiepiscopo restauravit. Quicumque enim paganorum reliquias, vel sacras vestes, vel vasa sanctuarii possidebat, vel cadu-
cus eum morbus vel insania terribilis agitabat;[3] unde Dei
magnificencia tremefacti, captivo archidiacono cuncta reddere
sunt coacti. Ipse quoque sanus et incolumis archidiaconus de
Pomoravia remeavit, sicque suis omnibus restauratis archiepiscopus Deum *mirabilem in suis operibus*[4] collaudavit. Ex ea die
Pomorani paulatim incipiunt annullari, nec ita sunt ausi postea
per Poloniam evagari.[5]

[a] *add* non *Mal*

---

[1] Or: 'where only a young man would dare to.' It is not made clear where the
old man climbs to.

[2] Apparently the priest was about to say mass before the bishop's planned
departure, and hence was already dressed in ecclesiastical vestments.

Meanwhile the archbishop had said his prayers and vows and placed himself in God's hands, blessing himself with the holy sign of the cross, and did not hesitate to climb, a tremulous old man, where even a young man would fear to.[1] Miraculous to relate, the powers which old age had denied him were ministered by sudden fear and the danger of death. The priest, however, lay down behind the altar, robed as he was,[2] and thus both bishop and priest through God's aid escaped the hands of the enemy. For the pagans were so blinded by the majesty of God when they burst into the church that none of them thought either to climb up or look behind the altar. Nevertheless, they took away the archbishop's travelling altar and the relics in the church, and at once left, taking these and the archdeacon whom they had seized. But Almighty God, just as he had delivered the bishop, the priest, and the church, so He afterwards restored to the archbishop the relics and all the contents of the sacristy, undefiled and inviolate. For whichever of the pagans had about him the relics or the sacred vestments or the vessels from the sacristy was possessed by the falling sickness or by a terrible madness.[3] So in terror at the greatness of God they were driven to return all these to the captive archdeacon. The archdeacon himself made his way back from Pomerania safe and sound, and so, with all his treasures returned, the archbishop gave praise to God who *is wondrous in all his works*.[4] From that day the Pomeranians began little by little to decline to nothing, and did not venture to range in this way through Poland thereafter.[5]

---

[3] On such standard miracles of vengeance see Gábor Klaniczay, "Miracoli di punizione e *maleficia*," in *Miracoli: Dai segni alle storia*, ed. S. Boesch-Gajano and M. Modica (Rome: Viella, 1999), pp. 109–36, with bibliography.

[4] Ps. 144:17.

[5] See, however, ch. 49, below!

(44)

Igitur inpiger Bolezlauus iterum Pomoraniam est ingressus et castellum obsessurus Carnkou[1] magnis viribus est aggressus; machinis diversi generis preparatis, turribusque castellana munitione preminencioribus elevatis, armis tamdiu ac instrumentis oppidum inpugnavit, donec illud facta dedicione suo dominio mancipavit. Insuper etiam ad fidem multos ab infidelitate revocavit, ipsumque dominum castelli de fonte baptismatis elevavit. Audientes autem hoc pagani, ipseque dominus paganorum, sic facile videlicet corruisse contumaciam Charncorum, ipse dux[2] Bolezlauuo primus omnium se inclinavit, sed eorum neuter longo tempore fidelitatem observavit. Nam postea baptisatus ille Bolezlaui filius spiritalis tradiciones fecit multimodas dignas sentencie capitalis. Sed ista suo loco recitanda presentialiter sub silencio contegamus, donec imperatorem de Vngaria, Bolezlauum vero de Bohemia reducamus et si qua prius fieri contigerit inducamus.

(45)

Nunc autem de Pomoranis ad Bohemos convertamur, ne diutius circa idem immorantes pigritari videamur. Igitur Bolezlauo in terre custodia persistente et honori patrie totis viribus insistente, contigit forte Morauienses advenire, volentes castrum Kosle, Polonis nescientibus, prevenire. Tunc quoque Bolezlauus quosdam probos milites ad Ratibor,[3] si possibile sit capiendum misit, ipse tamen propterea vel venari, vel quiescere non dimisit. Illi vero probi milites abeuntes et certamen cum Morauiensibus ineuntes, ibi probi quidam de Polonis in prelio corruerunt, socii

[1] On the river Noteć.

[2] Gumplowicz (Zbigniew, p. 68) suggests that this duke was Gniewomir, probably of the Strzegoca clan. Note that our author implies that there was one supreme duke at that time in Pomerania, which is quite unlikely.

44 [BAPTISM OF THE POMERANIANS]

So the restless Bolesław once again entered Pomerania and advanced with large forces on the castle of Czarnków,[1] in preparation for a siege. Engines of various kinds were made ready, towers were raised which rose above the level of the castle battlements, and he attacked the town by arms and machines until it surrendered and he subjected it to his lordship. In addition, Bolesław also turned many from paganism to the faith, and raised the lord of the castle himself from the baptismal font. When the pagans and the lord of the pagans himself heard of this–namely, that the pride of the people of Czarnków had been humbled so easily–the duke himself was the first of all to bow down to Bolesław.[2] But neither abided long in his fealty. For after being baptized as Bolesław's spiritual son, the lord of the castle perpetrated many treasonous deeds worthy of capital punishment. But these must be recounted in their proper place; for the present let us pass over them in silence, and meanwhile bring back the Emperor from Hungary and Bolesław from Bohemia, and recount whatever may have happened earlier.

45 [WAR WITH THE MORAVIANS]

Now let us turn from the Pomeranians to the Czechs, lest it seem that we are idling, ever treating these same matters. So, while Bolesław remained on guard over his land, preserving the honor of his country with all his strength, it happened that the Moravians advanced, hoping to seize the fortress of Koźle before the Poles found out. Once again Bolesław chose certain reliable knights and sent them to Racibórz[3] with orders to take the town if possible. However, he himself did not leave off hunting and recreation because of this. These select knights set out and engaged the Moravians in battle. Some valiant Poles fell in this

---

[3] On the river Oder.

tamen eorum et victorie campum et castellum habuerunt. Sic
sunt in prelio Morauienses interempti et sic illi de castello ignorantes interempti.[1] Interea Henricus imperator quartus Vngariam introivit, ubi parum utilitatis vel honoris acquisivit.[2] Nos
autem de gestis imperatorum vel Vngarorum ad presens non
tractamus, sed hec commemorando Bolezlaui fidem et audaciam
predicamus.

(46)

Erat enim inter regem Vngarorum Colmannum et ducem Polonie Bolezlauum coniuratum, quod si regnum alterius imperator
introiret, alter eorum interim Bohemiam prepediret.[3] Quando
ergo cesar Ungariam introivit, Bolezlauus quoque, fidem ser-
vans, in medio silvarum prelio commisso, victor Bohemiam
prepedivit, ubi tribus diebus et noctibus comburendo tres cas-
tellanias unumque suburbium dissipavit[4] et sic cito pro Pomoranis per traditionem sua castra capientibus remeavit.

(47)

Iam eo absente Pomorani Vscze Bolezlaui castrum[5] obsederant
et illud Poloni Pomoranis iam Gneuomir per traditionem suggerente reddiderant. Erat enim iste Gneuomir[6] de castello
Charncou, quod Bolezlauus expugnavit et quem ipse de fonte

---

[1] It is unclear what *ignorantes* implies; perhaps, that they were killed before
they even were aware of the outcome of the battle.

[2] Emperor Henry V entered Hungary in September 1108 in support of Duke
Álmos, and attempted to besiege Pozsony/Pressburg (today's Bratislava); at
the same time, Duke Svatopluk of Bohemia wasted northern Hungary. King
Coloman forced the emperor to retreat and made peace with him, and Svatopluk had to return home to deal with Bolesław's incursion; see Cosmas, *Chron.
Boh.* III:25, p. 193. The *Chron. Hung. comp. saec xiv* (*SRH*, ch. 150, pp. 429–30)
wrongly dates the emperor's campaign to 1113.

[3] This agreement was made in 1107; see *KMTL*, p. 315.

conflict, but their comrades remained in control of the battlefield and the castle. So the Moravians were destroyed in the battle, and so those who held the castle were destroyed before they knew it.[1] Meanwhile, Emperor Henry IV entered Hungary, but there he gained little profit or honor.[2] However, we are not concerned at this point with the deeds of the emperors or the Hungarians, but report these matters in order to commemorate Bolesław's good faith and boldness.

46 [WAR AGAINST THE CZECHS]

For King Coloman of Hungary and Duke Bolesław of Poland had sworn between them that if the emperor entered the kingdom of either of them, the other would at the same time counter with an attack against Bohemia.[3] So when the emperor marched into Hungary, Bolesław kept his word and beginning with a battle in the middle of the forests mounted a victorious campaign against Bohemia, where in the course of three days and nights he burnt and laid waste three castellanies[4] and a suburb. Thereupon he swiftly returned, because the Pomeranians were treacherously seizing his own castles.

47 [THE POMERANIANS REBEL]

In his absence the Pomeranians had besieged a castle of Bolesław's called Ujście,[5] and on the treacherous advice of Gniewomir the Poles surrendered it to the Pomeranians. This Gniewomir[6] was from the castle of Czarnków, the fortress Bolesław

---

[4] The size of a "castellany" in medieval Bohemia depended upon the size of an estate and the number of castles on it, according to which it would be divided into such units; see Vincenc Brandl, *Glossarium illustrans bohemico-moravicae historiae fontes* (Brno: Winiker, 1876), pp. 392–94 and 404.

[5] On the river Noteć.

[6] See above, p. 200, n. 2.

baptismatis elevavit et ceteris interemptis vite reservavit et in ipso castello dominum collocavit. Hic vero perfidus, periurus, immemor beneficii, perverso consilio castrum reddere consuluit castellanis, menciendo Bolezlauum superatum a Bohemis et iam redditum Alemannis. Exercitu itaque tam laborioso itinere tamque periculoso de Bohemia redeunte, nec sibi, nec viris fatigatis, nec equis macillentis pepercit, nec die noctuque quievit, donec illuc festinans cum paucis, quos de multis eligere potuit advenit et si non aliud fecit se velle iniuriam vindicare saltim innotuit eumque sanum et non superatum apparuit. Nullus enim se contra eum ad bellum preparavit, nullus enim eunti vel redeunti pugnaturus obviavit et sic nec dampnum faciens nec recipiens remeavit.

(48)

Iterum aliquantulum equis et militibus recreatis in Pomoraniam redire parat Bolezlaus iterum ad bellum cohortibus instauratis. Hostium ergo terram ingrediens, non predas sequitur vel armenta, sed castrum Velun[1] obsidens, machinas prepapat ac diversi generis instrumenta. At contra castellani vite diffidentes, solummodo in armis confidentes, propugnacula relevant, destructa reparant, sudes preacutas et lapides sursum elevant, obstruere portas festinant. Machinis itaque preparatis et universis adarmatis Poloni castrum undique viriliter invadunt, Pomorani vero non minus defendunt. Poloni pro iustitia et victoria sic acriter insistebant, Pomorani pro naturali perfidia et pro salute defendenda resistebant. Poloni gloriam appetebant, Pomorani libertatem defendebant.[2] Ad extremum tamen Pomorani con-

---

[1] Wieleń at the river Noteć.

[2] It is peculiar and surprising that the author grants the possession of "liberty" to the oft-despised barbarians (see also III:1, p. 223, below). The phrase resembles closely the words of Widukind, *Res gestae Sax.* II:20 (ed. Bauer–Rau, pp. 106–7) about one side fighting for glory the other for survival, and both may have their model in Sallust, *Jug.* 94. See also p. lvi, n. 121.

had taken; he raised Gniewomir from the baptismal font, spared his life when others forfeited theirs, and placed him as lord of this castle. But this perfidious, ungrateful perjurer by wicked counsel advised the garrison to surrender the castle, lyingly affirming that Bolesław was defeated by the Czechs and had by now been handed over to the Germans. When his army returned from its very laborious and dangerous march through Bohemia, Bolesław spared neither himself nor his exhausted men nor their wasted mounts nor did he rest by day or night until he had made his way there in haste with a selection of men chosen from the many available. And if he did nothing else, at least it was made known that he intended to avenge the injury, and it was clear that he was safe and had not been defeated. In fact no one attempted to make war on him, no one challenged him to fight either on his coming or on his return. So he returned home without either receiving or inflicting harm.

48 [BOLESŁAW PUNISHES THE REBELLIOUS POMERANIANS AFTER SEIZING THE CASTLE OF WIELEŃ]

Bolesław gave his horses and his men some little time to rest, and after again making his forces ready for war he prepared to march back into Pomerania. As he entered the territory of the enemy he did not go after plunder or cattle but laid siege to the castle of Wieleń,[1] making ready engines and devices of different kinds. In response, the townsmen, fearing for their lives and placing their hopes in arms alone, speedily raised battlements, repaired damaged ones, hauled up sharpened stakes and stones, and barricaded the gates. Once the machines were ready and every-one armed, the Poles attacked the castle valiantly from all sides, while the Pomeranians defended it with no less vigor. The Poles pressed on so strongly from a sense of justice and desire for victory, the Pomeranians resisted out of natural treachery and self-preservation. The Poles sought glory, the Pomeranians were defending their liberty.[2] But in the end the Pomeranians, ex-

tinuis laboribus et vigiliis fatigati, se non posse tantis resistere viribus meditati, de primo fastu superbie descendentes, sese castellumque, recepta Bolezlaui ciroteca[1] pro pignore, reddiderunt. At Poloni tot labores, tot mortes, tot asperas hiemes, tot traditiones et insidias memorantes, omnes occidunt, nulli parcentes, nec ipsum etiam Bolezlauum hoc prohibentem audientes. Sicque paulatim rebelles et contumaces Pomorani per Bolezlaum destruuntur, sicut iure perfidi destrui debent. Castellum vero Bolezlauus melius ad retinendum affirmavit, eoque munito necessariis, suos ibi milites collocavit.

(49) SEXCENTI POMORANI IN MAZOUIA SUNT PEREMPTI

Sequenti tamen estate congregati transierunt in Mazouiam predam capere Pomorani.[2] Sed sicut sibi Mazouienses predam facere sunt conati, sic ab ipsis Mazouiensibus preda fieri sunt coacti. Ipsi nempe per Mazouiam cursitantes, predam et captivos congregantes et edificia concremantes, iam securi cum preda stabant, nec de bello dubitabant. Et ecce comes nomine Magnus, qui tunc Mazouiam regebat,[3] cum Mazouiensibus, paucis quidem numero, probitate vero numerosis, contra plures et innumerabiles paganos horribile prelium intravit, ubi Deus suam omnipotenciam revelavit; namque de paganis ibi plus quam sexcentos aiunt interisse, predamque totam illis et captivos Mazouienses abstulisse; residuos quoque vel capi, non est dubium, vel fugisse. Quippe Symon, illius regionis presul,[4] oves suas lupinis morsibus

---

[1] While this form of pledging in Poland is not known from elsewhere, for the manifold symbolic uses of the gauntlet see Berendt Schwineköper, *Der Handschuh im Recht, Ämterwesen, Brauch und Volksglauben,* with a foreword by P. E. Schramm (Berlin: Junker und Dünnhaupt, 1938).

[2] The summer of 1109.

hausted by their ceaseless efforts and lack of sleep, began to think that they could not resist a force of such strength. Abandoning their previous lofty pride, they surrendered themselves and their castle after receiving Bolesław's gauntlet as a pledge.[1] But the Poles, unable to forget their many toils, their many dead, the bitter winters, the repeated treachery and ambushes, killed them to a man, sparing no one, and refusing to listen even to Bolesław when he tried to stop them. And so little by little the rebellious and stiff-necked Pomeranians were destroyed by Bolesław, paying the rightful price for perfidy. The fortress he thought it better to retain, so he fortified it with necessities and placed his men in it.

49 SIX HUNDRED POMERANIANS DESTROYED IN MAZOVIA

However, next summer the Pomeranians gathered and crossed into Mazovia in search of plunder.[2] But as they attempted to make plunder of the Mazovians, they themselves became unwilling plunder at the hands of the Mazovians. For as they ranged through Mazovia, rounding up plunder and captives and burning buildings, they stayed with their plunder unconcerned and not expecting to fight. But lo, a *comes* named Magnus, who was then ruling Mazovia,[3] took a group of Mazovians small in number but numerous in valor and engaged the larger and innumerable force of pagans in a fearful battle. Here God revealed His omnipotence, for in the battle they say that more than six hundred pagans lost their lives, and the Mazovians seized all their plunder and the captives, and that the survivors, too—there can be no doubt— either were captured or fled. For Simon, the bishop of those parts,[4] donned his priestly vestments and in company with

---

[3] Magnus of Mazovia, of the Powała kindred, may be identical with the like-named *comes* of Wrocław (above II:4, p.124); see also Fedor von Heydebrand u. d. Lasa, "Die staatsrechtliche Stellung," pp. 14–68.

[4] Simon, bishop of Płock (see above, I:Epist., p. 1, n. 4).

laceratas luctuosis vocibus cum suis clericis infulis indutus sac-
erdotalibus sequebatur et, quod armis sibi materialibus non
licebat, hoc armis perficere spiritalibus et orationibus satagebat.
Et sicut antiquitus filii Israel Amalechitas orationibus Moysi
devicerunt,[1] ita nunc Mazouienses de Pomoranis victoriam, sui
pontificis adiuti precibus, habuerunt. Sequenti etiam die due
mulieres, fraga per devia legentes, uno milite Pomoranorum
invento novam victoriam retulerunt, quem armis exutum, reli-
gatis post tergum manibus in presentiam comitis et pontificis
adduxerunt.[2]

(50)

Zbigneui quoque milites cum Bohemis per regionem Zleznen-
sem depredantes et concremantes,[3] simili infortunio ab ipsis
affinibus superati, quidam vero capti quidam gladio iugulati. Hiis
autem minoribus pretaxatis, aliquantisper quiescamus, ut con-
textum de maioribus librum tercium adeamus.

EXPLICIT SECUNDUS LIBER

---

[1] The Amalekites and Moses are mentioned together at Num. 14:43, but there
it is the Amalekites who smite the Israelites as punishment for their sins.

[2] Jacek Banaszkiewicz points to an Indo-European triadic pattern in this story
(cf. e.g. George Dumézil, "La tripartition indo-européenne," *Psyché* 2, 1947,
1348–56): first warriors, then clergy, and finally peasant women defeat the
enemy; see his "Potrójne zwycięstwo Mazowszan nad Pomorzanami—Gall,
II, 49—czyli historyk między 'rzeczywistością prawdziwą' a schematem
porządkującym [A threefold victory of Mazovians over Pomeranians—Gallus

his clerics followed his sheep who had be torn by the teeth of the wolves, mourning loudly, and strove to accomplish with spiritual arms and prayers what he was not permitted to do with material weapons. And as in ancient days the sons of Israel smote the Amalekites through the prayers of Moses,[1] so now the Mazovians won victory over the Pomeranians with the help of their bishop's prayers. What is more, on the following day two women picking strawberries in the woods came across a Pomeranian soldier and won a novel victory: they stripped him of his arms, bound his hands behind his back, and brought him before the *comes* and the bishop.[2]

50 [DEFEAT OF THE CZECHS AND ZBIGNIEW]

Zbigniew's soldiers, too, who were plundering and burning the region of Silesia in company with the Czechs,[3] met with a similar fate at the hands of the local inhabitants. Some were captured, some put to death with the sword. But now that we have recounted these lesser events, let us take a brief pause, that we may begin on our third book, which is woven together from greater deeds.

END OF THE SECOND BOOK

II, 49—or a historian between "real reality" and an arranged scheme], in *Kultura średniowieczna i staropolska*, ed. D. Gawinowa (Warsaw: PWN 1991), p. 305–31. One may also think here of the "three orders" (*bellatores, oratores, laboratores*) of medieval social thought; see e.g. Georges Duby, *The Three Orders: Feudal Society Imagined*, trans. Arthur Goldhammer, with a foreword by Thomas N. Bisson (Chicago: University of Chicago Press, 1980).

[3] See Cosmas, *Chron. Boh.* III:28, p. 198.

INCIPIT TERCIUS LIBER

INCIPIT EPISTOLA TERTII LIBRI

Capellanis ducalibus venerandis aliisque bonis clericis per Poloniam memorandis, presentis auctor opusculi sic bona temporalia preterire, ut liceat expedite de caducis ad permanentia transilire. Primum omnium vos scire volo fratres karissimi, quia tantum opus non ideo cepi, ut per hoc *fimbrias* mee pusillanimitatis *dilatarem*,[1] nec ut patriam vel parentes meos exul apud vos et peregrinus[2] exaltarem, sed ut aliquem fructum mei laboris ad locum mee professionis reportarem.[3] Item aliud vestre discretioni manifesto, quia non, ut me quasi ceteris preferendo, vel quasi facundiorem in sermone referendo, hunc laborem suscepi; sed ut otium evitarem et dictandi consuetudinem conservarem et *ne frustra panem* Polonie *manducarem*.[4] Insuper etiam copiosa bellorum materia ad presumendum onus viribus inequale meam ignoranciam excitavit, ipsiusque Bolezlaui belligeri ducis probitas ac magnanimitas audendi fiduciam ministravit. Quocirca

> Non mea sed vestra percipite,
> Non fabrum sed aurum perpendite,
> Non vasa sed vinum ebibite.

Et si forsan in hoc opere verborum nuditatem accusatis, ex hiis saltim materiam tractandi profundius et argumentosius habeatis.

---

[1] Matt. 23:5 (as at I:Epist., p. 1).

[2] Cf. e.g. Gen. 23:4.

[3] This passage is our most explicit information on the person of the author, see above, pp. xxvi.

BEGINNING OF THE THIRD BOOK

THE LETTER OF THE THIRD BOOK BEGINS

To the venerable ducal chaplains and the other good and worthy clergy throughout Poland, the author of the present modest work wishes that they may so pass through secular fortune that from the perishable they may readily pass to the eternal. First of all, my most dear brothers, I would have you know that I did not embark on such a great task in order to *make broad the fringes*[1] of my poor spirit, nor, an exile and *a sojourner among you*,[2] to exalt my country or my parentage; but that I might take back to the place of my profession some fruit of my labor.[3] Likewise another thing I would make plain to your understanding, that I undertook this task not as if I held myself to be better than others, or to have more proficiency in language, but so as to avoid being unoccupied, and to keep up my practice in composing, and *not to eat* Poland's *bread in vain*.[4] In addition, the wealth of material concerning the wars spurred me, ignorant as I am, to venture upon a task beyond my powers. It was the valor and noble spirit of the warlike Duke Bolesław himself that gave me the courage to dare. Therefore:

> Yours and not mine is here all the merit
> Test the gold not the craftsman who works it
> Drink the wine not the vessels that hold it

And if perchance you find fault with the bareness of the language in this work, at least you will have in it the material for a deeper and better-argued treatment. On the other hand, if you judge

---

[4] 2 Thess. 3:8.

Quodsi reges Polonos vel duces fastis indignos annalibus iudi-
catis, regnum Polonie procul dubio quibuslibet incultis barbarorum nationibus addicatis.[1] Et si forte proponitis me talem
talisque vite indignum talia presumpsisse, respondebo bella
regum atque ducum non euuangelium me scripsisse. Numquid
enim fama vel militia Romanorum vel Gallorum sic celeberrima
per mundum haberetur, nisi scriptorum testimoniis memorie
posterorum et imitationi servaretur. Maxima quoque Troia,
quamvis destructa iacet et deserta, eterne tamen memorie po-
etarum titulis est inserta. Muri coequati, turres destructe iacent,
loca spaciosa et amena habitatore carent, in palatiis regum et
principum lustra ferarum et cubilia secreta latent,[2] Troie tamen
Pergama ubique terrarum scriptura clamante predicantur. Hector et Priamus plus in pulvere, quam in regni solio recitantur.
Quid de Alexandro Magno, quid de Antiocho, quid de Medorum
atque Persarum regibus, quid de tyrannis barbarorum memora-
rem, quorum si tantum nomina recitarem, opus hodiernum in
diem crastinum prolongarem. Horum tamen fama veterum
vatum preconiis inmortalis, quorum vita non est perpetua sed
penalis.[a,3] Nam sicut sancti viri bonis operibus et miraculis celebrantur, ita mundani reges et principes bellis triumphalibus et
victoriis sublimantur. Et sicut vitas sanctorum et passiones re-
ligiosum est in ecclesiis predicare, ita gloriosum est in scolis vel
in palatiis regum ac ducum triumphos vel victorias recitare. Et
sicut vite sanctorum vel passiones ad religionem mentes fidelium

---

[a] pennalis *Mal*

---

[1] While this motive—destined to have a long modern history—that equates
people without history with barbarians, and vice versa, does not appear to be
widespread among medieval chroniclers (not being listed, e.g., in Simon,
Topik), something approaching this is found in the Prologus of Theodoric the
Monk's (fl. 1188) *Historia de antiquitate regum norwagiensium*, where he says
hardly any nation is so primitive it does not hand on some record of its
ancestors to posterity (... *paene nulla natio est tam rudis et inculta, quae non*

the kings and dukes of Poland unworthy of record in the annals of history, you would surely class the kingdom of Poland among the uncouth barbarian nations.[1] And if you hold me, being what I am and of such a way of life, to be unworthy to presume upon such matters, I would reply that I have been writing about the wars of kings and dukes and not a gospel. For would the fame and martial exploits of the Romans or the Gauls ever have been so celebrated throughout the world if they were not preserved in the testimony of writers for posterity to remember and imitate? Troy, too, that greatest of cities, though she lies ruined and deserted, has been enshrined in eternal memory by the writings of the poets. Her walls are leveled, her towers cast down, her broad and pleasant quarters are uninhabited and in the palaces of her kings and princes lurk the hidden lairs and trails of wild beasts;[2] yet writings loudly proclaim the fame of Troy and her citadel the world over. Hector and Priam are more sung now that they are in the dust than when they sat on the throne. What need I mention Alexander the Great, or Antiochus, or the kings of the Medes and the Persians, or barbarian despots. If I but read out their names, today's tale would stretch into the morrow. But their fame is immortal through the praises of the bards of old, though their life is not eternal but subject to punishment.[3] For as holy men are celebrated for their good works and miracles, so the kings and princes of this world are exalted in triumphal wars and victories. And as it is a holy task to preach in church of the lives and passions of the saints, so it is a glorious one to recite in schools and in palaces the triumphs and victories of dukes and kings. And as the lives and passions

---

aliqua monumenta suorum antecessorum ad posteros transmiserit—Gustav Storm, ed., *Monumenta historiae Norvegiae* (Kristiania: Norsk Historisk Kjeldeskrift-Inst., 1880, p. 3). On Theodoric's work, see Sverre Bagge, "Theodoricus Monachus: Clerical Historiography in Twelfth-Century Norway," *Scandinavian Journal of History* 14 (1989): 113–33.

[2] See above, I:19, p. 80, n. 1.

[3] We follow the reading of the MSS; Mal. reads *pennalis*, taken to mean 'transient (like a feather).'

instruunt in ecclesiis predicate, ita militie vel victorie regum atque ducum ad virtutem militum animos accendunt, in scolis vel in capitoliis recitate.[1] Sicut enim pastores ecclesie fructum animarum querere debent spiritalem, sic defensores honorem patrie famamque dilatare student et gloriam temporalem. Oportet enim Dei ministros in hiis, *que Dei sunt,* Deo spiritualiter obedire et in hiis, *que sunt cesaris,*[2] honorem et servicium mundi principibus exhibere. Quid enim mirum, si viri triumphatores et incliti famam et gloriam appetunt ex virtute, cum etiam Cleopatra Cartaginis regina[3] imperium Romanum avida laudis transferre voluit virili audacia, non naturali sive feminea probitate. Et si femina querens imperium, navali prelio superata, morte terribili semet ipsam perimere maluit quam servire, quid est mirum, si patriam vel hereditatem paternam defendentes, vel illatam iniuriam persequentes, in bello famosa non venenosa morte magis appetunt interire, quam ignominose suis obnoxiis obedire. Constat ergo ex hiis superius approbatis rebus gestis Polonorum principum non[a] in vacuum recitatis, constat quoque vestro iudicio confirmandum, vero presens opus interpreti[b] recitandum.[4] Insuper illud causa Dei causaque Polonie provideat vestre discrecio probitatis, ne mercedem tanti laboris impediat vel odium vel occasio mee cuiuslibet vanitatis. Nam si bonum et

---

[a] *om.* Z H
[b] interprete Z H

---

[1] The word *capitolia* is otherwise not used in the *GpP* and may refer to castles or palaces of the ducal centers. This passage has been seen as evidence that the author expected his *gesta* to be "performed," but the formulation suggests that the sense is more general. On the possible performance of this chronicle and others, see Karolina Targosz, "Galla Anonima i mistrza Wincentego *Gesta Principum*/Czyny polskich książąt" [The *Gesta Principum*/Deeds of the Polish princes of Gallus Anonymus and Master Vincent], in *Korzenie i kształty teatru do 1500 roku w perspektywie Krakowa* [The roots and forms of theatre till 1500 from the perspective of Cracow] (Cracow: Secesja, 1995), pp. 68–88.

of the saints when preached in churches instruct the minds of the faithful in religion, so the exploits and victories of the dukes and kings fire the hearts of soldiers to bravery when they are recited in schools and capitols.[1] For as the shepherds of the church ought to seek the spiritual profit of souls, so a country's defenders should seek to spread its honor and fame and temporal glory. For God's ministers should obey God spiritually *in the things which are of God*, and show honor and service to the princes of the world *in the things which are Caesar's*.[2] For what is surprising if men of renown and triumph seek to gain fame and glory by their courage, when even Cleopatra, queen of Carthage,[3] in her thirst for praise sought to transfer the Roman empire, with the boldness of a man, not with the natural or womanly virtues? And if a woman in her quest for empire preferred after being defeated in a naval battle to take her own life by a terrible death rather than to be a slave, what wonder if in defense of their country or their paternal inheritance or in vengeance for slights inflicted, men prefer to perish in battle not through poison but by a glorious death rather than shamefully to submit to their inferiors. So it is clear on the strength of these above confirmed deeds of the princes of Poland, which have not been recited in vain, it is clear, too, that your judgement must confirm this, that the present work must be recited by a true interpreter.[4] Moreover, in God's cause and in the cause of Poland may you in your discretion and probity see to it that such a task is not denied its reward through any ill-will or through any chanced vanity on my part. For if my work is judged by persons

[2] Matt. 22:21, Luke 20:25.

[3] This surprising identification has been explained by saying that Carthage stands here for Africa; one might rather suspect that it is a simple slip, Cleopatra being confused with the other famous African queen, Dido. For this appraisal of Cleopatra, cf. Horace, *Carm.* 1.37.

[4] Cf. the first lines of II:Epil., above, p. 115. The request for a judgment as to whether a work should be "published" or not is a commonplace in dedicatory letters, see Simon, Topik, II:118–21. The whole sentence, however, is obscure and has been variously emended; see Mal. p. 123, n. h-m.

utile meum opus honori patrie a sapientibus iudicatur, indignum
est et inconveniens, si consilio quorundam artifici merces operis
auferatur.[1]

EXPLICIT EPISTOLA

INCIPIT EPILOGUS[2]

Deo vero laus et *honor,* regnum, virtus, *gloria*[3]
Pomorania subiugatur cuius sub potentia
Bolezlauo triumphanti salus et victoria.

Ad honorem Ihesu Christi referamus omnia,
Qui gubernat totum mundum sua sapiencia.
Non hec fecit vis humana sed neque militia.

Bolezlaus obsidebat castrum antiquissimum,
Viris, armis et nature situ munitissimum
Et ad dampnum sui regni periculosissimum.

Pomorani venientes obsessis succurrere
In incautos obsessores properant irruere,
Sed inani spe decepti, sunt acti corruere.

Per opaca deviando cuncti fere pedites,
Fugiendi ne spem ponant in caballis milites,
Ex occulto per ignotos emersere tramites.

Bolezlaus dux armatus cum paucis militibus,
Scarbimirus palatinus cum collateralibus
Septingenti conflixere cum XXX milibus.

---

[1] Simon, Topik II:95–7, cites other examples of authors hoping to receive a
"wage" (*merces*) for their writing, most referring to divine or spiritual rewards.

of wisdom to be good and useful to the honor of this country,
it is unworthy and unfitting if through certain persons' counsel
the craftsman should be deprived of price of his work.[1]

END OF THE LETTER

BEGINNING OF THE EPILOG[2]

To God be honor, kingdom, *glory, praise*,[3]
Captured was Pomerania by His grace,
To Bolesław victory and health always!

To Jesus Christ this verse its tribute pays,
Whose wisdom rules the world in all its ways.
This deed no mortal strength or skill displays.

An ancient fortress Bolesław attacked,
Which neither arms nor Nature's vantage lacked,
A danger to his realm which must be sacked.

The Pomeranians a ruse began:
To ambush the besiegers was their plan.
Inept, their hopes deceived, they turned and ran.

Through darkness, furtive, crept the men on foot,
That mounted troops no trust in horses put.
From secret haunts and pathways they burst out.

Duke Bolesław commands few men that night,
His count Skarbimir musters all his might
So seven hundred thirty thousand fight.

[2] The events summarized in the Epilogus are detailed below in Book III.
[3] 1 Tim. 1:17.

Namque nocte precedente fecerant excubias
Et audito, quod venirent, miserant insidias.
Sic habebat dux transmissas huc et illuc copias.

Illi vero recurvati ordinarunt prelium,
Hastis suis circumquaque plectentes ericium
Nec procedunt catervatim, sed stant per cyrcinnium.

Bolezlaus dux de tali causa satis callidus
Transgirando vertit eos usquequaque providus,
Ut vir audax, bellicosus atque laudis avidus.

Scarbimirus ex adverso se confert in medios
Et hortatur et confortat ad pugnandum socios.
Tales, inquit, Pomorani, non sensistis gladios.

Sed quid plura? Terga vertunt Pomorani prelio,
Neque fuit super illos tanta cedes alio.
Septem castra conquisivit dux de belli premio.

In hiis ergo collaudemus Deum et Laurencium,
Die cuius sacrosancto factum est hoc prelium,
Inde sibi fiat ibi dignum edificium.

Tam preclara Bolezlaui descripta victoria,
Assignetur cum augusto pax et amicitia,
Confirmetur, sicut decet, fraterna concordia.

Qua de causa palam constat imperator venerat,
Quanto fastu, qua virtute regnum hoc intraverat,
Quos deponi, quos preponi, iamiam disposuerat.

Sed quid valet contra Deum virtus vel consilium,
Sine cuius nutu nil fit, nec movetur folium,
Qui convertit in convalles, si vult, iuga montium.

The night before the duke a watch had set.
Hearing the foe, of traps he laid a net
And forces placed both here and there, to wait.

The foes deploy a circle, not a line,
With spears it bristles like a porcupine;
They do not march but, cowering, intertwine.

The duke, a shrewd tactician born and made,
Circles them constantly and plans ahead,
Eager for fame, warlike and unafraid.

Skarbimir, on the other side, plunged in,
Exhorting, urging on his men to win;
"Such swords", he said, "you pagans have not seen!"

The Pomeranians turned and fled. What more?
Never such slaughter had been seen before.
The duke gained seven towns as spoils of war.

To God and to St Lawrence thanks let's say.
This deed was done upon his holy day.
A monument to him our debt will pay.

Bolesław's triumph having been proclaimed,
Let friendship with the Emperor be framed,
Fraternal concord, too, as justly aimed.

For sure Augustus, as has been disclosed,
Entered our realm with pomp and there disposed
Who should promoted be and who deposed.

But what can wisdom, bravery confer?
Unless God nods, naught is, no leaf can stir.
To vales He changes what once mountains were.

Bolezlauus stat in regno magnus dux et dominus
Et paratus est ad bellum sicut leo cominus,
Qui resistit, superatur, sed non fugit protinus.

Bohemenses quid tardatis colla vestra subdere,
Cum cernatis ipsum regem Bolezlauo cedere
Et sciatis vos non posse viribus resistere.

Non est hostis tanto duci congredi qui valeat
Et qui parem profiteri sese palam audeat,
Nec vicinus, qui cum eo de pace non gaudeat.

Nam in hostes triumphator existit mirificus,
Erga cunctos cum honore dator est munificus,
Vngarorum rex per eum consistit pacificus.

Non est tempus, quanta fecit, enarrandi singula,
Que noverunt, que senserunt carceres et vincula,[1]
Nos ad laudes, non ad fraudes, damus hec munuscula.[2]

INCIPIT III^us LIBER DE GESTIS BOLESLAUI III

(1)

Multis et innumerabilibus Bolezlaui tercii gestis militaribus
memorandis intitulandum precipue, qualiter sancti Laurentij
die[3] contigerit Pomoranis, utpote repressa sit ira cesaris et ut
inpetuosis obstitum fuerit Alemannis. Quoddam namque castrum nomine Nakel in confinio Polonie ac Pomoranie paludibus
et opere firmum constat, ad quod capiendum dux belliger cum
exercitu suo sedens, armis et machinis laborabat. Cumque oppi-

---

[1] A veiled reference, it seems, to the imprisonment and blinding of Zbigniew.

[2] Translated by Dr. Barbara Reynolds.

A mighty lord is Bolesław the great,
Ready for war, a very lion to meet.
Opponents vanquished are, he won't retreat.

Bohemians, surrender now straightway!
The king himself has yielded: why delay?
You know your forces cannot ours gainsay.

No foe with such a leader can contend,
None yet to be his equal dare pretend,
No neighbor but is glad to be his friend.

A conqueror he stands, magnificent,
Honoring all, he is munificent,
And Hungary's king at peace remains content.

There is no time to tell all he has done,
What prisons could recount, what chains have known.[1]
Praise, not deceit, we chronicle alone.[2]

BEGINNING OF THE THIRD BOOK
OF THE DEEDS OF BOLESŁAW III

1 [VICTORY OVER THE POMERANIANS]

Numerous beyond counting are Bolesław the Third's martial
deeds of renown, but in particular it is worthy of record how the
Pomeranians fared on St. Lawrence's Day,[3] and how the Emperor's anger was tamed and resistance offered to the furious
Germans. For there was a castle called Nakło on the border of
Poland and Pomerania, well protected by swamps and works,
which the warlike duke and his army had settled down to besiege,
plying arms and engines. When the townsmen saw that they

[3] 10 August, probably of 1109.

dani non posse tante multitudini resistere se vidissent et cum tamen a suis auxilium principibus expectassent, inducias quesierunt, diemque certum indiderunt, infra quem, si sui eos non iuvarent, in potestatem hostium et oppidum et se darent. Inducie quidem eos assultandi conceduntur, sed apparatus tamen expugnandi minime differuntur. Interim oppidanorum nuntii Pomoranorum exercitum convenerunt, eisque pactionem suorum factam cum hostibus retulerunt. Tunc vero Pomorani, audita legacione stupefacti, coniurant insimul pro patria vel se mori,[1] vel victoriam de Polonis adipisci. Dimissis igitur equis, ut adequato periculo fiducia cunctis et audacia maior esset, nullam viam vel semitam gradientes, sed ferarum lustra condensaque silvarum irrumpentes, non in die statuto, sed in sancti Laurentij sacrosancto, quasi sorices de latibulis emerserunt, indicioque suo non humana, sed manu divina, perierunt.[2] Gloriosus *Deus in sanctis suis;*[3] venerabilis enim dies sancti Laurentij martiris existebat et in illa hora christianorum concio de missarum sollempniis exiebat, et ecce subito barbarorum exercitus ibi cominus imminebat.

Martir Laurenti, populo succurre merenti!

Quid nunc faciant christiani, quo se vertant. Exercitus hostium inprovisus, acies ordinandi non est tempus, ipsi pauci, hostes multi, fuga tarda, numquam placita Bolezlauo.

Martir Laurenti, populo vim tolle furenti!

Igitur militibus quotquot erant in duobus tantum agminibus ordinatis, alterum agmen rexit ipse belliger Bolezlauus, alterum

---

[1] Horace, *Carm.* 3.2.13; see also E. H. Kantorowicz, "Pro patria mori," in *Selected Studies* (Locust Valley: Augustin, 1965), pp. 308–24. For high ideals credited to pagan enemies, see above II:48, p. 204, cf. Bisson, "On not eating," pp. 279 and 284.

[2] Cf. Terence, *Eun.* 5.7.23: *Egomet meo indicio quasi sorex hodie perii.*

could not resist such a great number, but yet were expecting help from their leaders, they sought a truce and nominated a day by which if their people had not come to their aid, they would surrender both themselves and their town into the power of the enemy. A cessation in the assaults was granted, but the siege preparations were in no way suspended. Meanwhile, messengers of the townsmen met the Pomeranian army and told them about the truce arranged between their fellows and the enemy. Hearing this news the Pomeranians were thunderstruck, and on the spot they swore that they would either wrest victory from the Poles or die for their country.[1] So they abandoned their horses, that all would be the braver and more confident when the danger was shared equally, and following not roads and pathways, pushed through the depths of the forests along the trails of wild beasts. It was not on the appointed day but on the holy day of St. Lawrence that they emerged from their hiding places like field-mice,[2] only to perish by their own disclosure at God's hand and not at the hands of men. For *God is* glorious *in his saints,*[3] and it was the blessed day of the martyr St. Lawrence, and at that hour a crowd of Christians had come out from celebrating the solemnity of the mass, when, lo, suddenly the barbarians' army appeared close at hand.

Come, St. Lawrence, come to the aid of your meriting people!

What are the Christians now to do, where should they turn? An enemy army unforeseen, and no time to draw up a battle line; they are few, the foe are many; too late to run, and flight was never Bolesław's way!

Lawrence, O Lawrence, destroy the power of this furious people!

So such warriors as were at hand drew up in two ranks, one line under the warlike Bolesław himself, the other under his flag-

[3] Gps. 67:36.

vero eius signifer Scarbimirus.[1] Nam cetere multitudinis alii pabulum equorum, alii victualia queritabant, alii vero vias et tramites et adventum hostium observabant. Nec mora Bolezlauus inpiger educit agmina, sic verbis paucissimis commonendo: Vestra probitas et imminentis periculi necessitas, amorque patrie magis quam oracio mea, vos invictissimi iuvenes, exhortentur. Hodie, Deo favente, sanctoque Laurencio deprecante, Pomoranorum ydolatria ac militaris superbia vestris ensibus conteretur. Nec plura locutus cepit hostes in circuitu transgirare, quia sic in terra hastas suas versis cuspidibus in hostes affixerant, seseque simul constipaverant, quod nullus poterat ad eos virtute nisi cum ingenio penetrare. Erant enim, ut dictum est superius, pedites fere cuncti, nec ad prelium more christianorum ordinati, sed sicut lupi insidiantes ovibus in terram poplitibus recurvati. Dumque magis inpiger Bolezlauus circumquaque volitare videretur quam currere, transversis in eum hostibus, Scarbimirus intrandi locum inveniens ex adverso, non differt in cuneos diutius confertissimos penetrare. Penetratis itaque barbaris ac vallatis, acriter inprimis resistunt, sed coacti tandem fugam petunt. De christianis ibi quidam probi milites cadunt, paganorum vero de XL[a] milibus decem milia vix evadunt.[2] Testor Deum, ope cuius sanctumque Laurentium, prece cuius facta fuerit ista cedes. Ammirabantur, qui aderant, quomodo tam subito a militibus minus mille peracta fuerit tanta strages. Dicuntur enim ipsi Pomorani certo numero computasse de suis ibi XXVII milia corruisse, quod[b] in paludibus interessent, nec illi quidem sic evadere potuissent.[3] Oppidani vero videntes se totam spem amisisse, nec auxilium aliunde vel a quolibet

[a] triginta *Mal*

[b] quot *H*, qui *Mal*

---

[1] See above II:29, p. 174, n. 4.

[2] 'Forty thousand' according to the MSS here, but the Epilogus (above, p. 217) gives the total of enemy combatants as thirty thousand. The figure of forty thousand better fits the Pomeranian estimate that (subtracting the ten thousand who escaped) the dead numbered twenty-seven thousand.

bearer, Skarbimir.[1] For the rest of the host were elsewhere, some in search of provisions, others of fodder for the horses, while others were watching the roads and paths against the arrival of the enemy. Without delay restless Bolesław leads out his ranks, giving them the briefest of exhortation: "My unconquerable young friends, let your mettle and the pressing danger and your love of your country, rather than any words from me, stir your hearts. Today, with God's favor and the intercession of St. Lawrence, may the idolatry of the Pomeranians and their martial pride be crushed by your swords." Saying no more, he began to circle the enemy, for they had driven their spears into the ground with the points turned towards the enemy and were crowded together in tight formation which could not be penetrated by courage alone without cunning as well. For, as was said above, they were almost all foot soldiers, and were not drawn up for battle in Christian fashion, but were crouching on the ground with bent legs, like wolves in wait for sheep. Restless Bolesław seemed more to fly on all sides than to ride, and while he was turning the enemy against himself, Skarbimir found a point to break through from the side, and waited no longer to burst into the thickest of their ranks. So the barbarians' line was broken and surrounded. At first they resisted fiercely, but finally they were forced to flee. A few brave warriors fell among the Christians, but of the pagans barely ten thousand out of the forty thousand escaped.[2] I call to witness God, by whose help, and St. Lawrence, by whose prayers this slaughter was brought about. Those present were amazed how such a great slaughter could so quickly have been made by less than a thousand warriors. For the Pomeranians themselves are said to have calculated that for sure twenty seven thousand of their men fell there, because they were in the marshes and thus could not have escaped.[3] The townsmen, seeing that all hope was lost, and that no help could be expected from any other quarter or anyone, surrendered the

[3] The exact sense of the Latin is unclear.

expectare, civitatem vita donata reddiderunt. Audientes autem
hec de sex aliis castellis oppidani consilium itidem inierunt, se
ipsos videlicet municionesque tradiderunt.[1]

(2) EPISTOLA IMPERATORIS AD BOLEZLAUM

Dum hec aguntur, Henricus imperator IIII[us], Rome nondum
coronatus, secundo quidem anno coronandus,[2] cum verbis huiuscemodi Bolezlauo legationem premisit, cum exercitu violenti
Poloniam invasurus, dicens: Indignum est enim imperatori
legibusque Romanis inhibitum fines hostis presertimque sui
militis prius hostiliter introire,[3] quam eum sciscitari de pace, si
voluerit obedire, vel de bello, si resisterit, ut se valeat premunire.
Quapropter aut oportet te fratrem tuum in regni medietatem
recipere, mihique CCC[as] marcas annuatim tributarias, vel
totidem milites in expedicionem dare, vel mecum, si vales, ense
Polonorum regnum dividere. Ad hec Bolezlauus, dux septentrionalis, respondit: Si pecuniam nostram vel Polonos milites pro
tributo requiris, si libertatem nostram non defendimus, pro
feminis nos habeas, non pro viris. Hominem vero seditiosum
recipere, vel unicum cum eo regnum dividere, non me coget
ullius violencia potestatis, nisi meorum commune consilium[4] et
arbitrium mee proprie voluntatis. Quodsi bonitate, non ferocitate pecuniam vel milites in auxilium Romane ecclesie postu-

---

[1] Gumplowicz, Zbigniew, p. 75, suggests, on later evidence, that at least five
castles (Vandsburg, Raciąż, Zieten, Wissek, and Prochy) belonged to the
district of Nakło.

[2] In fact, Emperor Henry V (1091–1125), consecrated emperor on April 13
1111.

[3] The reference to Roman law may be to the archaic tradition that it was
ungodly (*impius*) for Rome to wage war unless the *fetiales* (a special college of
priests) had warned the enemy and given them time to redress the alleged
wrong; see Adolf Berger, *Encyclopedic Dictionary of Roman Law* (Philadel-

city in return for their lives. On hearing this, the people of six other castles made the same decision, namely to surrender themselves and their fortifications.[1]

2 THE EMPEROR'S LETTER TO BOLESŁAW

While this was happening, the emperor Henry the Fourth—who had not yet been crowned in Rome but was due to be crowned only in the following year[2]—sent an embassy to Bolesław with the following message, while planning to invade Poland in force: "It is improper for an emperor, and forbidden by Roman laws, to enter the territory of a foe, and especially one who is his knight,[3] in hostile fashion before asking him to choose peace should he wish to obey, or war should he resist, so that he be able to prepare himself. Therefore you must either grant your brother the half of the kingdom, and give me 300 marks yearly in tribute or the same number of fighting men for campaigns, or else divide the kingdom of Poland with me by the sword, if you can." To this answered Bolesław, duke of the north: "If it is our money or Polish troops that you seek as tribute, you may call us women, not men, if we do not defend our liberty. To take back a person who caused sedition, or to partition an undivided kingdom with him, is not something that any person's violence and power will force me to do, unless it be the common counsel of my men[4] and my own will and decision. Now if you had called for money or troops in aid of the Church of Rome, amicably,

---

phia: The American Philosophical Society, 1953), s.v. "Bellum." The author may have learned about this custom through his readings of Livy or Cicero, who refer to it. The expression 'suus miles' is reminiscent of the feudal vocabulary of vassalage. However, as mentioned before, the term miles has a complicated history, and it might not have been applied in a technical sense in early twelfth-century Central Europe.

[4] The mention here of a commune consilium is an early hint at some kind of curia regis consultations in twelfth-century Poland.

lasses, non minus auxilii vel consilii[1] forsan apud nos, quam tui antecessores apud nostros impetrares.

> Ergo provideas, cui minaris,
> Bellum invenies, si bellaris.

(3)

Ex qua responsione cesar pernimium ad iracundiam provocatus, talia mente concipit, talemque viam incipit, unde non exibit, neque redibit, nisi se ipso suoque dampno quam maximo castigatus.[2] Zbigneus quoque cesarem iratum ex hoc multo magis incitabat, quia paucos de Polonis sibi resistere promittebat. Insuper etiam Bohemi, vivere predis et rapinis assueti, cesarem Poloniam intrare animabant, quia se scire vias et tramites per silvas Polonie iactitabant. Cesar ergo talibus monitis et consiliis superandi Poloniam in spem ductus, ingrediens, Bytomque[3] perveniens, in hiis omnibus est seductus. Namque castrum Bytom sic armatum sicque munitum aspexit, quod Zbigneum iratus cum verbis indignacionis respexit. Zbigneue, cesar inquit, sic te Poloni pro domino recognoscunt, sic fratrem relinquere tuumque dominium sic deposcunt. Cumque castrum Bytom municione situque nature et aquarum circuicione inexpugnabile cum aciebus ordinatis preterire voluisset, quidam de suis famosi milites ad castrum declinaverunt, volentes in Polonia suam miliciam comprobari, viresque Polonorum et audaciam experiri. At contra castellani portis apertis et extractis ensibus exierunt,

---

[1] *Auxilium et consilium* was a standard formula regarding the obligations of retainers and vassals (cf. p. 226, n. 3, above).

[2] The translation is uncertain, and several emendations to the Latin have been proposed; see Mal. 131, nn. a-d.

[3] Bytom Odrzański in Lower Silesia, see the emperor's itinerary; according to Karl-Friedrich Stumpf-Brentano, *Die Reichskanzler vornehmlich des X., XI.*

not violently, you might perhaps receive no less aid and counsel[1]
from us than your forebears did from ours.

> So take good care to whom you threat;
> If war you want, it's war you'll get."

3 [BEGINNING OF THE WAR WITH HENRY]

This retort threw the emperor into an exceeding rage. He devised
a plan and entered upon a course with no way out nor back
without punishment and most severe loss to himself and his
people.[2] Zbigniew was also inciting the emperor in his anger yet
further because he assured that few of the Poles would resist him.
Moreover, the Czechs, too, accustomed to living off raiding and
plunder, were urging the emperor to invade Poland, boasting
that they were familiar with all the ways and paths through the
forests of Poland. So with this advice and encouragement the
emperor was led to hope that he could conquer Poland, and he
crossed the border and came to Bytom.[3] In all this he had been
led astray. For at the sight of the castle Bytom he realized that
it was well armed and fortified. He turned angrily to Zbignew
and exclaimed in indignation: "Zbigniew! Is this how the Poles
acknowledge you as lord? Is this how they plan to abandon your
brother and call for your lordship?" Indeed, with its defenses and
its natural position, surrounded by waters, the castle of Bytom
was impregnable, and the emperor decided to bypass it with his
columns of troops. But some of his knights of repute rode off
to the castle, wishing to prove their martial prowess in Poland
and to test the strength and the courage of the Poles. However,
the garrison in response opened the gates and sallied forth with
swords at the ready. Undaunted either by the numerous host of

und XII. Jahrhunderts (Innsbruck: Wagner, 1865), Nr. 3035, the campaign
began around 15 August 1109. Cosmas, *Chron. Boh.* III:27, p. 195, says the
emperor entered Poland in September. For the general context, see Stefan
Weinfurter, *The Salian Century: Main Currents in an Age of Transition*, trans.
Barbara M. Bowlus (Philadelphia: University of Pennsylvania Press, 1999).

nec multitudinem tam diversarum gentium,[1] nec impetum Alemannorum, nec presentiam cesaris metuentes, sed in frontibus eis audacter ac viriliter resistentes. Quod considerans imperator, vehementer est miratus homines scilicet nudos contra clipeatos, vel clipeatos contra loricatos nudis ensibus decertare et tam alacriter ad pugnam velud ad epulas properare.[2] Tunc quasi suorum presumpcioni militum indignans, suos balistarios et sagittarios illuc misit, quorum terrore castellani saltim sic cederent et in castrum sese reciperent. At Poloni pila vel sagittas, que undique volitabant, quasi nivem vel guttas pluvie computabant. Ibi vero cesar primum Polonorum audaciam comprobavit, quia suos inde cunctos non incolumes revocavit. Nunc autem paulisper cesarem spatiari per silvas Polonie permittamus[3], donec draconem flammivomum[4] de Pomorania reducamus.

(4)

Igitur inpiger Bolezlauus in Pomorania superato prelio supradicto, septemque castellis acquisitis, audito pro certo, quod cesar Poloniam introisset, viris et equis obsessione diutina fatigatis, quibusdam militum interemptis, quibusdam etiam sauciatis, aliisque domum cum eis dimissis, cum quibus potuit equitavit et obstruere transitus et vada fluminis Odre modis omnibus comendavit. Obstrusa sunt itaque loca quecumque poterant vel sicco flumine transvadari, vel si que poterant ab ipsis incolis occulta forsitan attemptari. Quosdam etiam probos milites ad Glogow et ad fluminis transitus observandos premisit, qui cesari tam diu resisterent, donec ipso succurrente super ripam fluminis aut omnino victoriam obtinerent, aut saltim, eum ibi detinendo,

---

[1] The emperor's army included Bavarians, Allemans, Franks, Rhinelanders, and Saxons, as well as Czechs, according to Cosmas, *Chron. Boh.* III:27, p. 195.

[2] Cf. Justin, *Epitome* 1.8: *veluti ad epulas non ad bellum venissent.*

[3] While it cannot be proved that the verb *spatiari* is used ironically, we would like to think it is. Elsewhere the author's humor—a topic deserving further

diverse peoples[1] or the charge of the Germans or the presence of the emperor, they faced them boldly and resisted manfully. The sight of this greatly amazed the emperor: how could unprotected men face foot soldiers, or foot soldiers face knights in armor with bare swords, and go into battle as cheerfully as if they were going to a feast?[2] He felt in a way angry at the presumption of his men, and sent up archers and crossbow men, feeling sure that this at least would frighten off the defenders and compel them to withdraw into the castle. But the spears and arrows that flew from all sides were like snow or raindrops to the Poles. Now for the first time the emperor appreciated the Poles' courage, and called his men back, not all unharmed. But let us leave the emperor for a little while to enjoy his stroll through the forests of Poland,[3] while we bring back the fire-breathing dragon[4] from Pomerania.

4 [BOLESŁAW READIES FOR WAR]

Restless Bolesław, who had won the aforementioned battle in Pomerania and gained seven fortresses, as soon as he heard the news that the emperor had marched into Poland, although his men and horses were exhausted from the long siege, and some of his warriors had been killed, some wounded, and others sent back home with them, rode out with the soldiers that he could muster, and ordered that all means be used to block the fords and crossings of the river Oder. So all places were blocked that could be forded if the river was dry, or any hidden crossings where one might possibly attempt to cross with the help of the local inhabitants. He also sent some picked warriors ahead to Głogów to guard the river crossings. They were to oppose the emperor's advance as long as they could, and while he was coming to their aid, either win outright victory or at least hold

study—ranges from the ghoulish (III:9 below) to slapstick (I:26); see further above, p. xlii–iii.

[4] See II:39, p. 191, above.

exercitum et auxilium expectarent. Ibi vero Bolezlauus, non longe remotus a Glogow, cum exercitu parvo stabat, neque mirum, quia suos diutissime fatigarat. Ibi rumores et legationes audiebat, ibi suum exercitum expectabat, inde exploratores huc illucque transmittebat, inde camerarios pro suis et pro Ruthenis et Pannonicis delegabat.[1]

(5)

Cesar autem iter faciens, non sursum sive deorsum vada temptando declinavit, sed iuxta civitatem Glogow cum impetu per locum inestimabilem, nullo prius ibi transitum presciente, nulloque sibi resistente, cum densis agminibus et armatis, non preparatis civibus, transvadavit, per illum locum numquam castellanis dubitantibus nec sperantibus dubitandum. Erat enim sancti Bartholomei apostoli dies festus, quando cesar fluvium transiebat[2] et tunc totus civitatis populus divinum officium audiebat. Unde constat, quia securus et sine periculo pertransivit, predamque multam et homines et etiam tentoria circa oppidum acquisivit. Eorum quoque plurimi, qui castrum defendere venerant et extra castrum in tentoriis residebant, a cesare castrum sunt intrare prohibiti; quidam ibi subito retenti, quidam vero fuga subveniente liberati. Quorum unus Bolezlauo fugiens obviavit, qui cuncta, que contigerant, enarravit. Tunc vero Bolezlauus non sicut lepus formidolosus evanuit, sed suos sicut miles animosus ammonuit. O fortissimi milites, inquiens, in multis mecum bellis et expedicionibus fatigati, nunc quoque mecum estote pro libertate Polonie vel mori vel vivere[3] preparati. Ego quidem iam cum tam parva manu prelium libens contra cesarem inirem, si scirem pro certo, quod etiam ibi me moriente discrimen patrie diffinirem. Sed quoniam ad unum de nostris

---

[1] The role of auxiliaries from Rus' and Hungary is debated and, in fact, they are not mentioned elsewhere in connection with this campaign. The Hungarians' presence is also doubtful in view of the peace made by King Coloman with the emperor (see above p. 202, n. 2).

up the emperor there and await the army and reinforcement. Bolesław stationed himself not far from Głogów, with, not surprisingly, a small force, since he had driven his men to exhaustion over a very long period. There he could listen to rumors and messages, wait for his army, send out scouts hither and thither, and dispatch his chamberlains for his own people and the Ruthenians and Hungarians.[1]

5 [THE SIEGE OF GŁOGÓW]

Marching on, the emperor did not, however, turn aside to test the fords either upstream or downstream, but crossed the river near the city of Głogów in force, in dense columns, in full armor, at an unforeseen place where no one previously knew that one could cross. He met with no resistance, as the townsmen were unprepared and the garrison had no suspicion nor thought to have any suspicions about that place. It was the feast-day of St. Bartholomew the Apostle when the emperor was crossing,[2] and the whole population of the city was hearing divine service. Accordingly, he crossed over without trouble or danger, capturing a great deal of booty and captives near the town, as well as tents. Many of the men who had come to defend the castle and were encamped in tents outside the castle were prevented by the emperor from entering the castle. Some were seized right away, some managed to escape by flight. One of the fugitives met Bolesław and told him everything that had happened. At this point Bolesław did not bolt like a frightened rabbit, but as a spirited warrior urged his men on. "O bravest of warriors! You have worn yourselves out in many battles and campaigns with me. Now again stand by me, ready to live or die[3] for Poland's liberty. For my part I would willingly take on the emperor with so few troops if I knew for sure that even if I died here I would end the tribulations of our country. But since for every one of

[2] 24 August 1109.
[3] 1 Macc. 4:35.

restant de hostibus plus quam centum, hic est honestius residen-
dum,[a] quam illuc cum paucis eundo presumptuose moriendum.
Hic enim nobis residentibus,[b,1] eisque transitum prohibentibus,
satis pro victoria reputabitur. Hec dixit et rivulum, super quem
stabat, arboribus cesis obstruere cepit.

(6)

Interim vero cesar a Glogouiensibus obsides tali condicione sub
iureiurando recepit, quod si pacem vel aliquam paccionem infra
spatium quinque dierum missa legacione cives efficerent, reddita
responsione vel pace composita vel prohibita, cives tamen suos
obsides rehaberent. Et hoc utique per ingenium factum fuit. Ob
hoc utique cesar obsides cum iuramento recepit, quia per eos
civitatem, licet cum periurio, consequi se reputavit. Ob hoc
etiam Glogouienses illos obsides posuerunt, quia loca civitatis
interim vetustate consumpta munierunt.

(7)

At Bolezlauus audita legacione de datis obsidibus indignatus,
crucem civibus, si propter ipsos castrum reddiderint, est mi-
natus, adiciens esse melius et honestius et cives et obsides gladio
pro patria morituros, quam facta dedicione vitam inhonestam
redimentes, alienis gentibus servituros.[2] Recepta responsione,
cives Bolezlauum pacem sic fieri nolle referunt, obsidesque suos,
sicut iuraverant, requirunt. Ad hec cesar respondit: obsides
quidem, si mihi castrum reddideritis, non tenebo, sed si rebelles

---

[a] resistendum *Z H*
[b] resistentibus *Z H*

---

[1] The MSS reading *resistentibus* would slightly change the meaning to 'if we
oppose him'; similarly in the previous sentence.

us there is a hundred of the enemy, it is more honorable to hold back than to venture there with few and die a reckless death. If we remain[1] here and block their crossing this will be deemed as good as a victory." So he spoke, and set about cutting down trees to block the stream by which he was standing.

6 [A TRUCE WITH THE PEOPLE OF GŁOGÓW]

In the meantime, however, the emperor accepted hostages under oath from the people of Głogów on the understanding that if the townsmen sent an embassy with an offer of peace and a treaty within the space of five days, they would receive a reply and, whether peace was agreed to or not, they would still receive back their hostages. In fact, all this was a trick. The emperor's reason for receiving hostages under oath was that he thought he could gain possession of the city through them even if it meant perjuring himself. And the reason the people of Głogów handed over the hostages was that they had in the meantime fortified those parts of the city which had crumbled with age.

7 [THE TRUCE BROKEN]

But when Bolesław heard of the embassy and the giving of hostages, he was outraged. He threatened to crucify the townspeople if they surrendered the castle for the sake of them, adding that it was better and more honorable for both the townsmen and the hostages to perish by the sword for their country's sake than by surrender to purchase a life of disgrace and live as slaves to foreign peoples.[2] When they heard his response the townsmen sent back word that Bolesław refused to accept peace on these terms and called for the return of their hostages, as had been sworn to. The emperor's reply to this was: "If you surrender the castle, I will not keep the hostages; but if you are rebellious, I

[2] Cf. Regino, *Chronicon* ad a. 874, p.107: *melius nobiliter mori quam ignominia vitam servare.*

fueritis, et vos et obsides iugulabo. E contra castellani: tu quidem in obsidibus et periurium poteris et homicidium perpetrare, sed per ipsos, quod requiris, scias te nullatenus impetrare.

(8)

Hiis dictis cesar instrumenta fieri, arma capi, legiones dividi, civitatem vallari, signiferos[a] tubis canere precepit et urbem undique ferro, flamma, machinis expugnare cepit. E contra cives se ipsos per portas et turres dividunt, propugnacula muniunt, instrumenta parant, lapides et aquam super portas et turres comportant. Tunc imperator civium animos pietate filiorum et amicorum existimans posse flecti, precepit nobiliores ex obsidibus ipsius civitatis et filium comitis super machinas colligari, sic reputans sibi sine sanguine civitatem aperiri. At castellani non plus filiis vel propinquis, quam Bohemis vel Alemannis parcebant, sed eos abscedere a muro lapidibus et armis coercebant. Videns autem imperator, quod tali numquam ingenio civitatem superaret, nec umquam a proposito civium animos revocaret, viribus et armis obtinere nititur, quod ingenio denegatur. Igitur undique castrum appetitur et utrimque clamor ingens attollitur. Teutunici castrum inpetunt, Poloni se defendunt, undique tormenta moles emittunt, baliste crepant, iacula, sagitte per aera volant, clipei perforantur, lorice penetrantur, galee conquassantur, mortui corruunt, vulnerati cedunt, eorum loco sani succedunt. Theutonici balistas intorquebant, Poloni tormenta cum balistis; Theutonici sagittas, Poloni iacula cum sagittis; Theutonici fundas cum lapidibus rotabant, Poloni lapides molares cum sudibus preacutis; Theutonici trabibus protecti murum

---

[a] *add* prefici *Mal*

will kill both you and the hostages." The people of the town retorted: "Regarding the hostages you can commit both perjury and murder, but know this: in no way will you obtain what you want by using them."

8 [ATTACK ON THE CITY OF GŁOGÓW]

After this exchange the emperor gave orders for equipment to be prepared, arms donned, the legions divided, a rampart to be raised around the city, and the standard-bearers to sound the trumpets; he then launched an assault upon the city from all sides with iron, fire, and siege-engines. The townsfolk in turn deployed themselves upon the gates and towers, fortified the battlements, made ready their equipment, and stored rocks and water above the gates and towers. The emperor then had the idea that he might be able to sway the townspeople through their affection for their sons and friends, so he ordered the more noble among the hostages of the town, including the son of the *comes*, to be bound to siege-engines, thinking in this way the city would be opened without bloodshed. But the townsmen would no more spare their sons and relatives than the Czechs and Germans; instead, they drove them from the walls with stones and weapons. The emperor realizing that he would never win the city with such tactics or shake the townsmen in their resolve, and decided to win by force of arms what he had been denied by guile. So the castle was assaulted from all directions, and from both sides a ringing cry went up. The Germans charged the castle, the Poles kept them at bay, engines on all sides hurled boulders, crossbows twanged, spears and arrows flew through the air. Shields were shattered, armor pierced, helmets smashed apart. The dead fell, the wounded retired, fresh men took their place. The Germans cranked their crossbows, the Poles replied with engines and crossbows. The Germans fired arrows, the Poles arrows and spears as well. The Germans whirled stones from slings, the Poles hurled mill-stones along with sharpened stakes. The Germans tried to approach the walls under the cover of

subire temptabant, Poloni vero ignem comburentem aquamque ferventem illis pro balneo temperabant. Theutonici arietes ferreos turribus subducebant, Poloni vero rotas calibe stellatas desuper evolvebant. Theutonici scalis erectis superius ascendebant, Poloni vero uncis affixos ferreis eos in aera suspendebant.[1]

(9)

Interea Bolezlauus die noctuque non cessabat, sed quandoque de castris exeuntes pro victualibus agitabat, frequenter etiam ipsius castra cesaris territabat, modo huc modo illuc predatoribus vel combustoribus insidiando cursitabat. Talibus ergo modis cesar multisque diebus civitatem capere nitebatur, nec aliud quam carnem humanam suorum cottidie recentem lucrabatur. Cottidie namque viri nobiles ibi perimebantur, qui visceribus extractis sale vel aromatibus conditi in Bauariam ab imperatore vel in Saxoniam portandi, pro tributo Polonie curribus onustis servabantur.

(10)

Cumque vidisset cesar, quia nec armis, nec minis, nec muneribus, nec promissis cives flectere, neque diucius ibi stando quicquam proficere potuisset, inito consilio contra Wratislauiensem urbem castra movit, ubi quoque vires Bolezlai et ingenium recognovit. Nam quocumque cesar se vertebat, vel ubicumque castra vel stationes faciebat, Bolezlauus quoque quandoque anterius, quandoque posterius incedebat, semperque vicinus stacioni cesaris persistebat. Cumque cesar iter faciens sua castra dimovebat, Bolezlauus quoque comes itineris existebat, et si quisquam de ordinibus exiebat, redeundi statim memoriam amittebat et si

---

[1] Jacek Banaszkiewicz, in "Note sur le thème du siège triparti: Capitole, Narbonne et Głogów," *Annales ESC* 39 (1984): 776–82, compares this siege description with that of Rome by the Gauls in 390 BC in Livy, and of Narbonne in the *chanson de geste* known as *I Nerbonesi*; cf., however, Sallust, *Jug.* 57.

wooden beams, but the Poles prepared them a bath of boiling water and scorching flames. The Germans brought up iron rams to the towers, but the Poles rolled down wheels bristling with steel spikes. The Germans placed ladders and tried to climb up, but the Poles gaffed them with iron hooks and left them suspended in mid-air.[1]

9 [THE GERMANS GAIN WOUNDS AND DEAD FOR TRIBUTE]

Meanwhile Bolesław rested neither night nor day. At times he would harass those who left camp in search of supplies, often too he would even terrorise the emperor's camp, or range now here now there to lay traps for those intent on plundering and burning. So by these means the emperor spent many days in his efforts to take the city, and all he gained was the human flesh of his men, fresh each day. For every day noble men perished there, and their eviscerated bodies, preserved in salt and spices, were loaded onto carts to be sent back by the emperor to Bavaria or Saxony—this was his tribute from Poland!

10 [THE PANIC OF THE GERMANS AS THEY ARE HARASSED FRONT AND REAR]

When the emperor saw that the townspeople could neither be moved by force of arms, nor threats, nor bribes, nor promises, nor could he make any gains by staying there longer, he came up with a plan and moved his camp against the city of Wrocław. But here he again realized Bolesław's strength and ingenuity. For wherever the emperor turned, or wherever he set up camp or placed outposts, Bolesław too advanced, sometimes before him, sometimes after him, but always remaining the neighbor of the emperor in his quarters. And when the emperor set out and moved camp, Bolesław would always be his companion on his journey. If any one left their ranks and could not remember the

quandoque plures, victualia vel pabulum equorum querentes, freti multitudine longius a castris procedebant, inter eos et exercitum Bolezlauus se statim medium opponebat et sic predam capientes ipsi quoque Bolezlaui preda fiebant.[1] Unde tantum ac talem exercitum ad tantum pavorem redegerat, quod etiam ipsos Bohemos, naturaliter raptores, vel sua manducare, vel ieiunare coegerat. Nullus enim exire de castris audebat, nullus armiger herbam colligere, nullus etiam ad ventrem purgandum ire ultra constitutas custodum acies presumebat. Die noctuque Bolezlauus timebatur, ab omnibus in memoria habebatur: Bolezlauus non dormiens vocabatur. Si silvula, si frutectum erat, Cave tibi, ibi latitat, clamabatur. Non erat locus, ubi non putaretur Bolezlauus. Taliter eos assidue fatigabat, quandoque de capite, quandoque de cauda sicut lupus aliquos rapiebat, quandoque vero a lateribus insistebat. Sicque milites armati cottidie procedebant et assidue Bolezlauum quasi presentem expectabant. In nocte quoque cuncti loricati dormiebant, vel in stationibus residebant, alii vigilias faciebant, alii castra nocte continua circuibant, alii: vigilate, cavete, custodite, clamabant, alii cantilenas de Bolezlaui probitate decantabant, hoc modo.

(11)[2]

Bolezlaue, Bolezlaue dux gloriosissime,
Tu defendis terram tuam quam studiosissime.
Tu non dormis, nec permittis nos dormire paululum,
Nec per diem, nec per noctem, neque per diluculum.

[1] The Latin plays on two slightly different senses of *preda*, 'plunder' and 'prey.'
[2] While it is rather unlikely that the emperors' soldiers would really have sung such a song, it is noteworthy that the author does not leave it at that but adds (below) a whole story about the reaction of the emperor and his counselors to it. Elsewhere, too, the Polish duke is shown as being praised by his enemies,

way back immediately, or if ever a party of them, trusting in numbers, went further from camp in search of supplies or fodder for the horses, Bolesław would immediately move between them and the main force; so those in search of plunder themselves fell prey to Bolesław.[1] As a result, he reduced this large and fine army to such a state of fear that even the Czechs—born robbers—were forced to eat what they had or to go hungry. For none of them dared to set foot outside camp; no soldier would go to collect grass nor even venture beyond the lines of the watch in order to relieve themselves. Bolesław was feared day and night, he was in everyone's thoughts. "Bolesław who never sleeps" they called him. If there was a little grove or a patch of bushes, "Watch out," they would shout, "he's hiding in wait there!" There was no place where they might not imagine Bolesław to be. So he wore them down relentlessly, like a wolf, taking some at times from the front, at times from the rear, and at times moving in from the flanks. So every day the soldiers advanced fully armed, and at all times awaited Bolesław as if he were present. Even at night they all slept in armor or manned the outposts, some keeping watch and some moving about the camp all night. Some shouted, "Keep awake, watch out, be on guard!" Others would sing songs about Bolesław's bravery, like the following:

11 [SONG OF THE GERMANS IN PRAISE OF BOLESŁAW][2]

O Bolesław O Bolesław, famous prince and valiant,
With what zeal and matchless courage you defend your native land!
Day or night you neither sleep nor let us have a moment's rest,
Not at night or in the daytime, not at dawn and not at dusk.

even if not in as elaborate a form as here; e.g. at II:17, p. 153, he is styled "the wolf's son" by the Pomeranians, and is acknowledged as invincible at II:33, p. 179.

Et cum nos te putaremus de terra propellere,
Tu nos tenes ita quasi conclusos in carcere.
Talis princeps debet regnum atque terram regere,
Qui cum paucis tot et tantos ita scit corrigere.

Quid, si forte suos omnes simul congregaverit,
Numquam cesar sibi bello resistere poterit.
Talem virum condeceret regnum et imperium,
Qui cum paucis sic domabat tot catervas hostium.

Et cum nondum recreatus sit de Pomorania,
Sic per eum fatigatur nostra contumatia.
Et cum illi cum triumpho sit eundum obviam,
Nos e contra cogitamus expugnare patriam.

Ipse quidem cum paganis bella gerit licita,
Sed nos contra christianos gerimus illicita.
Unde Deus est cum eo faciens victoriam,
Nobis vero iuste reddit illatam iniuriam.

(12)

Quidam vero viri nobiles et discreti hec audientes, mirabantur
inter se referentes: Nisi Deus hunc hominem adiuvaret, nunquam tantam de paganis victoriam ei daret, neque nobis ita
viriliter contra staret. Et ni Deus eum ita potencialiter exaltaret,
numquam eum noster populus sic laudaret. Sed Deus secreto
forsan consilio hec agebat, qui laudes cesaris ad Bolezlaum transferebat. Vox enim populi semper solet voci dominice convenire.[1]
Unde constat Dei voluntati populum cantantem obedire. Cesari
vero cantilena populi displicebat, eamque cantari sepissime pro-

---

[1] Cf. George Boas, *Vox Dei, vox populi: Essays in the History of an Idea*
(Baltimore: Johns Hopkins UP, 1969).

Thinking that we'd quickly drive you out of Poland and prevail,
We're the ones whom you've encircled and enclosed as in a jail.
Such a prince should have a kingdom and a land beneath his sway,
Who can with so few beside him teach so many to obey.

What would it be like if he could ever muster all his might:
Never would the emperor prevail against him in a fight!
He would well deserve a kingdom, nay even imperial rights
Who can tame such hordes of warriors with a handful of his knights!

Back from Pomerania hardly had he time to rest again,
Now he comes to punish us for being arrogant and vain;
While a fitter meeting would be at his triumphal entry,
We do what we can to conquer him and seize his own country.

He is fighting wars against the pagans, which is right and just,
Whereas we attack our fellow Christians, which is quite unjust;
That's why God is on his side and gives to him the victory,
That he justly can repay us for insult and injury.

12 [THE EMPEROR FORCED
TO SUE FOR PEACE]

When they heard such things, certain men of worth and pru-
dence marveled and said to each other: "If God were not with
this man, He would never grant him so great a victory over the
pagans, nor would he stand against us so stoutly. If God did not
exalt him so powerfully, our people would never sing his praises
like this. But perhaps all this was a secret plan of God's to transfer
the emperor's praises to Bolesław; for the voice of the people
normally always accords with the voice of the Lord.[1] Hence it is
clear that the people by their singing are obeying the will of
God." However, this song annoyed the emperor, and time and

hibebat, sed eo magis ad tantam procacitatem populum prorsus commovebat. Cesar vero exemplis et operibus recognoscens, quia frustra laborando populum affligebat, nec divine voluntati resistere valebat, aliud secrecius cogitavit et aliud se facturum simulavit. Perpendebat utique, quia tantus populus sine preda diucius vivere nequibat et quia Bolezlauus eos assidue, sicut leo rugiens[1] circuibat. Equi moriebantur, viri vigiliis, labore, fame cruciabantur, silve condense, paludes tenaces, musce pungentes, sagitte acute, rustici mordaces[2] compleri propositum non sinebant. Unde se Cracow simulans ire velle, legatos de pace Bolezlauo misit et pecuniam non tantam, nec tam superbe, sicut prius quesierat, in hec verba.

(13) EPISTOLA CESARIS AD REGEM[a,3] POLONICUM BOLEZLAUM

Cesar Bolezlauo duci Polonie gratiam et salutem. Tua probitate comperta, meorum principum consiliis acquiesco et CCC marcas recipiens, hinc pacifice remeabo. Hoc mihi satis sufficit ad honorem, si pacem simul habuerimus et amorem. Sin autem hoc tibi placuerit reprobare, in sede cito Cracouiensi me poteris expectare.

(14) RESCRIPTUM AD CESAREM

Ad hec dux septentrionalis remandavit: Cesari Bolezlauus dux Polonorum pacem quidem, sed non in spe denariorum. Vestre quidem cesaree potestati ire consistit vel redire,[4] sed apud me

---

[a] ducem *Mal*

---

[1] For the lion-simile, see above, I:7, p. 46; II:33, p. 177; II:36, p. 185; II:37, p. 187; III:Epil., p. 221; etc.

[2] Literally: 'biting.'

again he forbade it to be sung, but this merely encouraged the people further to such insolence. Nevertheless, by these examples and actions the emperor recognized that by these vain labors he was afflicting the people and that he was unable to resist the divine will. So he devised a secret plan, while pretending to be going to do something else. He was aware that without raiding so large a multitude could not live much longer, but that Bolesław was circling them continually, like a roaring lion.[1] The horses were dying, the men were tormented with lack of sleep, labor, and starvation, and the dense woods, the mud of the swamps, stinging flies, sharp arrows, and vicious[2] peasants were frustrating his plans. So he pretended he wanted to go to Cracow, but he sent peace negotiators to Bolesław, demanding money, but not as much as previously, nor so high-handedly. This was the message:

13 THE EMPEROR'S LETTER TO BOLESŁAW THE POLISH KING[3]

"The emperor to Duke Bolesław of Poland: grace and greetings. Having discovered your qualities, I am acquiescing to the advice of my princes, and on receipt of 300 marks I will withdraw from here in peace. This is enough to satisfy my honor if we have peace and love at the same time. However, if you choose to reject this offer, you can soon expect me in the city of Cracow."

14 THE ANSWER TO THE EMPEROR

To this the duke of the north sent the following reply. "Bolesław duke of the Poles to the emperor: peace indeed, but not in hope of money. It rests in your imperial power to proceed or return,[4]

[3] So according to the MSS; as the author otherwise does not style Bolesław "king," the critical edition emends to "duke," but the wording of the chapter-titles was the choice of the scribe who added these, and not the author's.

[4] I.e. to proceed on to Cracow, or go home; in other words, to pursue the war or not.

tamen pro timore vel condicione nec ullum poteris vilem obulum invenire. Malo enim ad horam regnum Polonie salva libertate perdere, quam semper pacifice cum infamia retinere.[1]

(15)

Hiis auditis cesar urbem Wratislauiensem adivit, ubi nichil nisi de vivis mortuos acquisivit. Cumque diucius ire se Cracow simulando, huc illucque circa fluvium circumviaret et Bolezlauo sic terrorem incutere eiusque animum revocare cogitaret, Bolezlaus ideo nichil omnino diffidebat, nec aliud legatis, quam superius respondebat.[2] Videns ergo cesar diu stando sibi pocius dampnum et dedecus quam honorem vel proficuum imminere, disposuit, pro tributo nichil portans nisi cadavera, se redire. Unde quia prius superbe magnam pecuniam requisivit, ad extremum pauca querens, neque denarium acquisivit.[3] Et quoniam superbe libertatem antiquam Polonie subigere cogitavit, *iustus iudex* illud *consilium fatuavit* et iniuriam in Suatopolc consiliarium et illam et aliam vindicavit.[4]

---

[1] *Ad horam* can mean either 'at once' or 'for the time being.' The Latin leaves open whether "freedom" refers to Poland or the person of the ruler (in the sense of his being a free agent?); we follow the more commonly accepted interpretation.

[2] On the negotiations between Bolesław and the emperor, see Gerald Meyer von Knonau, *Jahrbücher des Deutschen Reiches unter Heinrich IV. und Heinrich V.* (Lepizig: Duncker & Humblot, 1907), 6:96–101.

[3] According to Ekkehard of Aura, *Chronica*, ad a. 1109, the emperor did return with tribute; see Franz-Josef Schmale, ed., *Frutolfs und Ekkehards Chroniken und die Anonyme Kaiserchronik*, FvS 15 (Darmstadt: Wissenschaftliche Buchgesellschaft, 1972), pp. 298–9. Also according to Cosmas, *Chron. Boh.* III:27, p. 195, the emperor initially at least acquired "*magna preda.*"

but from me you will get not a single farthing, whether through
threats or bargaining. I would rather lose at this hour the kingdom of Poland while keeping its freedom,[1] than retain it peacefully forever in shame."

15 [THE EMPEROR RETURNING CARRYING CORPSES INSTEAD OF TRIBUTE]

Having heard this the emperor headed to Wrocław, but all he
obtained there were dead men for living. For some while he
pretended as if he was going to Cracow and marched hither and
thither near the river, thinking thus to unnerve Bolesław and
make him change his mind. But Bolesław was not in the least
dismayed for all that, and kept replying to the emperor's emissaries exactly as before.[2] The emperor realized that staying there
longer threatened to bring him loss and disgrace rather than
honor and profit, so he resolved to turn back—taking as tribute
nothing but the corpses. Before in his pride he had demanded a
great deal of money, so in the end he asked for little, and gained
not a penny.[3] And since in his pride he had thought to crush
Poland's ancient liberty, the *Righteous Judge* turned that *counsel
into foolishness*[4]—and repaid both this and another injury upon
his counselor Svatopluk.

[4] Ps. 7:12, 2 Sam. 15:31. The author seems to mean that by Svatopulk's murder,
elaborated in the next chapter, God kills two birds with one stone (so to speak).
In the first instance, Svatopulk himself is punished for his disloyalty (to
Bolesław) as well as sundry misdeeds—it is this to which "another injury"
refers—while at the same time the Emperor is indirectly punished for his
arrogance ("this" injury) by suffering the loss of his 'counselor.' The latter title
may in part be a wordplay on the Biblical citation, and the moral of the story
would be easier to grasp if the author had made the emperor's relation to
Svatopulk plainer. In fact, according to Cosmas, *Chron. Boh.* III:27, p. 197,
Svatopulk was not just duke of Bohemia but the emperor's godfather, and was
taking part in the campaign and in the emperor's camp when he was murdered.
For Cosmas's version of the murder, see *Chron. Boh.* III:27, pp. 195–6.
However, unlike Cosmas our author is interested less in the political than the
moral aspects of the story.

(16) DE MORTE SWANTOPOLC

Et quia forte Suantopolc ad memoriam revocamus, opere precium est, ut aliquid de vita et morte ipsius ad correccionem aliorum inducamus. Igitur Suatopolc dux Morauiensis[1] hereditarie prius extitit, postea vero ducatum Bohemie Boriuoy[2] suo dominio plenus ambicione supplantavit, genere quidem nobilis, natura ferox,[3] militia strennuus, sed modice fidei et ingenio versutus.[4] Huius enim consilio cesar Poloniam intravit, qui Bolezlauo non semel sed frequenter iuraverat, qui cum Bolezlao unum scutum coniunxerat,[5] qui virtute Bolezlaui et auxilio regnum Bohemicum acquisierat. Numquid non Bolezlaus pro Suatopolc Prage ponendo cum rege Vngarorum Colummanno Morauiam intravit,[6] silvas Bohemie rege redeunte penetravit. Utique fecit. Nec sic inde remearet, nisi Boriuoy castrum Kamenez pro paccione sibi daret.[7] Insuper etiam Bolezlauus de Bohemia multos ad ipsum iam fugientes preocupaturos gratiam, ipsum ducem fore sperantes, et retinebat et pascebat, quia Suatopolc parvam terram, paucasque divitias tunc habebat. E contra Suatopolc Bolezlauo iuravit, quia si dux Bohemorum quocumque modo vel quocumque ingenio quandoque fieret, semper fidus eius amicus unumque scutum utriusque persisteret, castra de confinio regni vel Bolezlauo redderet, vel omnino destrueret. Sed ducatum adeptus nec fidem tenuit iurata violando, nec Deum timuit *homicidia perpetrando*.[8] Unde Deus ad exemplum aliorum sibi dignam pro factis reconpensationem exhibuit, cum securus,

---

[1] See above, II:25, p. 163.

[2] Bořivoj, duke of Bohemia ca. 1100–7.

[3] Cf. Sallust, *Cat.* 43.4: *natura ferox, vehemens, manu promptus erat.*

[4] See Cosmas, *Chron. Boh.* III:19, p. 183, on Svatopluk's love of trickery.

[5] Here and below the phrase "to be of one shield" is used symbolically of close friendship or alliance, but is not otherwise known from medieval Poland. The author, however, may have read in Gregory of Tours how Childebert expresses his friendship with Guntram with these words: "*Una nos parma protegat unaque asta defendat*"; see *Hist. Franc.* V:17, ed. R. Buchner, FvS 2 (Darmstadt: Wiss. Buchgesellschaft, 1955), 1:310.

16 THE DEATH OF SVATOPLUK

As we happen to be recalling Svatopluk to mind, it is worth relating something of his life and death for the edification of others. Originally Svatopluk was the hereditary duke of Moravia,[1] but being full of ambition he later subjugated Bořivoj's[2] duchy of Bohemia to his own rule; he was of noble stock, a fierce man,[3] a fine soldier, but sly of mind and not particularly trustworthy.[4] For it was on his counsel that the emperor invaded Poland, though he had sworn an oath to Bolesław not once but several times and had joined in one shield with him,[5] and it was by Bolesław' help and might that he had won the kingdom of Bohemia. Did not Bolesław enter Moravia[6] with King Coloman of Hungary in order to install Svatopluk in Prague and march through the forests of Bohemia after the king turned back? Indeed he did. Nor would he return from there unless Bořivoj surrendered to him the castle of Kamienec as a condition.[7] In addition, Bolesław had also welcomed and supported many who fled to him from Bohemia and were looking to secure favor with him, hoping that he would one day be duke; for Svatopluk at that time had only a small territory and little wealth. Svatopluk in return swore an oath to Bolesław that if by any means or stratagem he should ever become the duke of Bohemia he would always be a faithful friend and remain in one shield with him, and he would either return to Bolesław the castles on the borders of the country or pull them down altogether. But once he obtained the duchy he did not keep his word and violated his oaths, nor did he fear God, *for there was blood shed by him*.[8] So as an example to others God inflicted a deserved retribution on him for his deeds; for he died after he was stabbed

---

[6] October 1105.

[7] Cosmas, *Chron. Boh.* III:4, p. 164, tells of the founding of this castle on the river Nysa by Duke Vratislav in 1096.

[8] Exod. 22:3. Svatopluk obtained the duchy on 14 May 1107.

inermis, in mula residens in medio suorum ab uno vili milite venabulo perforatus occubuit, nec ullus suorum ad eum vindicandum manus adhibuit. Taliter cesar de Polonia rediens triumphavit, videlicet luctum pro gaudio,[1] mortuorum cadavera pro tributo memorialiter reportavit. Bolezlauus vero dux Polonorum parum presentem, sed minus abentem procul dubio dubitavit.

(17) CAPITULUM DE BOHEMIS

Igitur post tantum laborem dux septentrionalis aliquantulum recreatus, super Bohemos equitare non diutius est retardatus. Cogitabat enim et suam iniuriam de Bohemis vindicare et suum amicum Boriuoy in sede supplantata restaurare[2]. Dum autem iter faciens in medio silvarum cum Bohemis obviantibus prelio commisso victoriam obtineret, iamque pars exercitus in campis Bohemie resideret, Boriuoy a Bohemis iam receptus[3] Bolezlao grates pro fide tanta retulit et labore et sic inpiger Bolezlauus duplici de Bohemia rediit cum honore. Sed quid rediens egerit audiamus, ut exemplo probitatis tante fructum aliquem capiamus.

(18) CAPITULUM DE POMORANIS

Non enim statim exercitum tanto itinere fatigatum ire domum permisit, nec ipsemet in deliciis vel in conviviis asperitate yemis irruente requievit, sed terram Pomoranorum cum electis de exercitu militibus requisivit. Quamdiu ibi steterit, vel quanta per terram incendia vel predas fecerit, non est opus per singula scriptitando demonstrari, sed summam rei, nobis ad maiora festinantibus, sufficiat explanari. Illa namque vice Bolezlauus in

---

[1] Cf. Jer. 31:13: *convertam luctum eorum in gaudium*.

[2] After Svatopluk's murder Bořivoj's younger brother Vladislav was elevated to the duchy; see Cosmas, *Chron. Boh.* III:27–8, pp.197–8.

with a hunting-spear by a common soldier while sitting on a mule in the midst of his people, unarmed and unsuspecting, and not one of his people raised a hand to avenge him. In this manner the emperor had his triumph returning from Poland, when memorably he brought back mourning for joy[1] and corpses for tribute. Bolesław, duke of the Poles, feared him little when he was around, but without a doubt even less when he was gone.

17 A CHAPTER ABOUT THE CZECHS

So after such labors the duke of the north took a little recreation but did not delay before riding against the Czechs. For he intended to avenge the injury done to him by the Czechs and restore his friend Bořivoj to the seat he had been ousted from.[2] While he was crossing through the middle of the forests he joined battle with the Czechs who were coming against him and won a victory. With part of his army already encamped in the fields of Bohemia, the Czechs now accepted Bořivoj back.[3] Bořivoj gave thanks to Bolesław for such great loyalty and efforts; and so the restless Bolesław returned from Bohemia with double honor. But now let us hear what he did on his return, that we may have some profit from such an example of prowess.

18 A CHAPTER CONCERNING THE POMERANIANS

For he did not allow his army weary from such a long march to go home at once, nor with the onset of the winter cold did he relax in soft living and banquets, but he set out once again for the land of the Pomeranians with a select warriors from his army. There is no need to recount how long he stayed there or to list in detail how he burnt and pillaged the land; let it be enough to give a summary as we hasten on to greater matters. This time

[3] 24 December 1109. Cf. Cosmas, *Chron. Boh.* III:28, p.198, who makes no mention of Bolesław's role.

Pomorania tria castella cepit,[1] quibus combustis et coequatis solummodo predam et captivos excepit. Postea vero sine bello Bolezlauus aliquantulum repausavit, suasque civitates interim, ubi cesar fuerat, inexpugnabiles preparavit.

(19) CAPITULUM DE BOHEMIS ET POLONIS

Cum autem Bolezlauus civitatem Glogou muniens ibi cum exercitu resideret, milites Zbigneui cum Bohemis depredaturi per Poloniam exierunt, qui statim Bolezlauuo nesciente, ipsius loci marchionibus[2] congregatis, sicut mures de latibulis exeuntes, ibidem capti vel mortui remanserunt, exceptis paucis, qui silve, latronum amice, subsidium petierunt.

(20) DE FRAUDE BOHEMORUM

Paulo superius memini me dixisse Bohemos in sede supplantata Boriuoy ducem recepisse, ideoque de Bohemia Bolezlauum ita subito redivisse. Sed quia fides Bohemica volubilis est sicut rota, qualiter prius Boriuoy expellendo traditorie deceperunt, taliterque eum iterum decepturi traditorie receperunt. Nam brevi tempore non solum honore caruit a fratre medio supplantatus,[3] verum etiam acquirendi facultatem amisit, ab imperatore captivatus.[4] Tertium quoque fratrem habebat,[5] etate quidem minorem, probitate vero non inferiorem, quem dux Bolezlaus in fidelitate fratris persistentem in Polonia retinebat, eique calumpniandi maioris fratris honorem et consilium et auxilium impendebat.

---

[1] These castles cannot be identified.

[2] The use of the term *marchio* for a castellan of the border regions of Poland is otherwise documented only later, e.g. in a charter of Emperor Lothar in 1134, see MGH DD 8, Dipl. Loth., ed. E. von Ottenthal and H. Hirsch (Berlin: Weidmann, 1927), Nr. 66, p. 103, where a *marchio de Glogow* appears as a witness.

[3] Vladislav, duke of Bohemia 1109–25.

Bolesław seized three castles in Pomerania,[1] which he burnt and leveled, sparing only the captives and the booty. Thereafter, however, Bolesław rested a while from warfare, and in the meantime fortified his cities where the emperor had been, to make them impregnable.

19 A CHAPTER ON THE CZECHS AND POLES

While Bolesław was fortifying the city of Głogów and was staying there with his army, Zbigniew's troops together with the Czechs went out on a plundering raid through Poland. But the local margraves[2] at once gathered their forces without Bolesław even knowing, and they were all captured or killed on the spot, like mice emerging from their holes, excepting a few who fled for safety to the forest, the friend of brigands.

20 THE DECEIT OF THE CZECHS

I recall mentioning a little earlier that the Czechs took back Bořivoj as duke to his seat that he had been ousted from, and it was for this reason that Bolesław returned so suddenly from Bohemia. But the faith of the Czechs goes up and down like a wheel; and so, as previously they had treacherously deceived Bořivoj and driven him out, in the same spirit of treachery they took him back, intending to deceive him again. For in little time he had not only been ousted by his middle brother[3] and deprived of his position, but even lost the possibility of winning it back, for he was taken prisoner by the emperor.[4] He had a third brother as well,[5] younger than him but in no way his inferior in worth, but as he remained loyal to his brother, Bolesław kept him in Poland and extended to him counsel and aid in attacking the position of the older brother.

[4] Cf. Cosmas, *Chron. Boh.* III:32, p. 203.
[5] Soběslav, duke of Bohemia 1125–40.

(21) DE BELLO ET VICTORIA
CONTRA BOHEMOS

Inde belliger Bolezlauus, collecta multitudine militari, novam viam aperuit in Bohemiam, quo potest Hannibali facto mirabili comparari. Nam sicut ille Romam impugnaturus per montem Iouis[1] primus viam fecit, ita Bolezlauus per locum horribilem, intemptatum prius, Bohemiam invasurus penetravit. Ille montem unum laboriose transeundo tantam famam et memoriam acquisivit, Bolezlauus vero non unum sed plures nubiferos quasi supinus[2] ascendit. Ille solummodo cavando montem, coequando scopulos laborabat, iste truncos et saxa volvendo, montes arduos ascendendo, per silvas tenebrosas iter aperiendo, in paludibus profundis pontes faciendo, non cessabat. Tanto itaque labore Bolezlauus pro iustitia Boriuoy et amicitia tribus diebus et noctibus iter faciens fatigatus, tale quid in Bohemia fecit, unde semper erit triumphali memoria recordatus. Postquam tandem Bolezlauus tanto discrimine Bohemiam est ingressus,[3] non statim, predam faciens, ut Bohemi de Polonia, quasi lupus rapiens est regressus, immo vexillis erectis, tubis canentibus, agminibus ordinatis, tympanis resonantibus, paulatim per campos Bohemie patentes, bellum querens et non inveniens, incedebat, nec predam, nec incendia prius, quam finem bello fieri, cupiebat. Interim Bohemi per turmas aliquociens apparebant, sed statim Polonis irruentibus cursu prepeti[4] fugiebant. De castellis quoque contiguis multi milites exiebant, qui Polonis irruentibus obviantes[a] occasionem suburbia comburendi faciebant.[5] Frater vero Bori-

---

[a] redeuntes Z

---

[1] The peak next to the Great St. Bernard Pass was called *Mons Iovis* after the local cult of Juppiter Poeninus whose temple was built there—see Pauly-Wissowa, *Realencyclopädie der classischen Altertumswissenschaft* (Stuttgart: Metzler, 1951), 21:1155–62, s.v. "Poeninus"; *ibid.* 1:1608, s.v. "Alpis Poenina."

[2] *Supinus*, lit. 'on his back, horizontal.'

21 WAR AND VICTORY OVER THE CZECHS

Then Bolesław the warrior gathered a host of warriors and opened a new path into Bohemia, a marvelous deed for which he can be compared to Hannibal. For as Hannibal in his march against Rome forged a way through the Jovian Mount[1] for the first time, so in order to invade Bohemia Bolesław made his way through fearsome paths untried before. The former by crossing with great labor just one mountain acquired such fame and renown, but Bolesław crossed not one but several cloud-covered peaks, ascending almost vertically.[2] The former merely struggled to hollow out a mountain and level crags; the latter rolled away stones and tree-trunks, climbed towering mountains, opened a way through gloomy forests, and built bridges over bottomless marshes, never resting. Such labour did Bolesław undertake on behalf of justice and his friendship for Bořivoj; after three days and nights of marching he was exhausted, but such were his exploits in Bohemia that the memory of his triumph will always be recalled. After such perils Bolesław entered Bohemia at last,[3] but he did not plunder and then, like a wolf seizing its prey, at once retreat, as the Czechs did in Poland. Instead, he raised his banners and to the sound of trumpets and the beating of drums he advanced slowly with orderly ranks through the open plains of Bohemia, inviting battle but not finding it, and not wishing to burn or plunder until he had brought the war to a close. Meanwhile, detachments of Czechs appeared occasionally, but made off in haste[4] when the Poles fell upon them. Numerous troops also came out from the nearby castles, but when they met the onslaught of the Poles this offered the opportunity to burn down the suburbs.[5] Bořivoj's youngest brother, whom I men-

---

[3] On Wenceslas Day (28 September) 1110, according to Cosmas, *Chron. Boh.* III:35, p. 206.

[4] Cf. Seneca, *Phaedra*, 1061: *praepeti cursu evolat.*

[5] The meaning of this sentence is not entirely clear, and the Latin may be faulty; for *obviantes* 'when they met' Z reads *redeuntes* 'when they retreated (before).'

uoy minimus, quem predixi, predas capi, incendia fieri, terram destrui, Bolezlauo supplicans prohibebat, quia regnum acquirere sine bello puerili simplicitate verbis traditorum sine victoriis se credebat. Cumque iam die quarto bellum expectans Bolezlauus ad Pragam recto tramite properaret, fluvioque cuidam, non magno quidem sed difficili transitu,[1] propinquaret, ex altera parte fluminis exercitu congregato dux Bohemorum residebat, qui Bolezlauum ibi, non ausus alibi, difficultate loci confisus, transitum prohibiturus expectabat. At Bolezlauus repertis hostibus, quos querebat, quasi leo visa preda septis conclusa stomachabatur, quia pugnandi copiam non habebat. Nam sicubi Poloni modo sursum, modo deorsum transire reputabant, ex altera parte fluminis ibi Bohemi contra stabant. Erat enim fluvius Bohemis, qui cum eo erant, mentientibus, paludosus, tante multitudini nullo resistente periculosus. Videns autem Bolezlauus, quod sic agens tempus in vacuum expendebat et quod dies sole ad occasum vergente declinabat, eleccionem audacie militaris duci Bohemico proponit, videlicet: aut Bolezlauus sibi locum dabit, ut transeat, vel illuc transibit, si dux Bohemicus loco cedat; asserens etiam occupandi causa sedem se Bohemicam non venisse, sed more solito iustitiam fugitivorum causamque miserorum, sicut quondam sibi fecerat, defendendam suscepisse.[2] Quapropter aut suum fratrem in sorte hereditatis paterne pacifice revocaret, aut *iustus iudex*[3] omnium inter sese prelio campestri veram iustitiam declararet. Ad hec dux Bohemicus respondit: Fratrem quidem meum libens recipere, si tuum receperis, sum paratus, sed cum eo regnum dividere, nisi consilio cesaris, non sum ausus.[4] Si vero voluntatem vel facultatem

---

[1] Apparently the river Cidling, see Cosmas, *Chron. Boh.* III:35, p. 206.

[2] The reference is confused, as Bolesław had helped not Vladislav but his older—and then his younger—brother in the struggle for the Czech throne.

[3] Ps. 7:12 (as at II:5, p. 129, and III:15, p. 247).

tioned before, begged Bolesław to stop the plundering, burning, and destruction of the land. For with a child's simplicity he thought he could win the country without war, and believed the words of traitors that there was no need for victories. It was now the fourth day and Bolesław, hastening directly to Prague in expectation of battle, came to a river which was small but difficult to cross.[1] Here the duke of Bohemia had taken up a position on the other side of the river with his assembled army and was waiting for him; relying on the difficulty of the position he intended to oppose Bolesław's crossing there, for he would not have dared to do so elsewhere. But when Bolesław discovered the enemy he had been searching for, he chaffed and raged like a lion beholding a penned-up prey, for he could not come to grips with them. For each time the Poles marched up- or downstream thinking to cross, the Czechs stood opposite them on the other side of the river. For according to the lies of the Czechs who were with him the river was marshy and dangerous for such a large force even if they were unopposed. When Bolesław saw that he was wasting his time in these efforts, and that the day was declining and sunset approaching, Bolesław proposed a chivalrous challenge to the duke of Bohemia: either Bolesław would give him the opportunity to cross, or he would cross to him, if the duke would move back. He added that he had not come in order to seize the Czech throne, but, as was normal, to seek justice for exiles and to take up the cause of the afflicted, as he had done for him once.[2] Therefore he should either call his brother back peacefully to take his inheritance, or the *Righteous Judge*[3] of us all should determine true justice between them on the field of battle. To this the Czech duke replied: "I am indeed willing and ready to recall my brother, if you will recall yours; but I have not dared[4] to divide my kingdom with him unless on

---

[4] Or, with the emendation *non sim ausus*, 'I would not dare.' It is worth noting that according to the author the decision about joint rulership in Poland would have to be decided by the duke and "common counsel" alone (above, III:2, p. 227, n. 4), while in Bohemia, which was regarded as part of the Empire, the need for imperial assent is assumed.

habuissem vobiscum cominus confligendi, non vestram licentiam expectarem, cum longe habuerim prius licentiam transeundi.

(22) CAPITULUM DE VASTATIONE TERRE BOHEMICE PER POLONOS

Videns autem Bolezlauus, quia dux Bohemicus in hiis responsionibus, quas mandaret, nullam certam rationem nisi verba solummodo nuda daret, crepusculo diei, tempore requiei, castra movit, nec ab illius ripa fluminis ad Labe[1] flumen descendendo se removit. Ibi vero iuxta Labe flumen illum fluviolum sine obstaculo pertransivit et festinans ibi bellum, ubi dimiserat, requisivit. Cum autem ad Bohemorum staciones perveniret, nec aliud de ipsis, quam vestigia, reperiret, convocatis senioribus consilium inivit,[2] ubi satis, quod salubrius et honestius esse videbatur, cum ratione diffinivit. Quidam enim de senioribus aiebant: Tribus diebus satis sufficit per virtutem in terra hostium nos stetisse, nec bellum illis omnibus congregatis et presentibus invenisse. Iterum alii dicebant: Iudicia *Dei vera sunt*[3] et hominibus occultata; bene processimus usque modo, sed si diucius immoramur, in dubio pendet, quo se verterint ista fata. Econtra Bolezlauus et iuvenes seniorum consilia postponebant et ire Pragam ut in antea conlaudabant. Et vere vicisset seniorum consilia consilium iuvenile, nisi panis defecisset, qui plus potest, quam possit facere ius civile. Collaudato vix itaque consilio Bolezlauus redeundi, redeundo comburendi dedit licenciam et predandi. Ipse vero semper ordinatis cohortibus incedebat, plerumque cum extremis agminibus pro subsidio subsistebat. Habebat etiam acies militum ordinatas, qui combustoribus et predatoribus anteirent et a Bohemis supervenientibus providerent.

---

[1] The author uses the Czech name, Labe, for the river instead of the usual Latinised Albis (or the Polish Łaba), one of the proofs of his at least rudimentary knowledge of Slavic languages.

[2] According to Cosmas, *Chron. Boh.* III:35, p. 207, this council took place at the bridge near Crivici.

the emperor's counsel. However, if I had had the desire or the opportunity to join battle with you, I would not wait for your permission, since I long ago had the authority to cross."

22 A CHAPTER ON THE POLES LAYING WASTE THE LAND OF BOHEMIA

When Bolesław saw that the answers that the Duke of Bohemia sent amounted to nothing definite, that they were just words and nothing else, he moved camp at twilight, the hour of rest, and without abandoning the course of the river moved downstream towards the Elbe.[1] Then near the Elbe he crossed the little stream without opposition and hastened to resume war where he had left it. When he reached the Czech outposts, and found no trace of them but their footprints, he called his elders to ask their advice.[2] Here he came to a reasonable conclusion about what it seemed could be done prudently and honorably. For some of the elders declared, "Three days has been enough time for us to be standing in enemy territory to show our valor, and we have not encountered their full force gathered ready to face us in battle." Others said, "*God's* judgements *are true*,[3] and they are hidden from men; our advance has succeeded up to now, but if we linger longer, it is not clear which way fate will turn in all this." Bolesław and the younger members, on the other hand, thought less of their elders' advice and were in favor of the previous plan of pressing on to Prague. In fact, the younger faction would have prevailed over their elders had it not been that bread was running out—and bread always prevails over politics. So the decision to return was reluctantly approved, and Bolesław gave permission to loot and burn as they did. He himself, however, was always careful to advance in ordered ranks, and for most of the way he stayed behind with the last columns to protect them. For he kept his divisions in formation, to go ahead of those responsible for looting and burning, and also kept an eye out for a sudden attack

[3] Cf. Dan. 3:27.

Cumque tam prudenter tamque sagaciter exercitum duxisset ac
reduxisset et ad silvarum introitum VI^a feria iam stationem
posuisset,[1] vigilias crebriores fieri, paraciores esse unamquam-
que legionem, si tumultus forte fieret, in sua stacione persistere
precepit. Eadem nocte Bolezlauo post matutinas orationibus
persistente, forte quidam horror universam stacionem occupavit
et clamorem subitaneum per totum exercitum excitavit. Tum
queque provincia, queque cohors armata, sicut constitutum
fuerat, in sua stacione perstitit, suum locum defensura; acies vero
curialis curialiter armata circa Bolezlauum astitit, ibi victura, vel
ibidem moritura. At Bolezlauus audito clamore populi statim
iuvenum multitudine circumstantium coronatus, ascendit in locum locuturus aliquantulum altiorem, ibique sua locucione probis auxit audaciam, timidis horrorem ademit pariter et timorem,
sit exorsus:

(23) CAPITULUM DE AUDACIA BOLEZLAY ET PROVIDENTIA

O iuventus inclita moribus et natura, mecum semper erudita
bello, mecum assueta labore; securi sustinete, pariter expectate
leti diem hodiernum, qui vos triumphali *coronabit honore*.[2] Hactenus Bohemi sicut monstra marina vel silvatica de gregibus
nostris aliquid rapuisse et cum eo per silvas aufugisse Polonis
insultabant et pro militia reputabant. Vos vero iam die VII°
terram eorum circuistis, villas et suburbia combussistis, eorum
ducem et exercitum congregatum vidistis, bellum quesistis nec
invenire potuistis. Quippe aut hodie Bohemi si bellum non
commiserint, aut si commiserint, hodie Deo iuvante Poloni suas
iniurias vindicabunt. Et cum prelium inieritis memores estote
predarum, captivorum, incendiorum; memores estote puellarum
raptarum, uxorum et matronarum; memores estote quociens vos
irritaverunt; memores estote quociens, ipsi fugientes, vos inse-

[1] 8 October 1110; see Cosmas, *Chron. Boh.* III:35, p. 207 and III:36, p. 209.
[2] Ps. 8:6; Heb. 2:7.

from the Czechs. So he led his army there and back so cautiously and prudently, and on the Friday set up a camp by the entrance to the forest.[1] He gave orders for more watches to be kept and for each division to remain at their posts on the ready in case any disturbance broke out. The same night while Bolesław was still at prayer after matins, by chance some panic seized the whole camp and the entire army broke into sudden uproar. Then each section and each body of men at arms remained at their posts as they had been ordered, ready to defend their position. The court guard in princely armor rallied around Bolesław, prepared to win or die there. But when Bolesław heard the uproar among his people, he at once ascended an elevation, ringed about by the multitude of his young followers, in order to address them. His words gave fresh courage to his seasoned men and allayed the fears and panic of the fearful ones. He spoke as follows.

23 A CHAPTER ON BOLESŁAW'S BOLDNESS AND FORESIGHT

"My young followers, renowned for your character and qualities! You who have been schooled in war with me, who with me have come to know its privations. Fear not, stand firm, and face this day joyfully together, for today is a day which will *crown* you with the *honor*[2] of triumph. Till now the Czechs like monsters from the deep or beasts from the forests have snatched something from our flocks and fled with it into the forest; they taunted the Poles over it, imagining these were martial deeds. But now for the seventh day you have been marching over their land, you have burnt their villages and the suburbs, you have seen their duke and their army drawn up, you have offered battle and they have refused it. Certainly, whether the Czechs decline battle today, or if they do fight, today is the day when with God's help the Poles will avenge their injuries. And as you go into battle, remember the plunder, the captives, the burning; remember the girls, the wives and the matrons ravished; remember how often they goaded you; remember the times they fled and you

quentes fatigaverunt. Ergo sustinete modicum fratres et milites gloriosi, estote fortes in bello iuvenes mei letabundi. Hodierna dies vobis conferet, quod semper optastis, hodierna dies dolorem delebit, quem tanto tempore comportastis. Iam aurora apparet, cito dies illa gloriosa exardebit, que tradicionem et infidelitatem Bohemorum revelabit et presumptionem et superbiam eorum conculcabit et que nostras et parentum iniurias vindicabit. Dies inquam, dies illa,[1] dies semper in Polonia recolenda; dies illa, dies magna et amara semper Bohemis et horrenda; dies illa, dies Polonis gloriosa; dies illa, dies Bohemis odiosa; dies, inquam, omni tripudio letabunda, que frontes hodie Bohemorum humotenus inclinabit,[2] in qua Deus omnipotens *cornu* humilitatis nostre *dextera sue magnitudinis exaltabit.*[3] Hac oratione completa missa generalis per omnem stationem celebratur, sermo divinus suis parrochianis ab episcopis predicatur, populus universus sacrosancta communione confirmatur. Quibus rite peractis, cum ordinatis agminibus more solito de stationibus exierunt et sic paulatim ad silvarum introitum pervenerunt. Cum autem ad silvas tanta multitudo pervenisset, neque loci notitiam, neque vie vestigium habuisset, unusquisque sibi viam per devia faciebat et sic signa vel ordinem retinere iam nequiebat. Obstrusam enim viam, qua venerant, et omnes alias audiebant et ideo per viam aliam, non capacem tante multitudinis, rediebant. Dux vero Bolezlaus retro de latere dextro cum acie curiali subsistebat, totumque suum exercitum sicut *pastor egregius*[4] premittebat. Comes quoque Scarbimirus ex altero latere in silva tenui Bolezlauo nesciente latitabat, ibique Bohemos, si forte sequerentur, in insidiis expectabat. Gneznensis etiam acies, patrono

[1] Cf. Zeph. 1:15.

[2] The gesture of submission by 'bow[ing] their foreheads to the very earth' that Bolesław expects of the Czechs after their hoped-for defeat reminds one of the *chelobitie* (often "translated" with the Chinese noun 'kowtow') expected in later times mainly by rulers of Russia, though there is no explicit reference to it in Slavic lands before the fourteenth century; see Donald Ostrowski, *Muscovy and the Mongols: Cross Cultural Influences on the Steppe Frontier* (Cambridge, Cambridge UP, 1998), pp. 89–90. To be sure, various forms of proskynesis were known since antiquity. See also above, II:39, p. 192 and II:44, p. 201.

grew weary pursuing them. So stand firm a little longer, my brothers, my glorious warriors; be brave in the battle, my joyful young men. For today is the day that will give you what you have always longed for, and will cancel the pain that you've carried so long. Now dawn is showing; and soon that day of glory will burst forth, the day that will reveal the faithlessness and treachery of the Czechs, that will trample their pride and their presumption, that will avenge the insults done to us and our parents. This day, I tell you,[1] this day will ever be a day to be remembered in Poland, and a great and bitter day will this day be and ever a day of horror for the Czechs. A day of glory this will be for the Poles; for the Czechs it will be a day of loathing. Today, I tell you, you will leap and dance for joy, today will bring the Czechs to bow their foreheads to the very earth,[2] today is the day when the lord God Almighty will *exalt the horn* of our humility *in the might of his arm*."[3] After this speech was finished a general mass was celebrated throughout the camp, the bishops delivered the divine word to those of their diocese, and the whole people were strengthened by Holy Communion. When all this was properly performed, they advanced from the encampments in their ordered ranks according to custom and so gradually made their way to the entrance of the woods. But when so large a multitude reached the woods, having no knowledge of the area and finding no trace of a path, each man had to make his own way through the pathless terrain. Thus they were unable to keep to their ranks or standards. For they heard that the way they had come along and all the others were blocked, so they went back by another path, which could not accommodate such a multitude. But Duke Bolesław remained behind with the princely guard on the right flank, ushering the whole of his army through like *a faithful shepherd*.[4] But as well on the other side and unbeknown to Bolesław *Comes* Skarbimir was in hiding in light woodland, in wait to ambush any Czechs who might be following. The unit

[3] 1 Sam. 2:1; 2 Macc. 15:23.

[4] Isa. 40:11–12; Jer. 43:12, etc.

Polonie[1] dedicata cum quibusdam palatinis aliisque militibus animosis in planicie quadam parva dominum subsistentem expectabat, que planities silvas maiores a minori silva prostante dividebat. Cumque Bolezlauus ex obliquo suum exercitum per silvam tenuem sequeretur, videns suos et a suis visus, hostes reputavit suos, a suis etiam hostis similiter estimatus; sed propius ad invicem accedentes et arma subtilius contemplantes, signa Polonica[2] cognoverunt et sic a pene cepto scelere desierunt. Interim Bohemi, quasi iam certi de victoria, non ordinati ut[a] prius catervatim,[3] sed unus ante alium properabant, quia Polonos in silva iam receptos, ad prelium irrevocabiles, inordinatos, latitantes, dispersos se capere sicut lepores reputabant. At belliger Bolezlauus, visis hostibus iam vicinis, exclamavit: Iuvenes, feriendi nostrum sit inicium, noster quoque finis. Hoc dicto, statim venabulo primum in acie de dextrario supinavit et cum eo simul Dirsek pincerna potum alteri mortiferum propinavit. Tum vero iuventus Polonica certatim irruunt, lanceis prius bellum inferunt, quibus expletis enses exerunt; clipei paucos de Bohemis accedentes ibi clepunt,[4] lorice pondus non subsidium illis reddunt, galee honorem ibi capitibus non salutem acquirunt. Ibi ferro ferrum acuitur, ibi miles audax cognoscitur, ibi virtus virtute vincitur. Corpora strata iacent, sudore vultus et pectora madent, sanguine rivi manant, iuvenes Poloni clamant: sic est virtus approbanda viris, sic famam querendo non predam furtim rapiendo silvamque petendo rapidorum more luporum. Ibi fulgens lorica-

---

[a] ut] *om. Z H Mal*

---

[1] St. Adalbert.

[2] The reference here and above may be to some otherwise unknown proto-heraldic signs or standards, as well perhaps as to the different dress of Polish troops; see Władysław Semkowicz, *Encyklopedia nauk pomocniczych historii* [An encyclopedia of the auxiliary sciences of history], ed. B. Wyrozumska (Cracow: Universitas, 1999), pp. 165–6, 185.

from Gniezno as well, dedicated to the patron of Poland,[1] with certain of the palatines and other doughty warriors stood in wait on a small plain for their lord as he stayed back. This plain separated the main forest from a smaller wood that stood out. As Bolesław moved obliquely through this light woodland to keep up with his main force, he could see his men and they could see him. But he mistook his own men for the enemy and his men similarly thought that he was the enemy. But as they drew closer to each other and could see their arms more distinctly, they recognized the Polish standards[2] just in time to avoid committing a terrible deed. Meanwhile the Czechs, now feeling almost certain of victory, were racing ahead of each other, no longer in rank and units as before,[3] imagining that now that the Poles had retreated into the forest they could not be called back to fight, and dispersed, out of their ranks, and cowering, they could be caught like hares. But Bolesław the warrior, seeing the enemy close by, cried out, "My young men, let us be the ones to strike first, and us the ones to finish." So saying, immediately with his hunting spear he struck the first man in the enemy line to the ground from his horse, while at the same time as he did so, his cup-bearer Dzierżek served a fatal drink to another. Then indeed the Polish youth fell upon them in earnest, clashing first with lances, then when these gave out drawing swords. Shields shielded[4] few of the Czechs who approached, their armor was more weight then help, their helmets gave their heads distinction but no safety. Iron on iron is sharpened here, the daring warrior is recognized here; brave men by brave are vanquished here. Bodies lie in heaps, faces and chests are pouring sweat, streams run with blood, the young Poles cry, "This is how men's courage is proven, by thus winning fame and not stealthily snatching plunder and running for the woods in the way of greedy wolves."

[3] With the reading of the MSS the text would mean: 'without having first drawn up in rank.'

[4] The word *clepunt* is unknown; we take it as a verb derived in some manner from the noun *clipeus* 'shield.'

torum acies Bohemorum et Theutonicorum, que prima fuit, prima corruit, gravata pondere, non adiuta.[1] Adhuc tamen dux Bohemorum vice secunda, tercia, iam flore milicie prostrata iacente, suum dampnum catervas retorquens vindicare nitebatur, semperque suorum congeries corruencium augebatur. Scarbimirus quoque cum acie palatina, silvula dividente, cum aliis Bohemorum agminibus dimicabat, ita quod Bolezlauus de Scarbimiro vel Scarbimirus de Bolezlauo penitus, ubi staret, vel si prelium ageret, ignorabat. Ex utraque parte Mars suas vires exercet, fortuna ludit, rota Bohemorum eversatur, a Parcis fila Bohemorum secantur, Cerberus ora vorantia laxat, portitor Acheronti navigando laborat, Proserpina ridet, Furie viperinas illis vestes explicant, Eumenides balnea sulphurea parant, Pluto iubet Ciclopes dignas fabricare coronas militibus merito venerandis, dentibus anguinis, linguis nec non draconinis.[2] Quid multis moramur? Videntes Bohemi suam causam divino iudicio[3] non placere et Polonorum audaciam cum iusticia prevalere, suorum ibi meliorum acie prostrata, catervatim, divisim fugam arripiunt, nec eos fugere Poloni statim percipiunt, sed fugam simulare credunt. Convallis enim media quedam et silva Bohemos adiuvabat, que fugam eorum vel insidias occultabat. Ideo dux Polonorum Bolezlauus milites impetuosos presumptuose persequi prohibebat, quia cautelam Bohemorum et insidias dubitabat. Comperta tandem Poloni vera fuga Bohemorum, insequentes statim laxant suorum habenas equorum. Ergo potiti Poloni victoria triumphali, redeundi Poloniam iter inceptum non differunt, suos sauciatos in Bohemia redeuntes secum ferunt, superioribus

---

[1] This troop may have been the one lead by Detrisek, son of Busa; see the description of this battle in Cosmas, *Chron. Boh.* III:36, pp. 207–8. The references to the weight of armor tallies well with the author's explanation about why the Poles earlier abandoned the wearing of it (above, I:24, p. 93).

[2] This passage rich in classical mythology may derive from the author's reading of Statius, *Theb.* 8.9–13 and 8.97–8, as well as of the *Ecloga Theoduli* (93–94), popular in medieval schools, although some of its elements are grouped in an unusual way (e.g. the crowns made by the Cyclops, the Eumenides' sulphur baths).

Those Czechs and Germans in their gleaming armor who were the first in line were the first to fall, encumbered rather than helped by the weight.[1] Yet the duke of the Czechs, though the flower of his knighthood lay fallen, attempted a second and still a third time by turning round his troops to make good his losses; but ever the heap of his slain grew higher. Skarbimir, too, with the palatine guard was battling other Czech detachments, but they were separated by a small wood, so that Bolesław had no idea where Skarbimir stood nor Skarbimir Bolesław, or even if the other was engaged in battle. On both sides Mars showed his strength, Fortune played, the wheel turned against the Czechs, the Fates cut the threads of the Czechs. Cerberus opened his devouring mouths, the ferryman of Acheron labored at his portage, Proserpina laughed, the Furies spread their viper garments, the Eumenides made ready baths of sulphur, Pluto commanded the Cyclops to fashion fit crowns for soldiers who truly deserved them, with the teeth of serpents and the tongues of dragons.[2] Why go on at length? When the Czechs saw that their cause was not favored by the judgment of God[3] and that the boldness of the Poles as well as justice was prevailing and the ranks of their best soldiers had fallen, they broke in flight, unit by unit and man by man. The Poles at first did not realize they actually were fleeing, and thought the rout was feigned. For a valley in the middle and the woods helped the Czechs, hiding whether this was a rout or a trick. Consequently Bolesław duke of the Poles checked his eager soldiers from overconfidently pursuing them, fearing deceit on the part of the Czechs and an ambush. When at last the Poles discovered that the Czech flight was genuine, they at once set off in pursuit as fast as their horses could carry them. The Poles, having thus won a triumphant victory, made no delay in continuing their journey home to Poland, taking back with them their comrades who had been wounded in Bohemia and making, with the addition of those

[3] On the judgment of God in battles, see above, 1:21, p. 86, n. 1; II:5, p. 129.

adiectis denarium profectionis numerum impleverunt.[1] Ad hoc enim detrimentum et dedecus bellica gens Bohemorum traditorum faccionibus est redacta, quod pene militibus probis et nobilioribus, Polonorum conculcata sub pedibus, est exacta. Ibi quoque cum Bohemis Zbigneus interfuit, cui fugisse similiter, quam ibi stetisse, plus profuit. Poloni vero de Bohemia cum ingenti tripudio remeantes, omnipotenti Deo grates rependunt eternales et Bolezlauo triumphanti laudes referunt triumphales.

(24) CAPITULUM DE VASTACIONE TERRE PRUSSIE PER POLONOS

Item inpiger Bolezlauus yemali tempore non quasi desidiosus in otio requievit, sed Prussiam terram aquiloni contiguam, gelu constrictam, introivit,[2] cum etiam Romani principes in barbaris nationibus debellantes, in preparatis munitionibus yemarent, neque tota yeme militarent. Illuc enim introiens, glacie lacuum et paludum pro ponte utebatur, quia nullus aditus alius in illam patriam nisi lacubus et paludibus invenitur. Qui cum lacus et paludes pertransisset et in terram habitabilem pervenisset, non in uno loco resedit, non castella, non civitates, quia ibi nulla, sibi obsedit, quippe situ loci et naturali positione regio ista per insulas lacubus et paludibus est munita et per sortes hereditarias ruricolis et habitatoribus dispartita. Igitur belliger Bolezlauus per illam barbaram nationem passim discurrens predam inmensam cepit, viros et mulieres, pueros et puellas, servos et ancillas innumerabiles captivavit, edificia villasque multas concremavit, cum quibus omnibus in Poloniam sine prelio remeavit, quod prelium tamen invenire plus hiis omnibus exoptavit.

---

[1] The wording of the Latin is peculiar, and we follow the standard interpretation. According to Cosmas, *Chron. Boh.* III:36, p. 208, this battle was fought by a small river, the Trutina, near Smířice.

above, the number (of days) for their journey to ten.[1] For the warlike Czech race had suffered such loss and shame through cliques of traitors that it was practically bereft of its experienced and nobler fighting men after being crushed beneath the feet of the Poles. There, too, among the Czechs was Zbigniew, who like them found it more advantage to flee than to stand firm there. The Poles arrived back from Bohemia with enormous celebration, offering up eternal thanks to Almighty God and voicing praises in triumph to Bolesław the triumphant.

24 A CHAPTER ON THE WASTING OF THE LAND OF PRUSSIA BY THE POLES

Restless Bolesław would not repose in ease during the winter season like an idle person, but marched into the frozen land of Prussia to the north.[2] Yet even the Roman emperors when waging war among barbarian peoples would winter in fortifications prepared in advance, and did not campaign throughout the winter. So he entered their land, using the ice on lakes and marshes as his bridge, for no other way can be found into that country save by lake and marsh. And when he had crossed the lakes and marshes and reached habitable land, he did not pause in one place, nor did he besiege castles and cities, for there were none there. For by the lie of the land and its natural location this region on islands is protected by lakes and marshes, and divided among peasants and inhabitants into hereditary portions. So Bolesław the warrior marched far and wide through this barbarous nation, collecting immense plunder, seizing men, women, boys, girls, servant men and servant women in countless numbers, burnt down numerous buildings and villages, and with all these he returned to Poland without even fighting. Yet he would have given all these to be offered a battle.

[2] In the winter of 1110–1.

(25) CAPITULUM DE CONCORDIA ZBIGNEY FALSA CUM BOLEZLAO

Hostibus itaque Bolezlauus, sicut dictum est, refrenatis, ducem Bohemicum coegit fratrem minimum, quem supra diximus, in hereditatis sortem recipere, quibusdam civitatibus sibi datis.[1] Quo facto Zbigneus Bolezlauo fratri suo legationem misit misericorditer supplicando, quatinus aliquam particulam hereditatis paterne, sicut dux Bohemorum suo fratri, sibi quoque concederet, ea condicione, quod nullatenus in aliquibus illi coequaret, sed sicut miles domino semper et in omnibus obediret. Iam enim nec per cesarem, nec per Bohemos, nec per Pomoranos se posse vincere confidebat, sed quod viribus et armis obtinere non poterat, humilitate saltim et fraterna karitate presumebat. Verba quidem satis bona et pacifica videbantur, sed *aliud promptum in lingua forsan et aliud clausum in pectore tenebatur.*[2] Sed hec dicenda suo loco differamus, et Bolezlaui responsionem audiamus. Audita fama fratris tam humillima supplicatione, Bolezlaus a periuriis tot transactis, ab iniuriis tot illatis, ab alienis gentibus in Poloniam introductis ignoscendo, suum animum mitigavit et Zbigneum cum verbis huiuscemodi condicionis in Poloniam revocavit; videlicet si verbis sue legacionis mens humilis concordaret et si se pro milite non pro domino reputaret, nec ullam superbiam deinceps, nec ullum dominium ostentaret, fraterna karitate quedam castella sibi daret. Et si veram humilitatem in eo veramque karitatem prospiceret, semper eum in melius *die cottidie*[3] promoveret; sin vero contumatiam illam antiquam in corde discordem[a] occultaret, melius esset aperta discordia,[b] quam iterum novam seditionem in Poloniam reportaret.[4] At Zbigneus

---

[a] discordiam *Z H Mal*

[b] apertam discordiam *H Mal*

---

[1] According to Cosmas, *Chron. Boh.* III:37, p. 209, Soběslav received the castle of Žateč.

[2] Sallust, *Cat.* 10:5.

25 A CHAPTER ON ZBIGNIEW'S FALSE RECONCILIATION WITH BOLESŁAW

So Bolesław, having brought the enemy to heel, as has been told, compelled the Czech duke to receive his youngest brother (whom we have mentioned previously) into his hereditary portion and to grant certain cities to him.[1] Thereupon Zbigniew sent an embassy to his brother Bolesław humbly pleading to grant to him, too, some small part of their paternal inheritance, as the duke of the Czechs had to his brother. He accepted the condition that he should not be his equal in any respect, but would always obey him as a knight his lord in every regard. For now he believed that neither emperor, Czechs, nor Pomeranians could help him prevail, but what by strength of arms he could not obtain he might hope to gain by humility and a brother's love. Indeed, the words seemed very fine and peaceable, but it could be that he had "one thing concealed in the breast, and another ready on the tongue."[2] But let us postpone the story of this to its rightful place, and listen to the answer Bolesław gave. When Bolesław had word of his brother's most humble plea, Bolesław overlooked all the perjuries he had committed and the injuries he had inflicted, all the times he had brought foreign nations into Poland; he softened his anger and let Zbigniew return to Poland. His terms were these. If the humility of his mind was in keeping with the words of his envoys, and if he would regard himself as a knight and not as lord, nor make display of any pride or lordship in future, out of brotherly love he would give him certain castles; and if he could see in him true humility and true love, he would always advance him *daily and every day*,[3] but if he concealed in his heart that ancient divisive pride, then open discord would be better than bringing back new sedition to Poland again.[4] Yet Zbigniew gave in to the advice of fools. He recalled

---

[3] Ps. 68 (67):20: *benedictus Dominus die cotidie*. The same phrase appears in I:16.

[4] The Latin as transmitted is problematic, but the general sense seems clear.

stultorum consiliis acquiescens promisse subieccionis et humilitatis minime recordatus, ad Bolezlauum non humiliter sed arro-
ganter est ingressus, nec sicut homo longo tam exilio castigatus,
tantisque laboribus et miseriis fatigatus, ymmo sicut dominus
cum ense precedente, cum simphonia musicorum tympanis et
cytharis modulantium precinente, non se serviturum sed regnaturum designabat, non se sub fratre militaturum, sed super
fratrem imperaturum pretendebat. Quod quidam sapientes in
partem aliam, quam Zbigneus forsan cogitaverat, moverunt et
consilium Bolezlauo tale suggesserunt, quod se statim credidisse
penituit, semperque se fecisse penitebit;[1] talibus videlicet verbis
mentem humanam accendentes: Hic homo tantis calamitatibus
contritus, tam longo exilio detrusus, aditu primo cum tanto fastu
superbie de singulis adhuc incertus ingreditur; quid faciet in
futuro, si sibi potestas aliqua de regno Polonie concedatur. Aliud
quoque maius et periculosius asserentes, quod ipse videlicet
Zbigneus quemlibet cuiusque generis, divitem sive pauperem,
iam repertum et constitutum haberet, qui Bolezlauum oportuno
sibi loco considerato vel cultello vel alio quolibet ferramento
confoderet; quem homicidam ipse, si tunc mortis periculum
evitaret, honoris magni culmine sicut unum de principibus exaltaret. Sed nos magis credimus ab ipsis malis consiliatoribus hoc
fuisse machinatum, quam umquam ab ipso Zbigneuo, satis hu-
mili satisque simplici tale facinus cogitatum. Ideoque minus
mirandum iuvenem etate florentem, in imperio consistentem,
iracundia stimulante, sapientum quoque consilio suggerente,
quodlibet facinus perpetrare, quo mortis periculum evitaret et
securus a cunctis insidiis imperaret. Nullus tamen credat illud
peccatum inspiratione fuisse perpetratum, sed ex presumptione,
non ex deliberatione, sed ex occasione propagatum. Si enim
Zbigneus humiliter et sapienter adveniret, sicut homo misericor-

---

[1] This passage, though the only one where the author actually refers to Bolesław
III as a living figure, is sufficient to disprove assumptions about his having
written the *GpP* after the duke's death (see above, p. xxxi, n. 41). Indeed, the

not at all his promises of submission and humility; his approach to Bolesław was not humble but arrogant. He behaved not like a man whom long exile had punished and toils and hardship had worn out, but indeed like a lord with a sword carried before him, and a band of musicians playing drums and cythers ahead. He indicated that he would not be coming to serve but to rule, he made as if he would not be a knight at his brother's command but his brother's lord and master. This was twisted by certain wise men in a way that may not have been foreseen by Zbigniew, and they gave Bolesław counsel, which he immediately regretted believing, and will always regret having done.[1] For they stirred his human sensibility with such words: "This man, tried by so many calamities and having suffered such a long exile, arrives at the outset in such height of pride, when he is still uncertain of any single thing: what will he do in the future, if he is granted some degree of power over the kingdom of Poland?" They asserted another even more dangerous thing, that he, namely Zbigniew, had already found and commissioned someone of whatever origin, rich or poor, who having determined a place suitable for him would stab Bolesław with a dagger or some other iron object, and he would then raise this murderer to a place of high honor as one of the princes if he should at that moment escape the threat to his life. But we rather believe that this was fabricated by the evil counsellors themselves rather than that such a crime was ever planned by Zbigniew, a quite humble and quite simple man. And so it is hardly surprising that a young man in the prime of life, occupying supreme power, moved by ire but also counseled so by wise men, would commit any crime to avoid a threat to his life and to be able to rule without fear of any plots. But let no one believe that that sin was committed out of calculation and not through impetuousness, that it was done by premeditation and not on the spur of the moment. For if Zbigniew came humbly and prudently, like a man intending to ask for

surprisingly strong implicit censure of the hero of the work may have even have been a factor behind the evidently hasty termination of the work.

diam petiturus, non sicut dominus quasi vanitatis fascibus reg-
naturus, nec ipsemet in dampnum irreparabile corruisset, nec
alios in crimen lamentabile posuisset.[1] Quid ergo? Accusamus
Zbigneuum et excusamus Bolezlauum? Nequaquam. Sed minus
est peccatum ira precipitacionis ex occasione data perpetrare,
quam illud faciendum ipsa deliberatione pertractare. Nos vero
nec peccato deliberationis penitentiam denegamus, sed in penitentia tamen personam, etatem, oportunitatem perpendamus.
Non enim convenit post malum irreparabiliter perpetratum malum peius evenire,[2] sed illi, qui sanari potest, decet medicum
discretionis medicamine subvenire. Quapropter, quia quod factum
est in altera parte non potest in statum pristinum restaurari,
oportet partem infirmam, medicine capacem, in statu dignitatis
vigilanti studio discrecionis conservari. Unde constat infirmo
corporaliter corporali subsidio ministrari et infirmum spiritaliter
spiritali medicamine sustentari. Sed qui Bolezlauum in hoc, quod
tale quid egerit, accusamus, in hoc tamen, quod digne penituerit
et satis humiliaverit, collaudamus. Vidimus enim talem virum,[3]
tantum principem, tam deliciosum iuvenem primam karinam
ieiunantem, assidue *in cinere et cilicio*[4] humi provolutum, lacri-
mosis suspiriis irrigatum, ab humano consortio et colloquio
separatum,[5] humum pro mensa, herbam pro mantili, panem
atrum pro deliciis, aquam pro nectare reputantem. Preterea pon-
tifices, abbates, presbiteri missis et ieiuniis eum quisque pro suis

---

[1] This is evidently an oblique reference to the blinding of Zbigniew, which
seems to have occured before July 1110, since the entry under that date in
Cosmas, *Chron. Boh*. III:34, p. 205, presents the act as an event of the past.
However, the date of 1111 is argued by Bieniak, "Polska elita", 2:49, note 156.
Both Karol Maleczyński, *Bolesław III Krzywousty* [Bolesław III Wrymouth]
(Wrocław: Zakład Narodowy im. Ossolińskich, 1975), p. 75, and Bieniak, *loc.
cit*., p. 48, argue that there is no reason to accept the hypothesis, often repeated
in the older literature, that Zbigniew died shortly thereafter.

mercy and not like a lord who wants to rule with the rod of vanity, he would not have incurred irreparable damage on himself and drawn others into a lamentable crime.[1] What then? Do we accuse Zbigniew and excuse Bolesław? In no way. But it is less to commit a sin propelled by anger on the spur of the moment, than to contemplate doing it wilfully. Now we do not deny penance even for wilful sin, but nevertheless in the penance let us weigh carefully the person, his age, and the circumstances. It is not right, namely, that after the commission of irreparable wrong a worse evil should follow;[2] rather, the physician should with judicious medication bring succor to him who is capable of being healed. Wherefore, since what has been done to the other cannot be repaired to its pristine state, it is necessary to preserve the part that is sick but capable of treatment in the state of its dignity by vigilant and prudent care. Hence it is accepted that those ailing corporally are ministered corporal assistance, and those ailing spiritually are to be sustained with spiritual medicine. Still, we who accuse Bolesław in this, that he did such a thing, nevertheless praise him for worthily repenting and properly humbling himself. For we have seen such a man,[3] such a prince, such a favored youth fasting from the beginning of Lent, ever prostrate on the earth *in sackcloth and ashes*,[4] washed in tearful sighs, bereft of human company and conversation,[5] regarding the earth as his table, grass as his tablecloth, black bread as fine fare, and water as nectar. Furthermore, bishops, abbots,

[2] Mal. p. 157, n. 1, speculates that "worse evil" here refers to the possibility of Bolesław's abdication, which may have been mooted at this time.

[3] Some have regarded this sentence as proof that the author was himself an eye-witness to these acts of penitence; however, whether he really had seen Bolesław under these circumstances is doubtful, and the phrasing may be merely rhetorical.

[4] Matth. 11:21.

[5] These words may imply that Bolesław was excommunicated (by Archbishop Martin?) because of the blinding of his brother, though there is no independent evidence for this.

viribus adiuvabant et in omni sollempnitate precipua vel in ecclesiarum consecrationibus aliquid sibi de penitentia canonica auctoritate relaxabant. Insuper ipse missas cottidie pro peccatis, pro defunctis celebrari, psalteriaque cantari faciebat et in pascendis et vestiendis pauperibus magne caritatis solatium impendebat. Et quod maius hiis omnibus et precipuum in penitentia reputatur, auctoritate dominica fratri suo satisfaciens, concessa venia concordatur.[1] Unum quoque Bolezlauus fructum tulit penitentie satis dignum, quod potest reputari de tanto principe cunctis penitentibus quasi signum. Nam cum ipse non ducatum, sed regnum magnificum gubernaret ac de diversis et christianorum et paganorum nationibus hostium dubitaret, semet ipsum regnumque suum servandum divine potentie commendavit et iter peregrinacionis ad sanctum Egidium sanctumque regem Stephanum[2] occasione colloquii, paucissimis hoc rescientibus,[3] summa devotione consumavit. Omnibus quippe diebus illius quadragesime, sola contentus panis et aque refeccione ieiunaret, nisi tanti laboris occasione discrecio presulum et abbatum missis et orationibus illud ieiunium caritatis obsequio violaret. Singulis quoque diebus ab hospitio tam diu pedibus quandoque nudis cum episcopis et capellanis incedebat, donec horas perpetue Virginis dieique canonicas, VII que psalmos cum letania penitentiales adimplebat et plerumque cursum psalterii

---

[1] The formulation of this sentence is problematic (but certainly, given the nominative participle *satisfaciens*, the main verb *concordatur* cannot be impersonal, qs. 'there was reconciliation,' as others have translated, and one must therefore asssume that the subject in both cases is "Boleslaw"). In all likelihood, the author did not wish to go into details about the (probably quite short-lived) final peace between the brothers. It is, however, the proper completion of a penance of this kind that at the end comes reconciliation. Much depends on the meaning of *satisfactio*, which has clearly more than legal implications; see also above, n. 2, p. 146.

[2] The reference is to the daughter-house of St. Gilles in Somogyvár (Monasterium Sancti Egidii, in Somogy county, South-Western Hungary), and the burial place of St. Stephen in Fehérvár (Alba Regia, today Székesfehérvár). Somogyvár was founded by King Ladislas I in 1091—see György Györffy, ed. *Diplomata Hungariae Antiquissima* (Budapest: Akadémiai, 1992), pp. 266–8—

and priests assisted him, each as he might, with masses and fasts, and at every special feast and at church consecrations granted him by canonical authority indulgence for a part of his penance. Moreover, he himself had masses celebrated and psalms sung each day for sinners and the dead, and exhibited great works of mercy in feeding and clothing the poor. And what is regarded as greater than all this and most essential in penance, he offered satisfaction to his brother by lordly authority, and once pardon was given he was reconciled.[1] And Bolesław also bore one quite worthy fruit of penitence, which from such a prince may be regarded as an example to all penitents. For although he ruled not a duchy but a magnificent kingdom and had to fear from diverse enemy nations, Christian and pagan alike, he commended himself and his realm to the care of God's power and with deepest devotion undertook a journey of pilgrimage to St. Giles and St. Stephen the King,[2] which involved a talk, something about which only very few knew.[3] On all the days of that Lent he would have fasted, satisfied with taking only bread and water, had the wisdom of the bishops and abbots in view of such tribulation not interrupted this fast by masses and prayers in the indulgence of mercy. Every day, too, he would walk from his hostel, often barefoot, with the bishops and chaplains so long till he completed the canonical Hours of the perpetual Virgin, the seven penitentiary palms with a litany, and added most of the

and received as a rule only Frenchmen, as was still the case in the time of Alberic of Troisfontaines (see idem, *Chronica*, ed. G. Pertz, MGH SS 23:798, 50). On the cult of St. Stephen at Székesfehérvár, see Gábor Klaniczay, *Holy Rulers and Blessed Princesses: Dynastic Cults in Medieval Central Europe* (Cambridge: Cambridge UP, 2002), pp. 114–54.

[3] The last words may refer to the talk of the two rulers or the whole pilgrimage; in either case, the author may have received his information from chancellor Michael. Regarding the talk—for which no other evidence exists, but sources are scarce for this period—one suggestion has been that this was connected with the fact that Coloman had blinded his own brother, Duke Álmos; but for this the chronology is problematic. Others (e.g. Mal., p. 158, n. 6.) speculate that Bolesław asked Coloman to intervene against his (assumed) excommunication.

post defunctorum vigilias adiungebat. In pedibus etiam pauperum abluendis, in elemosinis faciendis ita devotus et studiosus
per totam viam illius peregrinacionis existebat, quod nullus in-
digens ab eo misericordiam querens sine misericordia recedebat.
Ad quemcumque locum episcopalem, vel abbaciam, vel preposi-
turam dux septentrionalis veniebat, episcopus ipsius loci, vel
abbas, vel prepositus et ipse rex Vngarorum Colummannus
aliquociens obviam Bolezlauo cum ordinata processione procedebat. Ipse autem Bolezlauus ubique semper aliquid per ecclesias offerebat, sed in illis locis principalibus nonnisi aurum et
pallia proferebat. Et sicut religiose per totam Vngariam ab episcopis et abbatibus et prepositis recipiebatur, ita munifice sibi
corporale servitium ab ipsis cum summa diligentia parabatur et
ipsos ipse donabat et ipse ab ipsis donabatur. Ubique tamen eum
ministri regis et servitium sequebatur et ubi Bolezlauus diligentius vel negligentius reciperetur, notificandum regi a suis familiaribus notabatur. Et quicumque diligentius eum et honestius
recipere videbatur, amicus esse regis, vel gratiam inde consequi
sine dubio dicebatur. Cum tali devocione spiritali, talique vener-
acione temporali Bolezlauus de sua peregrinacione remeavit;
neque tamen in regnum suum rediens vitam penitentis habi-
tumque peregrinacionis abnegavit, sed ad sepulchrum usque
beati martiris Adalberti, pascha Domini celebraturus, cum
eodem peregrinacionis proposito perduravit.[1] Et sicut cottidie
propius ad locum sancti martiris accedebat, tanto devotius cum
lacrimis et orationibus nudis pedibus incedebat. Cum autem ad
urbem et sepulchrum sancti martiris pervenisset, quantas
elemosinas in pauperibus erogavit, quanta per ecclesiam et in
altaribus ornamenta presentavit, opus aureum existit operationis

---

[1] 3 April 1113. The shrine of St. Adalbert had in fact been in Prague since 1039,
but from the context it is clear that Bolesław's pilgrimage was to the saint's
original resting place in Gniezno, where his cult as patron of Poland—see
above, III:23, p. 265—was maintained even after the loss of the main relics.
His cult was revived in the late eleventh century after relics were discovered in
the cathedral; see Gerard Labuda, "Posłowie" (Afterword) to H. Likowski,

entire sequence of the Psalter after the vigil for the dead. Moreover, during the entire course of that pilgrimage he was so devoted and diligent in washing the feet of the poor and giving out alms that no needy person requesting his mercy would leave without receiving it. Whichever episcopal see, abbey or priory the duke of the north came to, the bishop of that place, or the abbot or prior, and even Coloman, the king of the Hungarians, on occasion came out to meet Bolesław in a formal procession. Bolesław himself everywhere always offered something in the churches, but in the principal places he presented nothing but gold and vestments. And as he was received devoutly through all of Hungary by the bishops, abbots, and priors, just so they generously supplied him material services with the greatest of attention; and he gave them gifts and received gifts from them. Yet everywhere the king's officers and servitors accompanied him, and wherever Bolesław was received either with particular care or with excessive negligence, this was noted by the retainers to be reported to the king. And whoever was seen to have received him with special honor and diligence was called a friend of the king, who would doubtlessly receive favor as a result. Bolesław returned from his pilgrimage with such spiritual devotion, with such temporal veneration, yet once back in his own country he did not give up the life of a penitent and a habit of a pilgrim. Rather, he persevered in the plan of pilgrimage as far as the grave of the blessed martyr Adalbert, intending to celebrate the feast of Easter.[1] And as he came daily the closer to the place of the holy martyr, ever more devotedly he proceeded, with tears and prayers and on bare feet. And when he had reached the city and the grave of the holy martyr, how many alms he gave to the poor, how many treasures he presented in the church and on the altars is evidenced materially by the golden object which

"Geneza święta 'translatio s. Adalberti' w Kościele polskim: Rozwiązanie sprawy o relikwie św. Wojciecha" (The origin of the feast of *translatio s. Adalberti* in the Polish church: A solution to the problem of St. Adalbert's relics), in *Święty Wojciech w polskiej tradycji historiograficznej: Antologia tekstów*, ed. G. Labuda (Warsaw: PAX, 1997), p. 151.

argumentum, quod fecit Bolezlauus reliquiis sancti martiris in sue devocionis et penitentie testamentum. In illo namque feretro auri purissimi octoginta marce continentur, exceptis perlis gemmisque preciosis, que minoris quam aurum pretii non videntur. In episcopis vero suis, in principibus, in capellanis, in militbus innumeris ita magnifice ac munifice pascha sanctum illud gloriosissimum celebravit, quod singulos maiorum et pene minorum pretiosis vestibus adornavit. De canonicis autem beati martiris, de custodibus ecclesie vel ministris, vel de civibus ipsius civitatis ita liberaliter ordinavit, quod omnes, nullo pretermisso, vel vestibus, vel equis, vel aliis muneribus unumquemque pro qualitate dignitatis et ordinis honoravit. Hac itaque peregrinatione tam religiosa devocione completa,[1] non ideo tamen est obsessio facta prius de cordis nostri memoria sic deleta, nec debet quisquam illud[2] preposterum ordinem reputare, quod, si fuerit intersertum, poterit cepte narrationis totam seriem perturbare.

(26) POMORANI TRADIDERUNT CASTRUM NAKEL POLONIS[3]

Igitur castrum Nakel, ubi prelium illud fuisse maximum superius memoratur et unde dampnum semper Polonis laborque continuus generatur, Bolezlauus cuidam Pomorano, genere sibi propinquo, Suatopolc[4] vocabulo, concesserat cum aliis castellis pluribus sub tali fidelitatis condicione retinere, quod nunquam deberet ei suum servitium vel castella, causa pro qualibet, prohibere. Sed postea numquam iuratam sibi fidelitatem retinuit,

---

[1] A penny depicting a person with a stick kneeling in front of a bishop has been identified as a coin struck to commemorate this penitential pilgrimage by Marian Gumowski, *Handbuch der polnischen Numismatik* (Graz: Akademische Verlagsanstalt, 1960), Tafel III, fig. 81, on p. 16. However, this assignment has been seriously questioned.

[2] I.e. the order of events as here given; in other words, the insertion of the siege of Nakło at its proper chronological place in the narrative would have meant interrupting the account of the events leading up to the pilgrimage, which belong together with it.

Bolesław had made for the holy martyr's relics in witness of his devotion and penitence. For in that shrine there are eighty marks of purest gold, besides pearls and precious stones hardly less valuable than the gold. And regarding his bishops, princes, chaplains and countless warriors he celebrated that most glorious Holy Easter in such a magnificent and munificent way that every one of the greater men and almost all the lesser ones received precious garments. Regarding the canons of the holy martyr and the guardians and servitors of the church, as well as the citizens of the town, he made such generous provision that all without exception were honored either by vestments or horses or other gifts, each according to his rank and estate. Thus was the pilgrimage completed with such religious devotion.[1] Yet the siege previously undertaken has not simply been deleted from the memory of our heart because of this, nor should that[2] be seen as a reversal of order which, if inserted, would disturb the full sequence of the story already started.

26 THE POMERANIANS HAND OVER NAKŁO CASTLE TO THE POLES[3]

Thus the castle of Nakło, where, as mentioned earlier, that very great battle took place and whence endless trouble and loss was constantly being occasioned to the Poles, had been entrusted by Bolesław to a certain Pomeranian close to him in kin called Świętopołk,[4] together with several other castles. He was to hold these under such condition of fealty that he would never for any reason refuse Bolesław service or access to the castles. But later

[3] As the chapter in fact does not describe the handing over of Nakło but the capture of two other towns or castles, the heading has been seen by some (e.g. Mal., p. 160, n. 3) as a proof of the incompleteness of the surviving MSS or even of the original; see above, p. xliv. However, since it has been accepted that the headings were added later, the misleading title may have been a misunderstanding of the scribe or a copyist.

[4] Probably the son or father of Sobichor; but the genealogy and the identity of Pomeranian dukes is highly uncertain—see further Mal., p. 160, n. 4.

neque promissam servitutem exhibuit, neque venientibus portas castellorum aperuit, ymmo sicut perfidus hostis et traditor viribus et armis sua seseque prohibuit. Unde Bolezlaus dux septentrionalis ad iracundiam concitatus, convocatis bellatorum cohortibus, castrum Nakel fortissimum obsedit, suam vindicare contumeliam meditatus. Ibique de festo sancti Michaelis ad Nativitatem[1] usque dominicam sedens et in bello contra castrum cottidie studiosus incedens, laborem suum in vanum penitus expendebat, quia humidum per locum aquosum et paludosum machinas et instrumenta ducere non sinebat. Insuper castellum erat et viris et rebus necessariis sic firmatum, quod non esset armis vel necessitate rei cuiuslibet per annum continuum expugnatum.[2] Ipse quoque Bolezlauus, cum ibi fuerit sagittatus, ad se vindicandum est maioris ire stimulis agitatus. Unde Suatopolc pacem semper vel pactum aliquod per amicos et familiares Bolezlaui requirebat et pecuniam illi magnam cum obsidibus offerebat. Quibus rebus perpensis, Bolezlauus obsessionem dimisit, redeundi suamque contumeliam vindicandi tempus ydoneum expectando remeavit, partemque pecunie secum obsidemque filium ipsius primogenitum asportavit.[3] Item anno sequenti, cum ipse Suatopolc neque fidem datam neque paccionem factam observaret, neque de periculo filii cogitaret, nec ad colloquium cum Bolezlauo constitutum venire, vel causam excusacionis mittere procuraret, suum Bolezlauus exercitum congregavit, hostemque perfidum aliquantulum *in virga ferrea,*[4] sed non plenarie, visitavit. Qui cum ad confinium Pomoranie pervenisset, ubi quilibet princeps alius cum tota multitudine timuisset, exercitu relicto cum electis militibus in antea properavit et castellum Wysegrad impetuose capere, castellanis non

---

[1] 29 September till 25 December 1112.

[2] The *Annales Cracovienses Priores* record for the year 1113 (*MPH* n.s. 5, p. 55): *Boleslaw III Nakel et alia castra obtinuit,* suggesting that the siege of Nakło was finally successful.

he never kept his sworn fealty, nor did he perform the promised service, nor did he open the gates of the castles when they came. He even withheld himself and his resources by force of arms, as a perfidious enemy and traitor. Therefore Bolesław, the duke of the north, stirred to anger, called up his cohorts of warriors and besieged the mighty castle of Nakło, intending to avenge the affront against him. Although he stayed there from Michaelmas till Christmas[1] and every day waged war vigorously against the castle, his efforts were completely in vain, because the moist ground did not allow siege machines and engines to be brought across the wet and marshy terrain. Moreover, the castle was so well supplied with men and necessities that it could not have been taken within a full year by arms or for shortage of any thing.[2] Bolesław, after being wounded by an arrow there, was goaded by even greater anger to avenge himself. Therefore, Świętopołk constantly tried to arrange peace or some agreement through friends and retainers of Bolesław, and offered him a large amount of money and hostages. Bolesław, having given this thought, broke off the siege and went back, in order to wait for a suitable time to return and avenge the affront; he took with him a part of the money and the first-born son of the prince as hostage.[3] Then in the following year, because Świętopołk neither kept the pledge he had given nor the agreements he had made, nor cared for the danger to his son, nor did he bother to come to a parley agreed to with Bolesław nor even send an excuse in explanation, Bolesław again called up his army. He afflicted the treacherous enemy *with a rod of iron*,[4] though not fully. When he reached the borders of Pomerania, where any other prince even with a full force would have felt fear, he left the army behind and pushed ahead with selected warriors, planning to take the castle of Wyszogród by storm, for the townsmen were neither expecting

---

[3] This hostage cannot be identified; but cf. *Mal.*, p. 161, n. 5.

[4] Apoc. 2:27.

premeditantibus, nec premunitis, cogitavit. Ubi vero ventum est ad fluvium, qui iunctus Wisle flumini castellum illud in angulo situm fluviorum[1] ab eis ex altera parte dividebat, alii fluvium illum cursim, alius ante alium, transnatabant, alii vero Mazouiensium per Wislam fluvium navigio veniebant.[2] Sicque contigit ignoranter in bello dampnum fieri plus civili, quam VIII diebus expugnando castrum illud assultu fuerat ex hostili. Exercitu tandem toto circa castrum congregato, iamque diversorum instrumentorum apparatu oppidi expugnandi preparato, oppidani pertinacem in hostes obstinanciam Bolezlaui metuentes, recepta fide dedicionem fecerunt, sicque manus Bolezlaui mortemque evaserunt. Illud vero castrum Bolezlauus VIII° diebus acquisivit, VIII° que diebus aliis sibi retinendum, ibi residens, premunivit; ibi derelictis presidiis, inde progrediens, obsidione castrum aliud circuivit. Illud namque castrum cum maiori labore prolixiorique dilatione Bolezlauus expugnavit, quia plures et forciores ibi pugnatores locumque municiorem assultu bellico exprobavit. Paratis igitur a Polonis instrumentis ac machinationibus expugnandi, Pomorani similiter instrumenta modis omnibus repugnandi fecerunt. Poloni foveas equant, terram lignaque comportant, quo levius ac planius ad castrum cum turribus ligneis accedant; Pomorani contra lardum lignaque picea parant, quibus paulatim congeriem illam comburant. Tribus enim castellani vicibus instrumenta omnia de muro descendentes furtive combusserunt, tribusque vicibus iterum illa Poloni construxerunt. Ita nempe turres lignee Bolezlaui castello vicine stabant, quod castellani de propugnaculi cuneis[a,3] armis et ignibus repugnabant. Si quandoque Poloni castellum armis, igne, lapidibus, sagittis inpetebant,

---

[a] cum eis Z

---

[1] Wyszogród is located at the confluence of the rivers Brda and Vistula; see further *Zantoch, eine Burg,* as n. 6, p. 9.

[2] Pairing the Latin words differently produces an alternative translation: 'others were ferried down the Vistula by the Masovians.' The present transla-

it nor prepared. There, however, they reached a river, which joined the Vistula and separated them on one side from that castle, which was located in the confluence of the two rivers.[1] Then some swam swiftly across, one after the other, while other Masovians came down the Vistula by boat.[2] Thus, out of ignorance greater harm was done in a battle by civil war than what was caused by the hostilities during that castle's eight-day-long siege. When finally the entire army was assembled around the castle, and the equipment for the various siege-engines for the attack on the town was ready, the townspeople, fearing Bolesław's unyielding stubbornness towards his enemies, on receiving a pledge surrendered, thus evading the death at Bolesław's hands. So Bolesław obtained that castle in eight days, and within another eight days, while residing there, he fortified it in order to hold it. Then, having left a guard there, he proceeded thence and surrounded another castle in siege. That castle, however, he took with greater effort and longer delay, for there in armed assault he encountered more numerous and powerful warriors and a better fortified place. So the Poles prepared engines and siege devices, and the Pomeranians similarly built engines in order to fight back in every way. The Poles filled in ditches and brought up earth and timber, so that they might approach the castle with their siege towers over smoother and more level ground. The Pomeranians in turn prepared lard and pieces of wood dipped in pitch, and with these they gradually burnt down these structures. For the townspeople three times crept down from the wall and burnt all the engines, and three times the Poles rebuilt them. For Bolesław's wooden towers stood so near the castle that the townsmen could attack them from the projections[3] of the battlements with weapons and fire. If ever the Poles attacked the castle with weapons, fire, stones and arrows, the defenders paid

---

tion implies that subsequent reference to "civil war" was to a conflict between two groups of Masovians who failed to recognize each other, in contrast to two groups of Bolesław's Poles.

[3] Or, with the reading *cum eis* (Z): 'with their (weapons, etc.)'.

castellani similiter modis omnibus vicem contrariam repende-
bant. De Polonis multos castellani sagittis et lapidibus vulnera-
bant, de castellanis vero Poloni plures cottidie perimebant. Erant
enim pagani de morte securi, si virtute bellica caperentur, et ideo
malebant, ut cum fama se defendentes quam collum extenden-
tes[1] cum ignavia morerentur. Interdum tamen cum Bolezlauo
pactum facere castrumque reddere cogitabant, interdum indutias
petentes, vel auxilium expectantes, illud consilium differebant.
Interea Poloni nunquam ociosi, nunquam desidiosi tot laboribus
et vigiliis fatigati desistebant,[a] sed castrum capere vi vel insidiis
insistebant. Pomorani vero talem Bolezlaui mentem et inten-
cionem cognoscebant, quod nullatenus evadere manus ipsius,
nisi castro reddito, prevalebant, et ex hoc quam maxime diffide-
bant, quia de Suatopolc, suo domino, nullum auxilium expectabant. Unde pro tempore consilium partibus utrisque[b] satis
ydoneum inierunt, castellum videlicet fide recepta tradiderunt,
ipsique sani cum suis omnibus incolumes, quo sibi libuit,
abierunt.[2]

[a] non desistebant *H Mal*
[b] utrique *H Mal*

them back similarly in every way. The defenders wounded many of the Poles with arrows and stones, but day by day the Poles killed larger numbers of the defenders. For the pagans were assured of death if they were captured fighting, and so they preferred to die defending themselves honorably than to stretch out their necks[1] and perish as cowards. However, at times they considered making a pact with Bolesław and surrendering the castle, but at others they would change their minds, seeking a truce, perhaps hoping for relief. Meanwhile the Poles were never idle, never resting, nor ever ceased because wearied by such labors and wakefulness, but pressed on to take the castle by force or trickery. But the Pomeranians knew Bolesław's mind and his will, that they would in no way be able to escape his hands except by surrendering the castle, and they were particularly unconfident because they were expecting no help from their master Świętopołk. So in the circumstances they formed a plan suitable enough to both sides, that they handed over the castle on receipt of a pledge, and they departed safe and unharmed with all that belonged to them, wherever they wanted.[2]

[1] This expression *collum extendere*, not commonly used in Latin, may mean something similar to the English "risking their necks," but implying submission.

[2] The fullest MSS (Z, S) end here. On the problem of the completeness of the text as we know it, see above, p. xliv.

SELECTED BIBLIOGRAPHY

(for titles cited in abbreviation, see above, pp. xii–xv)

EDITIONS AND TRANSLATIONS OF THE *GpP*

Araki, M. "Tokumei no Garu Nendaiki, Dai Ikkan, Hon'yaku to chushaku" (The Chronicle of Gallus Anonymus, volume 1, translation and notes). *Okayama Daigaku Hogaku-kai Zasshi* 42 (1993): 178–212; 44 (1994): 287–334.

Bandtkie, Joannes Vincentius, ed. *Martini Galli Chronicon ad fidem codicum : qui servantur in Pulaviensi tabulario celsissimi Adami principis Czartoryscii, palatini regni Poloniarum / denuo recensuit . . . Joannes Vincentius Bandtkie.* Warsaw: Regia Societas Philomathicae Varsoviensis, 1824.

Bujnoch, Josef. *Polens Anfänge: Gallus Anonymus, Chronik und Taten der Herzöge und Fürsten von Polen.* Slawische Geschichtsschreiber, 10. Graz: Styria, 1978.

Chronicae Polonorum. Ed. J. Szlachtowski and P. Koepke. MPL 160:833–936.

Chronicon Polonorum usque ad a. 1113, ed. J. Szlachtowski and P. Koepke. In *Chronica et annales aevi Salici,* ed. Georg Heinrich Pertz, MGH SS IX, pp. 418–78. Hanover: Hahn, 1851. Reprint, 1983.

Finkel, Ludovicus, and Stanislaus Kętrzyński, ed. *Galli anonymi chronicon.* Fontes rerum Polonicarum in usum scholarum 1. Lviv: Societas Historica Leopolitana, 1899.

Galla kronika. Ed. August Bielowski. MPH 1/1, pp. 379–484. Lviv: Gubrynowicz i Schmidt, 1864.

Krzyżanowski, Julian, ed. *Galla Anonima Kronika. Podobizna fotograficzna rękopisu Zamoyskich z wieku XIV/Galli*

Anonymi Chronica codicis saec. XIV. Zamoscianus appellati reproductio palaeographica. Warsaw: Towarzystwo Naukowe Warszawskie, 1946.

Lengnich, Gottfried, ed. *Vincentius Kadlubko et Martinus Gallus scriptores historiae Polonae vetustissimi cum duobus anonymis ex ms. bibliothecae episcopalis Heilsbergensis editi.* Gdańsk: n.p., 1749.

Mizlerus De Kolof, Laurentius, ed. *Historiarum Poloniae Et Magni Ducatus Lithuaniae Scriptorum Quotquot Ab Initio Reipublicae Polonae Ad Nostra Usque Tempora Extant.* Warsaw: Mizler, 1776.

Popova, Ljudmila Mikhailovna, ed. and trans., *Gall Anonim, Khronika u deianiia kniazei ili pravitelei polskikh.* Pamiatniki srednevekovoi istorii narodov Tsentralnoi i Vostochnoi Evropy. Moscow: Akad. Nauk SSSR, 1961.

Woś, J. W. "La cronaca di Gallo Anonymo." *Annali della Scuola Normale Superiore di Pisa, Classe di lettere e filosofia,* ser. 3, vol. 11 (1981): 165–79.

PRIMARY SOURCES

Annales Cracovienses priores cum calendario. Ed. Zofia Kozłowska-Budkowa. MPH, n.s., 5. Warsaw: PWN, 1978. Pp. 3–105.

Bak, J. M., Gy. Bónis, and J. R. Sweeney, ed. *The Laws of the Medieval Kingdom of Hungary/Decreta Regni Mediaevalis Hungariae.* Vol. 1 (1000–1301). 2d ed. Idyllwild, CA: Schlacks, 1999.

Chronica Poloniae Maioris. Ed. Brygida Kürbis. MPH, n.s., 8. Warsaw: PWN, 1970.

Constantine Porphyrogennetos. *De administrando imperio.* Ed. Gyula Moravcsik, English trans. R. I. H. Jenkins. Budapest: Pázmány Péter Tudományegyetem, 1949.

Cross, Samuel Hazzard, and Olgerd P. Sterbowitz-Wetzor. *The Russian Primary Chronicle: Laurentian Text*. Cambridge, MA: The Medieval Academy of America, 1953.

Długosz, Jan. *Annales seu Cronicae incliti Regni Poloniae, lib. 1–2*. Ed. Jan Dąbrowski. 2 vols. Warsaw: PWN, 1964.

Frutolfs und Ekkehards Chroniken und die Anonyme Kaiserchronik. Ed. Franz-Josef Schmale. FvS 15. Darmstadt: Wissenschaftliche Buchgesellschaft, 1972.

The Gesta Normanorum ducum *of William of Jumiège, Orderic Vitalis and Robert of Toringny*. Ed. and trans. Elisabeth M. C. Van Houts. 2 vols. Oxford: Oxford UP, 1992–5.

Goiffon, Etienne. *Bullaire de l'abbaye de St Gilles*. Nimes: · Comité de l'art chrétienne, 1882.

Györffy, György, ed. *Diplomata Hungariae antiquissima: Accedunt epistolae et acta ad historiam Hungariae pertinentia*. Vol. 1, *Ab anno 1000 usque ad annum 1131*. Budapest: Akadémiai Kiadó, 1992.

Herbordi Dialogus de Vita Ottonis episcopi Babenbergensis. Ed. J. Wikavjak and K. Liman. Wrocław: PWN, 1974.

Honorius Augustodunensis. *De imagine mundi*. MPL 172: 115–86.

Jacobus de Voragine. *The Golden Legend: Readings on the Saints*. Trans. William G. Ryan. 2 vols. Princeton: Princeton UP, 1993.

Kozłowska-Budkowa, Zofia. *Repertorjum polskich dokumentów doby piastowskiej* (Repertory of Polish documents of the Piast age). Cracow: PAU, 1937.

Liber S. Jacobi: Codex Calixtinus. Ed. Klaus Herbers and Manuel Santos Noia. Santiago de Compostella: Xunta de Galicia, 1999.

Magistri Vincentii dicti Kadłubek Chronica Polonorum. Ed. Marianus Plezia. MPH, n.s., 11. Cracow: Secesja, 1994.

Passio S. Adalberti martiris. Ed. August Bielowski. MPH 4:206–21. Cracow: Nakładem Własnym, 1864.

Quellen zur Geschichte Kaiser Heinrichs IV: Die Briefe Heinrichs IV. Ed. Franz-Josef Schmale. Darmstadt: Wissenschaftliche Buchgesellschaft, 1963.

Simon of Kéza. *The Deeds of the Hungarians/Gesta Ungarorum.* Ed. and trans. László Veszprémy and Frank Schaer. Central European Medieval Texts, 1. Budapest: CEU Press, 1999.

Stumpf-Brentano, Karl-Friedrich. *Die Reichskanzler vornehmlich des X., XI. und XII. Jahrhunderts.* Innsbruck: Wagner, 1865.

Vita Minor S. Stanislai. Ed. Wojciech Kętrzyński. MPH 4. Lviv: Nakładem Akademii Własnym, 1884. Pp. 238–85.

Vita Maior Sancti Stanislai. Ed. Wojciech Ktrzyński. MPH 4. Lviv: Nakładem Akademii Własnym, 1884. Pp. 319–438.

Widukind of Corvey. *Res gestae Saxonum.* In *Quellen zur Geschichte der Sächsischen Kaiserzeit,* ed. Albert Bauer and Reinhold Rau, pp. 1–184. FvS 8. Darmstadt: Wissenschaftliche Buchgesellschaft, 1977.

SECONDARY LITERATURE

Adamska, Anna. "'From Memory to Written Record' in the Periphery of Medieval Latinitas: The Case of Poland in the Eleventh and Twelfth Centuries." In *Charters and the Use of the Written Word in Medieval Society,* ed. K. Heidecker, pp. 83–100. Turnhout: Brepols, 2000.

Adamus, Jan. *O monarchii Gallowej* (On the monarchy in Gallus). Warsaw: Towarzystwo Naukowe Warszawskie, 1952.

Althoff, Gerd. *Amicitiae und Pacta: Bündnis, Einung, Politik und Gebetsgedenken im beginnenden 10. Jh.* MGH Schriften 37. Hanover: Hahn, 1992.

———. *Otto III.* Darmstadt: Primus-Verlag, 1997.

———. "Symbolische Kommunikation zwischen Piasten und Ottonen." In *Polen und Deutschland vor 1000 Jahren: Die Berliner Tagung über den "Akt von Gnesen,"* ed. Michael Borgolte, pp. 293–308. Berlin: Akademie Verlag, 2002.

Banaszkiewicz, Jacek. "L'affabulation de l'espace: L'exemple médiéval des frontières." *APH* 45 (1982): 5–28.

———. "Bolesław i Peredsława: Uwagi o uroczystości stanowienia władcy w związku z wejściem Chrobrego do Kijowa" (Bolesław and Peredsława: Remarks on the ceremony of constituting the ruler with regard to Chrobry's entry into Kiev). *Kwartalnik Historyczny* 97, no. 3–4 (1990): 3–35.

———. "Königliche Karrieren von Hirten, Gärtnern und Pflügern: Zu einem mittelalterlichen Erzählthema vom Erwerb der Königsherrschaft." *Saeculum* 33 (1982): 265–86.

———. *Kronika Dzierzwy: XIV-wieczne kompendium historii ojczystej* (The chronicle of Dzierzwa: A fourteenth-century compendium of national history). Wrocław: Zakład Narodowy im. Ossolińskich, 1979.

———. "Die Mäusethurmsage: the symbolism of annihilation of an evil ruler." *APH* 51 (1985): 5–32.

———. "Note sur le thème du siège triparti: Capitole, Narbonne et Głogów." *Annales ESC* 39 (1984): 776–82.

———. *Podanie o Piascie i Popielu: studium porównawcze nad wczesnośredniowiecznymi tradycjami dynastycznymi* (The legend of Piast and Popiel: A comparative study on early medieval dynastic traditions). Warsaw: PWN, 1986.

Banaszkiewicz, Jacek. "Potrójne zwycięstwo Mazowszan nad Pomorzanami – Gall, II, 49 – czyli historyk między 'rzeczywistością prawdziwą' a schematem porządkującym (A threefold victory of Mazovians over Pomeranians – Gallus II, 49 – or a historian between "real reality" and an arranged scheme). In *Kultura średniowieczna i staropolska: studia ofiarowane Aleksandrowi Gieysztorowi w pięćdziesięciolecie pracy naukowej,* ed. Danuta Gawinowa, pp. 305–31. Warsaw: PWN, 1991.

———. "Slavonic *origines regni*: hero the lawgiver and founder of monarchy (introductory survey of problems)." *APH* 60 (1989): 97–131.

———. "Złota ręka komesa Żelisława" (The golden hand of *comes* Żelisław). In *Imagines potestatis: Rytuały, symbole i konteksty fabularne władzy zwierzchniej, Polska X–XV w.* (*Imagines potestatis*: rituals, symbols and narrative contexts of supreme power—Poland, the tenth to the fifteenth centuries), ed. Jacek Banaszkiewicz, pp. 228–48. Colloquia Medievalia Varsaviensia, 1. Instytut Historii PAN. Warsaw: PAN, 1994.

Bańkowski, Andrzej. "Imiona przodków Bolesława Chrobrego u Galla Anonima: rozważania etymologiczne" (The names of the ancestors of Bolesław Chrobry in *Gallus Anonymus*: Etymological considerations). *Onomastica* 34 (1989): 109–11.

Barford, P. M. *The Early Slavs: Culture and Society in Early Medieval Eastern Europe.* London: The British Museum Press, 2000.

Barnat, R. "Siły zbrojne Bolesława Chrobrego w świetle relacji Galla Anonima" (The forces of Bolesław the Brave in the light of the account of Gallus Anonymous). *Przegląd Historyczny* 88 (1997), 223–35.

Bieniak, Janusz. *Państwo Miecława: Studium analityczne* (The dominion of Miecław: An analytical study). Warsaw: PWN, 1963.

———. "Polska elita polityczna XII wieku" (The Polish political elite in the twelfth century). In *Społeczeństwo Polski średniowiecznej: Zbiór studiów* (The society of medieval Poland: A collection of studies), ed. Stefan K. Kuczyński, 3:2–49. Warsaw: PWN, 1985.

Bisson, Thomas, N. "The 'feudal revolution.'" *Past & Present* 142 (February 1994): 6–42.

———. "Medieval lordship." *Speculum* 70 (1995): 743–59.

———. "On not eating Polish bread in vain: Resonance and Conjuncture in the Deeds of the Princes of Poland (1109–1113)." *Viator* 29 (1998): 279–88.

———. "Princely Nobility in an Age of Ambition (c. 1050–1150)." In *Nobles and Nobility in Mediaeval Europe*, ed. A. J. Duggan, pp. 101–13. Woodbridge: Boydell, 2000.

Bogucki, Ambroży. "The administrative structure of Poland in the eleventh and twelfth century." *APH* 72 (1995): 5–32.

Borawska, Dorota. "Gallus Anonim czy Italus Anonim" (Gallus Anonymus or Italus Anonymus). *Przegląd Historyczny* 56 (1965): 111–9.

Brachmann, Hansjürgen, ed. *Burg – Burgstadt – Stadt: Zur Genese mittelalterlicher nichtagrarischer Zentren in Ostmitteleuropa*. Forschungen zur Geschichte und Kultur des östlichen Mitteleuropa. Berlin: Akademie-Verlag, 1995.

Brackmann, Albert, ed. *Zantoch, eine Burg im deutschen Osten*. Leipzig: Hirzel, 1936.

Breeze, Andrew. "The Crowland *Planctus de morte Lanfranci* and the Polish *Galli Anonymi Cronica*." *Revue bénédictine* 101 (1994): 419–23.

Bresslau, Harry. *Jahrbücher des Deutschen Reiches unter Konrad II*. 3 vols. Leipzig: Duncker & Humblot, 1884. Reprint, 1967.

Brückner, Alexander. "Pierwsza powieść historyczna" (The first historical novel). *Przegląd Humanistyczny* 3 (1924): 116–36.

———. *Słownik etymologiczy języka polskiego* (Etymological dictionary of the Polish language). Warsaw: Wiedza Powszechna, 1985.

Bujnoch, Josef. "Gallus Anonymus und Cosmas von Prag: Zwei Geschichtsschreiber und Zeitgenossen." In *Osteuropa in Geschichte und Gegenwart*, ed. H. Lemberg, P. Nitsche, and E. Oberländer, pp. 301–15. Cologne and Vienna: Böhlau, 1977.

Charvát, Petr. "Bohemia, Moravia and Long-Distance Trade in the 10th–11th Centuries." *QMAeN* 5 (2000): 255–66.

Chudziak, Wojciech, "The Early Romanesque Building from Kałdus, Voivodship of Toruń: Chronology and Function," *QMAeN* 4 (1999): 197–210.

Curtius, Ernst Robert. *European Literature and the Latin Middle Ages*. Trans. Willard R. Trask. Bollingen Series 36. Princeton: Princeton UP, 1953.

Dąbrowski, J. *Dawne dziejopisarstwo polskie (do roku 1480)* (Early Polish historiography, to 1480). Wrocław: Zakład Narodowy imienia Ossolińskich, 1964.

Dalewski, Zbigniew. "Die heilige Lanze und die polnischen Insignien." In *Europas Mitte*, 2:907–11. Cf. "The Holy Lance and Polish Insignia." In *Europe's Center*, pp. 602–5.

———. "The Knighting of Polish Dukes in the Early Middle Ages: Ideological and Political Significance." *APH* 80 (1999): 15–43.

David, Pierre. *Les sources de l'histoire de Pologne à l'époque des Piasts (963–1386)*. Paris: Les belles lettres, 1934.

Davies, Norman. *God's Playground: A History of Poland*. 2 vols. Oxford: Clarendon, 1982.

Dembińska (Dębińska), Maria. *Food and Drink in Medieval Poland: Rediscovering a Cuisine of the Past*. Revised and adapted by William Woys Weaver. Philadelphia: University of Pennsylvania Press, 1999.

Deptuła, Czesław. *Galla Anonima mit genezy Polski: Studium z historiozofii i hermeneutyki symboli dziejopisarstwa średniowiecznego* (The myth of the origin of Poland in Gallus Anonymus: A study in historiosophy and the hermeneutics of the symbols of medieval historiography). Lublin: Instytut Europy Środkowo-Wschodniej, 2000.

———. "Ideologia Polski jako państwa morskiego w średniowiecznym dziejopisarstwie polskim" (The ideology of Poland as a marine country in medieval Polish historiography). *Zeszyty Naukowe Katolickiego Uniwersytetu Lubelskiego* 18, no. 4 (1975): 3–17.

Derwich, Marek. "Die ersten Klöster auf dem polnischen Gebiet." In *Europas Mitte*, 1:515–8. Cf. *Europe's Centre*, pp. 332–4.

Engel, Pál. *The Realm of St. Stephen: A History of Medieval Hungary 895–1526*. Ed. Andrew Ayton, trans. T. Pálosfalvi. London: Tauris, 2001.

Fried, Johannes. "Gnesen-Aachen-Rom, Otto III. und der Kult des heiligen Adalberts: Beobachtungen zum Älteren Adalbertsleben." In *Polen und Deutschland vor 1000 Jahren: Die Berliner Tagung über den "Akt von Gnesen,"* ed. Michael Borgolte, pp. 235–80. Berlin: Akademie-Verlag, 2002.

———. *Otto III. und Boleslaw Chrobry: Das Widmungsbild des Aachener Evangeliars, der "Akt von Gnesen" und das frühe polnische und ungarische Königtum*. 2nd ed. Stuttgart: Steiner, 2001.

Gieysztor, Aleksander. "Die Herrschaft der Piasten in Gnesen." *Bohemia* 40 (1999): 79–86.

———. "Récherches sur les fondements de la Pologne médiévale: état actuel des problèmes." *APH* 4 (1961): 7–33.

———. "*Sanctus et gloriosissimus martyr Christi Adalbertus*: un état et une église missionaires aux alentours de l'an mille." In *La conversione al christianismo nell'Europa dell'Alto Medioevo*, pp. 611–47. Settimane di Studio, 14. Spoleto: Centro di Studio, 1967.

———, ed. *History of Poland*. Warsaw: PAN, 1968.

Górecki, Piotr. "A Historian as a Source of Law: Abbot Peter of Henryków and the Invocation of Norms in Medieval Poland, c. 1200–1270." *Law & History Review* 18 (2000): 479–523.

Görich, Knut. "Ein Erzbistum in Prag oder in Gnesen." *Zeitschrift für Ostforschung* 40 (1991): 10–27.

Grabski, A. F. "Polska wobec idei wypraw krzyżowych na przełomie XI i XII w.: 'Duch krzyżowy' Anonima Galla" (Poland and the idea of crusade at the turn of the eleventh to the twelfth century: The 'crusading soul' of Gallus Anonymus). *Zapiski Historyczne* 26 (1961): 4, 49–64.

Graus, František. "Der Heilige als Schlachtenhelfer: Zur Nationalisierung einer Wundererzählung in der mittelalterlichen Chronistik." In *Festschrift für Helmut Beumann zum 65. Geburtstag*, ed. Kurt-Ulrich Jäschke and Reinhard Wenskus, pp. 330–48. Sigmaringen: Thorbecke, 1977.

———. *Die Nationenbildung der Westslawen im Mittelalter*. Nationes: Historische und philologische Untersuchungen zur Entstehung der europäischen Nationen im Mittelalter, 3. Sigmaringen: Thorbecke, 1980.

Grodecki, Roman. "Zbigniew książę Polski" (Zbigniew, a Polish prince). In *Studia staropolskie: Księga ku czci Aleksandra*

Brücknera (Old Polish studies: Festschrift for Alexander Brückner), 71–105. Cracow: Krakowska Spółka Wydawnicza, 1928.

Grudziński, Tadeusz. *Boleslaus the Bold, Called Also the Bountiful, and Bishop Stanislaus: The Story of a Conflict.* Trans. Lech Petrowicz. Warsaw: Interpress, 1985.

Gumowski, Marian. *Handbuch der polnischen Numismatik.* Graz: Akademische Verlagsanstalt, 1960.

Gumplowicz, Maximilian Ernst. *Bischof Balduin Gallus von Kruszwica, Polens erster lateinischer Chronist.* Sitzungsberichte der Kaiserlichen Akademie der Wissenschaften in Wien, Philosophisch Historische Classe, vol. 132, H. 9. Vienna: Tempsky, 1895.

Györffy, György. *Krónikáink és a magyar őstörténet: Régi kérdések új válaszok* (Hungarian chronicles and ancient history: Old questions, new answers). Budapest: Balassi Kiadó, 1993.

———. *St Stephen of Hungary.* Boulder, CO: Social Science Monograph, 1994.

Hamann, Richard. "Der Schrein des heiligen Aegidius." *Marburger Zeitschrift für Kunstwissenschaft* 6 (1931): 114–36.

Hensel, Witold. *La naissance de la Pologne.* Wrocław: Ossolineum-PAN, 1966.

Herrmann, Joachim. *Ralswiek auf Rügen: Die slawisch-wendischen Siedlungen und deren Hinterland.* 2 vols. Lübstorf: Archäologisches Landesmuseum für Mecklenburg-Vorpommern, 1997–8.

Heydebrand, Fedor von u .d. Lasa. "Die staatsrechtliche Stellung des comes nomine Magnus Wratislawensis." *Zeitschrift des Vereins für Geschichte Schlesiens* 74 (1940): 14–68.

Hlawitscka, Eduard. "Königin Richenza von Polen: Enkelin Herzog Konrads von Schwaben, nicht Kaiser Ottos II." In *Institution, Kultur und Gesellschaft im Mittelalter: Festschrift für Josef Fleckenstein*, ed. L. Fenske, W. Rösener, and T. Zotz, pp. 221–44. Sigmaringen: Thorbecke, 1984.

Janowski, Rudolf, Christian Lübke, and Michael G. Müller, ed. *Eine kleine Geschichte Polens*. Frankfurt: Suhrkamp, 2000.

Janson, T. *Prose Rhythm in Medieval Latin from the 9th to the 13th Century*. Studia Latina Stockholmiensia, vol. 20. Stockholm: Almquist & Wiksell, 1975.

Jasiński, Kazimierz. *Rodowód pierwszych Piastów* (The genealogy of the first Piasts). Warsaw and Wrocław: Uniw. Wrocławski, 1993.

Jurek, Tomasz. "Fremde Ritter im mittelalterlichen Polen." *QMAeN* 3 (1998): 19–49.

———. "Kim był komes wrocławski Magnus" (Who was Magnus the *comes* of Wrocław). In *Venerabiles, nobiles et honesti, Studia z dziejów Polski średniowiecznej: Prace ofiarowane Profesorowi Januszowi Bieniakowi w siedemdziesiątą rocznicę urodzin i czterdziestopięciolecie pracy naukowej* (*Venerabiles, nobiles et honesti*—studies on the history of medieval Poland: Works offered to Prof. Janusz Bieniak on his 60th birthday and the 40th year of his scholarly activities), ed. A. Radzimiński, A. Supruniuk, and J. Wroniszewski, pp. 181–92. Toruń: Uniwersytet Mikołaja Kopernika, 1997.

Kara, Michał. "Anfänge der Bildung des Piastenstaates in Lichte neuer archäologischer Ermittlungen." *QMAeN* 5 (2000): 58–85.

Karp, Hans-Jürgen. *Grenzen in Ostmitteleuropa während des Mittelalters*. Cologne: Böhlau, 1972.

Karp, Marek J. "Więź ogólnopolska i regionalna w średniowiecznych mitach początku" (The all-Polish and regional ties in the medieval myths of origin). *Przegląd Historyczny* 72 (1982): 211–27.

Kersken, Norbert. *Geschichtschreibung im Europa der "nationes:" Nationalgeschichtliche Gesamtdarstellungen im Mittelalter*. Münstersche Historische Forschungen, 8. Cologne: Böhlau, 1995.

Kiersnowska, Teresa. "O pochodzeniu rodu Awdańców" (Concerning the provenance of the Awdańcy family). In *Społeczeństwo Polski średniowiecznej* (The society of medieval Poland), ed. Stefan K. Kuczyński, 5:57–72. Warsaw: PWN, 1992.

Kiersnowski, Ryszard. "Znaki graniczne w Polsce średniowiecznej" (Border signs in medieval Poland). *Archeologia Polski* 5.2 (1960): 257–87.

Klaniczay, Gábor. *Holy Rulers and Blessed Princesses: Dynastic Cults in Medieval Central Europe*. Cambridge: Cambridge UP, 2002.

Kłoczowski, Jerzy. *La Pologne dans l'Eglise mediévale*. Aldershot: Variorum, 1993.

———, ed. *Histoire réligeuse de la Pologne*. Trans. K. T. Michel. Paris: Centurion, 1987.

Knonau, Gerald Meyer von. *Jahrbücher des Deutschen Reiches unter Heinrich IV. und Heinrich V.* 7 vols. Leipzig: Duncker & Humblot, 1907.

Kras, Robert J. "Dzieła Sallustiusza w warsztacie Anonima zw. Gallem" (The works of Sallust in the workshop of the Anonymous called Gallus). *Roczniki Humanistyczne* 50 (2002), fasc. 2: 3–51.

Kristó, Gyula. "Les relations des Hongrois et des Polonais au Xᵉ-XIIᵉ siècles d'après les sources." *QMAeN* 7 (2002): 127–44.

Krystofiak, Teresa. "Giecz." In *Europas Mitte*, 1:464–7. Cf. *Europe's Center*, pp. 299–300.

Krzemieńska, Barbara, and Dušán Třeštik. "Wirtschaftliche Grundlagen des frühmittelalterlichen Staates in Mitteleuropa (Böhmen, Polen, Ungarn im 10.–11. Jahrhundert)." *APH* 40 (1979): 5–32.

Kürbis, Brygida. "Kształtowanie się pojęć geograficznych o Słowiańszczyźnie w polskich kronikach przeddługoszowych" (The development of geographical notions concerning Slavic territories in the Polish chronicles before Długosz). *Slavia Antiqua* 4 (1953): 262–82.

———. "'Sacrum' and 'profanum' in Polish Mediaeval Historiography: Views on Social Order." *Questiones Medii Aevi* 2 (1981): 19–40.

———. "Zum Herrscherlob in der Chronik des Gallus Anonymus (Anfang 11. Jahrhundert): '*Laudes regiae*' am polnischen Hof?" In *Patronage und Klientel: Ergebnisse einer polnisch-deutschen Konferenz*, ed. H-H. Nolte, pp. 51–67. Beihefte zum Archiv für Kulturgeschichte, 29. Cologne: Böhlau, 1989.

Kurnatowska, Zofia. "Die Christianisierung Polens im Lichte der archäologischen Quellen." In *Europeas Mitte*, 1:490–4. Cf. "The Christianisation of Poland as Reflected in the Archaeological Record." In *Europe's Center*, pp. 317–9.

Labuda, Gerhard. "Der 'Akt von Gnesen' vom Jahre 1000: Bericht über die Forschungsvorhaben und -ergebnisse." *QMAeN* 5 (2000): 145–88.

———. "Bazoar Anonymus Gallus krónikájában" (Bazoar in the Chronicle of Gallus Anonymus). *Századok* 104 (1970): 173–7.

Labuda, Gerard. *Studia nad początkami państwa polskiego* (Studies on the beginnings of the Polish state). Vol. 2. Poznań: Wydawnictwo Uniwersytetu im. A. Mickiewicza, 1988.

Labuda, Gerard. *Święty Stanisław biskup krakowski, patron Polski: Śladami zabójstwa – męczeństwa – kanonizacji* (St. Stanislas, bishop of Cracow, patron of Poland: Evidence on his murder, martyrdom, and canonisation). Poznań: Instytut Historii UAM, 2000.

———. "Zatargi z Czechami i Pomorzami w pierwszym okresie rządów Bolesława Śmiałego (1058–1073)" (Battles with Czechs and Pomeranians in the first period of Bolesław the Bold's reign [1058–73]). *Zapiski Historyczne* 50 (1985): 33–49.

Lanckrońska, Karolina. "A Cyrillo-Methodian See in Poland." In *Studies on the Roman-Slavonic Rite in Poland*. Orientalia Christiana Analecta, 161. Rome: PIO, 1961.

Leciejewicz, Lech. "Die Pomoranen und der Piastenstaat im 10.–111. Jahrhundert." *Zeitschrift für Archäologie* 18 (1984): 107–16.

———. "Zur Entwicklung der Frühstädte an der südlichen Ostseeküste." *Zeitschrift für Archäologie* 3 (1969): 182–210.

Łowmiański, Henryk. "Economic problems of the early feudal Polish state." *APH* 3 (1960): 7–32.

Lübke, Christian. "Das 'junge Europa' in der Krise: Gentilreligiöse Herausforderung um 1000." *Zeitschrift für Ostmitteleuropaforschung* 50 (2001): 475–96.

Maleczyński, Karol. *Bolesław III Krzywousty* (Bolesław III Wrymouth). Wrocław: Zakład Narodowy im. Ossolińskich, 1975.

Manteuffel, Taddeusz . *The Formation of the Polish State: The Period of Ducal Rule, 963–1194*. Tr. Andrew Gorski. Detroit: Wayne State UP, 1982.

Meyer von Knonau, Gerald. *Jahrbücher des Deutschen Reiches unter Heinrich IV. und Heinrich V*. Vol. 6. Leipzig: Duncker & Humblot, 1907.

Michałowski, R. *"Restauratio Poloniae* dans l'idéologie dynastique de Gallus Anonymus." *APH* 52 (1985): 5–43.

Modzelewski, Karol. "Comites, Principes, Nobiles: The structure of the ruling class as reflected in the terminology used by Gallus Anonymus." In *The Polish nobility in the Middle Ages: Anthologies*, ed. A. Gąsiorowski, pp. 177–206. Polish Historical Library, 5. Wrocław: Zakład Narodowy im. Ossolińskich, 1984.

―――. *"Ius aratorum* na tle praw grupowych ludności chłopskiej"* (The *ius aratorum* in the context of the group rights of the rural population). In *Społeczeństwo Polski średniowiecznej: Zbiór studiów* (Polish medieval society: Selected studies), ed. S. K. Kuczyński, 1:86–127. Warsaw: PWN, 1981.

―――. *Organizacja gospodarcza państwa piastowskiego: X-XIII wiek* (The economic organisation of the Piast state: Tenth to thirteenth centuries), 2d ed. Poznań: Poznańskie Towarzystwo Przyjaciół Nauk, 2000.

Petersohn, Jürgen. *Der südliche Ostseeraum im kirchlich-politischen Kräftespiel des Reiches, Polens und Dänemarks vom 10. bis 13. Jahrhundertt: Mission, Kirchenorganisation, Kultpolitik.* Ostmitteleuropa in Vergangenheit und Gegenwart, Bd. 17. Cologne: Böhlau, 1979.

Piskorski, Jan M. *Pommern im Wandel der Zeiten.* Szczecin: Zamek Książąt Pomorskich, 1999.

―――. *Pomorze plemienne: Historia – Archeologia – Językoznanwstwo* (Tribal Pomerania: History, archaeology, linguistics). Poznań and Szczecin: Sorus, 2002.

Plezia, Marian. *Kronika Galla na tle historiografii XII w.* (The chronicle of Gallus in the context of the historiography of the twelfth century). Rozprawy Wydziału Historyczno-Filozoficznego PAU, ser. 2, vol. 46, no. 3. Cracow: PAU, 1947.

Plezia, Marian. "Księgozbiór katedry krakowskiej wedle inwentarza z r. 1110" (The library of the cathedral of Cracow according to an inventory from 1110). *Silva Rerum*, n.s. 1 (1981): 16–29.

―――. "Nowe studia nad Gallem Anonimem" (New studies on Gallus Anonymus). In *Mente et litteris: O kulturze i społeczeństwie wieków średnich* (*Mente et litteris*: On the culture and society of the Middle Ages), ed. H. Chłopocka, pp. 111–20. Poznań: Wydawnictwo Naukowe Uniwersytetu im. Adama Mickiewicza w Poznaniu, 1984.

―――. "Les relations littéraires entre la France et la Pologne au XIIe siècle." *Bulletin de l'Association Guillaume Budé* 1 (1983): 67–78.

―――. "Ungarische Beziehungen des ältesten polnischen Chronisten." *Acta Antiqua Academiae Scientiarum Hungaricae* 7 (1959): 285–95.

Polak, Wojciech. "Czas w najstarszej polskiej kronice" (Time in the oldest Polish chronicle). *Zeszyty Naukowe Katolickiego Uniwersytetu Lubelskiego* 39, no. 3–4 (1996): 47–72.

―――. "Uwagi w sprawie rocznikarskiego źródła *Kroniki* Galla Anonima (Remarks about annalistic sources of the chronicle of Gallus Anonymus). *Roczniki Humanistyczne*, 47 (2000) fasc. 2: 447–60.

Polheim, K. *Die lateinische Reimprosa.* Berlin: Weidmann, 1925.

Polska technika wojskowa do roku 1500 (Polish military technique before A.D. 1500). Ed. Andrzej Nadolski. Warsaw: Oficyna Naukowa, 1994.

Powierski, Jan, Błażej Śliwiński, and Klemens Bruski, ed. *Studia z dziejów Pomorza w XII wieku* (Studies on the history of Pomerania in the twelfth century). Biblioteka Słupska, 35. Słupsk: Polskie Towarzystwo Historyczne, Oddział w Słupsku, 1993.

Rhode, Gotthold. "Die ehernen Grenzsäulen Boleslaus des Tapferen von Polen: Wege einer Legende." *Jahrbücher für Geschichte Osteuropas*, NF 8 (1960): 331–53.

———. *Kleine Geschichte Polens*. Darmstadt: Wissenschaftliche Buchgesellschaft, 1965.

Roeppel, Richard. *Geschichte Polens*. Hamburg: Friedrich Perthes, 1840.

Sappok, G. *Die Anfänge des Bistums Posen und die Liste ihrer ersten Bischöfe*. Leipzig: Hirzel, 1937.

Schich, Winfried. "Die pommersche Frühstadt im 11. und frühen 12. Jahrhundert am Beispiel von Kolberg (Kołobrzeg)." In *Die Frühgeschichte der europäischen Stadt im 11. Jahrhundert*, ed. J. Jarnut and P. Johanek, pp. 273–304. Cologne: Böhlau, 1998.

Schramm, Percy Ernst. "Die 'Heilige Lanze,' Reliquie und Herrschaftszeichen des Reiches und ihre Replik in Krakau." In *Herrschaftszeichen und Staatsymbolik*, 2:492–537. MGH Schriften 13/2. Stuttgart: Hiersemann, 1955.

Semkowicz, Władysław. *Encyklopedia nauk pomocniczych historii* (An encyclopedia of the auxiliary sciences of history). Ed. B. Wyrozumska. Cracow: Universitas, 1999.

Sobel, Leopold. "Ruler and Society in Early Medieval Western Pomerania." *Antemurale* 25 (1981): 19–142.

Targosz, Karolina. "*Gesta principum recitata*: 'Teatr czynów polskich władców' Galla Anonima" (*Gesta principum recitata*: Gallus Anonymus's "theatre of the deeds of the Polish rulers"). *Pamiętnik Teatralny* 29 (1980): 141–78.

Uhlirz, Karl. *Jahrbücher des Deutschen Reiches unter Otto II. und Otto III*. Ed. Margaret Uhlirz. Berlin: Duncker and Humblot, 1902. Reprint, 1967.

Warnke, Charlotte. *Die Anfänge des Fernhandels in Polen*. Würzburg: Holzner, 1964.

Wasilewski, Tadeusz. "Poland's administrative structure in early Piast times: *Castra* ruled by *comites* as centres of territorial administration." *APH* 44 (1981): 5–31.

Weinfurter, Stefan. *The Salian Century: Main Currents in an Age of Transition*. Trans. Barbara M. Bowlus. Philadelphia: University of Pennsylvania Press, 1999.

Wenskus, Reinhard. *Studien zur historisch-politischen Gedankenwelt Brunos von Querfurt*. Mitteldeutsche Forschungen, 5. Munich and Cologne: Böhlau, 1956.

Wiesiołowski, Jacek. *Kolekcje historyczne w Polsce średniowiecznej XIV-XV wieku* (Historical collections in medieval Poland, fourteenth-fifteenth centuries). Wrocław: Zakład Narodowy im. Ossolińskich, 1967.

Wojciechowski, Tadeusz. *Szkice historyczne jedenastego wieku* (Historical sketches of the eleventh century). Cracow: Akademia Umiejętności, 1904. Reprint, with a foreword by A. Gieysztor, 1951.

Wojciechowski, Z. *Mieszko I and the Rise of the Polish State*. Warsaw: PWN, 1971.

Wood, Ian. *The Missionary Life: Saints and the Evangelisation of Europe 400–1050*. Turnholt: Brepols, 2001.

Zeissberg, Heinrich. *Die polnische Geschichtsschreibung des Mittelalters*. Leipzig: Hirzel, 1873. Reprint, Cologne: Böhlau, 1968.

Zernack, Klaus. *Die burgstädtischen Volksversammlungen bei den Ost- und Westslawen: Studien zur verfassungsgeschichtlichen Bedeutung des Veče*. Wiesbaden: Harrasowitz, 1967.

INDEX OF PROPER NAMES

(includes persons unnamed in the text
but identifiable [in brackets]; biographical details
appear at the first citation)

INDEX OF GEOGRAPHICAL NAMES

INDEX OF NAMES OF PEOPLES

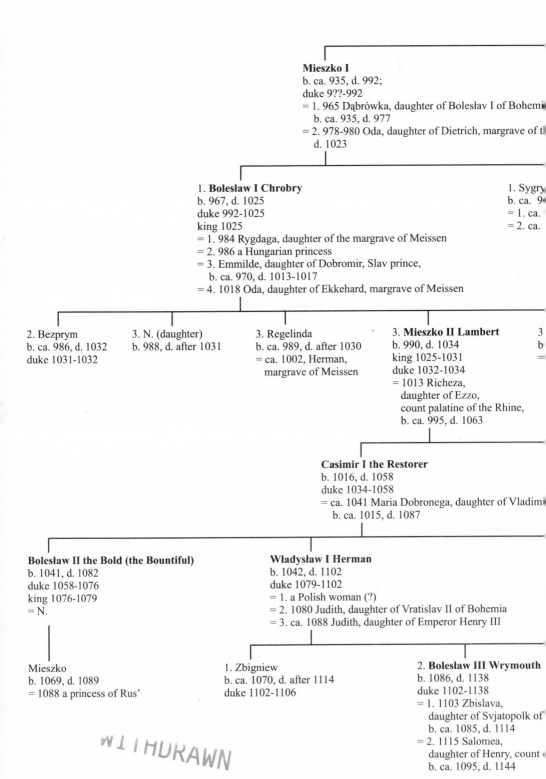

Mieszko I
b. ca. 935, d. 992;
duke 9??-992
= 1. 965 Dąbrówka, daughter of Bolesłav I of Bohemi░
  b. ca. 935, d. 977
= 2. 978-980 Oda, daughter of Dietrich, margrave of t░
  d. 1023

1. **Bolesław I Chrobry**
b. 967, d. 1025
duke 992-1025
king 1025
= 1. 984 Rygdaga, daughter of the margrave of Meissen
= 2. 986 a Hungarian princess
= 3. Emmilde, daughter of Dobromir, Slav prince,
  b. ca. 970, d. 1013-1017
= 4. 1018 Oda, daughter of Ekkehard, margrave of Meissen

1. Sygry░
b. ca. 9░
= 1. ca. ░
= 2. ca. ░

2. Bezprym
b. ca. 986, d. 1032
duke 1031-1032

3. N. (daughter)
b. 988, d. after 1031

3. Regelinda
b. ca. 989, d. after 1030
= ca. 1002, Herman,
  margrave of Meissen

3. **Mieszko II Lambert**
b. 990, d. 1034
king 1025-1031
duke 1032-1034
= 1013 Richeza,
  daughter of Ezzo,
  count palatine of the Rhine,
  b. ca. 995, d. 1063

3░
b░
=░

Casimir I the Restorer
b. 1016, d. 1058
duke 1034-1058
= ca. 1041 Maria Dobronega, daughter of Vladimi░
  b. ca. 1015, d. 1087

Bolesław II the Bold (the Bountiful)
b. 1041, d. 1082
duke 1058-1076
king 1076-1079
= N.

Władysław I Herman
b. 1042, d. 1102
duke 1079-1102
= 1. a Polish woman (?)
= 2. 1080 Judith, daughter of Vratislav II of Bohemia
= 3. ca. 1088 Judith, daughter of Emperor Henry III

Mieszko
b. 1069, d. 1089
= 1088 a princess of Rus'

1. Zbigniew
b. ca. 1070, d. after 1114
duke 1102-1106

2. **Bolesław III Wrymouth**
b. 1086, d. 1138
duke 1102-1138
= 1. 1103 Zbislava,
  daughter of Svjatopolk of░
  b. ca. 1085, d. 1114
= 2. 1115 Salomea,
  daughter of Henry, count ░
  b. ca. 1095, d. 1144